Praise for *The Last Places on Earth: Journeys in Our Disappearing World*

Gary Mancuso had the itch you can't scratch except by getting out there. He left a high-dollar job to face tropic heat, bad cops, and former cannibals. His extraordinary account, *The Last Places on Earth*, breathes one message from every page: *Go while you still can—while it's still there to see.*

> —Robert Ankony, author of *LURPS: A Ranger's Diary of Tet, Khe Sanh, A Shau, and Quang Tri*, nominated for Army Historical Foundation's Distinguished Writing Award, 2006, 2009

If you ever plan to travel where few have dared set foot and where the nearest consulate is several days distant, read *The Last Places on Earth* before you go. It will enthrall you, make you laugh, and teach you much about how to get "out there" and back without losing too much skin in the process.

> —Michael J. Carr, multiple *New York Times* best-selling editor

What child hasn't dreamed of going to the wildest, most pristine places on earth and meeting people who have never ridden in a car, touched ice, or seen television? Gary Mancuso had these dreams. But unlike the rest of us, he never outgrew them—*he went!* Even better, he wrote it down in *The Last Places on Earth*. His story will keep you up late, spellbound.

> —Gwen White, Re'D Regional Vice President Encyclopedia Brittanica/ Honorary Board Member American Film Institute

What possesses someone to take a rattletrap car over the Khyber Pass into post-9/11 Afghanistan? Spend the night among reformed headhunters and dine with onetime cannibals in Stone Age New

Guinea? Drink with Muslim separatists in the Caucasus, party with an exhumed corpse in the Madagascan highlands, and learn a little voodoo from a Togolese witch doctor? Ask Gary Mancuso. If you thought the Age of Exploration was over, *The Last Places on Earth* will make you think again.

—Peter Russell, UCLA Entertainment Division of the Extension School's Teacher of the Year 2009, founder of HowMoviesWork.com, a film and television story school based in Venice, California

A fantastic firsthand account of the author's courageous and almost devil-may-care approach to traveling some of the remotest, most exotic destinations left on the map. Gary Mancuso's story is filled with wonder, excitement, and, at times, real physical danger. Never taking himself too seriously, the author tells this epic tale with great descriptions and humor, making the book itself an unforgettable travel experience.

—Michael W. Silvey, military knife authority and author of several well-known books including *Knives of the United States Military: World War II* and *Knives of the United States Military in Vietnam: 1961 1975*

JOURNEYS
in Our Disappearing World

The
LAST
PLACES
on
EARTH

GARY MANCUSO

The Last Places on Earth: Journeys in Our Disappearing World
by Gary Mancuso

Published by:
Great Lands Publishing Co., LLC
Los Angeles, CA
www.thelastplacesonearth.com

ISBN: 978-0-9912271-0-5

Library of Congress Control Number: 2013955499

Book Design: Nick Zelinger, www.NZGraphics.com
Editor: Michael J. Carr, www.book-editing.com

First Edition

Printed in the United States of America

To the Salonites family
L'audace, l'audace, toujours l'audace!

Contents

Prologue

January 2005
Peshawar
Federally Administered Tribal Areas, Northwestern Pakistan

The muezzin's first call to prayer, blaring through my open window, felt like a bullhorn in my ear. It was five o' clock and still dark. Though it happened every morning of the world in all Muslim lands, I would never get used to this jolting predawn wakeup call. Amplifying the effect, my room in the Afghan-run guesthouse faced the muezzin's high-wattage loudspeaker in an old mosque in downtown Peshawar. For just a moment, I longed to be back home in West Los Angeles, which I pictured lying silent and peaceful under a blanket of coastal fog.

"*Allahu Akbar!*" came crackling over the loudspeaker again.

No matter. I could use the time to ponder an important decision. After the prayer call's infernal blaring, the street was quiet again except for the occasional clop-clop and creak of a nag and wagon plodding over the cobblestones. The peacefulness belied Peshawar's status as the hub of Pakistan's notorious, semiautonomous Northwest Territories. This was the real Wild West—a haven for al-Qaeda forces fighting the coalition army in Afghanistan.

My thoughts turned to yesterday afternoon's conversation with Alam, the guesthouse's jovial young manager.

"You should do the journey by land, not flying," Alam had said when I mentioned my intent to fly from Peshawar to Kabul, Afghanistan. Tall and clean-shaven, he hailed from a Pashtun tribe of the porous Afghan borderlands. "It will be a most scenic trip."

When I asked whether it was safe to make the road journey, what with the war going on, he told me he had friends who had made the trip from Peshawar, over the Khyber Pass, to Kabul. "They tell me, for the most part, it is reasonably safe to go by land," Alam assured me.

As I lay awake in my room calculating how to get to Kabul, I was glad Achara, my wife, was not with me at the moment. In our six years together, she had endured—mostly—my penchant for long treks in the back of beyond, with surprising good humor. She knew I had to see things up close, not separated from them by some TV documentarian's telephoto lens. But apparently, she had concerns. One evening before this latest trip, she had told me she worried sometimes about suddenly and unexpectedly being without me.

I had originally planned to fly into Kabul from Peshawar, hoping to leapfrog over the worst risks of travel in the war zone. I figured that Kabul, with its huge presence of coalition forces, would be reasonably safe. But a land trip through the Khyber Pass would be much more interesting than flying. I would be journeying along the same route taken by Darius the Great, Alexander of Macedon, Genghis Khan, and Tamerlane. I would be seeing the same mountainous vistas that those famous conquerors had seen, essentially unchanged over the centuries. Afghanistan offered a chance to glimpse ways of living and thinking far removed from the norm in today's fast-homogenizing world. It fit my general travel aim of experiencing the gamut of traditional, or "primitive," lifestyles in a world where they were quickly being subsumed by rampant globalization.

Alam had explained that a foreigner needed to get a permit from the Pakistani military and pay a small fee for an armed soldier escort through the Khyber Pass, to the Afghan border. I felt that I would have been fine without the armed protection. In Peshawar, I had picked up a handmade wool shawl and a flat wool cap, called a *chitrali*, that looked a bit like a potato pancake—the traditional male dress in the region. And to blend in while in Pakistan, I had quit shaving, grown my hair longer, and adopted the *shalwar kameez* (loose-fitting trousers and long-sleeved upper tunic). Since I was tall and lean with relatively dark hair, my Pakistani clothing and new shawl and cap made me look like a Pathan from Northern Afghanistan. But the first few days wearing my new shawl, I had only managed to look ridiculous because it kept falling off, exposing me as an obvious foreigner.

That morning, with the muezzin's distorted, crackling tones still ringing in my head, I realized that I couldn't pass up this opportunity to go to Kabul by land. In truth, though, I wasn't sure whether I was taking this added risk because of my genuine desire to experience the fabled Khyber Pass and get a glimpse of the northern Afghan landscape, or because of my lifelong tendency to choose the option with the most adrenaline.

The day I set out for Kabul, Alam joined me for the ride through the pass. He wanted to make sure I had no problems getting to the Afghan border, where he also hoped to arrange safe transport for me to Kabul. Shortly after sunrise, we were off in a tiny white Honda Civic taxi to the Pakistani military office just outside Peshawar, where I got my armed soldier escort and my permit to travel through the Khyber region. We all then crammed into the Honda and drove through a dusty, rocky landscape, arriving shortly at a military checkpoint. The sign read, "ATTENTION: ENTRY OF FOREIGNERS IS PROHIBITED BEYOND THIS POINT." There, after looking at my permit, the border guards let us pass.

The drive from that point was through an area that felt bleak, lawless, and at the same time puritanical—and utterly alien to me. The terrain was rocky, dry, and flat, with scattered scrub. We passed low-rise rectangular mud-walled compounds and, occasionally, a woman in black burka, or a bearded man in flowing white shalwar kameez. After passing a small, dusty town and turning onto a winding road toward the mountains, we came to a huge compound with high white concrete walls. Alam asked the driver to stop.

"This is the home of an important man in the region," he explained. "The owner is a powerful and famous drug lord. We can have an iced tea here and hopefully meet him if he is at home."

Entering the compound, I found myself in what I imagined a drug lord's home to be like. It was palatial, with a pretty garden and well-tended green lawn, and several liveried servants bustling about. I half expected to see gorgeous women lounging about as part of the decor, but we were in a strictly fundamentalist Muslim land. Since the owner was not at home, Alam and I had our iced tea quickly in a garden patio decorated with colorful ceramic tile, before moving on.

The drive through the Khyber Pass was a slog along winding roads through high, desolate mountains. We were often stuck behind big, lumbering Pakistani trucks painted in a garish kaleidoscope of bright colors. They chugged along, barely making it up the steep hills while spewing a constant plume of choking black exhaust. Our compensation for the glacial pace and near asphyxiation was an endless series of grand vistas, each more spectacular than the last, of rugged peaks stretching into the purple distance. These views, and the many old military posts, markers, and monuments we passed, were a reminder of the strategic barrier to armies that these mountains had always presented.

Finally, we came to a sere, barren settlement in a valley on the other side of the pass, with several small stone or concrete buildings and a flagpole flying the Pakistani flag. This was the Pakistani/Afghan border. A high chicken-wire fence, with a simple opening manned by two armed guards, ran along the boundary.

The exit procedures went surprisingly quickly, without even a bribe, and I walked to a gap in the fence. It struck me that I was about to cross a line beyond which I couldn't change my mind.

"Wait here," Alam said as I stood looking through the gap in the fence. "I will go through the border crossing and find a taxi driver with a good, reliable car that can get you to Kabul."

Alam then talked the border guard into letting him cross the border for a moment, with the promise that he would return shortly. The guard must have known that Alam would come back. After all, Afghanistan was a desperate war zone, where no one would want to stay given the choice. I also speculated about who the guard must think I was in wanting to go into such a place voluntarily.

I began to wonder this myself—and also to worry about the time. Alam had explained to me that the drive from the border to Kabul was a race against time since it was dangerous to be out after five p.m., when it got dark. Road bandits and Taliban made the place literally deadly after sundown, especially for a Western foreigner. It was only about a 135-mile stretch, he had said, but the road was terrible to nonexistent in many places, and the trip would take over six hours. Alam and I had taken far longer than we planned to get to the border crossing, arriving there around twelve forty-five p.m. It was late to start out for Kabul, which meant that I would be making at least part of the journey in darkness.

Returning after a brief while, Alam pointed to a car a hundred yards off, on the other side of the chicken-wire fence. "I found you a good, reliable car," he said enthusiastically. "The driver is a good man. His name is Jacob, and he is from the same tribe as I, so you can trust him, too. He swore on his honor to protect you with his life."

So I grabbed my bags, said good-bye to Alam, turned and waved to my armed soldier and the Pakistani cab driver, and walked through the gap in the fence, toward the only car visible on the Afghani side of the border. My fate was now tied to the total stranger standing silhouetted beside his car.

Jacob, my new Afghan driver and protector, spoke not a word of English. He was short and lean with longish, unkempt dark hair and dark sunburned complexion and was wearing a dirty shirt with a few holes. My worry increased when I saw that his "good, reliable car" looked ready for the junkyard. This was not unusual—indeed, most vehicles in this region were in varying states of disrepair and unutterably dirty. Jacob's car was a small, old Toyota that had once been tan. All four tires were bald, the windshield was cracked, and a wire hanger stuck up out of a broken radio antenna perch. The whole car was completely caked in dirt and mud.

Seeing my dubious expression, Jacob flashed a big smile and gave me a thumbs-up sign. Still in doubt, I heaved my luggage into the dusty, dank-smelling trunk and hopped into the front passenger seat. But before I could get comfortable, Jacob motioned me to the back. Puzzled, I got out and started to get into the backseat. But no, that wasn't what he meant. He made a shoving motion, indicating that I had to push-start the car. I now realized why he had parked so far away from the border: he was at the top of a gentle rise and wanted the momentum going down to help push-start the car. So, I pushed until it got rolling, then jumped in after it started, and off we went.

I started to fasten the grubby shoulder harness, but Jacob waved his hand no to this—a seat belt would make me stand out as a foreigner.

Jacob drove a short way along a wide dirt road to a bare area ringed by falling-down huts. The circular patch of dirt was filled with unwashed people and a bedlam of cars, trucks, buses, and jitneys. Jacob then got out of the car and disappeared into the disarray. Eventually, I figured out that the place was the auto-fixing area nearest the border for guys like my driver. Jacob had come here to find a mechanic to fix his starter.

As I sat in the car alone for a while, trying to keep myself calm while precious time ticked away, I realized that we had never actually passed through a border checkpoint into Afghanistan after leaving Pakistan. So we must be in some kind of no-man's land between border checkpoints. Jacob soon returned, and we both sat there waiting for someone to come and start working on his car. Despite my rising anxiety, I almost laughed out loud at the stupid situation. Our precious daylight was slipping rapidly away, not a soul around me spoke English, and I was stuck in a broken-down car on the edge of a war zone.

At 1:45 p.m., I was relieved when we finally got started again and were speeding at full throttle along a wide dirt track—the "highway" toward Kabul. As if to emphasize that we were in a tortured land, we passed "wanted" posters of bin Laden and other al-Qaeda and Taliban leaders, military and police convoys, and signs warning not to pick up various pictured items such as mines, artillery shells, and bullets. In our first hour along the way, we passed a bombed-out Soviet tank, several military outposts and forts, and a U.S. military patrol.

The U.S. soldiers, compared to their Afghan counterparts, appeared to be straight out of a Hollywood action adventure movie. Their two vehicles, a desert camouflage Humvee and an armored fighting vehicle, were very clean and BIG. The soldiers all looked buffed in their stylish designer-looking camouflage, sharp berets, and wide-brimmed soft hats and sported longish, smart haircuts. They all carried big, scary-looking automatic weapons. I was glad they were on our side.

The terrain was stark: vast stretches of rocks and more rocks as far as the eye could see, with a backdrop of high, rugged, parched-looking mountains on both sides of the road. And over everything and everyone, a liberal coating of dust. Here and there in the distance, colorfully dressed people herded their goats or gathered firewood. Some lived in large mud compounds, others in houses of sticks and mud. With nothing in sight but rocks, dust, scrub, and sand, I couldn't see how they managed to scrape up anything to eat.

Not far off the roadside, I saw a small girl carrying firewood. She wore heavy woolen clothing of faded orange and brown checks and had so much brush piled on her head, she looked like a huge, walking tumbleweed. What future did she face, I wondered? This innocent young girl had gotten a cruel draw in the birth lottery: born in the middle of a perpetual war zone, in one of the worst places on the planet to be a woman.

The horrible irony was that this stifling suppression of women was supposedly dictated by God. I had been raised with the conception of an all-knowing, all-powerful, all-loving God. But that this girl could, through no fault of her own, be placed in this predicament made a mockery of these ideas. What sort of God could knowingly inflict such wretched circumstances on a child? It would take a God who was not all that loving or, perhaps, was just too busy to care.

The only city of any size that we passed through was Jalalabad. It was mostly ramshackle old buildings and streets choked with cars, horse-drawn carts and rickshaws, human-powered rickshaws, bikes, motorbikes, jitneys, buses, and trucks of every shape and size, all painted with bright, gaudy designs. Otherwise, the whole journey was essentially a breakneck race against both time and other drivers along this dirt and rock track.

With no concept of lanes, everyone along the way seemed intent on cutting each other off, as if this were a point of pride. The whole trip involved constantly weaving back and forth, dodging the countless potholes, bumps, and rocks the size of engine blocks. It was a free-for-all with only two speeds: full throttle and slamming on the brakes.

At one point, in a scene typical for the journey, we were beasting up a hill at full speed in our beat-up wreck, trying to pass another wreck that was also hurtling uphill at full speed, both cars sending up choking plumes of dust on the unpaved road. As Jacob veered into the oncoming lane starting to pass the other car, we neared the crest of the hill. A huge truck suddenly appeared, charging us head-on since we were in the wrong lane. In a blast of mental clarity born of the sudden awareness that my life was in mortal danger, my right foot stomped the floorboard as if to hit the brakes. The driver of the truck looked forward impassively. He had the Goliath vehicle—the sure winner if we should collide.

Of course, my stomping of the phantom brake pedal produced no effect. Jacob continued the game of high-speed chicken with the other driver to his right, veering back over to the correct lane and cutting the other car off at the last split second. The huge truck barreled past us, and we felt the small shock wave of its passing.

Looking over at me, Jacob flashed an impish grin with two left front teeth prominently missing. For him, the near-death encounter with the truck, this constant game of chicken with other drivers, was just part of the daily routine.

Unlike in a professional road race, though, there would be no crowds cheering the winner, nor any beautiful, adoring women scrambling to meet us. Rather, the reward would be something much more banal: arriving in a city with huge sections in rubble, and military patrols regularly cruising the streets. And most of the women would be burka-clad, looking like so many large, moving black bowling pins.

As our precious sunlight dwindled toward dusk, we had a flat tire, and Jacob pulled over to change it with an even balder spare. But that was not the end of this unforeseen delay—we still had to get the punctured tire repaired. Otherwise, we would really be up a creek if another tire went flat. So, despite the approaching darkness and a long stretch before we reached the relative safety of Kabul, we stopped at a small hut along the way. Inside, a lone worker did a brisk trade patching bald tires. Every delay added to the risk of the situation, stretching out the time we would spend traveling in darkness, vulnerable to bandits and Taliban fanatics.

We made it to Kabul at seven p.m., two hours after nightfall. The dark, war-shattered, crumbling city felt like a lush oasis of calm and safety.

Introduction

This is a story of a long journey that lasted almost six years. Midway through the first decade of this century, I put my reasonably happy and fulfilling life on hold to take this journey. My travels took me to many of the wildest, most remote places on the planet, visiting some of the last, least Westernized traditional societies remaining on earth. I left the promising career path I was on in a bank trading room, sold my beautifully decorated home near the ocean in West Los Angeles, and put everything I owned in long-term storage. We sold both my wife's and my cars and automated all my accounts and obligations as much as possible. My commitment to my travel project was total.

When, during my travels, I told people what I was doing, two questions almost inevitably arose: What was it like to do such a long journey, especially into the wilder, rougher parts of the planet? And why do it at all?

These were surprisingly hard questions to answer. Not because I didn't know the answers, but because, well, it's complicated. First of all, independent travel into remote and unfamiliar places, as most of my destinations were, often involved a big leap of faith into the goodness of complete strangers. Going into a place where I didn't know the language, customs, or even such basics as what were the safe places to stay and what were the absolute no-go areas, was often the *only* way, since only someone local really knew. In the end, although the adventurer must sometimes put his faith in strangers, most independent travel is still largely an exercise in self-preservation. Along the way, I goofed myself up countless times, had to fend off vicious robbery attempts, was physically attacked in the streets more than once, had to endure a standoff with armed police on a dark street, and dealt with an endless train of crooked police and corrupt government officials. And without question, it was worth every hardship and misadventure.

My long journey brought a thousand occasions of sheer joy at seeing the best of humanity; at receiving the innumerable warm welcomes, smiles, and hospitality almost everywhere I went; and at realizing my lifelong dream: to experience the great wonders and see some of the last traditional peoples on earth. It was also a journey shot through with moments of sadness and anger—anger at the world for being so unfair to all those who drew the short stick in the birth lottery. Those many millions were born into impossible circumstances, whether women under an oppressive cultural system, whole populations under authoritarian kleptocracies that are still the norm in much of the world, or those unfortunate enough to be stuck under the earth's truly horrific regimes and open prisons such as North Korea.

At times, my journey included episodes of indignation against those who interfere with and bully those ill equipped to resist them. I have railed, both inwardly and out loud, against the countless meddlers from rich countries who descend like vultures on the developing world, whether missionaries pushing alien and culturally disruptive religious beliefs, developers and extractors who bring quick wealth to a few while further impoverishing the many, or those not-for-profit organizations that thrive on human disaster and misery by overpaying their executives while underdelivering to those who should be benefiting from their efforts.

One of the aspects of my long journey that I reveled in—for the earlier part, at least—was that my day-to-day experience was so far out of the norm for most people of the developed world. Sometimes during my travels, people would ask me where I lived, to which I happily replied, "Nowhere." It was such a joy—again, especially in the earlier travels—to escape those routine mundane activities of normal life, such as checking my e-mail in-box every morning or making sure I got credited correctly on the gas bill I paid last month.

It was certainly strange and, in some ways, even fun to be totally gone and unavailable to all who knew me, with no one knowing my whereabouts. And when I did contact people I knew, usually by Skype Internet phone during my travels, I seldom got the perfunctory "How are you?" or "What's happening?" as a greeting. Instead, more often than not, the question was a genuinely curious "*Where are you now?*" to which I usually had an answer very different from the last one I gave that particular questioner.

I found another curious aspect of my travels unexpectedly fun. Wherever travelers go, they are usually unknown. A traveler just shows up from who knows where and will leave into the same unknown. This mysterious coming and going, I found, often convinces the people one meets to imbue the traveler with an exaggerated importance. This occurs, in part, because so many of the world's people still really do not have the luxury of travel and have never been more than a few miles from their home town or village. So the traveler is often seen and treated as a sort of star or celebrity. This contrasts with how it is at home, where we are just average Joes going about our daily business. And, to gain this elevated status, the traveler did nothing beyond the simple act of showing up in a place far from home.

Finally, though, the main reason for my long journey is summed up in the title of this book. It was a bittersweet quest to know firsthand some of the earth's remaining wildernesses and its pockets of colorful and traditional cultures steeped in beliefs and worldviews that hark back to earlier epochs of humanity.

Throughout history, many people have made long journeys. Some are even household names. But one thing that is crucially different for today's traveler is how fast globalization is changing the world, and how quickly natural places are being exploited beyond recognition. In my earlier travels, before this long project, I saw firsthand how fast the world's biological and cultural diversity was being obliterated by rapidly spreading modernization. So today, unlike when history's great travelers embarked for distant lands, my journey was also an exercise in profound sadness at witnessing the rapid and relentless conquest of wonderment and mystery that we humans have naively assumed would always be there. It was the desire to know and experience this disappearing richness of our world that ultimately drove me on this long journey.

This book is my attempt to tell some small bit of what I found.

CHAPTER I

Papua New Guinea: First Journey Into a Disappearing World

They must be our ancestors from the place of the dead . . .
We believed our dead went over there, turned white and
came back as spirits. Our own dead had returned.

—Old New Guinea tribesman, on what the native people thought
when Australian gold prospectors first came to their highland village
in early 1930. (Recounted in the 1982 Australian documentary
First Contact.)

November 2005
Southern Highlands Province, Papua New Guinea

I gazed out the window of the old Air Niugini Dash 8 twin turboprop
at the endless green carpet of dense mountainous forest below. It
was a bumpy flight as storm clouds on the horizon moved fast toward
us. The only interruptions to the monotone green were the curving
strips of brown river that switched back and forth through the dense
forest. The battered Canadian-built thirty-six-passenger craft, with
its cracked blue and white vinyl seats, was a noisy place—and smelly,
too, with the pungent whiff of days-old sweat. My wife, Achara, sitting
in the window seat next to me, was busily snapping pictures. She
always diligently recorded our adventures.

The geography below looked forbidding, and I could easily see how isolating it was for the huge diversity of peoples living there. It was not long ago—as late as 1930—that people looking down at these same vast tracts of Papua New Guinea's Highlands assumed them to be uninhabited. A chance encounter by three Australian brothers, prospecting for gold inland from the coastal region, led to the discovery of over a million native highlanders living in this region. The indigenous people of that time thought that the white-skinned prospectors were spirits of their ancestors, and that the first airplanes they saw were gigantic birds that had ferried them here.[1]

I was excited about this first big trip of my travel project and thought Papua New Guinea (PNG) the perfect place to begin. Going into these dense rain forests with their amazing biodiversity would be a time-travel experience into an earlier stage of humanity's long journey. Starting as a youngster—perhaps because of my social awkwardness through early youth—understanding human nature became a passionate amateur pursuit of mine. Beyond the intellectual satisfaction, I reasoned that this would have the practical effect of helping me get along better with people. In this pursuit, I figured that if I really wanted to understand human nature, I could learn a lot from those whose lifestyles, thought patterns, mythologies, and religions were from a much earlier chapter in the story of humankind. PNG, with its hundreds of distinct cultural groups still following neolithic folkways, seemed the best place left on earth to do this.

I first visited PNG, which occupies the eastern half of the vast island of New Guinea, north of Australia, in the late 1990s. I was on a scuba diving excursion on a live-aboard dive boat, exploring the extraordinary marine life and coral-rich waters surrounding PNG. We did go ashore, though. During that brief sortie, wandering off on my own, I stumbled onto a hilltop cave filled with perhaps two hundred human skulls. Examining the skulls in the dank, almost

---

[1] *First Contact*, directed by Robin Anderson and Bob Connolly, 1983.

pitch black cave, I noticed that each one had a roughly one-inch hole. Later, the dive boat's skipper told me that these skull holes were from a traditional ritual still practiced in parts of New Guinea. The brains of deceased elders were sucked out through a straw inserted into the hole, and eaten, in the belief that the participant would gain the wisdom of the deceased. I was hooked—I had to come back and experience such a place.

I was doubly excited to be here with Achara. To realize my lifelong dream of traveling the world with the woman I loved seemed almost too much to wish for. And yet, here I was, having it all. I couldn't have been happier.

Achara would not at first strike anyone as a likely candidate for this type of travel endeavor. She was several years younger than I and had come from a well-connected background in Thailand, with a powerful uncle high in the government, and was somewhat accustomed to privilege. But she was game to try new things, had done several trips with me into remote places, and had enjoyed the experience.

Our plane circled in for landing at the airport, which was basically a wide strip of low-cut grass and bare dirt. Looking out the window, Achara said that an airplane landing in Tari appeared to be a major event. About two hundred people, many holding big, bright umbrellas as protection from the beating sun, were pressed against the chain-link fence enclosing the landing strip below.

Our plane landed to a festive reception. As we and the other passengers got off and waited for our baggage to be unloaded onto the grass, villagers streamed onto the airfield, excitedly greeting the passengers.

"I hope Steven is here," said Achara as we picked up our luggage off the ground. She was referring to a local Huli tribesman who was supposed to meet us. My research on PNG's Southern Highlands had been sketchy because there simply was not much current information out there, but I came across the name of a prominent member of a local clan of Huli people inhabiting the area. This man, who went by the English name Steven Wari, apparently ran a small jungle lodge about fifteen miles from the airport. The only other accommodation in the entire region was a terribly expensive eco lodge that did three-day packaged tours of the area—not really our style.

Steven had a P.O. box address in the town of Mount Hagen, about four hours' drive from Tari. I had written several months earlier, asking him if he could meet us at the airport and put us up in his lodge for the week. I never got a reply, though. It was another of those many times when, as a traveler in an alien land, I took that leap of faith, putting my fate totally in the hands of a stranger. In this case, I didn't even know whether the stranger knew of my existence.

Through the excited crowd, I spotted a man who seemed to be approaching Achara and me. "That's him, I think," I said hopefully, pointing to a compact but powerfully built fellow with very dark skin and short, curly black hair.

"You Gary?" the man asked. "I am Steven. Welcome to Tari!"

Relieved that Achara and I were not to be stranded here in the middle of this highland rain forest, I introduced Steven to Achara. "I am glad you spotted us," I said.

"I saw you as soon as you got off the plane," Steven replied cheerfully in fair English. "I think when I see you, 'That is the only Westerner. It must be Gary. The other Westerners getting off the plane are missionary peoples that work in this area.'" (The only other tourists were Japanese, on a package tour with the expensive eco lodge.)

Steven grabbed Achara's backpack, and we hauled our stuff to his dilapidated yellow Toyota Land Cruiser parked nearby. Then began a bumpy uphill ride along the winding dirt track that served as the main road in the Tari area, heading to his lodge. Our ride was through rolling green hills, with large patches of highland tropical forest and lush green scrub. Along the way, we passed run-down wooden shacks and thatch-roofed field huts neatly woven from bands of fibrous wood. Though the region felt raw, it had an air of abundance from a bountiful environment.

The jeep ride gave me a chance to know Steven a little. Achara and I had immediately liked this good-natured man, and he seemed to feel the same about us. He was a prominent member of a large clan known as the Huli Wigmen, that lived near Tari. It appeared that Steven was well off by Huli standards. "I recently married my third wife," he said as we zoomed blind around a sharp uphill corner. "She is a good woman and cost me a bride price of thirty-six pigs."

This seemed quite a price on an island where people generally had a protein-deficient diet. I asked him if thirty-six pigs was a lot in the Highlands.

"Yes, it is a big amount," he said. "Pigs are one of the main forms of wealth in the Highlands—more useful than money."

After a half hour, we came around a bend to a compound of several rectangular woven wood-band huts with thatched roofs, set off the roadside by a packed-dirt berm several feet high and fronted by a deep ditch. It was the Warili Lodge, Steven's place. The place looked well-tended and was in a pretty setting in the hills above Tari, at about seven thousand feet elevation and surrounded by highland tropical forest. The entry to the complex was through a stick-and-vine bridge over the ditch on one side of the complex—obviously a security measure.

Steven showed Achara and me around the inside of his place with evident pride. The grounds, simply landscaped with lush tropical foliage and flowering plants, had four guest rooms, a common toilet with a shower, and a large common room, all pleasantly cool due to the elevation. Adding to the welcome feeling of his place, Steven said that he had learned to cook Western-style food for his guests, lest they get bored of the normal starch-based Huli diet.

"The main food for Huli people is sweet potatoes," he said. "Many Huli eat sweet potatoes for breakfast, sweet potatoes for lunch, and for dinner, sweet potatoes."

For variety, his people also ate taro (another tuberous, starchy plant common in Oceania), sugar cane, watercress, a type of blood-leaf, and bananas, with an occasional meal of chicken or, on special occasions, pig. Achara and I were glad to hear that we would be spared this rather bland diet.

Early the next morning, Achara and I began a crash course in Huli culture. I had chosen to visit the Huli people because they were still relatively isolated from the modern world. During my research before the trip, I learned that the Huli, the second largest group in PNG, inhabited an area of about a thousand square miles in the center of the country. Their isolation was evident by the surrounding geography. The rugged Muller and Karius ranges to the south, and the Central Range system to the north acted as natural barriers. Because of this geographical isolation, the Southern Highlands were the last of the Highlands area to be explored by the outside world, remaining "undiscovered" until 1935. It was this isolation that interested me since it helped preserve the Huli culture into modern times.

Our first introduction to Huli culture was a welcoming "sing-sing" in our honor. This took place in a village set in a clearing a short walk through the forest from Steven's lodge. There, in a round dirt common area surrounded by several huts, five male dancers gathered. Their faces were painted in bright red and yellow ochre, and their bodies were decorated with cassowary bones, hornbill skulls, pig tusks, everlasting flowers, and other foliage. Their upper bodies were unclothed and oiled, giving their black skin a noticeable gleam. They had varying patterns and colors of paint on their shoulders, and all wore grass skirts ("ass grass," they drolly called it) and painted their legs in pastel hues.

Most striking, though, were the extravagant human-hair wigs they wore. The wig's hair was attached to an angular frame, sometimes at a dramatic angle like the tricorn hat of a pirate captain of old, and adorned with extravagant bird of paradise feathers, flowers, shells, and pigments. The plumage on some wigs rose several feet above the wearer's head. The whole scene had an enchanting, primal feel.

Our guide for the morning was Steven's assistant, a man named Peter, who looked to be around 35 years old. He explained that a sing-sing was traditional Huli dance. Different versions were done to welcome visitors, call the clan to war, intimidate the enemy during hostilities, and celebrate victory in war.

Peter said the men's ceremonial wigs were a defining part of Huli culture. They were made of the man's own hair, harvested over an extended time. Historically, it was believed that the wigs were head-dresses for war and, though made individually, expressed common elements of Huli culture. Making them sounded like an involved process.

The dancers lined up side by side, the leader then blew a whistle to set the beat, and they hopped lightly up and down, shaking their grass skirts while some clapped a drum they wore tied to them. This went on for a minute or so. The dancing then stopped and restarted again a moment later, to be repeated several times with no variation.

Peter explained that the welcome sing-sing we were watching was an imitation of a male bird of paradise trying to attract a mate. I confess to being inwardly surprised at how simple the dance routine was, given the elaborate, colorful costumes and wigs.

After the welcome sing-sing, the men who had danced invited us to their homes in the fields behind the clearing. There, Achara and I got a glimpse into the harsh reality of Huli society. During my research before the trip, I learned that the Huli people were very warlike and that the men traditionally fought for land, women, and pigs. This state of never-ending warfare in the Highlands appeared to continue to this day.

The homes were basic and uncomfortable looking, with several men living in each. They were small woven wood-band huts with several beds arranged around the dimly lit inside perimeter of the single rooms. A fire pit for baking sweet potatoes was dug into the dirt in the center of the room. When Achara and I peered into a couple of huts, I remarked that the beds looked very hard. Some were basically just a board. Peter interpreted my comment to the men in the local Huli language.

"Our beds are not comfortable," a smaller, tough-looking young man replied. "We prefer a bed full of ticks," he then joked, and everyone laughed. "But," he added seriously, "it is not a good idea to be too comfortable in bed and sleep too soundly. Otherwise, a sleeping man might not hear an enemy approaching."

A middle-aged man with a beard, who looked very strong and had big hands, explained that clan wars still went on. He told about a big interclan war in Tari just a few years earlier that was so bad, the airport was closed for a long time.

When I asked about some of the causes of wars, Peter explained that blood feuds were commonplace. "Justice is very much eye for eye," Peter said, adding that feuds could run on, tit for tat, for long periods, often escalating into larger battles and wars.

These feuds reminded me of the infamous Hatfield and McCoy feud on the West Virginia-Kentucky border during the latter part of the 1800s, except that the highlanders in PNG were still using arrows, spears, and axes rather than guns. This was one of the things that I had come to see in PNG. It was the time-travel aspect of my journey that I would value so much in my Disappearing World travel project, because it gave me a firsthand look at what large parts of humanity have gone through at various stages during human prehistory. The constant warfare was also a sad reminder that human nature hasn't changed much. Only the technology has changed in a modern world where conflict seems never ending and human butchery is conducted on an industrial scale.

Our glimpse into the martial culture of the Highlands continued when Achara and I were invited into the fields behind the village. The fields were dotted with low mounds of freshly hoed dirt from which grew taro, a starchy tuber with elephant ear-looking leaves. Standing in the middle of this bucolic setting, a group of boys were practicing with bow and arrows. One shirtless young boy barely three feet tall, wearing a tan canvas skirt and with his face painted in yellow ochre, shot his arrows with impressive accuracy into a pile of palm thatch across the taro field.

A short, muscular young man appeared to be instructing the boys. In his grass skirt, brown animal skin armbands, and colorful beaded headband, he looked every inch a warrior. Noticing me, the instructor motioned for me to give it a try. After demonstrating the proper technique, he handed me the long bow and helped position me in the correct stance. I pulled back hard on the taut string, concentrating on a target well across the field, and released the arrow.

Everybody burst out laughing. My arrow went straight and true, right into the ground about twenty-five feet away.

"Try again," Peter shouted as Achara rolled her eyes. After several attempts, I redeemed myself somewhat, managing to send my arrows well across the field, though I'm sure that any enemy would have felt quite safe.

After this humbling archery session, we walked through more fields into the village, where Steven was scheduled to pick us up. But it began to rain so hard that when he arrived, one couldn't see to drive. So we took shelter under the tin roof of a nearby shop, where some women invited us to join them in their home in a nearby hut.

Achara and I squeezed into the small space inside their hut, where seven women were sitting in a circle around a fire pit. Steam rose from a vat of boiling water slung over the fire pit. When we sat, a chubby woman in a white cotton smock offered us some food. As she handed me a piece of boiled pork fat held in a steamed bloodleaf, everyone beamed a welcoming smile. Not wanting to ruin this warm show of hospitality, I took the glob of dripping white fat with a smile, trying to suppress a shudder. Happily, it tasted better than it looked. Since none of the women spoke English, we all just smiled at each other while Achara and I sat there eating pork fat.

When the rain stopped, we got up to leave, smiling and rubbing our stomachs to convey our hearty thanks. This would be just one of many instances, during our week in the Highlands, when Huli people were quite open and friendly to us outsiders—and also quite curious about us.

We rejoined Steven and Peter outside, where a small group of villagers had also come around.

"They want to see and meet the white people," said Steven (referring to us both, though Achara is Asian). "They are very curious. It is most unusual to see tourists in their village."

They asked Achara and me several questions, with Steven eagerly interpreting. One question, though, really struck me: "Why are the tourists that we sometimes see always in vehicles being driven up or down the road?" one female villager asked. "Their vehicles never stop. How come the tourists don't come to talk to us, as you are doing?"

I could think of no good answer to this question. Should I suggest to these hospitable, friendly, and curious folks that perhaps some visitors might feel intimidated by them, or that the outside world had a view of traditional cultures as being dangerous? Could I somehow explain that some tourists only wanted to observe while staying in the creature comforts that reminded them of their homes in the rich world?

We ended up conversing with the villagers for about two hours. It was perhaps the first time any of them there had ever spoken with a foreigner.

That night at the lodge, our education into the martial life of the Highlanders continued. Over an excellent dinner of fire-roasted chicken with green vegetables and tea, which Steven had prepared, he explained how Huli boys were trained in the art of war.

"When boys are still young, around the age of nine, the education into warfare skills is begun," Steven said. "The young boys learn the use of the bow and arrow, spear throwing, and hand combat weapons such as axes and machetes."

"So they really start early," I noted.

"Yes. This is very important," he said. "Young boys may even participate in wars at very young ages—not as combatants, but as bystanders near the line of fire from arrows. Boys must learn how to see and dodge arrows while still young. If they do not develop this skill at a young age, it is hard to learn when they are grown."

This made good sense in the Highlands, of course. But I still found it an amazing reality when, just a couple of days' flight away, most of my friends' kids at home would be playing Little League baseball or video games.

Later that evening, I asked Steven to explain more about male and female interactions. I had read before the trip that in Huli culture, men and women were separated, with women living in totally separate villages. Even married women lived and slept in separate villages, where they raised the children: the boys until around age 9, and the girls until they got married. Women also tended the garden where the family food was grown, and raised the pigs. When I was much younger and had first learned about how strict Muslims segregated their women, I thought it extreme. But by Huli standards, even conservative Islam seemed mild.

"Women and marriage are considered to be specifically for procreation," said Steven. "The sex act is mainly to create pregnancy."

This little factoid I hadn't read, and it seemed out of character for the testosterone-driven Huli culture. So I asked how often sex took place and where—in the man's or the woman's home.

"Perhaps several times a year, the married couple will find a comfortable spot in the garden or bush and have sexual intercourse," he explained rather clinically. (I would learn later, perhaps to my relief, that Huli males were actually "regular" men after all. On an occasion when Steven and I were having a few beers in private, he mentioned that it was normal for men to have sexual relations with unmarried girlfriends. "Men have needs," he said (with a wink and a smile.)

Since sex did not seem to be a major draw, Achara asked what were the most important things a Huli man looked for in a wife.

"Unlike in modern societies, physical attractiveness is not the primary factor in choosing a wife," Steven continued. "The woman's capacity to work and raise children and pigs is most important. A man will evaluate a woman's suitability based on visual signs that she is a good and sturdy worker."

"How can you tell if a woman is a good worker?" Achara asked.

"Dirty, short fingernails show that a woman works in the garden a lot," Steven replied. "Another sign of a good working woman is that she will have a two-finger gap that starts a short way behind the hairline at the top of her forehead and runs across the top of her head." He motioned toward Achara's head to show where this gap in the hairline should run. "Women carry bundles or clothes baskets, called 'bilum,' attached to straps that are hoisted over their heads. Over time, this practice creates a gap or deep furrow in the hair across the woman's head."

"How about men?" Achara then asked. "What do women look for in a man?"

"Men are judged as attractive potential mates by their ability to provide and protect," Steven answered. "A man's prowess as a warrior and a sign that he is a diligent worker might be shown by him having hard, strong hands. His status and wealth are demonstrated by how many pigs and wives he has."

That evening, in a moment of levity, Achara decided to write a personal ad that a Huli male might post when seeking a mate:

HULI PERSONAL AD

Great Huli warrior with many pigs, hard strong hands, has been growing out beard for many moons, seeks ideal partner. Must be Huli, have dark, short, dirty fingernails, and at least a 2-finger gap between front hairline and back hair. Pig raising and gardening skills a plus!! Also has to be a good provider and self-sufficient.

Of course, Huli people didn't use personal ads to find mates. Instead, as Steven explained, this was arranged between parents. The prospective mates would be allowed to sit in the woods or garden together. There they would talk and learn about each other through stories they both told. If they should decide to marry, they must wait one year, apart from each other, before the courting ceremony took place. All this sounded efficient but not very romantic.

One of the things I loved about this trip into the Highlands of PNG was that life here was so thoroughly different from anything I had ever experienced. Every day brought new realizations of just how different. One day, we would be in the dense rain forest near the lodge, scouting for birds of paradise. New Guinea is famous for these beautiful birds, the males of which sport amazingly long, elaborate, brightly colored plumage extending from the head, wings, or tail.

Another day, we saw a woman made up in ghostlike disguise, with white powdery face makeup and wearing beads, a blanket and a tan-colored grass skirt, with clay spread all over her body. She was standing in a forest clearing, staring up at an elevated wooden platform set on six-foot stilts—a traditional Huli grave. Peter explained that she was grieving her dead husband in the Huli mourning ceremony. Her dress and appearance were a disguise so that her husband's spirit would not recognize her and take her with him. As I often did when hearing about premodern religious beliefs, I marveled at the simplicity and straightforward logic of those beliefs.

On another day, we were in a village clearing in the forest, surrounded by wooden dolls all dressed up and painted to look life-like, while watching the Huli "witch doctors" of the God Clan. The witch doctors did dances during the day to worship the sun and at night to cure people. They wore wigs of thick black hair flowing all the way down their backs, adorned with brown, black, and red feathers and topped off by a bed of fluffy snow white feathers, and long strands of white beads strung around them like Christmas tree lights. Like the welcome sing-sing, the "spirit dance" routine we watched was simple in its steps, though still fascinating. I was glad to see these traditional religious beliefs in action, still untainted by meddling Anglican and other Christian missionaries, who seemed to flock like vultures to PNG, bent on changing those they perceived as "backward" or too poor not to be swayed by whatever trivial goods they brought.

It was late morning, on a Tuesday, when Achara and I visited the witch doctors with Steven. After their performance, Steven took us on a walk through the forest to a local courthouse on Tari's dirt main drag. On Tuesdays, he explained, members of the village came to settle disputes in front of a judge. To me, the courthouse and judge seemed anachronistic—misshapen artifacts from the far-off "modern," ridiculously corrupt and inept government in PNG's dilapidated capital, Port Moresby.

The court was empty at the moment, because people were out to lunch. So, we walked to the local market, where I bought a few warm SP beers for Steven, Achara, and me to drink while passing the time. With no real place to sit, we just plopped down on the ground on the side of the dirt road.

Suddenly, we found ourselves at the center of a growing crowd of curious villagers: small kids with stripes on their faces; young men in faded old baseball caps and equally faded old shirts and shorts; a shirtless man in a grass skirt, with white-painted legs, wearing several bead necklaces and an old fishing hat wrapped with yellow beads; old men in beards; and even a guy in a hoodie. Within fifteen minutes, perhaps seventy people had gathered in front of us and began sitting on the ground, just staring at us. It felt as if Achara and I were the exotic attraction of a traveling carnival—every bit as strange as the bearded lady or the five-legged calf.

"They are curious about you and Achara," Steven said as more villagers came. "Most have never seen a white person sitting in their village."

With Steven interpreting, the villagers started asking us questions.

"Why are you here?" a young man with a round face and darkly stained teeth asked.

"What is the world like outside PNG?" a young woman in a plain peach sweatshirt wanted to know.

One asked self-consciously, what did we think of them? Another man in the crowd expressed embarrassment over their evident poverty and "backwardness."

Perhaps the most memorable statement came from a middle-aged woman with a kindly face. "We are all so surprised to see white people sit on the ground and drink beer with a local person," she said in earnest as Steven continued to interpret. "We all thought that white people had to always be in an air-conditioned bus and could only live in the lodge on the big hill" (the luxury eco lodge). "But here you are, sitting with us."

This went on for more than an hour. Achara and I did our best to answer each question and address each comment. The most delicate issue was the villagers' evident embarrassment over their poverty and "backwardness."

"Yes, I can see that people are very poor here," I replied. To deny the obvious would be silly, of course. These people were among the poorest in the world. "But you do have a type of great wealth. You are fortunate to live in such a beautiful natural world as this, here in the Southern Highlands of PNG." I also mentioned that many in the modern world spent most of their time working, often at labors they did not enjoy, and didn't have much free time to enjoy nature or relax with their friends and neighbors—things that the people here in this village did every day.

It eventually started to rain. So the villagers invited us into their local clubhouse to talk and have some more beers. The reality was that only Steven, Achara, and I were actually drinking. I told Steven that I could buy beers for everyone. "No!" he warned. "Drinking is dangerous for most men here. They can't stop, and fights happen."

The clubhouse was a large one-room shack a short way down the road. While there, Steven told us that many people expressed their surprise that Achara and I would sit on the ground and drink beers and actually interact with them. They also told Steven that we were the first white people they had ever had in their clubhouse. Steven said that in twenty-one years of hosting tourists and guiding in the area, he had never seen anything like this happen.

During the spontaneous party, the villagers sang us Huli songs about the rain and courtship. Then they asked if we could take their photos and show them the pictures. At first, they were hesitant to ask such a thing, fearing that we might run out of film. But their hesitancy evaporated when Achara showed them that we both had digital cameras with capacity to take 500 more pictures. Everyone eagerly started posing and hamming for the cameras.

The party lasted several hours and was a highlight of our trip. (Later, I sent stacks of photos from this occasion to Steven, for distribution to the villagers who were there.) I felt genuinely privileged to have had this type of interaction with people who were still, in many ways, from the Stone Age. I also knew that within a decade or two, this sort of experience would become all but impossible anywhere in our rapidly globalizing world.

One of the things I found most fascinating about Huli culture was the central prominence of elaborate male-hair wigs in their lives. This aspect of their culture seemed such a contrast to the humdrum straightforwardness of so many other aspects of day-to-day living. Naturally, I was eager to learn more about the rituals involved in making the wigs. On our last day in the Highlands, Peter brought us to an area in the forest where some bachelor boys were staying in wig school. A young man's progress to full manhood in Huli society had a number of elaborate ceremonies, Peter explained, and the final one was the bachelor's ritual, which was done in the late teens.

In an open area in the forest by a small creek, we were greeted by two "spell masters." These men were middle-aged and sported bushy black beards and large conical human-hair wigs. One of the spell masters had a long twig through his nose. Both were bare chested and wore woven grass skirts, animal-skin armbands, and various ring necklaces. They looked every bit as outlandish as I would imagine a spell master to be.

Peter said that spell masters were skilled elders who trained the bachelor boys in the wig school. As he explained this, one of the spell masters lit up a large wooden pipe, and a young man, one of the bachelors, came out to join us. The rules he lived under sounded onerous.

"The young men stay in wig school for around eighteen months," the spell master said, offering me his pipe. "During this period, they grow their hair for use in their wig. We have very strict rules. The bachelors must avoid all contact with women, especially sexual, and have no contact with family. No one can touch the young man's hair. They cannot walk behind a woman, cannot go anywhere alone, and must avoid sun and rain to protect their hair." The spell master went on to explain that the young had to live in the woods during this entire period and must not use main roads for travel, to prevent inadvertent contact with women.

"Here in wig school," he concluded, "the bachelors learn Huli traditions and train for manhood."

The other spell master then explained that after a young man grew his hair for eighteen months a spell master inspected it. If it was satisfactory, he received permission to see a specialist to cut the hair, which the young man would then use to construct his wig.

"Upon finishing this long initiation, the young man will now be considered a full adult," said the spell master with the pipe.

I saw in this whole centrality of male-hair wigs in Huli society a display of human nature at its most primal. We were not so different from many other species in the animal kingdom, in which the males had the more attractive ornamentation.

On our last morning in the Highlands, we bumped along the potholed dirt road in Steven's beat-up truck back to the Tari airport. Achara and I had to catch a flight to Wewak, along New Guinea's northeast coast, where we would arrange the next part of our journey, deep into the lowland jungles of the fabled Upper Sepik River.

Achara and I were sad to leave. We had been treated so hospitably during the whole experience, by just about everyone we met. And what we experienced was so different from anything in our normal lives. We were so impressed with our time in the Highlands that we made a plan with Steven to return in the foreseeable future. We wanted to trek into the nearby Mt. Bosavi range and visit several very isolated villages in that area.

"If you and Achara return a second time," Steven said solemnly, "You will no longer be visitors. I will welcome you like family."

We knew that he meant it.

CHAPTER 2

River of the Crocodile People

November 2005
Sepik River, Papua New Guinea

The hot, wet air felt almost too thick to breathe. Nothing moved but the mosquitoes, which seemed strangely impervious to the blazing equatorial sun. Achara and I had just come ashore after two hours by motorized canoe trip up the Sepik River and were standing by our gear on the dirt bank as the brown water slid silently by. Behind us, the thatch-roofed huts of Ambunti village backed away into the steaming rain forest. I was hoping to find a man who lived in this area and was known to be a reputable guide. It was the second time in two weeks, I realized, that we had arrived in these semi-Neolithic lands not knowing whether we would even find the person we were looking for.

Our journey so far had not gone smoothly. Yesterday, Achara and I had flown from Tari to Wewak, a pleasant backwater on PNG's northeast coastline. We had stayed in a bare-bones seaside lodge near the Wewak airport, in a concrete-walled room unfurnished but for two single beds with dirty sheets. I accepted this indignity because the hotel's owner could arrange the three-hour road transport to Pagwi, a tiny village on the Lower Sepik River, and then the motorized canoe ride upriver to Ambunti, on the Middle Sepik. He also owned the Ambunti Lodge in the village. I had paid him US$100 up front for one night's stay there, and US$600 altogether, which included the return ride to Wewak.

Nothing that the pudgy local lodge owner arranged worked out well, though. After his driver dropped us off in Pagwi, the motor canoe that I had prepaid to have waiting for us wasn't there. So I scrambled and found another one to take us upriver to Ambunti. Then, along the way, I found out that he had charged me triple the going rate from Wewak to Ambunti. The final insult was the Ambunti Lodge, which we were now looking at. The "lodge" was a termite-ridden old shack and not worth two dollars a night, let alone a hundred.

But no use fretting about it now. With Achara standing watch over our bags, I asked around for the reputable jungle guide. Just as in the Highlands, a small group of villagers soon congregated around Achara. Some were boys learning English in the mission station next to the village. One of the boys told me the jungle guide I had hoped to meet no longer lived here, that he had moved to a village far down-river. This news fit how things had been going thus far on our Sepik journey.

As the curious, friendly villagers gawked at us newly arrived aliens, I considered the curious aspect of being a traveler in this very remote, still lawless land. It was strange to think that back home in Los Angeles, there were "no-go zones" where people from nicer parts of the city wouldn't dream of just casually visiting and hanging around, let alone voluntarily stranding themselves deliberately. But here we were, in a place where everyone around us might well see us as vulnerable, naked, and plastered with hundred-dollar bills. And yet, except for the discomfort of the heat, humidity, and bugs, we felt completely at ease.

Standing here with Achara in the steam oven of the deep Sepik rain forest, I also mused that, after all, this was what real adventure travel was—you accepted the hassles and screw-ups or would do better to stay home. I always get a kick out of how the modern travel-and-tourism industry misuses and overuses the word "adventure," hanging it on excursions as tame and predictable as Universal Studios, or even a three-day cruise in the Caribbean, where the most unexpected thing that can occur is a different catch of the day at dinner. But real adventure travel is all about journeying into unfamiliar situations and locales where the traveler truly does not have control—or even knowledge of all the variables involved. And the reality often involves being dirty and sweat soaked in unrelenting heat, while constantly dodging scams and rip-offs, and where things seldom go right.

Since the guide I hoped to meet wasn't here, I asked the young boys to put out the word that I needed someone with passable English, who could guide us into the Upper Sepik region. Achara and I waited by the riverfront near the Ambunti Lodge as several men quickly appeared. Clearly, opportunities to make hard cash were scarce in a place like this. No one looked too promising, though—they were either drunk or sickly, or just had no experience as river guides. After wasting an hour with the ill-favored crop of applicants, I learned from a small boy that the guide I had come to meet had a son named Ronnie, who also guided on the river and lived in a nearby village in the forest.

The boy took us to Ronnie's home, a neat wood-and-thatch house in a forest clearing. Ronnie was also out of town, though, but his younger brother Robin was here. Robin, who appeared to be in his early thirties, was a sturdy chap and seemed amiable enough. He was a carpenter who did odd jobs in the village, but he didn't speak much English and had never been a guide or even gone very far up the Sepik River. But as we stood in the suffocating heat in the clearing by his small, tidy home, Robin explained, with the young boy interpreting, that he had grown up in the area and knew about the people on the river. He would bring his wife, Jacinda, along on the trip to interpret.

None of this sounded especially promising. But with no other options, Achara and I hired him and his wife, for US$2,000, to be our guides. Once again, as a traveler, I was entrusting our fate into the hands of utter strangers—in this case, strangers with no experience, who would be taking us for the next eight days into what were still some of the wildest, most remote rain forests on earth.

Early the next afternoon, we were chugging up the muddy waters of the Sepik. Our small wooden canoe, powered by a fifteen-horsepower outboard, managed to move along reasonably well despite being loaded with Achara and me, Robin and Jacinda, and supplies for the week-long trip, including several blue plastic five-gallon water jugs. Gliding past the endless green of the jungled shore, we were excited to be on our way upriver, into an area that had seen very few visitors from the outside world. Much of the Sepik Basin is still a true vast wilderness, inhabited by humans, yet with almost no development of any kind except for a few Missionary Air Force landing strips (which are perhaps the only useful thing that these alien intruders, with their culturally disruptive belief systems, bring to the island).

Like the rest of New Guinea, which has a mind-boggling range of strange creatures, from tree-climbing kangaroos to lizards with green blood and mushrooms that glow in the dark, the Sepik is a cornucopia of natural treasures, and a continual source of newly discovered species. As a child, I had grown up aware of a world that always seemed on the verge of annihilation by nuclear war between the Soviet Union and the United States. It was also a time when people started hearing about the wholesale destruction of the planet's tropical rain forests, especially the burning of the Amazon. I constantly worried that these wondrous places would be gone by the time I was old enough to go there, and vowed to see them when I grew up, if they were still around. One of the main goals for my Disappearing World project was to journey into the world's last great remaining tropical rain forests: the Amazon, the Congo Basin, and the Sepik River Basin. Being here now was a partial step toward fulfilling this lifelong goal.

The river journey, as with everything else since Achara and I left Tari, had not started smoothly. We began the day dead tired, having had no sleep the night before at the Ambunti Lodge. Achara later wrote in her trip journal: "The Ambunti Lodge was a filthy, smelly, oven-hot dump. Everything was dilapidated and disgusting. Our room was a dirty little box with no ventilation and a black, mold-encrusted screen riddled with holes to let the mosquitoes in. The mosquito net over the nasty bed was so full of holes, Gary and I thought it must be there just for decor. And the other guests, mostly drunk men, seemed to be in a marathon snoring contest for the night!" Indeed, we probably would have been more comfortable just to have camped outside and saved the hundred-dollar cost of the room.

After the sleepless night, we were up early in the unrelenting heat and humidity, working with Robin and Jacinda to load the canoe. In the process, I began to wonder if I had made a dreadful mistake entrusting the inexperienced Robin with our trip. The little dugout canoe, which had taken hours of searching the nearby forest villages yesterday afternoon to find, looked pretty forlorn. Overwhelmed by our cargo even without us aboard, it sat low in the water, looking ready to sink into the turbid brown water. I expressed my concern to Robin that the little craft was way too small for this trip, but he beamed confidently. Not to worry, he said, the canoe could hold more than it looked capable of.

My confidence in him evaporated once Achara and I took our "seats" and Robin and Jacinda stepped into the back. The gunwales were now only inches above the waterline. Robin started the engine, and we puttered toward a small hut a short distance away, where we would buy gasoline, adding yet more weight to our overladen craft. The canoe shook and groaned, and its bow kept swinging back and forth like a compass needle that couldn't find north.

"This won't work," I said to Robin again, quite alarmed now. "The canoe is too small."

But still he insisted that all was well. A moment later, though, as if to mock our new skipper, the boat swung precariously around, doing a complete 360 in the middle of the river when Robin tried to steer back toward the dock for the gasoline. At that moment, I thought, *This is it!*—the boat was about dump everything we had into the drink.

That was enough nonsense for me, and I demanded that we get a bigger boat and engine, period.

But all that was behind us now. We found a larger canoe and engine and were on our way a little before noon. We chugged all afternoon up the Sepik and then onto the April River, a Sepik tributary. Journeying upriver, we passed a profusion of river and forest birds the entire way. The most common were great egrets—elegant, slender creatures with black legs, that waded along the riverside, their daggerlike yellow beaks cocked and ready to spear a fish or frog in the river waters below. More sinister looking were the crocodiles sitting silently in the riverside brush, their half-open eyes watching for careless prey to wander by. Along the way, the primal rawness of the land was palpable. We were in untouched wilderness that had been this way forever.

The long ride gave Achara and me a chance to know Robin and Jacinda better. Petite, friendly Jacinda said they had two young children and lived on food they grew in a small garden near their home, and from fishing. The small carpentry jobs that Robin did around Ambunti helped with a little cash when needed. I gathered that the sum of money I was paying him for this journey, after expenses, was a nice windfall.

We arrived at Paru on the April River, Upper Sepik region, just after sunset. The small village had a dozen neat thatch-roofed houses built on stilts, some along the river. Several crude yet ornate hand-carved wooden benches, each with a smiling face carved into one end, were scattered around the settlement, giving the place a welcoming feel. Pigs, apparently as valuable here as in the Highlands, scampered about the place while friendly villagers showed us around.

Paru was in a naturally gorgeous Eden surrounded by lush jungle. At a waterfall where we bathed, dozens of blue-and-green butterflies and several iridescent reddish dragonflies flitted about. Green parrots and cockatoos rioted in the trees above. In a swamp near the village, a hornbill convention was in full swing as perhaps two dozen of the outlandish-looking birds bickered noisily in a large leafless tree.

Tempering the beauty of its surroundings, Paru was a perfect mosquito hell. They were so bad that Achara had to spend both our evenings there in our tent-shaped mosquito net. I had to bring her food there, and we jokingly began calling it "Achara's jail." But the mosquitoes were no joke for her. Even though she wore long pants and used strong deet repellent, she soon had big red welts on her legs from the nasty little beasts.

From Paru, we began our slow journey back downstream, a trip that would take us from village to village along the April and then the Sepik over the next six days. Starting out from Paru, we drifted into a magical spot full of large green shoots rising out of the water, each bearing dozens of almost hand-size yellow-green Venus flytraps. In some low brush by the shore, a bluish-gray bird with an elegant white-tipped blue lace crest watched us out of bright red eyes. The bird—a crowned pigeon, according to Robin—made a strange deep whooping sound far out of keeping with its size. Continuing downriver, we passed areas of almost deafening cacophony as loud as a machine shop, coming from untold numbers of cicadas droning in the dense jungle that lined the river. It all felt like some tropical Eden from an earlier geologic age.

Our first stop in this wonderland was less Edenic. The small village of Biaga was a collection of stilt houses built right in the swamp at the juncture of the April and Sepik Rivers. Not a single villager was in sight, and the place was so thick with mosquitoes that

Achara elected to stay in the canoe while I made a quick visit to the village's spirit house. Spirit houses were at the core of Sepik River culture, and I was eager to see one.

Biaga's Spirit House was a small one-room wooden structure built on stilts over the water. Inside, the dank room was filled with stylized likenesses of crocodiles and also more human-looking faces carved on the flat wooden statues. The faces were often shown smiling, which seemed oddly cheerful for such a dreary place.

From my readings and Robin's explanation, I learned that the spirit house was the most important building in any village. It housed wood carvings, masks, and figurines bearing likenesses of ancestors, nature spirits, and other mythical beings. The carvings were created to be inhabited by good spirits and to ward off malign spirits. The spirit house was also where rites of initiation into adulthood for young males took place. Robin had explained that in the past, only initiated warriors, or those going through initiation, could enter the spirit house. In some cases, violators faced the death penalty.

While looking over Biaga's dusty carvings, I wondered what would eventually become of these sacred and hallowed structures if modern eco- or "adventure" tourism got a foothold in these parts of the Sepik. It was sad to think that they would just become another tick on some tourist's bucket list. I envisioned visitors trampling through the spirit houses, snapping photos of these relics from perhaps one of the few surviving truly ancient human mythology and belief systems left in the world.

After the earthly purgatory of Biaga, our next stop was a genuinely strange place an hour downriver, on a small waterway just south of the Sepik. Swagup, a relatively large village of around two hundred people, was well regarded as a center of canoe making in the region.

As we glided through the dark water to the shoreline, the atmosphere couldn't have been more different from Biaga's. A swarm of eager kids welcomed us.

"Hey!" . . . "Hello, mister." . . . "Photo!" the eager, waving kids shouted at once. "Hello! Good-bye!" others yelled. All wanted their photos taken. After somber Biaga, it was endearing and quite refreshing.

Swagup's adults, however, were very different from the kids. As we walked around the neatly laid-out village of wooden houses on low-rise stilts, the adults we met were quite reserved, almost unfriendly. When we walked up to the spirit house, which had a steep, sway-backed thatch roof and large carved standing pillars supporting its thick ridge beam, the young men in front of it, surprisingly, turned us away. A few moments later, when I asked some men about the village outhouse, they waved me away, pointing to the woods. (As a guest in the village, I would have assumed it very rude just to take it upon myself to use the surrounding forest as a toilet.) This unwelcoming behavior was a stark contrast to anything that Achara and I had yet experienced in PNG, and Swagup took on an oppressive pall.

We continued onto the village's canoe-making area along the riverbank. Many large wooden canoes, dug out from freshly cut trees, were laid out over a wide area, all apparently organized according to their various stages of production. In what was a familiar motif for the Sepik, the ends of the canoes had very nice crocodile-head like-nesses. By the canoe-making area, I asked Robin why everyone in Swagup, except for the kids, was so unfriendly, and why the rude answer when I asked about an outhouse.

"It's a strange place," Robin replied in a low voice. "It was one of the last villages to give up cannibalism. The village also has some weird practices. One is that males must defecate in the forest behind the spirit house, hidden from the village women. The villagers believe that spirits eat the men's dung. They also believe that if a woman sees a man defecate, then that man must kill the woman."

Swagup had such a foreboding atmosphere that Achara and I were glad to leave. Later on the trip, we picked up Robin's brother, Ronnie, who joined us for the remainder of the journey. Ronnie, a tough, no-nonsense man in his early thirties, told us a grim story about Swagup's recent past, which perhaps helped explain the strange unfriendliness:

"Our grandfather was the leader of a village near Swagup," Ronnie said. "Sometime around the late 1960s, several children and teenagers from the village went missing. It was learned that some people from Swagup had eaten the missing people.

"So my grandfather and elders from other villages in the area organized a war party. They snuck up through the forest and surrounded Swagup one night," he said in an even voice. "Then they attacked and massacred every living person in Swagup."

"But a small amount of Swagup's villagers ran away and hid in the forest," he continued. "Eventually, they returned to their destroyed village to start it over again. The people today in Swagup are the descendants of those few survivors."

I had no way of verifying the accuracy of this story, but I felt that Ronnie had no reason to lie, and the history seemed to fit the village's grim, oppressive atmosphere.

After leaving Swagup, our group, with the addition of Ronnie, spent the next several days visiting more river villages in the primeval wilderness of the Upper Sepik. The villages were almost incomprehensibly remote, not only from the outside world but also from each other. In each village we visited, often just a mile or so downriver from the last one, a completely different, often unrelated language was spoken. To communicate, people from different villages would have to use pidgin, a sort of "contact language" made up of simplified borrowed words from different languages.

A major motif of our Sepik journey, besides the swarms of bugs and the endless steam bath, was the theme of crocodiles. The people of the Sepik in general held the giant, ancient saurians in high esteem, and the crocodile loomed large in much of the art we saw all along the way. Nearing our final major destination on the journey, we even visited a place whose inhabitants were known as the "crocodile people." This was in the village of Yenchen, near the Chambri Lakes on the Middle Sepik, a spectacular wetland of broad clearwater swamps and interconnecting canals that spread between many of the villages in the region.

Yenchen was a pleasant, orderly-looking village of small, neat wooden houses, many with small gardens of colorful flowers, laid out along a path fronting the river. It had an impressive seventy-five-year-old two-story spirit house, whose bottom floor doubled as a craftsmen's factory. On the rectangular ground floor, which was perhaps a hundred feet long and thirty-five feet wide, village men were hard at work making colorful masks of all sizes, placards, and figurines. Others were making larger pieces that covered the wearer's upper and middle body and were worn during traditional ceremonies. The crocodile, in symbolic and mythical forms and figures, was everywhere in the artworks. Most striking were the various scarifications and raised tattoos on many of the men's sparsely clothed bodies, resembling forms and patterns of crocodiles and crocodile skin.

Although the crocodile tattoos and scarring often gave the men a fierce aspect, everyone was very welcoming to Achara and me, and we ended up staying the night in Yenchen. We had dinner that evening with a group of crocodile men in a large community hut that was perhaps half the size of the spirit house. In the shadowed firelight of the hut, we were surrounded by lots of big, fierce-looking wooden masks in bold reds, shades of purple, black, and white. On the rough hardwood floor about us, ceremonial bell-shaped body masks, with large mythical faces carved and painted on them, watched in silence as we ate. It was a setting that fit the Sepik River, and about as exotic as any I could imagine.

While Achara once again sat inside her "jail" as protection from the mosquito swarms, our meal was rather more prosaic. As on much of the trip, it was a type of fish that the locals called "rubber-mouth"—a bland-tasting fish with so many fine little bones that eating it involved more time spent picking out the mouthful of bones than chewing. Unfortunately, in the Sepik this was becoming the main fish available, due to an unwelcome intrusion from the outside world.

"The rubber-mouth is an introduced invasive species to the Sepik," Ronnie had explained earlier. "Over time, it has displaced much of the native fish stocks."

Sitting that evening in the village of these still very traditional people, so far removed from the modern world, I found it hard to believe that such a widespread ecological change had already occurred in the Sepik River. This was not the only instance of spreading invasive species in the region, either. Traveling over the next two days in the Chambri Lakes area, we would see a type of water hyacinth choking the smaller water passages—also an invasive species, according to Ronnie.

The Crocodile People of Yenchen were not the only ones in the region to etch and scarify their bodies with crocodile motifs. Achara and I happened to visit a village called Kanganaman, near the Chambri Lakes, on the day that a ceremony initiating the village's young men into manhood was taking place. During my travels so far, I had begun, whenever possible, witnessing the major rites of passage so prevalent in traditional and premodern cultures. The equivalent of this in the Papua New Guinea Highlands, for instance, was the training of young boys for war, and wig school for adolescent males. These rites of passage were fundamental in holding these societies together. I theorized that perhaps they also aided in mitigating the rampant juvenile delinquency so prevalent in modern societies, most of which don't really have any such equivalent major life initiations for their young people.

We had stopped into Kanganaman because I wanted to buy some of the high-quality masks that the village was well known for. It was a casual place, spread across dry and wet lands into the forest, off the main river. Ducks waddled about on the deep-green wet grasses, and kids ran playing.

Our canoe pulled up to dry land at Kanganaman, and a village elder led us up long wooden stairs into the shaded second floor of the cavernous spirit house. Robin, Ronnie, Jacinda, Achara, and I followed him into the dimly lit room, where a haunting carving of an ancestral spirit gazed down at us from atop the thick central roof support pole. Across the long, rectangular room stood a line of naked men covered in a sawdust powder and holding large spears. The men's heads were shaved, and long-leafed foliage covered their genitals. The skin on their backs and exposed buttocks looked raw and almost sunburned because they all had recently been extensively scarred to resemble the hide of the crocodile. Narrow shafts of bright sunlight coming through cracks in the walls played on the sawdust powder on their bodies, giving them a ghostly appearance.

"The initiation rites take three months," the village elder said. "During this time, the initiates learn the various things men are expected to know, such as their traditions, important wisdom, and the arts of combat. The time also allows for healing of the scars."

To my surprise, the elder explained that the whole initiation course was 500 kina (about US$167) per man. I didn't think to ask then but later wondered what happened to young men who couldn't scrape up what was probably a large sum for the cost of this all-important ritual.

As the village elder led us around the room, the line of young men all kept an impressive solemn silence, standing like Marines at attention. I felt that these young men all understood the solemn passage that was occurring in their lives, from boyhood to manhood. I also sensed that they would go unhesitatingly into battle if ordered to do so by their elders. These disciplined-looking young men seemed a far cry from the less-directed "rascal" gangs that were becoming a common menace all across PNG, a land still largely in another epoch but fast becoming engulfed by the twenty-first century.

———————

The final part of the journey, getting back to Wewak, was another exercise in things gone wrong. We reached Pagwi late Saturday morning. The owner of the seaside lodge in Wewak was supposed to have arranged a truck for us. But no truck was there, and there were no vehicles anywhere that could take us. So Achara and I waited in Pagwi for hours under the blistering sun, wondering if we would end up having to camp out for the night (and then miss our flight back home). Finally, someone with an open-bed truck came along who was heading to Wewak. Achara and I gladly hopped onto the truck bed for the bumpy three-hour ride.

In Wewak, when Achara and I went to check in at the seaside lodge we had stayed in before the trip, we found that the owner had goofed us up again, forgetting to hold a room for us for the night (for which we had already paid). Hearing this, I asked to speak to the owner and was told that he was in his office in the back of his vanilla-processing warehouse on the lodge compound grounds.

Fuming, I left Achara at the front of the compound with our bags and went to the warehouse. There, I stalked through a large room with long tables, where several women were bundling strands of raw vanilla into packages. I stormed straight through the door of the owner's office without knocking and confronted him about the room, the missing ride back to Wewak, the missing boat ride from Pagwi to the Ambunti Lodge, and the overcharge for the truck ride to Pagwi. This became a loud shouting match, which was exactly my strategy— I wanted to deeply embarrass the dishonest creep in front of his staff. Achara told me later she heard us shouting all the way across the compound.

My strategy worked. To save face in front of his staff, the cheat refunded US$600 to me—*all* the money I had paid him. This was fair for the huge hassle he had caused us. All just another part of the experience with real adventure travel.

———

It was during this Sepik trip that I perhaps felt closer to Achara then at any time in our relationship so far. We had shared a special experience together in the Highlands and then again in the Sepik. The Sepik has to be one of the most unpleasant, uncomfortable places on the planet for a modern Western person, especially for a woman. But the visual feast of craftsmanship styles, and the primal experience of the various river cultures that continued to follow their ancient traditions, was a shared time to be treasured forever.

Unfortunately, when we returned to Los Angeles, the high of our shared adventure would quickly turn to impatient frustration. Our plan was to wrap up our affairs, put everything in storage, and get on with our long-planned travel project. I would make arrangements with the bank trading room where I was working, and resign after getting my replacement up to speed. But we hit an unexpected delay.

The year before, I had suffered serious injuries to my foot and knee from Krav Maga martial arts training. The foot injury was so severe that the only real solution offered was a potentially crippling joint replacement. So I had spent almost ten months before our Sepik trip in denial, pretending that with self-directed physical therapy and some other nontraditional medical treatments, the problems would just go away. But the nontraditional medical treatments proved to be nothing but costly quackery. While in PNG, I realized that it would be impossible to do several years of world travel into remote and rugged areas without first fixing my problems.

So, reluctantly, we put our plans on hold, and I spent months searching for a reasonable medical solution for my foot problem, meanwhile undergoing knee surgery. By summer 2006, I had found a doctor who suggested what was, at the time, an innovative answer to my problem, and I had surgery with her. The recovery took months, but the problem was miraculously solved without a joint replacement.

The delay took a major toll on Achara. I was at that midcareer point in life when a professional might be evaluating the chances of making it to the top executive suites or, perhaps instead, embarking on an entrepreneurial route. But Achara, who was considerably younger than I, had just recently finished her master's degree at the University of Southern California and was itching to get started on her career path. She had dreamed all her life of working in the Thai foreign ministry but had given that dream up to live with me in the United States. To do the long travel project, she had accepted a three-year delay in starting a different type of career path in the States. But the additional delay—likely a year, though we didn't actually know how long it would last—meant that she just sat in a sort of bored and frustrated limbo, waiting for me to recover. It was enormously frustrating for her. She worried constantly that the chances for a successful career in the paths she envisioned would close to her because she would be too old when we completed our travels.

Despite the frustration of the long unexpected delay, I stayed laser focused on starting back on the travel project as soon as possible. One of my traits in life, for good or ill, was always to focus in on a big project and see it through at all costs. We finally did get started again in November 2006, beginning with a quick stop in Beijing. But my directed focus during the long unplanned delay had perhaps blinded me to my wife's very real frustrations and would come back to haunt me later during my travels.

CHAPTER 3

Getting Started Again:
Can Anything Else Go Wrong?

Anything that can go wrong will.
—Murphy

December 31, 2007
A police station somewhere in Beijing

The concrete holding cell's walls were covered with lime green paint. At one end was a small iron-barred window, at the other a scratched gray metal desk and chair, and in the middle a single bare lightbulb hanging from a wire. The officer in charge had left the cell a moment ago through the steel door by the desk, leaving Achara and me alone, sitting on two metal folding chairs set against the wall.

It was New Year's Eve, and Achara and I were supposed to be celebrating the restart of our big travel project after a frustrating almost year-long delay following our journeys in Papua New Guinea. We had left Los Angeles two weeks ago after closing our affairs there, then spent some time in Bangkok with Achara's family. We then came to Beijing for a ten-day jaunt, after which we would fly on to Peru to begin our long—and long-awaited—travel project.

Beijing, in its headlong rush to transform itself into a clone of a modern Western city before the upcoming 2008 Olympics, seemed a fitting departure point for a journey into places that themselves were vanishing amid the scramble of globalization. Instead, we were experiencing one of those lessons a traveler must periodically endure: that underneath a thin veneer of modernity, life, in many ways, still goes on much as it has for ages.

Looking over at the empty desk where the officer had been sitting, I realized that he had not locked the steel door to the cell when he left a moment ago. Jumping up from my chair, I cracked the door and peered outside. All the police on duty in the cavernous, garagelike building were at the far end.

"Achara, I see a way out of here," I whispered. Walking back to where she sat, I outlined my plan.

All the cops were eating in the back of the garage. A dozen motorcycles were parked along the wall to a back door that opened to an alley. We could duck down behind the motorcycles, go quietly to the door, and make a run for it.

"I think the guy left the room because they just want to be rid of us," I said. "They don't know what to do about our situation. Let's help them with their problem."

Achara looked at me and giggled. She couldn't believe we were actually making a getaway from the police when we were the ones who had actually been the victims of a crime, and the police had been called in to aid us.

"Okay," she said enthusiastically. "Jail break!"

I opened the steel door just enough for us both to squeeze through. The garage had the smell of stale exhaust as we crouched behind the heavy police motorcycles parked along the wall, and slunk to the back door. Reaching the door, I turned the knob, and to my relief, it opened. We ducked quickly through the door and found ourselves in a darkened alley. Not knowing where we were, we ran down the alley to the lights of the nearest street. It was a major boulevard. Stepping into the street, I waved down an oncoming empty taxi, and we both jumped in the backseat.

The ordeal had begun that morning, in Tiananmen Square. Achara and I happened to meet two young local women who claimed to be university students. They asked if they could join us and practice their English. "We can show you around," said one, a perky lass with a smart, short hairstyle. "We can bring you to some nice art galleries and gift shops."

It sounded like a win for everyone, so we had them show us around.

"It is National Tea Week," the other girl explained. She was a little taller than her friend, with pale ivory skin and long, straight black hair. "Have you done a traditional tea ceremony yet?"

Achara and I thought it sounded fun, so they brought us to an exotic-looking wood and stucco teahouse in Beijing's old-fashioned Hutong District. There, a serving girl led us to a cozy low-lit private room on the second floor, where we sat on bright red floor pillows emblazoned with orange dragons, against backrests of polished wood. Delicate ceramic teacups were set out for each of us, incense holders were lit, and soon a spicy fragrance filled the room.

It was fun—the perfect diversion, I thought. The fun part was important in our travel plans, especially for Achara, who had suffered some nasty skin welts from bug bites on the New Guinea trip, which had taken almost six months to heal. So I wanted her to have some fun, comfortable, civilized moments to offset the rougher, more remote jaunts.

But the tea ceremony did not stay fun. After all of us had tasted tiny thimblefuls of ten different teas, I was presented with the bill. It was a whopping 1,500 Chinese yuan (about US$220). Angry at the extortionate charge, which should have amounted to maybe twenty or twenty-five U.S. dollars, I had our servant get the manager. A tough older woman with pinned-back graying hair appeared. After arguing with her for a while and getting nowhere, I realized that we were being ripped off because I was a foreigner. So I threatened to walk out of the teahouse without paying. The two students both started crying.

"We'll pay the bill," the girl with the short hairstyle sobbed. "We are so sorry to have caused you this problem. We are so ashamed. We'll pay it. My friend and I have lost so much face now."

"No! You are students," I said. "This is a lot of money to you." Then, after arguing with the manager for a while longer, we negotiated the bill down to US$160. They threw in several small boxes of tea for us to take home. It was still a ridiculous sum, but I paid it so we could be on our way.

After saying good-bye to the two students, Achara and I were walking back to our hotel, a well-known four-star business hotel called the Markham, when Achara blurted, "They were in on it, Gary! The two students—they set us up."

"You think?" I said. Then I realized that we had been completely scammed from the start. Though I felt stupid for being taken in by what, in retrospect, seemed such a transparent con, I ended up laughing with Achara about it, almost admiring how adroitly the girls had played us.

Back at our hotel, I mentioned the incident to the manager when he came over to greet us as we walked through the lobby.

"We must call the police!" he said indignantly. The manager was middle-aged man, elegantly dressed in a black business suit. "It is a scam, as you now know, and it happens all the time. I'll ask the police chief to go down to the teahouse with you and get your money back," he insisted.

Although I had to respect the girls' skill in conning me, I liked the idea of getting my money back. I wasn't eager to involve the police, though, especially in a country infamous for its corruption and mind-boggling bureaucracy. But the well-meaning manager insisted on getting the police involved, and brought Achara and me into a large conference room to wait for them. A half hour later, around four p.m., several police walked into the conference room to take our complaint. We all sat around a huge round polished hardwood conference table as Achara and I filled out a complaint form. This began a process that took on a life of its own and that only a visitor into an alien land would fall into.

The bureaucratic procedures of the Chinese police turned out to be elaborate, especially when involving foreigners. (I suspected this was due in part to China's push to polish its image to the outside world for the upcoming Olympics.) Over the next six hours, various officers, translators, tourist police, and bunko squad detectives came to the hotel to review our claim. Everyone agreed that there was a crime, but no one could decide on the actual charges. Several times during this process, I suggested, and then came almost to insist on, dropping the complaint. But as the drama grew ever more Kafkaesque, I was told that I couldn't let it go.

"Once a complaint process is started it must continue until completed," explained an attractive female police translator with perfect white teeth.

Achara and I were trapped by well-meaning bureaucrats running in futile circles, trying to aid us while following byzantine rules. We sat in that conference room the entire evening, watching the time tick away on what was supposed to be our New Year's Eve celebration. After six hours, the situation went from being merely ridiculous and inconvenient to ominous.

"They need you to go to the police station," said the by now exhausted hotel manager. "There, a special detective from another district will come and review your case to determine the appropriate charges against the teahouse." It was nine thirty p.m. Achara and I were hungry, and I would happily have paid another US$160 just to be able to go out on the town and celebrate New Year's Eve.

We were brought to the police station in the back of a police car, lights flashing, as if we were the suspects. We then waited an hour in the holding cell before finally grabbing our chance and slipping away.

Achara and I finally got back to Markham Hotel just before midnight, our evening ruined—an inauspicious start to the year and our big travel project.

———————

February 2007
Peruvian Andes

One of my favorite modes of travel is by train. You can see a lot and learn volumes about a country, in a mostly hassle-free manner, when moving through it by train. As the countryside rolls by, a rail traveler can meet and have in-depth conversations with all sorts of interesting people—something much harder to do when going by car. Stations and towns the train passes through are frequently places you would not drive or would simply pass through without stopping. And the scenery along the way can be glorious—and, in some cases, quite telling.

Ten days after flying into Peru from Asia, Achara and I were on the luxurious Andean Explorer for the nine-hour train ride from the scenic Andean city of Cuzco to Puno, on Lake Titicaca in the Southern Peruvian Altiplano. It was during this ride that I first sensed the wrenching change sweeping Peru as modernization took hold. I didn't get this insight from the natural scenery along the way, though. The rugged mountain tiers, stretching into the distance behind vast sweeps of highland plain dotted with small herds of fluffy llamas and alpacas, exuded a quiet, timeless beauty. And at each stop, indigenous women in colorfully patterned woolen capes descended on the train, selling embroidered woolen clothing, throw rugs, and tapestries. This, too, was a scene of timelessness, of deep traditional roots.

But I could see globalization crashing in on Peru in the enormous volume of trash that littered every kilometer along the way. Plastic bottles and bags and blister packs, chunks of Styrofoam, rusting cans, broken glass bottles, paper, and all the other detritus of modern consumption carpeted every right-of-way and roadside. The trash piled up beside the train tracks even in the sparsely populated highland plains, miles from the nearest town or road. From my previous travels, I had begun to recognize large amounts of trash in unlikely locales as a universal marker of regions struggling with wrenching change brought by sweeping modernization.

I first noticed this phenomenon in the late 1990s, in the idyllic tropical islands I visited on diving trips in the Pacific. I remembered, upon my initial arrival for a dive trip in Truk Lagoon in Micronesia, naively expecting island nature at its pristine purest. Instead, walking around near where the dive trip would start, I was shocked at the vast quantities of modern trash scattered and piled everywhere. As I walked along floral-scented dirt roads beneath swaying palms I commonly saw the rusted hulks of old cars abandoned beside the road. In other places, major piles of modern trash lay in open spaces surrounded by lush jungle. A year later, in 1999, on a dive trip in the Marshall Islands—in the tropical North Pacific and also part of Micronesia—I was surprised to notice precisely the same phenomenon.

This trash wasn't just in supposedly remote Pacific Island paradises. It was part of the landscape almost everywhere I went in the poorer world, especially those areas in the throes of rapid modernization. Everywhere in the poorer world, it seemed that the sheer mass of garbage strewn about varied directly with the speed of modernization.

This is perhaps simplistic—and surely ethnocentric—but I supposed this effect was largely because, in societies where modernization is crashing in, people don't have the knowledge, systems, and habitual patterns of how to deal with modern refuse. Trash, littered widely about, was an easily identifiable marker, like a human genetic marker for susceptibility to a disease, pointing to a society caught in the upheaval of rapid and often traumatic modernization. I soon grew to expect lots of trash in far-flung locales during my Disappearing World travels.

Before the train ride to Puno, Achara and I had already been in Peru for nine days. Peru interested us, both in its attractions such as Machu Picchu and Lake Titicaca and in its immense biodiversity. It also beckoned me because of its many still relatively intact traditional cultures.

Our first activity in Peru was a four-day trek up the Inca Trail to Machu Picchu. Along with the natural splendor of the trek, and the breathtaking vista from those famous Inca ruins, I was able to get a feel for the long struggle of the region's inhabitants, most of whom descend from the Inca people, to retain their indigenous cultural roots. Peru has been under major onslaught from the outside "modern" world ever since European conquistadors and colonialists invaded nearly five centuries ago. The indigenous peoples' attempts to resist the outside influences were subtle but apparent.

In starting our Machu Picchu trip, we also set off on this journey into a land of people trying to hold on to their cultural roots. Achara and I had started our trek from Cuzco, riding in a jeep along winding half-paved roads heading into the mountains. Our route took us through tropical cloud forests and past modest farmhouses and a few larger brick and stone haciendas. On the tiled roofs of most houses, or adorning the entry gateway, was a set of animal figurines—usually bulls, horses, or pigs—with a Catholic cross placed between them.

Our guide, an amiable young man named Miguel, explained that the model animals were an artifact of the syncretic blending of the indigenous people's traditional beliefs with Spanish-imposed Catholicism. The model animals were there to protect the home and bring good luck, he said, and the Catholic cross was there "just in case."

During our Inca Trail trek, I got an intellectual feel for this practical drive of the Andean peoples to retain their cultural roots. Miguel, a handsome young man with light brown skin and dark, serious eyes, himself of native origin, had pointed out other aspects of this effort. He explained that the Spanish colonists had tried to stamp out all facets of Incan heritage from his ancestors. But important cultural traits were kept and passed along to future generations, including the Quechua language, the native religion, and coca cultivation and consumption. Since these insights came to me cocooned within a package tour of Cuzco and the Inca Trail, it wasn't until I saw the enormous amount of litter on the train ride to Puno that I got a feel for the change overtaking Peru.

———

The morning after our train arrived in Puno, a shabby smallish city on the shores of Lake Titicaca, Achara and I set out early on a boat I had hired to explore the famous lake. The air was crisp and skies clear, and looking out from shore, the lake seemed an ocean.

Straddling the border between Peru and Bolivia, Titicaca, at over 12,000 feet (3,900 meters), is the highest navigable lake in the world. I was especially interested in the lake's many tiny manmade islands, built in the 1400s by people escaping the warfare between the conquering Incas and a resisting local tribe. I had read that the invading Incas apparently thought it not worth bothering with a few hundred people who chose to live in the lake, and left them alone. Amazingly to me, those people created a way of life that continues to this day.

Our boat puttered into the lake through green grasses and tall reeds. I had asked the skipper, a muscular fellow with a bushy mustache, named Esteban, who spoke mostly only Spanish, to bring us to the islands farthest away from Puno and well off the tourist circuit.

On the half-hour journey over open water to the first island, Esteban explained that these unique islands were woven from lake reeds. What I found interesting, though, was that they had to be continually rebuilt by their inhabitants: Every few months, as the reeds at the island's bottom rot away, more reeds are piled on top in a never-ending cycle of rebuilding and rotting. I tried to imagine how many times over the past six centuries each of these islands had been laboriously rebuilt by the generations dwelling there.

We visited two islands, where the families lived isolated but practical lifestyles. The islands were tiny indeed—no more than fifty to seventy-five yards in diameter. Seven families lived on one island, ten on the other—some twenty-five to thirty people on each, eking out a living by fishing and making small handicrafts to sell on the mainland. What struck me most, though, was what future awaited the many children and young teens on these little spaces. Their life horizons were shaped in childhood playgrounds of a few square yards, separated from humanity by a vast barrier of water. I suspected that many of those youngsters, after seeing the more modern lifestyles of Puno, would opt for a life onshore. Indeed, I could be looking at one of the Altiplano's last generations of lake dwellers.

After a few days among the islands of Lake Titicaca, Achara and I returned to Puno and stayed a night in a small hotel. While checking my e-mail at the hotel's Internet café that evening, I learned of a distressing loss.

Several years earlier, I had invested what for me was a significant sum, in an Orange County, California, company that I had felt comfortable with. But the e-mail message I read showed that my comfort level with the organization's management was badly misplaced. The company, a financial services firm, had gone bankrupt almost overnight in the first weeks of 2007—an early victim of the upcoming Great Recession and fraudulent accounting. The money that I had invested with them—half the funds I had set aside to pay for my travel project—was wiped out. Devastated, I went with Achara back upstairs to the room, cursing myself for ignoring the warning signs I had seen of the coming calamity. The huge financial blow threatened my entire travel project.

Achara, with a maturity surprising in someone so young, tried to comfort me. "You lost a diamond," she said. "But you are resourceful. At some point, you'll find another diamond to replace it."

I appreciated Achara's pragmatic mind-set, though I knew it would be a long time before I came to peace with such a huge loss.

Early the next morning, bleary-eyed from a lack of sleep, I went with Achara to the Puno bus station. I had stayed awake all night, worrying about the financing of my travel project. But our travels were still going on, at least for the moment, and we were going to catch the bus for the eight-hour ride to the city of Arequipa. The bus station only made my depression worse. It was a cheerless, bare-bones affair—a large building with rows of cheap blue plastic seats and a few booths for various bus company vendors. After buying our tickets for the 8:40 a.m. bus, Achara and I sat near the end of the station.

Just after taking our seats, Achara left for a moment to go to the toilet. As she walked away she left her handbag, which contained our two pairs of expensive German binoculars and her compact camera, on the seat two chairs down from me. At the same time, I sneezed, looking away for just an instant. When I turned, a plump middle-aged Peruvian woman was sitting where Achara's handbag had been.

"*¡Disculpe, usted está sentar en mi bolsa!*" I said in my dependably bad Spanish.

"*¡No, señor, no hay bolsa!*" she replied, startled, jumping up and pointing to the chair.

There was no bag under her. The most valuable things we were carrying had been stolen the instant that I turned away!

Immediately realizing this, I jumped up.

"*Por favor, mira mi bolsas*" (roughly, "Please watch my bags"), I said excitedly to the woman, pointing to our other luggage. I took off at a sprint, passing row after row of mostly empty seats. Then, halfway down the terminal, I saw him out of the corner of my eye. Somehow, instinctively, I knew he was the thief.

He was a middle-aged indigenous man of medium height and squat build, wearing a shabby long gray coat, walking fast with his head down, toward the exits. He was carrying a large yellow plastic shopping bag that looked heavy. I veered in his direction, zigzagging down a row of chairs. Within a moment, I was almost even with him.

Reaching forward while still running, I grabbed one end of the yellow shopping bag he carried. The man kept hold of the other end of the bag, causing it to open up. Inside, to my relief, was Achara's handbag.

Furious, I pounced on the guy. He stumbled backward, looking really scared, not resisting. Grabbing him around the neck with one arm while holding Achara's bag with the other and yelling "*¡Ladrón!*" (thief), I dragged him toward a bus counter, continuing to yell "*¡Ladrón!*" in the hope that some police in the terminal would hear me and come. Each time he struggled, I tightened my arm around his neck, choking him till he stopped squirming. Some private terminal security guards came up to me. I told them I wanted real police and wouldn't release the thief to anyone else. I didn't trust the security guards to actually help me or arrest the thief.

With a procession of private terminal security behind me, I continued to drag the thief back through the terminal to where Achara and I had been sitting, with everyone around me looking on in startled curiosity. As I got near our seats by the end of the terminal, several efficient-looking police in crisp blue uniforms came up to me.

With my arm still firmly around the thief's neck, I struggled to explain in Spanish to the officers, who turned out to be tourist police, what had happened.

"You must come with us to file a complaint," the lead officer said in perfect English (to my relief) as they took custody of the subdued thief.

"I don't have time, though," I said. "My bus is about to leave for Arequipa."

"Don't worry," the lead officer said. "We'll tell it to wait!"

The police then led the thief and me away to the nearby police station to file a complaint. The station was as bare-bones as the bus station—a squat concrete structure painted in pastel yellow inside and out. It appeared to have three almost empty cubical rooms, with a desk and a few cheap chairs in each. Belying the crisp, efficient appearance of the tourist police, the complaint process was laborious. The officers had to fill out the report and complaint by hand.

"I am sorry about the slow process," the lead officer said as he sat down behind his desk. "We don't have computers."

The process seemed to take forever. They needed four copies of the complaint, which they had to do all by hand since they also had no carbon paper. I couldn't believe how ridiculously antiquated the whole process was, and had to restrain myself from voicing my rising impatience. Finally, I was able to sign all four copies of the complaint. They then videotaped me while I made a verbal explanation of what had occurred. In the meantime, I heard shouting that I could not understand coming from the next room, where they were holding the thief. Thinking the process was finally done, I said good-bye and started to leave.

"Please, mister, just a little more time," the lead officer said. "We have to make four more copies of the signed complaint with a copy machine, and you must sign those copies, too. But we don't have a copy machine. So, we need to go to a service in the city to make our copies."

Exasperated, I walked with the lead officer through town to a local faxing/copy service. This took even more time than expected since the machines in the first two copy shops we went to were not working. Finally, at the third place we visited, we got the job done.

A few moments later, with Achara's rescued bag in hand and two hours after the ordeal had begun, I felt embarrassed while walking back onto the bus. But to my relief, everyone was polite toward me even after sitting for so long under the hot sun.

Achara rolled her eyes when I took my seat next to her. "This is the second time in two months we've sat in a foreign police station!" she said. "What strange luck."

Our next stop, Arequipa, was quite pleasant compared to shabby Puno and the hassle at the bus station. Our first evening there, Achara and I walked to the central town square, with its big fountain in the center, and admired the striking colonial-era buildings facing it. These buildings, made of a whitish-pink volcanic stone called sillar, for which the city is famous, spoke of another era of wrenching globalization, over four and a half centuries earlier.

The city's imposing central square, the Plaza de Armas, was where the armories stood, where the government stocked weapons for distribution to citizen defenders in the event of an indigenous uprising. This seemed particularly apt for Arequipa, Peru's second-most important city after Lima, for it has been the center of recurrent separatist movements. The Arequipeños even tried once, albeit unsuccessfully, to get their own flag and issue their own passports.

For me, the most interesting of the city's attractions was its infamously luxurious old convent for the nuns of the Order of Santa Catalina. The huge high-walled complex near the city's center is itself the size of a small city. We walked through arched colonnades into surrounding courtyards, some with fountains and gardens. Nuns' private rooms had small patios, and some had lovely paintings and other art. Our guide explained that the riches of the monastery came from the families of nuns who entered the order. Most came from upper-class Spanish families who paid a large fee, or dowry, to the convent to have their daughters accepted.

The luxurious lives of the nuns became scandalous, our guide told us. Young upper-class women lived here with servants, had parties, and even held private concerts. It was easy to imagine such ostentatious wealth arousing feelings of resentment among the indigenous and poor peoples. It was a good time-travel experience, giving me a sense of why Latin America in general has had such a turbulent relationship with the Church. It was also an appropriate ending to our Peru trip. We had started it by seeing the ghostly ruins of Machu Picchu, the skeletal architectural remains of a society obliterated by the globalization taking place at the end of the Middle Ages. And we left not knowing what would be the result of the current wave of globalization sweeping · Peru.

From Arequipa, Achara and I went to Peru's capital, Lima. There we took a flight to Salvador, Brazil, where we would attend its big Carnival celebration.

———

February 2007
Salvador, Brazil

It was the opening evening of Carnival in Salvador, and the lively, raucous music of the slowly approaching procession could be heard from afar. Crowds thronged the wide boulevard along the main parade route in the old Portuguese colonial city. Countless small street vendors had set up shop on the beach side of the boulevard, many using portable vinyl tables to serve the Carnival revelers. Colorful banners flapped in the sultry evening breeze, and trash blew around the streets and pockmarked sidewalks. As I stood on the wide boulevard with Achara and our good friend Clark, a pilot from San Francisco who had come down to join us for the festivities, the crowd's excitement and anticipation were palpable.

As the Carnival procession of Trio-electricos—the main attraction of Carnival in Salvador—drew closer, the noise became almost deafening. Trio-electricos, which look from the front like oversize trucks, have huge built-in sound systems, and an electric band performing atop the open bed. While the lead Trio-electrico was inching closer to where we stood, none of us quite realized that we were becoming enveloped in the massive sea of heaving humanity lining the boulevard. Clark, who was standing to my left with Achara, made a somewhat alarmed comment about the crowds. I looked over. My friend stands five-eleven and is of medium build with graying hair and should have been easy to spot, but he seemed to have gotten separated from Achara and me as several people jostled to a place in front of him. It didn't help that night was falling and this poor coastal city had little in the way of street lighting.

The crowds became so crushingly dense, I couldn't see anything except the bodies around me and the darkening sky above. Thousands of people crammed together, closer and closer, like sardines as the parade of blaring Trio-electricos came closer. Then two tall, lanky, dark young men abruptly pushed through the crowd and stood directly in front of me.

A little miffed at their rudeness, I tried to adjust my position to keep from being swept along in the suffocating crush surrounding me.

Then the two young men backed into me, seemingly unaware of my presence. At the same time, the masses behind me crowded forward, squeezing me.

Suddenly, I felt the surge of adrenaline that comes with the realization that one is being attacked.

Achara could be in danger! I suddenly realized that she wasn't beside me—I had been separated from her. Lashing out immediately at the two young men in front of me, I began to twirl in a furious circular motion with my elbows out horizontally. Indiscriminately pushing through whatever dark figures were about me, I shoved and fought to get back to where I sensed that Achara was. I felt a brief sensation of a frantic and almost violent jab on my left leg pocket of my cargo pants.

It was not Achara who was being attacked. *It was me.*

And then it was over. A pocket of space had developed around me. I grabbed at Achara, who was standing next to Clark, and pulled her away from where we had been standing.

"Are you okay?" I shouted, relieved that she appeared unharmed.

Both Clark and Achara looked flushed and agitated. "Are you okay?" they shouted at me above the rising din.

"Of course," I said. "What happened?"

"Didn't you see them?" they both asked me. "Four guys surrounded you and tried to rob you!"

"I started hitting one of them from behind!" shouted Achara. "I was screaming your name, but you didn't hear me."

"I saw them come at you, too!" Clark shouted. "I grabbed one of 'em by the hair from behind and yanked his head back."

Clark then pointed at my now opened cargo pant pocket. A local tourist map, the only thing in it, lay trampled on the ground near me.

"They thought you had a wallet in that pocket," he said.

"Well, we're okay now," I said. Incredibly, the small camera that Achara was holding in her hand had not been the target of the pick-pocket gang. Illogically, they had picked me, the biggest person of our group, to attack.

The huge Trio-electrico procession was now very near. It was getting darker, and the crowds had once again enveloped us. It was impossible for us to get away to a clear spot. But I figured that we were probably fine now.

Wrong.

They hit me again a few moments later. This time, they were less subtle. They came right up directly facing me. I didn't recognize them right away, since I hadn't really seen them in the first attack. All four slammed into me from each direction, pressing hard while they rifled my pockets. I lashed out as viciously as I could, elbowing and punching. Clark and Achara hit them frantically from behind. Some other bystanders in the crowd also helped shove the assailants away.

They plowed through the crowd away from me, retreating again after this second assault. I pushed and shoved after them, swearing like a longshoreman, trying to grab one of them. After a moment, I gave up and shoved my way back through the crowd toward my little group.

"We need to move to a safer spot, where we can see them if they come back," I said. There was no way out through the huge crowds stretching endlessly up and down the street. "Here, we're vulnerable to a knife attack from these assholes." I pointed to a high concrete wall that lined the sidewalk behind us. "Let's go back toward that wall."

As we shoved our way hurriedly through the crowds, I explained that against a wall is not usually the best place to be in a fight. But in this case, with the wall behind us, the attackers would have to come head-on, and we would be able to see them and thus have a better chance to fight back.

While pushing through the crowd, I tried to think why the attackers had come back on me the second time. The only thing I could figure out was that perhaps I stood out as an easy target: a professional-looking white North American—by definition, "rich" to them.

We forced our way through the jam of people to the wall lining the side of the boulevard. The parade procession was almost directly in front of us, and the high wall behind us. The hot, sweaty crowd had us completely hemmed in. There was nowhere else to go. The crowd stretched endlessly in all directions.

I had to get Achara out of here! But how?

Near the wall where we had retreated to, I saw three big guys—black men who looked like football players or bodybuilders. They were wearing tank tops and baseball caps turned backward in the fashion often seen on the streets. I shoved my way over to them.

"Hello, we're in trouble!" I explained. "Can you help me? We are being attacked, and I am afraid for my wife," I said, pointing to Achara.

The biggest man, who looked like a small mountain, grinned at me, as if this looked like fun. "Sure. We're glad to help."

And they did. The street gang came on yet again. At first, our new helpers didn't see what was going on. But then they rushed at the attackers and commanded Achara, Clark, and me to get behind them, which we did. They crouched down and held their arms out, forearms horizontal to the ground, lining up like a rugby scrum in the darkness.

Then I finally got a clear look at the attackers. Livid, I shoved forward onto one of them and punched him solidly in the face. He ducked back into the crowd and moved frantically away. My new comrades had blocked off the other three attackers. Then the biggest two of the three remaining attackers also evaporated into the heaving mass of people. Somehow, though, the smallest of the thugs got left behind. He tried to look nonchalant and blend into the crowd. I chased and shoved my way toward him. I hadn't really seen him clearly, but I sensed him. I got to him just as an opening in the crowd magically appeared.

He had long, light-colored surfer-style hair, dark cream-colored skin, and a torn shirt.

Swearing, I punched him hard in the ribs. He started to run away, and I grabbed at him. Squirming from my grasp, he cursed and spat back at me and continued to run, knocking people out of his way as he went. I went after him for about a hundred meters before giving up. I had lost him in the seething mass of bodies.

The parade had passed us now, and the street started to clear as the crowd moved on, following the parade.

I ran back to where Achara and Clark were standing. We thanked our new comrades who had so graciously helped us, and I offered to buy them all drinks from one of the street vendors. They thanked me but said they didn't drink.

"Be careful!" they warned.

Achara, Clark, and I called it a night and went back to our hotel.

Back in our comfortable bed-and-breakfast near the beach, Achara and I marveled at all the mishaps we had experienced in our brief two months of travel so far.

"Starting in Beijing," Achara noted, "We've had four robbery attempts of some sort, including this one. Two of these even involved the police!"(Along with the tea-ceremony rip-off in Beijing and attempted robberies in Peru and at Carnival, I was pickpocketed for a small sum while in Beijing.)

Along with this, I added, was the serious personal financial setback I had learned of in Peru—in a way, a robbery of another sort.

"Maybe it's a good omen to get all the bad luck out of the way at the beginning of our travels," Achara remarked hopefully. Somehow, we both actually managed to laugh about all the bad luck.

Inwardly, I knew that these misadventures were a part of traveling and had to be accepted as such. But all the logic and philosophical acceptance of this would never dim my memory of the visceral concern I had felt over Achara's safety earlier that evening, during the pickpocket gang's attacks. I resolved to be doubly vigilant, to preempt such a situation from ever happening again.

Achara's hope that our bad luck had run its course after the events in Brazil was a little premature. After Carnival in Salvador, we said good-bye to our friend Clark and flew to Buenos Aires, planning to enjoy the cosmopolitan delights of the Argentine capital for a few days. Unfortunately, I got really sick, apparently from swimming unsuspectingly in polluted waters in Salvador, and spent most of our time in Buenos Aires in bed, staring at my hotel room ceiling.

The next two months I would come to remember with a sad fondness. I didn't know then, but it would be one of the last long stretches of time that Achara and I would spend together. Our travels were mostly tourist oriented, which I figured would make the time more fun for her. We trekked in Chile's southern Patagonia and visited its famous large Magellanic penguin colony, then flew to Ushuaia, a charming town surrounded by majestic glaciers at the southernmost point in Argentina, to look into a future Antarctic trip. After a quick stop at Easter Island to see its famous stone statues,[2] and wine tasting in Chile's renowned vineyards, we finished our South American trip in Ecuador, a country that Achara and I both loved from previous travels.

But amid all these fun travels, I was sad that Achara had come to realize that long-term travel was not for her. She explained that she enjoyed traveling for two or three weeks at a time but that she needed a place to call home, where she could have a daily routine. She also continued to worry about the long delay in starting her career.

I had not expected her to want to abandon the great adventure we had set out to experience. Our travel project plan had initially grown from my lifelong desire to know and experience the world through extended travel and from my conviction that many of the world's great wonders were fast disappearing. And Achara had seemed a perfect fit for this project. In her young life, she had traveled much with her family, once even joking that for her, hotels were like home. After we met in 1999 in Long Beach, we had begun an international courtship that lasted almost three years. During our entire relationship, travel was a major theme, and we had planned this long travel project for years. The realization that I would have to carry on without her robbed the vision of some of its joy.

After our travels in Ecuador, Achara and I returned to Thailand and revamped our plans. Achara would do one more trip with me, meeting me in the highlands of Papua New Guinea for our second journey together there. Then she would live in Bangkok with her family and do an internship in the Thai government. This would give her valuable work experience for her future career during the time I traveled. I would continue my travel project alone. Despite all the setbacks, quitting was not an option I ever seriously considered.

---

[2] In Easter Island, the most notable part of the trip for me was not the colossal stone statues from the mysterious culture that disappeared centuries ago. Rather, it was the enormous amounts of trash that had washed up from the Pacific Ocean and accumulated on some of the island's otherwise gorgeous sandy beaches.

CHAPTER 4

Nomination Time in the Southern Highlands

Steeped in traditional magic and innocent of modern economies, PNG's citizens prove easy marks for Ponzi schemes which proliferate throughout the country. Now it's election time . . . and the politicians are dusting off their bottles of snake oil. Viewed from afar or from a national perspective, it's an appalling spectacle of disregard for governance.
—Confidential cable from U.S. embassy in PNG, entitled "Ponzi Politics," leaked by WikiLeaks

Papua New Guinea rates 2.2 on a scale of 0 (highly corrupt) to 10 (very clean), ranking it 154th out of 182 countries, the same level as the tragically dysfunctional corrupt government in Zimbabwe.
—Statistics from 2011 Transparency International Corruption Perception Index Ratings

May 2007
Tari, Southern Highlands of Papua New Guinea

As the Fokker twin turboprop circled above the landing strip at Tari, I looked out the window and saw the familiar site. An airplane landing in the Southern Highlands of Papua New Guinea was still as big an event as it was when I flew here with Achara sixteen months ago. Crowds of people, many holding brightly colored parasols, lined the chain-link fence around the airfield, waiting for the plane.

I looked at the man sitting next to me, who had introduced himself as Charles at the start of the one-hour flight from Port Moresby. He was perhaps the blackest man I had ever seen. Charles had coal black skin and a bushy jet-black beard and wore a shiny black dress suit, black cowboy hat, and tall black stovepipe cowboy boots. Incongruously for a man so elegantly dressed, his suit smelled like stale sweat. I figured that it was difficult to keep a dress suit properly dry-cleaned in a place like this, which probably had three dry cleaners in the entire country. During the flight, I had learned from Charles that I may have come to PNG at an interesting time.

"Are you here on business?" he had asked me at the start of the flight. "Or for the elections?"

"No," I said. "I'm here to trek the Mount Bosavi area with my wife, who will come to join me next week." It was Sunday of the first week in May. Achara had gotten unexpectedly delayed in Bangkok and would fly to Tari to join me the following Friday.

"I also came to see a big festival that is supposed to happen with all the tribes from the Southern Highlands participating," I said. "What kind of elections are going on?"

"The festival is not going to happen, but you are in for a much bigger treat!" Charles answered enthusiastically. "It is nomination time in the Southern Highlands Province, to choose candidates to compete for its open Parliament seat in the upcoming national elections."

"Really?" I said. "This is a special event, huh?"

"Yes, I can tell you for sure," he said. "I am a campaign manager for one of the candidates. PNG doesn't have anything like a strong national party that penetrates into these remote areas. Elections in the Southern Highlands are very colorful, with large amounts of candidates. There will probably be twenty candidates nominated to run for their single open seat in the upcoming national election."

"It is not like your elections in the West," Charles continued in a lowered voice, winking at me. "Elections here are raw, free-for-all events with all kinds of shenanigans."

After our plane landed, I wished Charles good luck in the upcoming elections.

Steven Wari, whose lodge we stayed at on our previous visit, picked me up again at the airstrip. As we loaded my things into his truck, it seemed that things had changed a bit in the Tari area since my last visit, not even a year and a half ago. For one thing, Steven was driving a less beat-up truck than before. Then, to my astonishment, as we bumped along the still-lousy dirt road to his lodge, I heard the ring of a cell phone.

"Where is that coming from?" I asked, reaching for my small backpack to see if my cell phone was somehow ringing.

"It is mine," Steven said. Beaming with pride, he pulled a cheap Nokia phone from his pocket. After talking to someone in his native language, he explained that cell service had just come to the Tari area in the past year. It wasn't very reliable, though, and not many people had it, because it was too expensive for most. But Steven was happy to have it.

I thought it remarkable, to say the least, that cell service should be here at all.

As I got over my great surprise at seeing this twenty-first century tool in these still mostly neolithic lands, Steven explained that he needed the phone this week to handle all the people coming to his lodge. He assured me, though, that he had kept for me the same room I stayed in last time. He did let me know that it would be much noisier this time, though, and he hoped I wouldn't mind.

"That is good news," I replied happily. "Business must be good for you!"

"No, business is bad. Only this week is good, because of the nomination ceremonies. I have the only lodge in the area besides the expensive eco-lodge. So several of the candidates for parliament are staying with me this week. They each have their campaign manager and helpers. So I had to put five people in the small room next to you because I have only a few rooms to rent."

I then asked Steven to tell me about the elections, which, until the flight, I hadn't even known took place in the Highlands.

Steven explained that the elections were becoming serious business in the Southern Highlands. Some areas had a lot of oil and gas, and the tribes who lived there didn't want the wealth under their lands taken and squandered by the corrupt government in Port Moresby.

"The government takes the oil for years, but we get nothing in return," he said. "We still don't even have a decent road that comes here to Tari. People are beginning to understand that to make change, elections are important," he concluded.

We arrived at the lodge to find it jam-packed and indeed noisy, with an increasingly festive air as evening approached. Several of the candidates and their staffs staying there gathered around the lodge deck, drinking and talking. During this gathering, I met several of the candidates, including one named Francis, who seemed to have a special charisma. My favorite of the candidates here, he was considered honest and competent and, indeed, came across that way. He had a real chance of winning the election.

After the hubbub of the gathering died down some, I learned of an ominous change in the area since my last visit. I retired to my room for the night but noticed several mosquitoes. So I went to get a mosquito coil from Steven. I wasn't worried about malaria, because of the high altitude; I just didn't want the annoying creatures buzzing in my ears all night.

I was wrong about the malaria.

"It is important now to be careful with mosquitoes," Steven warned when I got a coil from him. He explained that as far back as anyone remembered, the altitude in the Highlands made it too cool for the type of mosquitoes that carry malaria. But now, with global warming, it was getting noticeably warmer in the Tari Highlands.

"Just this past year, malarial mosquitos are more common, and more Highlanders are getting sick," he said.

I found this new situation disturbing, though it was just one of several instances in my travels so far where global warming seemed to be causing unprecedented changes to a local situation.

The next morning, Monday, Steven and I were off in his truck early to see the opening nomination festivities. It also happened to be the day that Francis was putting in his nomination. I was excited to see what a relatively modern political process would be like in a society with one foot in the Stone Age and the other in the twenty-first century. We drove for about two hours along a dirt road, crossing a high pass above the Tari Highlands and coming down onto a dusty highland plain. Steven explained the process along the way.

We were headed to a small town called Margarima, he said. In the town was a missionary house, where all candidates would come over the next few days to put in their nomination papers and pay a fee. To be nominated as a candidate sounded surprisingly easy. A potential candidate need only present a petition, with at least twenty signatures supporting his candidacy, to the registrar at the mission house and pay a nominal fee of 1,000 kina (US$300).

As we neared Margarima, our road intersected another dirt road going into the village. In the distance, approaching the town along the other road, I saw what looked like a big dust cloud. As it got closer I understood what Charles had meant, on the airplane ride to Tari, by saying I was in for a treat. It was an amazing spectacle.

Dozens of tribesmen, their facial features outlined with yellow and white paint, wearing rust-colored pineapple-shaped feather head-pieces, white smocks lined with yellow flowers around their waists, and long green banana leaves fluttering off their backsides, were carrying long spears hewn from bamboo poles. They were leading a crowd of people in a candidates' procession. The procession crowd walked alongside a small caravan of trucks. Looking completely out of place in the procession was the candidate himself. He was a man with a big beard, wearing a Western-style dark business suit and standing on the open bed of the lead truck. He had a microphone and amplifier and was shouting rally cries to his procession as it inched along. It looked like nothing I could have come up with in my wildest imaginings.

Steven, grinning as he saw my face light up with excitement, explained that I was watching a procession from the Enga tribe and their candidate. The Enga came from another part of the Southern Highlands.

Soon, another similar candidate procession came down the road from a different direction. Differently clad but equally colorful tribespeople led this procession. As with the Enga tribe's procession, it was easy to spot the candidate: He and his campaign staff members stuck out as the only people in the procession in Western business dress. I found it interesting that the candidates deemed it necessary to mimic the dress of the outside modern world for this process. The dark business suits on the candidates and their staffs looked like torture in the sticky tropical heat.

We soon arrived at the missionary house where each candidate would come. It was a rectangular ranch-style bungalow with a long, narrow covered front porch, set three feet above ground level. The house fronted a large grass lawn, where people from different villages were beginning to gather.

Soon the first procession, that of the Enga tribe, marched into the front yard. Several tribal warriors escorted the candidate as he walked ceremoniously through the crowd, up the steps of the porch and into the house, to pay his fee and present the registrar with his nomination petition. He then reappeared back on the porch to give a rally speech, and his followers in warrior dress broke into a boisterous sing-sing. Lining up in two rows facing each other, the warriors hopped while chanting, beating on long drums, and shaking the banana leaves on their backsides. The lead warrior blew a loud whistle, setting the beat, while the candidate, looking as if he were about to melt in his heavy suit, stood looking out from the elevated porch.

The crowd grew, and the event took on a carnival atmosphere. Eventually, it was Francis's turn. He led his procession onto the yard and into the house to pay the nomination fee, reappearing a moment later to rally his supporters. Tall and dignified looking with a neatly trimmed, longish beard and somehow managing to appear comfortable in his dark suit, he looked like a credible candidate.

Some people standing with Francis on the porch noticed me, the only pale-skinned foreigner in the entire crowd, and started waving to me.

"They want you to go up there, Gary," Steven said. "Do it—you'll get a great view!"

So I walked up onto the porch as a sort of guest of honor to the event and stood behind Francis while he gave his speech. The porch, being a few feet higher than ground level, afforded me a great view of all the tribal members doing their sing-sing routines. Some of the spectators, wondering who the lone white face on the porch was, came over to Francis's chief of staff, who was out in the yard at the time. Later, he told me what occurred:

"Who is that white man?" a spectator associated with another candidate had asked.

Francis's chief of staff was a clever man with large local land holdings and oil interests. With a perfectly straight face, he replied, "He is an adviser from America, sent by the George Bush team to help with Francis's campaign."

The spectator gasped, duly impressed that Francis was so well connected to have such powerful international allies. Later that week, Francis's chief of staff told me that his answer had gotten around and had made quite a splash. Laughing so hard that he almost doubled over, he said he had heard that, as a consequence of this rumor, a couple of candidates may actually have dropped out of the election, deciding not to run against such a well-connected opponent!

One of the fun things about my status, while here in the Tari Highlands, as something akin to an alien from another planet was that so many great surprises seemed to happen regularly. The next day, Tuesday, brought one of those surprises. Steven and I were off early again to see more nomination rallies at another small village in the opposite direction from Margarima. We drove under partly cloudy skies, along a fairly decent dirt road, past the Tari airport and turned onto a rough dirt road into some hills. We bounced along a track enclosed on both sides by high, smooth walls of hard-packed dirt. The lines of these sturdy-looking walls were broken intermittently by walls that turned inland, away from the road. In front of some of these walls was a ditch with running water.

These sturdy dirt walls, Steven explained, surrounded living areas and were PNG's version of medieval European moats and protective walls. We stopped at one that was under construction, and I took a careful look. It was about twenty feet high, very smooth, and quite hard. Steven said that the wall would be very difficult for an intruder or attacker to climb. I looked up and imagined village defenders raining rocks and arrows down on any attackers trying to scale the wall.

We continued down the road, eventually turning onto a wide dirt path and passing a small village. Just ahead was my second amazing spectacle in two days. A long, broad column of armed tribal warriors, many shirtless and wearing grass skirts and human-hair wigs, was running straight at us. They were carrying spears, machetes, hatchets, axes, rusty old guns, and sticks. I wasn't sure whether to be excited about another fascinating spectacle, or to urge Steven to do a bootleg turn in the narrow road and flee.

Steven looked concerned and pulled his truck off the road, out of the way of the approaching column of warriors.

"Wait here and don't get out of the truck," he said as he got out to find out what was going on.

The column rumbled past us, kicking up dust as it passed, the warriors looking straight forward, their jaws set in determination.

"You are in luck, Gary!" Steven said, climbing back into the truck. "I think it is a compensation ceremony."

I didn't know what he was talking about, but I figured it had to be interesting.

Driving ahead, Steven stopped at a local road junction just past a wooden bridge and asked some of the locals about the event. He then explained that a young man in the village we had just passed was killed by some rascals from the next village down the road. ("Rascals" are thugs—a rough equivalent of gangbangers—who are a real menace in some areas of PNG.) During the mourning period for the dead young man, some people from the victim's village came over and killed a young man from the culprits' village in revenge. (Revenge killings often target a random person associated with the culprit— often an innocent member of the culprit's clan.)

"To prevent an all-out clan war," Steven said, "the tribal chiefs from the two villages got together and negotiated a mutual compensation agreement."

In this agreement, Steven explained, the family in the village of the first man killed would be compensated by the killer's village in the amount of forty pigs and some cash and other goods. And the family of the man slain in the revenge killing, who lived in the original killers' village, would be compensated by the first victim's village in the amount of thirty pigs, some cash, and other goods.

The idea of compensating for a crime through some form of payment has existed since time immemorial, of course, and is familiar to modern Westerners in the concept of civil liability damages. It seemed imaginatively practical, though, to use this concept to have both criminally liable sides give each other almost mutually canceling payments.

Since everyone was friendly to Steven and me, we decided to watch the action and followed several warriors who were carrying pigs. The pigs had been cut in half lengthwise, each half tied by the legs to a wooden pole, and the pole ends hoisted on the shoulders of two warriors. They brought the pigs to an area by a hut on the side of the road to prepare them for presentation to the other village.

Despite the seriousness of the event, the hundred or so warriors there stopped and looked at me as I walked up with Steven. Then a rugged-looking man wearing a black cowboy hat and carrying an old rifle motioned me to come over. Pointing to the camera, he posed next to me. I gave my camera to Steven to shoot the photo as the entire group stopped working to watch their fellow warrior have his picture taken with the alien. Then several others did the same, and soon boys were hamming it up for the camera. For a moment, the presence of a being from the faraway modern world trumped whatever solemnity was involved in their proceedings.

Finally, after lots of photos, the warriors got back to work preparing the pigs for the ceremonial exchange. This involved first splitting any still-whole pigs. The half pigs were then hoisted on long poles and carried in procession by the men of the village to the other village (and vice versa, in this case). The procession was led and flanked by weapon-carrying tribesmen, many in warrior dress. Despite the jocularity during the impromptu photo session, the facial expressions on the men in the procession looked as if they could easily spring into savage battle mode in an instant.

Steven and I walked back to the road juncture and the wooden bridge. A crowd of villagers there had gathered to witness the unusual sight of the foreigner who just happened to appear in their midst. Behind the crowd, five women, all dressed in long, white smocks over long black skirts, with white powder on their faces and bare arms, were performing a mourning ceremony. They were flanked by several more women dressed in dark clothing, with white-powdered faces and arms. They, too, stopped to look at me with eager curiosity as I walked over with Steven. I sensed that for them, it was just as fun a surprise to see the unexpected alien as it was for me to find myself at a compensation ceremony.

Later, as Steven and I drove back to his lodge, we passed the Tari airport and came upon yet another strange site. Six women were standing in a field next to a fire and gazing upward while chanting and appearing to pray to the sky. I half expected to see an apparition floating above them.

Steven said that the women were doing another type of mourning ceremony. He stopped the truck and walked over to find out the details, then came back and told me:

"A local man had died in Port Moresby (PNG's capital)," Steven said. "His body was to be flown back to the Highlands for burial later this week. In this ceremonial ritual, the women are praying for spirits to bring the body of the dead man back home for burial—to be assisted by Air Niugini [the national airline], of course," he jokingly concluded.

As we continued to drive toward Steven's lodge, we passed a colorfully dressed woman with yellow and orange slashes of paint on her face. She was leading a procession of pigs down the road.

"This is a newly married woman," Steven said. "The pigs are part of her bride price, which is paid in pigs and cash, and she is leading them back home to her village."

He then stopped his vehicle in a small village we came to, at a simple outdoor restaurant and bar. I had offered to buy him some beers to bring back to the lodge for dinner.

"Let's drink here for a while," Steven suggested. "I have a girlfriend who lives in this village."

As we drank warm SP lager, the only beer available in the highlands, I chided Steven for having time for a girlfriend when he had three wives.

Laughing, he replied, "I now actually have only two wives. I divorced my second wife recently."

"Oh, I'm sorry to hear that," I said. "I did not know that people got divorced here. Why did you divorce your second wife?"

"Of course, sometimes married people get divorced," Steven said. "But it is still the responsibility of the man to make sure his ex-wife has a good home and enough food to eat. My second wife was very difficult and we did not get along. She wanted her freedom."

"But I have a girlfriend because I am a man," Steven said, giving me a wink and a smile. "As you know, in our culture a man has sex with his wife for procreation only. So, as a man, I have needs. It is normal for men to have unmarried girlfriends for this purpose."

Steven also went on to tell me the latest on his several children. Achara and I had met a few of his sons on our previous visit, when they came to the lodge. "One of my sons is now of age to learn the arts of war," Steven told me, referring to his youngest (who was about 10 years old at the time).

"I am proud to teach him how to fight," Steven continued. Back when we first met, Steven had proudly demonstrated for me some martial arts moves that he knew. "I am teaching him how to fight both with his hands and with weapons."

On Wednesday and again on Thursday, Steven and I went to Margarima for nomination rallies. Thursday was the last day of the nomination period, and the culmination of the rally festivities. Steven assured me that it would be spectacular.

The day started with parade after parade of traditionally dressed supporters from different tribes descending on Margarima—a procession for each of the almost twenty candidates. Thousands of people from all over the province thronged the wide fields around the missionary house. As on both Monday and Wednesday, someone noticed that I was the only foreigner at the event, and, of course, I was again invited as a guest of honor onto the porch with the candidates.

One after another, the candidates came up on the porch and gave rousing speeches. The themes of the speeches were easy to sympathize with.

"We must keep part of the royalties for resources from our traditional lands—this is a main theme of many of the speeches," a young
campaign staffer in Western dress, who spoke English, told me.
"Another big theme is that the government must respect the Highlanders' way of life and promote development in the Highlands.
Proper roads and schools should be given for the revenues from oil
and gas taken from our lands."

The young staffer pointed out another candidate. "He is speaking
mostly about how the Highlands must have someone strong to protect
us from the corrupt government in Port Moresby."

During and after each candidate's speech, his supporters would
chant and cheer boisterously. Loud sing-sing dances would break out:
whistles blowing, drums beating, women in long grass skirts shaking
their bare breasts, high headdresses of colorful exotic bird feathers
undulating in the air. Someone in the crowd held up a branch with a
live tree kangaroo, dancing with his mascot. The Huli witch doctors,
with their long black wigs flowing down their backs to their waists,
did a rambunctious circular dance.

As a traveler with no real connection to the local people, I felt truly
blessed to have shown up in the Tari Highlands during the nomination-
week ceremonies. The only way it could have been more perfect would
be to have Achara with me to see it all.

The next day, Achara flew into Tari. Though she had missed the
exciting events that week, Steven took us to a sing-sing in celebration
of a village school opening. Driving there in his truck, we happened
across a bride price ceremony, in which the families of the newly
married bride were dividing up the spoils.

We pulled up our truck at the edge of the village where this was
going on. It was a very hot day, with the sun blazing down on us.

"The various clan members related to the bride are negotiating their shares of the pigs and cash paid by the groom's family for the bride," Steven said. The whole situation looked strident and petty, even comical.

"That family member, the young man there," Steven said, pointing to a tall, scrawny light-skinned guy with a narrow face who was talking in a heated voice. "He thinks he should get more pigs because he is a first cousin of the bride. And that man there is another member of the extended family, who wants a bigger pig than the one he got."

Two short, muscular young men, one wearing a torn burgundy gym shirt, were loudly expressing their indignation. Laughing, Steven explained, "Those two boys are distant cousins of the bride. They got only twenty kina [about US$7] each and are really angry at the insult." Steven had trouble talking, he was laughing so hard. "They are arguing that they are very close to the bride—more like brothers to her than distant cousins. So they should get more money!"

It was all quite entertaining. Getting back into our truck, we attracted some attention. A sizable crowd of locals, who had been watching or participating in the serious negotiations over the bride price spoils, gathered around the truck. Some of the younger boys were eyeing Achara, now sitting in the backseat, as an attractive potential mate.

"How much do you want for her?" one of the boys shouted in English. They then suggested various sums of money and pigs.

"I'll give you one million kina for her [about US$300,000]!" an older teenage boy yelled.

I looked to Achara as if this were a tempting offer. She was not amused.

Achara and I would spend another two weeks in Papua New Guinea. We had to cancel our plan to trek in the Mount Bosavi area, though— I had badly sprained my knee during the week of the nomination ceremonies.

Instead, we scuba dived off PNG's northeastern shores. We tried to make the most of our time together, enjoying the country's famous world-class diving in pristine waters off Edenic palm-lined beaches.

I didn't know it, but this would be the last real travel adventure for Achara and me. In so many ways, our relationship had been intertwined with travel. Our long intercontinental courtship had by definition involved a lot of travel. During that period and after being married, travel was one of the major activities we shared together. Many of our most cherished memories occurred while in some faraway place. How ironic that travel was to be a big part of what pulled our relationship apart.

CHAPTER 5

Indonesia: Death Rituals, (Ex-)Headhunters, and "Where Are You From?"

17,508: The total number of islands that make up the Indonesian Archipelago, according to the Indonesian Naval Hydro-Oceanographic Office

June 2007
Jakarta

"Exasperation, pure exasperation—that's what it's like getting anything done in Indonesia," said Nadia, a friendly woman in her early thirties. It was my first evening in country, and I was in the Cork and Screw, a popular wine bar and restaurant catering to Jakarta's professional set. From my online reading, it sounded like a good place to meet educated people or expats and gain some insights into this sprawling island country. Nadia and her friend Eva, both Indonesians who worked with a large international accounting firm, had taken seats beside me at the bar and were giving me an insight of sorts: that perhaps the quality a traveler in Indonesia needed most was patience.

Nadia was stylishly dressed in a short red skirt and light purple blouse. She fit right into the general crowd at this chic eatery, which was packed with what could be yuppies from about any major Western city.

"The red tape, bureaucracy, ridiculous procedures, and outmoded thinking make doing even simple things, like buying a ticket or paying bills, an infuriating process," Nadia complained above the din. "And scheduled things, like airplanes or buses, never run on time!"

"Be careful in Jakarta," warned Eva, also stylishly dressed and in her thirties, and a little heavier than her coworker. While the three of us sipped our Australian red wine, Eva cautioned me, "Take special care with taxis! Only use Blue Bird or Silver Bird. I was robbed once in a car masquerading as a Blue Bird taxi. When I got in I didn't notice that the usual signature identification card with a picture of the driver wasn't on the dashboard. When I did notice, the driver had a gun on me. He took my purse with all my credit cards, money, and national ID card."

I promised her I would check the dashboard before getting in any taxis.

I spent a few days in Jakarta, a city with a deserved reputation as a dirty, polluted, crowded, unlivable mess. I stayed in the modern, fashionable city core, with its high-rises, glittering malls, chic cafés, wine bars, nightclubs, and spa centers. The area felt like a modern island in a sea of pollution, chaos, traffic gridlock, and sprawling slums.

My original plan for Indonesia was to travel on the island of Borneo, one of the top priorities in my travel project. But my knee was still very sore from the sprain I got two weeks earlier in Papua New Guinea. So I reluctantly revised my travel plan for Indonesia with an itinerary not involving deep-jungle treks. I was terribly disappointed by this since Borneo was one of those places that I had wanted to see for as long as I could remember.

Despite my disappointment over the blown travel plan for Borneo, I was determined to make my time in Indonesia worthwhile. My revised plan was to visit the exotic island of Bali. It would be a tame place to nurse my sore knee, and interesting with its Indonesian Hindu culture (the rest of the country is predominantly Muslim). So on my second evening in Jakarta, I decided to buy an airline ticket to Bali—a routine task.

To buy a ticket, I booted up my laptop in my hotel room and chose one of the no-frills airlines with regular flights from Jakarta to Bali. Typical of the airlines in Indonesia, its Web site had a "click-and-fly" button for making an online reservation. Easy enough.

But after going through the steps to buy my ticket, I found that it was not possible to make payment online. Instead, the Web site instructed me to call a special call center and make the payment over the phone, or go to a designated bank ATM to pay—either of which seemed to defeat the purpose of doing the transaction online in the first place.

When I called the "special call center" the friendly agent happily informed me that she could take payment over the phone only after I went into their downtown office the next day to sign a form. Not wanting to waste half a day in Jakarta's legendary traffic, I decided to try instead using the designated ATM to pay for my airline ticket to Bali. After wasting twenty minutes wandering the streets near my hotel, I found the proper type of transactional ATM to pay for my ticket. I keyed my name, reservation number, and all the other necessary info onto the ATM screen, only to bring up a notice telling me that I must have an Indonesian bank credit or ATM debit card to use the machine— a requirement that necessarily excluded most foreigners.

So the next morning, I wasted almost two hours slogging through traffic and waiting in a long queue at the airline office to make the payment for my online transaction. While waiting, I learned that this ridiculous inability to make a simple online transaction actually applied to Indonesians, too. Apparently, after an Indonesian makes successful payment by telephone to a call center or via an ATM, the airline still cannot generate an itinerary. So, just like a foreigner, the Indonesian national has to trudge down to the airline office to get a printed itinerary for the "convenient" online click-and-fly transaction. My thoughts drifted back to Nadia's abiding sense of exasperation.

———

After arriving and settling into Bali, I had my first experience of the legendary corruption the country is so infamous for. This involved the daily petty graft that ordinary people must endure. I was staying in Ubud, a charming town in the hilly center of the island, and had hired a local guide to drive me around the countryside for a day. After breakfast, Gede, my guide and driver, picked me up at the small guesthouse where I was staying, and we set out.

We drove along a dusty winding road in the forested hills, passing several small villages, each with at least one Balinese Hindu temple. These stood out with their pyramidal structures, ornately decorated with mythological animals and deities and brightly colored ornamental gold, red, and peach motifs. About a half hour into our drive, we approached a police roadblock along a lonely stretch of road. Several motorcycle police, in uniforms of light gray shirt, brown pants, and white helmet, were standing about. Two officers who were similarly clad but wore white soft caps held up their hands as we approached, indicating for us to stop.

One of them stepped over to our car. Gede calmly stopped, rolled down his window, and handed him a small sum of Indonesian rupiah equivalent to about US$2.25. Then he drove on, not saying anything.

"What was that about?" I asked. "Just a normal daily bribe for taking a drive?"

"Yes, this is routine," said Gede. He was a stoic, friendly man around 25 years old, with bushy black hair and serious eyes. "We'll probably see roadblocks about every hour or so today. There is a big holiday at the end of this month [June], and the police officers need money for their families to celebrate the approaching holiday."

"Really?" I said. "This looks like it can add up. You paid that guy twenty thousand rupiah. If you do this hourly all day, it will cost you a quarter of your daily profit after subtracting the fuel cost from what I will pay you (we had agreed on US$80 for the day)."

"Yes, but there is nothing we can do about it," Gede said.

"I have an idea," I said. "At the next stop, just refuse to pay. I'll take out my big camera here and make it obvious that I am photographing them in the act of trying to extract a bribe. This way, we'll shame them into letting you pass without giving the bribe."

"It won't work," Gede said matter-of-factly. Then he grinned. "But we can try."

Within twenty minutes of the first police roadblock, we approached another. As Gede slowed to a stop, I pulled out my camera and zoom lens. Conspicuously, I pointed the camera through the windshield at the officers and started snapping photos.

Without hesitation, an olive-skinned male officer with "Sujaya" on the name tag of his gray uniform shirt came to the driver's window and asked Gede to step outside and to the rear of his car. I continued openly taking photos. A second officer, a stern-faced, squatly built female motorcycle cop, wearing a white helmet and a name tag that read "Diantari," stood outside my door. As I snapped photos, Gede handed the officer some cash while standing behind the car's trunk. He then got back into the car, and we drove off.

"I guess my plan didn't work very well," I said, deflated.

"No," Gede replied. "Who would we show the photos to, any-way—their boss? Their bosses, including probably the district police chief, all expect their share of the bribes these police will collect today. After all, they all need money to celebrate the holiday with their families."

The scenery in the Bali highlands we drove through was serene and gorgeous. Huge swaths of terraced rice paddies spread out over entire hillsides. The beautiful irrigated terrace fields, deep green even in the dry season, were dotted with homes, temples, and resting spots or shelters. Luckily, we came upon only one more police roadblock that day.

While enjoying the scenery, I realized how naive I was to think we could shame the police at the second roadblock into not taking the bribe. I knew better, having seen this thing in many poor places around the world. People in the rich West more or less see police as a benevolent force. For much of the world's population, though, the police are a scourge, a plague on humanity.

I enjoyed Bali, with its wonderful variety of spicy foods and countless lovely temples. But after six days there, the lure of nearby Borneo grew too much. Despite my sore knee, I impulsively bought an air ticket and flew there the next morning.

Kalimantan (Borneo)

I leaned over from the aisle seat of the Lion Air flight and peered out the window. The plane was cruising above the intermittent thick forest along the rugged southeastern coast of the island of Borneo. Below, the Java Sea's dark blue waters glistened under the tropic sun.

Borneo. Just the name of the world's third-largest island had always brought to mind exotic images. As a youngster, I would look at a map of the world and gaze at this mysterious island. Pictures of thick, endless jungles, dark hardwood longhouses, headhunters, orangutans, and strange birds filled my mind. At last, I was finally here.

My mind shifted from the romantic to the pragmatic as I thought about logistics for my journey in Borneo. I figured I would travel in the jungle wilderness mostly by boat or motorized canoe, since sitting in a boat would be easiest on my injured knee. I had two goals for this trip: to journey into the center of the island, an area infamous for its fierce headhunting cultures of the past, and to visit Tanjung Puting, the southern peat swamp national park famous for orangutans and prolific wildlife.

But since Borneo was not originally part of my revised travel plan for this trip to Indonesia, I hadn't brought my gear for heavy jungle travel. I had no mosquito netting, malaria prophylactic meds, rain tarp, or other outdoor items. Mostly, I had city stuff and the usual travel things. But I figured, perhaps optimistically, that I could just pick up a few necessities along the way.

Although I was quite excited to be finally coming to Borneo, I knew that the journey would likely be a sad experience. Its rain forests, among the most biodiverse places on earth, are estimated to be around 130 million years old—the oldest on the planet. But the island's ancient forests, which have withstood so many epochs and geological upheavals, have faced massive deforestation and other degradation in just the past few short decades, at a frightening rate. Sadly, it now fits the profile as a poster child for the Disappearing World.

My flight brought me into Balikpapan, a modern port city on the southeastern edge of Borneo, in East Kalimantan, an oil-rich province in the Indonesian part of the island. (Indonesia has about three-fourths of the island, with Malaysia and Brunei, to the north, occupying the rest.) Surprisingly, in Balikpapan, a city of three hundred thousand people, I couldn't find the outdoor gear I needed. So after two days, I left for Banjarmasin, a city in the south-central part of the island, and the capital of South Kalimantan province. From Banjarmasin, I would journey up the great Kahayan River, into the deep jungles of the island's center, home of the once-feared headhunting Dayak people. Unfortunately, because of the language barrier, I took the wrong buses to Banjarmasin and stretched a day's journey into three.

Banjarmasin was crowded, chaotic, and impoverished, but also colorful with a grimy, noisy charm. Situated on the Kahayan River delta just north of the Java Sea, it is crisscrossed with waterways and canals. Houses built on stilts or floating logs line the waterways in some areas, adding to the charm.

I spent a few days enjoying the bustle of this major river port, walking along its canals and waterways, which are major arteries of transport and commerce. At the floating market, just out of town, a huge jam of small boats had gathered, filled with colorful produce. Women dressed in bright, gaily colored headscarves and saris haggled over jackfruit, durian, spices, and all manner of vegetables brought in boats from outlying areas.

I found the people in Banjarmasin very hospitable and friendly. The main ethnicity of the city is Banjarese, a Muslim people closely related to the Dayak of the interior. While in Banjarmasin, I got lost a number of times. But, each time someone happily walked with me some of the way, taking me in the right direction, or called a motor-cycle taxi, giving it directions to get me where I wanted to go. It was a nice place to linger before starting my jungle journey.

I combed Banjarmasin for a mosquito net and rain tarp. Surprisingly, despite its being a trade center of nearly half a million people, I couldn't find these things anywhere after hunting through many shopping areas. So, my next plan was to travel north on the Kahayan River to the last large town, Palangkaraya. There, I hoped to outfit myself properly for the jungle trip into Dayak country. At a minimum, I needed mosquito netting and an English-speaking guide.

I ended up going to Palangkaraya by car instead, with a man I had met in the Banjarmasin service center for Garuda Airlines (Indonesia's national airline). He happened to be going to an area near Palangkaraya for the weekend to see his mistress and offered me a ride. As we drove there my new friend, a middle-aged man named Reza who managed a travel business in Banjarmasin, expressed surprise at my travel plan.

"I have lived here my whole life and have never been north of Palangkaraya into the wilderness," Reza said. "You are very brave, Gary, to be going there alone."

"Oh, I'll be fine," I said, laughing, "I have some experience in jungle wilderness. And I hear that cannibalism among the Dayak has been outlawed for some time."

"Well, this is true," he said. "My mistress happens to be Dayak. They have very beautiful women. Maybe you'll find yourself a mistress. They are very loyal, you know."

"Well, I'm happily married," I said, laughing again, "so that's not really on the agenda."

"Don't spend much time in Palangkaraya," Reza advised. "It is a boring government town with nothing to do. I don't know how you'll get around to find your mosquito net. There is no call-taxi service of any kind, and almost no one speaks English."

At Palangkaraya, Reza dropped me off at a small guesthouse he knew, and we said good-bye.

I spent my first full day in this last outpost of civilization walking tremendous distances under the blazing sun, searching for my camp needs. The town was drab—a few wide boulevards lined with nondescript low-rise buildings, many of them government oriented. There were no taxis, and I didn't know the city well enough to use the tuk-tuks (little three or four-wheeled vehicles that run regular routes around town, like informal buses). So I walked everywhere, communicating by pantomime gestures or by drawing on a notepad I carried.

I spent the day dripping in sweat from the saunalike heat, with nothing to show for my efforts. I couldn't find a mosquito net, an English-speaking guide, or anything else useful in the town. My face and arms were sunburned even though I had worn SPF 50 sunscreen, and my feet were sore. So that evening, to soothe body and soul, I decided to treat myself to a relaxing dinner at a decent, air-conditioned Indonesian restaurant.

Inside the restaurant, it was wonderfully cool. The main room had several small round tables covered with white cloths. I almost fell over in surprise when a friendly young waiter in a rust-colored uniform and white gloves greeted me in perfect English.

"Good evening, good sir, please sit here," the waiter said, motioning to a table while handing me a menu.

I couldn't read the menu, which was in Indonesian. As in many restaurants throughout East Asia, the menu had pretty little pictures of the various dishes. But since I was not familiar with Indonesian foods, this didn't help much. So I called over the friendly young waiter.

"Perhaps you can recommend some dishes to me," I said. "I don't know much about Indonesian food."

As I was finding in my travels around Indonesia, this simple inquiry often drew a guarded and thoroughly useless response from a waiter.

"That depends on whatever you desire, good sir," the friendly young man replied.

"Of course," I said in response to this useless answer. So I narrowed my inquiry. "What is this restaurant known for? What are the best things on the menu?"

"Well, um-m, ah . . . that depends on what you are in the mood for this evening, good sir," the waiter replied in an even more obsequious manner.

I thought to myself, Is this for real? *This is the first person I've met in over twenty-four hours who speaks English, and he can't just give me a simple opinion?*

So, trying not to betray my frustration and keeping a fake smile firmly plastered on my face, I pointed to some pictures of dishes on the menu.

"Out of these three dishes," I said, pointing strategically to three separate pictures on the menu, "which do you recommend?"

"Oh, they are all most excellent, sir!" my waiter replied.

I pictured myself leaping from the chair, putting my hands around the smiling waiter's neck, and squeezing till I got an answer. I would not give in, I vowed internally, not betraying any hint of these violent thoughts to my waiter. By now my frozen smile was no doubt beginning to look more like a grimace. I would get a straight answer from this guy yet!

Mustering my last dram of patience, I cleverly pointed to just one of the three pictures I had picked from the menu. Maintaining my grimace of a smile, I said, "From among these three dishes, would you choose *this* one?"

"Oh, yes sir, that would be a very good choice," he replied almost convincingly.

Then, just to make sure, I pointed to the next picture in my subset of three choices. "Would this one possibly be a better choice?" I asked, starting to feel the pressure lift.

"Actually, I think, as a foreigner, you would enjoy that one better, sir," the waiter replied, *finally* giving me something that resembled an opinion.

"I'll take it!" I said, jubilant at actually having accomplished something that day.

My dinner, fish stew in a savory black sauce, and vegetables, was excellent.

———

Early the next morning, I threw caution to the winds and grabbed the first speedboat river taxi heading north on the Kahayan. There seemed no point in staying any longer in Palangkaraya. I still had no guide, mosquito netting, or other camp equipment. I had forgotten to get water, and since I couldn't find anything in the food store that I wanted and was able to carry, I had no food. I also had no way to find out what was at the end of the day-long boat ride I was taking deep into the jungle. There was literally no one around who spoke good enough English to ask. But I hoped, somewhere along the way, to find an English-speaker I could hire as a guide, who would have an extra mosquito net and know where to sleep and get food. In other words, I was hoping for a miracle.

The speedboat taxi was medium size, perhaps twenty feet long, with a canvas sun awning and narrow vinyl-upholstered benches along each side. It was a service in impressively high demand: upon pulling up to Palangkaraya's dock, it filled immediately, mostly with young mothers and their children. The women, all light-brown skinned with black hair and rounded cheeks, smiled at me, the only alien aboard. Surprisingly, despite the high heat and humidity, every one of the women wore a denim jacket, sweater, or sweatshirt.

We started up the wide, mud-colored Kahayan River under azure skies dotted with puffy white clouds. A thick green wall of vegetation lined either side of the river, interrupted now and then by clusters of tin-roofed wooden houses, some built on stilts. The other interruptions to the greenery were ugly intrusions in the form of small gold-dredging operations. Crude setups built on wooden platforms over the water, they sounded like jackhammers and belched black, stinky exhaust. Unusually for a deep-jungle river, I saw almost no birds or wildlife of any kind. I assumed the profusion of gold-dredging monstrosities was part of the reason.

During the first hours of the journey, the boat engine ominously sputtered and stalled out several times. We would then drift in the brown waters, deprived of the breeze from our movement and sweltering in the intense heat and humidity. But to our crew's credit, each time the engine died the pilot and his engine man somehow managed to revive the engine, and to everyone's relief, we would speed upstream once more.

Our luck gave out, though, three hours into the normally seven-hour journey. The engine died for good, and we were dead in the water and drifting ignominiously back downriver. Luckily, a speedboat from upriver came by and towed us to a small village nearby. There, the pilot came to me and politely indicated that a replacement boat would eventually come from Palangkaraya. With nothing to do, I walked around the village and was relieved to find a small shop in a tin-roofed shack, where I could buy bottled water, peanuts, and eggs. I pantomimed to the shop's owner, a stooped old woman with skin the color and texture of beef jerky, that I wanted her to hard-boil some eggs for me to take upriver. She happily obliged, and I now had some food and water.

After several hours spent standing about in the heat and fanning away the bugs, a new speedboat came along. All the passengers hopped in, and we were on our way again. The boat stopped at several river villages along the way, dropping off passengers, until it was just the pilot, the engine man, and me. Just before dusk, the speedboat reached the end of the line, a village called Tewah.

As I stepped off the boat, onto a small wharf of waterlogged boards, I looked up a long flight of wooden steps running up the steep riverbank. To my amazement, a small, neat-looking guesthouse stood at the top. I couldn't believe my good luck. I had figured I would be whacking weeds to make a clearing to sleep in for the night, or maybe sleeping on a wooden floor in a common village shelter after getting permission from the village chief. So at that moment, the guesthouse looked to me like a Four Seasons resort.

I hauled my luggage up the steep, creaky steps to the guesthouse and was greeted by the proprietor, a petite, attractive young Muslim mother of two. She brought me into the tidy kitchen and introduced me to her all-female staff. The neat wooden house had a feminine touch, with vases of fresh flowers set about, and was astonishingly clean. Another welcome surprise was the air conditioner in my room, powered by a diesel generator. The proprietress conveyed that there was a small extra fee for this, which I gladly paid. It was quite a luxury to escape the oppressive heat and humidity of the jungle, if only for a night. Joyful at this turn of events, I then feasted on fried chicken and stir-fried vegetables made by the friendly staff.

After dinner, I communicated to the proprietress that I was looking for someone who spoke English. (No one at the hotel did.) She happened to know a man who spoke English, and sent a messenger to fetch him.

Later that evening, the English-speaking man came by the hotel. He was of medium height and slight build, with light brown skin and unkempt black hair, and looked to be in his mid-thirties.

"I Margee," the man said. "I teacher Inglish to chillan in village."

Though Margee could barely speak English himself, he seemed proud of being the village's English teacher.

"I need an English-speaking guide to take me upriver into Dayak villages," I said. "And I need a mosquito net."

After talking for an hour, we struck a deal. Margee himself would take me to a historically famous Dayak village called Tumbang Anoi, a day and a half upriver from Tewah. "You, me share my mosquito net at night," Margee offered. He had only one, and there was no place to buy another. (Going forward, I quote Margee using proper English, though much of what he said was unintelligible and took considerable effort for me to understand.)

Early the next morning, I walked around Tewah with Margee. It was a picturesque village set between the jungle and the river. We went along a dirt road, away from its small center, to the village cemetery—a traditional Dayak burial place and quite a sight. It had the combination of different grave marker styles often seen in the South Pacific. Some graves were marked by small houses about the size of a doghouse, topped with exaggerated extended rooflines. Other markers were thick, short poles with colorful scary masks carved into them. Some larger grave markers were carved wooden pole statues. One, my favorite, depicted a naked woman with one hand serving as a fig leaf.

At midday, we set off in a motorized canoe called a *klotok*. These contraptions make a great racket, sounding like high-speed jack-hammers. As we blasted along the river, spewing a cloudy trail of black smoke, the klotok effectively scared away any birds or other wildlife along the way. So, as on the speedboat ride to Tewah, I saw nothing but more green jungle monotony.

Actually, besides the green jungle, I saw something quite disturbing and remarked about it to Margee, above the engine's din.

"I cannot believe how much trash is here in this remote jungle," I said with amazement. Even in this sparsely populated area deep in the jungle, tremendous amounts of plastic trash were strewn everywhere.

"What are you talking about?" Margee asked, perplexed.

"There, and there—it's all around us," I said, pointing to plastic bags and debris hanging from low-lying branches along the shore and caught in rushes sticking up from the water. "I noticed trash like this at many places along the Kahayan River."

"Oh, yes, I see," Margee finally said, sounding surprised. "I never noticed this before!"

It was the time of the year when the river runs low. "There is so much trash," I said, pointing to pieces of garbage as we zipped along, "you can see, just by the trash line, how high the river got during the rainy season." (The trash line was fairly high, maybe twelve to fifteen feet above the current river level.)

"I really can't believe how much plastic trash I see everywhere," I said again.

After about three hours, the river became much rockier, with many rapids, and evening darkness was starting to set in. Since it was too dangerous to navigate any farther, we stopped at a medium-size village and checked into the one hotel.

The village was not attractive, consisting mostly of run-down wooden buildings with peeling paint and rusted metal roofs. The hotel where Margee and I stayed had all the hominess of a prison: a large, dank concrete structure with little ventilation in its dark and barely furnished rooms, peeling drab paint spotted with mold, and lots of mosquitoes and other insects for roommates. We didn't hang around too long before heading out for dinner.

As we walked back from a dinner of spicy fish and fried rice, Margee stopped to talk with a young man on a motorbike, who told him about a special ceremony for the recently dead in a nearby village. Margee explained that we were lucky, since this event happened only once every two years. So we hopped onto a couple of motorcycle taxis and sped off along a dirt track through the woods to the village.

After ten minutes, our motorcycle taxis arrived at the village hosting the ceremony for the dead. It sat in a forest clearing and had several small and medium-size wooden houses built on platforms a few feet above ground. In the village center was a type of wooden altar. It had a big center pole with lots of dried bamboo and wood poles surrounding it and was festooned with various colored flags. It looked like a perfect setup for burning heretics at the stake.

Darkness set in shortly after we arrived, and a fire was lit at the base of the altar. Soon, a sweet scent of burning incense filled the air, and a deep, primal booming sound, which seemed to resonate inside me, emanated from big gonglike instruments being played in a hut behind us. Crashing cymbals accompanied the boom of the gongs, and a complicated, dramatic melody ensued. Some villagers then began moving around the altar in a slow, circular line dance while chanting to the music.

Women wearing colorful batiks performed one of the dances. They would take a few steps in their circular path around the firelit altar, then stop and turn toward it. Facing the blazing altar, they flared out their batik clothes like gaudy butterfly wings. In the pitch darkness of the jungle, the firelight glowed through the batiks as they flapped their arms in ghostly slow-motion flight. It was at once graceful, primal, dramatic, and sensual.

"The ceremony honors those who have died in this and neighboring villages over the past two years," Margee said. "It helps the souls of the recently deceased find their way into the afterlife. The colored flags on the altar each represent someone who died."

Then, turning and pointing to some of the elevated wooden houses, Margee said, "See those houses with a flag hanging from them? Each of those shows that one of the deceased being honored in the ceremony lived in the house."

The eerie, graceful dances around the altar went on for two hours, with the fire raging brilliantly in the dark forest. In between the dances, people went to the altar and threw offerings of rice grains onto it. Many spectators passed around bottles of a local moonshine, or arak, and the event became progressively livelier.

When the ceremony ended around midnight, several friendly villagers invited Margee and me to stay and drink beers with them. Since it was late, we reluctantly declined so that we could return to our prisonlike hotel for the night.

The next morning, we were off at the crack of dawn in another klotok. This was fine with me since I hadn't slept the entire night, thanks to Margee's heroically loud snoring. For six hours, we sputtered upriver, enduring yet more earsplitting noise as the engine spewed its continuous plume of black smoke. A little after noon, we reached the historic village of Tumbang Anoi, a pleasant-looking fishing village built on a high bank along the river. It appeared as an oasis of quiet in what had so far been a noisy deep-forest experience.

Margee and I climbed a steep metal stairway from the river to the village and walked down the main road, a narrow strip of concrete running along the top of the riverbank. Lining the road on both sides were small, well-built wooden houses with high-quality wood shingle roofs. Most of the houses had a small entry porch with a couple of steps. A number of houses had lifelike carved and painted wooden statues standing in front of their tiny yards, and many had little picket fences along the main road in front, some with laundry draped over them. The village had a feeling of contentment in its lush green forest surroundings.

We walked by the village's longhouse. These structures, which Borneo is famous for, are built of hardwoods set on high stilts and can be a hundred feet or more in length. They can house large numbers of people, usually an entire extended family.

The longhouse in Tumbang Anoi was a historic place. Margee explained that in the late 1800s, Borneo's Dutch colonial masters used forceful persuasion to bring the warring regional Dayak tribal leaders together into a peace conference. The conference and negotiations were held in Tumbang Anoi's longhouse over several months in 1894. During the conference, with strong prodding from the Dutch, the tribal leaders finally reached a historic agreement to stop hunting the neighboring tribes' heads. In front of the famous longhouse, a memorial plaque was on display honoring the site and its historic meeting and agreement.

Margee suggested that we return to the longhouse later to see the inside since our first stop should be to visit the village headman. We continued walking to the far end of the village to a neat, modest-size wooden house and knocked on the front door. The village headman, a tall, sturdy-looking young man with neatly groomed black hair, who looked to be in his late twenties, answered our knock.

"Please come in for tea," he said, motioning to some chairs in front of a hardwood desk in the house's front room.

"Where are you from, and what brought you to my village?" the headman asked, with Margee interpreting. "We get only a trickle of foreign visitors—maybe one every couple of weeks. The last foreigner to visit his village was a Swiss researcher who visits Tumbang Anoi every month or two."

"I am interested in seeing remote areas and the people living there who still retain their traditional way of life," I said.

During the discussion, Margee and the headman talked a lot in their native Dayak language. Margee mentioned to him my amazement at all the plastic trash I saw along the river, and I could see the headman growing more animated as they discussed the trash situation.

"I never thought about the trash or was aware of it," the headman finally said to me.

"The trash can become a big problem," I politely explained. "This plastic trash is not degradable and will never go away. Instead, it will continue to pile up, causing low-level contamination of the drinking water (the river) and killing birds that feed on the trash, thinking it is food."

"Hm-m, yes, this makes sense," the headman said.

"Perhaps as headman," I suggested, "You may want to consider making a rule that your people no longer throw plastic bags into the river."

"I'll consider this idea," the young headman said. "This is something I never thought about before."

After our meeting with the headman, Margee gave me a tour of the longhouse, a sturdy building of dark hardwood. The inside was just one long, cavernous room, but the outside of the house was more interesting. In all the village, it was the only building on high stilts. In front of it were several carved wooden statues, some of human figures, others of scary masks with snakes coming out of fanged mouths. It reminded me of the rich spirit world that is part of the Dayak cosmology, and some of which I had witnessed at the death ceremony the night before.

After seeing the longhouse, Margee and I visited a nearby hut, where Margee said some of his relatives lived. They greeted us warmly and invited us into the hut. Soon, a spontaneous party was in full swing, with beer and some local varieties of brandy and arak being passed around. Of course, being the rich foreigner, I was expected to buy the beer and other alcohol, which was fine with me. The party lasted well into the evening. I could tell that even in the village's idyllic surroundings (if one looked past the trash), people welcomed any excuse to have fun and do something outside the usual daily routine.

After a couple of days in Tumbang Anoi, Margee and I had to return downriver. First, though, we took our klotok a short way along the river for a closer look at a small gold-dredging operation near Tumbang Anoi. Besides all the plastic trash, the dredging rigs were the next most common thing I saw along the river, and I wanted to see one up close.

As we rode out to the rig, Margee explained that people had been panning for gold along the river for the past couple of centuries but that the big modern push for gold on the river began in the late 1990s, when a partnership of Indonesian and Canadian mining companies reported that the Kahayan River region had big gold reserves. (I later read that estimates were as high as several million ounces of in situ gold—portending even more degradation of the region's ecology.)

The gold-dredging machines that I saw along the river, like the one Margee and I closely inspected, consisted of a diesel-powered engine connected to a pump with a long intake snout. The snout of the pump was dropped through the water to the river floor, where it sucked up the muck and spewed it out an exhaust pipe, into a forest clearing behind the riverbank. In the process, small amounts of gold were separated from the muck being dredged up.

It was depressing to see one of these crude, ugly contraptions up close. There was no disguising their damage to the environment. The huge amounts of muck they suck from the river bottom are just casually piled behind the shoreline, eventually forming unnatural hills. Worse, from what some people in the area told me, a fair amount of mercury (a common by-product from the mining) is released into the environment. Also, the big diesel engines themselves that power the dredging rigs are not just noisy but also very polluting, releasing steady streams of grayish-black exhaust into the air. To me, any hope for the long-term health of the mighty Kahayan River and its surroundings looked bleak in light of all the poisons from the gold operations, the trash buildup, and the awful emissions from all the various diesel engines in use.

My conversation with Margee on the journey back to Tewah did not improve my bleak prognosis for the river. He railed at length about what was perhaps the biggest problem facing the environment (and, indeed, the biggest obstacle to resolving any of Indonesia's deep problems): corruption.

"The government steals much of the island's wealth," Margee said with vehement frustration. "This is a huge sum because of Kalimantan's large oil and timber extraction industries."

"As proof," he continued, "just look at the poor condition of the island's roads. The few paved ones are crumbling, and the rest are nothing more than dirt and rock paths strewn with big craters that fill with water!" (Except for the better roads in Kalimantan's few bigger cities, this corresponded with what I had seen up to that point.)

"It is the same with Kalimantan's drinking water," Margee said, pointing out another insidious result of government corruption and misappropriation of funds. "There is a general lack of clean drinking water almost everywhere on the island. And this is a rain forest! The rape of our land for oil, minerals, gold, and timber has polluted so much of the island's rivers, streams, and other water sources. The bribery and corruption is so bad that laws protecting habitats and the environment are regularly violated or ignored."[3]

Back at Tewah, I decided to end my trip in Borneo early since I just wasn't properly outfitted for further jungle travel. Instead, I would go back to Palangkaraya and arrange a flight to the Indonesian Island of Sulawesi, another place I wanted to visit. Inquiring about a boat ride back, I found to my surprise that I could return to Palangkaraya by minivan bus if I wanted. This surprised me—I hadn't known that any roads actually came that far toward Central Borneo. But someone explained to me that the road was actually a logging route and not an "official" highway. I should have heard ominous overtones in this explanation, but instead, I opted to take the minivan bus that left the next morning. I looked forward to seeing nice jungle scenery by land.

---

[3] I would later read that this was the case with drinking water across Indonesia in general. The archipelago (still) has more intact rain forest left than anywhere else in Southeast Asia, which should provide ample fresh water from rain. Yet the water almost anywhere in the country is not considered potable, even by the locals.

Instead, the long ride back to Palangkaraya was a sad, depressing experience. The bus passed through an apocalyptic disaster area. The stretch that we drove through, once one of the most biodiverse rain forests on the planet, in some places resembled a moonscape. The logging highway proceeded south along a huge swath of dusty, dry wasteland.

Though I had read about the relentless deforestation taking place all over Borneo, seeing it firsthand was one of the most jarring experiences of my life. It helped me reaffirm my commitment to the Disappearing World travel project, reinforcing my belief that at humanity's current pace, it is only a matter of time before many more wildernesses resemble the dusty, depressing badlands that I passed through in Central Borneo.

Sulawesi

From Palangkaraya, I flew to the old historic port city of Makassar, on the southwest coast of Sulawesi. Sulawesi is a fairly large island southeast of Borneo, with high biodiversity and some interesting cultures. I came to the island to visit the Central Highlands of South Sulawesi, where the Toraja people live.

Makassar, or Ujung Pandang, was chaotic and noisy—apparently the norm in Indonesia. The capital of South Sulawesi province and the island's largest city, Makassar in the 1500s was a major spice trading center and one of Southeast Asia's largest cities. Indians, Chinese, Arabs, Siamese, Javanese, and Malays came to trade in the cosmopolitan entrepôt of Makassar. This ended in 1667, when the Dutch captured the city in a bid to dominate the spice trade in the region.

I found Makassar a friendly city—perhaps too friendly. After checking into a pleasant guesthouse on the shoreline, I set out to do some personal errands in the city. I hadn't walked more than ten paces down the sidewalk from my guesthouse entrance when I heard the by now familiar call of "Mister!" followed by another call of "Hey, where are you going?"

I looked over. Four pedicab drivers were sitting by the sidewalk on their old-fashioned tricycle rigs, looking hopefully at me. I smiled and waved, indicating I didn't need a ride.

After another dozen paces, I crossed the street onto a main avenue lined with lots of shops. "Where are you from?" someone from a storefront shouted. "Where are you going?" another person on the side of the street yelled.

"I am from the Congo! I am going this way," I called back, pointing straight ahead while continuing to walk. It would be like this my entire time in Makassar. The constant attention that I, as a foreigner, attracted merely by walking down the street was not unique to Makassar. It seemed to be the case in any town or city in Indonesia that I had passed through so far. It was another of those maddening things about being in this sprawling, chaotic, endlessly fascinating and endlessly exasperating country.

Seeing a small art boutique, I decided to step in and take a look. Not two seconds after walking in, I was greeted with this most constant and irritating of inquiries.

"Hi, where are you from?" asked the pudgy young salesman who approached me.

"Tonga," I said, walking over to look at the jewelry display case.

"Oh, that sounds nice," the salesman said as I looked around the store.

Later that evening, I had dinner with a highly educated French expat named Giles, who had lived and worked in Indonesia for the past thirteen years. The nice woman who managed my guesthouse had introduced us.

"'Where are you from?' is THE question I get everywhere I go in Indonesia!" I said at one point to Giles. We were sitting in the upstairs lounge of a popular seaside restaurant and enjoying the sunset over a bottle of Australian red before dinner.

"This question is starting to grate on me," I complained. "Everyone I come into contact with or who even sees me, even just walking down the street, feels compelled to call out this question! I bet I could be at a funeral, and somebody there would shout out, 'Hey, mister, where you from?'"

Giles, a tall, stocky man with longish, tousled hair and a scholar's demeanor, mentioned that he experienced the same thing when he first came to Indonesia. He assured me that I would get used to it after a while.

I then explained to Giles that at first I would reply to this question by saying "L.A." or "Los Angeles." But to my surprise, the inquiring person usually had no idea what I was talking about. So then I started replying, "California," which the inquiring person sometimes recognized but still often didn't. Usually, I would have to say "USA" or "America" for the person to really understand.

"I finally got so exasperated by the question that I started replying 'the Congo,' or 'Tonga,'" I told Giles. "I figured it didn't make any difference since the inquirer usually didn't know where these places are any more than they knew where L.A. or California is!"

Giles poured us each another glass of wine as we both had a good laugh at my tale of exasperation.

"It makes sense that people here are curious about outsiders," Giles said. "The vast majority of Indonesians are poor and have never been off the island where they were born, let alone out of the country. I have found Indonesian people in general to be very insular."

I mentioned that I had seen this insularity, too, and gave the example of Gede, the well-spoken guide I hired for the day in Bali. Gede had proudly pointed out the large banyan trees all over the central highlands of the island, telling me that they were considered sacred. He erroneously had said that in all the world, the banyan tree was unique to Bali. Gede had also done this with some other things, such as the star fruit, telling me that it grew nowhere but on Bali. But when I pointed out to him that banyan trees were common in Hawaii and Florida in the United States and were found in many other places in the world, such as India and Thailand, and that I myself had eaten star fruits and seen them growing in many islands in the South Pacific and Southeast Asia, he almost refused to believe me.

Giles explained that he felt that this insularity among the general population of Indonesia was partly related to the rampant corruption in Indonesian society. From my experiences in other parts of the world, I found his explanation a depressingly familiar tale.

The corruption here was so pervasive, he said, that it hit every level of society, including the educational system. Primary and secondary education in Indonesia were supposed to be free to all, and funded from a percentage of tax revenues was theoretically set aside for the school system. But in what seemed the norm in Indonesia, funds earmarked for education just sort of disappeared, with only a fraction ever getting to the schools.

Because of the disappearance of school funds, Giles continued, most families in Indonesia had to pay tuition to send their children to school. Worse, it was common for ill-trained teachers to extort funds from families throughout the school year. The families made payments for various contrived reasons, or else their child would not be taught properly.

"In a country where most people struggle to make ends meet, many Indonesians are barely educated above basic levels because they can't afford it," Giles added.

In such a system, it was hard to see how rigorous, high-quality education could occur. Though I was not surprised to hear what Giles discussed, it was still hard to imagine the sheer exasperation and frustration of being a parent facing such an obscene situation.

On my fourth day in Sulawesi, I left Makassar, taking an all-day bus ride to the Central Highlands of South Sulawesi. While there, I stayed at a small, neat guesthouse in a town called Rantepao, in the heart of Toraja lands. I was interested in the Toraja people after reading of their elaborate funeral rites and famous burial sites. Since my time on my Indonesian visa was starting to run out, I immediately looked for a driver and guide who would know Toraja funeral customs. I didn't have to look far; the manager of my guesthouse referred me to a man named Dirwan, who knew the Toraja well.

The next morning before breakfast, Dirwan came to the guesthouse to meet me. Casually dressed in Western clothes, he had a military-style crew cut and looked around thirty years old. He spoke excellent English. To my delight, he told me that a death celebration was taking place today. If we hurried, he said, we could get there for the start. So I hired Dirwan for 200,000 rupiah (US$21) plus gasoline expense for the day to take me to the ceremony.

Skipping breakfast, we hopped into his car, a several-year-old blue Mazda, and drove off. We passed through a lush, green, neatly tended rural valley that had an air of prosperity. The valley was surrounded by forested hills and low mountains, and its wide crop fields were rimmed by sturdy low-rise stone fences. In some sections, clusters of distinctive-looking Toraja homes stood out. The traditional Toraja house, called a *tongkonan,* has a roof in the shape of a stylized, old-fashioned ship's hull turned upside down. The rooflines were long and arched, incised with red, yellow, and black carvings and ending in a point at both ends of the house. With so many houses topped by upside-down boats, it felt like an exotic land indeed.

Driving through these strange, lovely surroundings, Dirwin talked about the Toraja funerals.

"The funerals, or death celebrations, are essentially huge parties," Dirwan said. "Funeral rites for the Toraja, especially the rich, can be very big events. The wealthy have death celebrations that last for days and can go as long as a week. The ceremony is a joyous celebration for the deceased, who, the Toraja believe, is passing on to a better life."

Dirwin then explained that I was lucky since the death celebration we were attending today was for a very wealthy man and would last for six or seven days. However, today was the second and most interesting day of the celebration. "It is Greetings Day, the day that guests bring presents to the family of the deceased," Dirwan explained. "The main presents are live pigs, water buffalo, and cash." He then suggested that a gift of ten dollars from me would be a nice gesture, which, of course, I was happy to do.

Arriving at a large L-shaped ceremonial compound set in a forest clearing, Dirwin and I followed a line of people in through an arched gate. Entering the compound was like going into the belly of a gigantic capsized boat. Jutting out overhead from both sides of the main thoroughfare was a line of high, dramatically arching roofs in the shape of upside-down wooden "boats," whose prows arced gracefully over the dirt walkway. Each of these roofs, replicas of those on real tongkonan houses, sheltered one of the open wooden pavilions lining each side of the route.

The brother of the deceased, who was the host of the event, greeted me, saying, "Welcome! I am happy to meet you." He was a gracious man of compact build, wearing a long black tunic and a thick gold watch. "Please, follow me and sit in my pavilion with members of my family."

My host, who gave off an air of quiet affluence, brought me up some steps into his pavilion by the compound entrance, where many people were eating soup. Some women sitting on small chairs invited me to join them. A chubby woman in a long black skirt gave me a bowl of soup as more people streamed into the compound.

My seat afforded me a great view, and I marveled at the elaborate ceremonial compound. A tall "totem pole" made of a stack of curved water buffalo horns stood as the main arch support for the roof in one large pavilion. Smaller, cross-shaped carvings, reminding me of Native American stylized wooden birds, hung from the high end of each arched roof. Short rattan-and-wood-pole fencing, with long red cloth banners stretched from end to end along the top, lined the front of each pavilion. The pavilions stretched seventy-five yards along the road, turned right, and continued around the entire L-shaped compound. In this grand compound, designed to look like a miniature traditional village, I felt enveloped in an idealized mythological Toraja reality.

The crowd was colorful, too. Many men wore long, dark tunics like the host's, some also wearing the cylindrical Muslim hat while others wore a white and red checked scarf tied around their head. Some women wore long, dark dresses with elaborate bright yellow bead necklaces. Others were in long dark gowns with red, orange, and blue trim.

Sitting in the pavilion eating my soup, I watched an impressive medieval-looking scene unfold. A procession of four-man teams trooped in, each man bearing one end of a thick green bamboo pole on one shoulder. At the midpoint of these two parallel poles, a shorter pole was tied by its two ends, roughly forming an H. Trussed and hanging from this shorter pole was a live pig. The procession of men carrying the pigs proceeded along a path inside the large compound. The pigs, their feet bound by rope, were laid down in groups toward the front of the compound.

Then came another procession of men, leading water buffaloes. They followed the same route as those bearing the pigs, and eventually led their animals to a place reserved for them. Some of the animals would later be slaughtered and consumed during the ceremonial feasting.

"The deceased was very rich," said Dirwan, sitting next to me. "There are many pigs and water buffalo being brought in as presents. It looks like at least sixty pigs!"

Dirwin explained that under Toraja custom, the giving of animals was a reciprocal process. A family that provided a certain number of animals at a funeral expected to receive a like number of animals in return during a funeral for one of its family members. I surmised that the large numbers of animals being brought as presents must have been worth tens of thousands of dollars, even in Indonesia. It was an impressive display attesting to the wealth of the deceased and his family.

After the animals were brought in, people went to the pavilion at the end of the main road, where the widow of the deceased greeted them. She was a pretty middle-aged woman with creamy white skin, a roundish face, and her hair done up in a bun. Wearing a red and orange checked headband, a long dark dress overlaid with a skirt woven of thick orange yarn, and a similar body-length "necklace" of thickly braided orange strands, she reminded me of some exotic noblewoman—which, I suppose, she was. A procession of women, all wearing powder blue embroidered silk tops and checkered tan saris, brought small gifts of food and cakes to the widow's pavilion.

The event soon had the atmosphere of a country fair, with music blaring from loudspeakers, and people socializing in the pavilions. Dirwan and I spent the day at the death celebration, where everyone treated me, the only foreigner there, like a special guest. The event was a touching display of a different view of death.

The next day, Dirwan took me to a traditional Toraja burial area. We parked the car by a small village near a lake at the foot of a mountain and hiked a path along the lake, into the surrounding forested hills. After crossing a flimsy bridge of wood slats and vine slung over a steep crevice, we came to a flat area in front of the mountain. There was a cave opening at the foot of the mountain. I looked up above the cave opening and saw an astounding sight.

Over two dozen extraordinarily lifelike statues of old men and women stared out from a perch set above the cave entrance. The statues were placed on a re-creation of a large house porch, built on a platform that jutted from the side of the mountain. The whole thing was so meticulously realistic that the "porch" even had a wood shingle roof above it. The front row of statues depicted old men and women sitting in a line of wooden chairs and dressed in normal farm-style clothing. A second row of fully dressed statues was standing behind the seated statues. The whole set looked like an extended family, gathered on the porch and posing for a photograph.

"The Toraja put the bodies of the dead in caskets that are then laid inside the cave," Dirwan said. "Richer people have these life-size statues carved and painted to bear a close resemblance to the dead person, and then placed in an elevated position outside the cave entrance. Often, these displays will be of entire families, who put up statues over time as various members pass away."

Later, we hiked back to the car. As we started to drive away, I looked across the lake at the burial site. In the distance, I could see the eerily realistic statues staring out at the world in motionless silence.

CHAPTER 6

Venezuela: Sticky-Fingered Cops and a Demagogue's "Revolution"

There have been 43,792 homicides in Venezuela since 2007 . . . compared with about 28,000 deaths from drug-related violence in Mexico since that country's assault on cartels began in late 2006.
—Grim statistics on exploding violence in Venezuela from the Venezuelan Observatory of Violence, an NGO that compiles figures based on police files, as reported in the *New York Times*, Aug. 22, 2010

I am convinced that the path to a new, better and possible world is not capitalism, the path is socialism.
—Hugo Chávez, Venezuelan president 1999–2013

August 2007
Caracas

" **S**ocialismo o Muerte" (Socialism or Death), proclaimed the red banners hanging from several downtown Caracas high-rises and fluttering in the morning breeze. I was red eyed from the red-eye flight I had just taken from Los Angeles into Caracas, Venezuela's crime-ridden capital. Under the rising sun, though, Caracas seemed pleasant. The city sits in an elongated valley between two forested mountain ranges, both running roughly parallel to the coast. I noted some scenic views of the mountains at several points along the way into town.

During my taxi ride into downtown Caracas, I remembered reading that many areas of the city were considered "no-go" zones for visitors. I also thought about the stern words my aunt Gwen had regarding the city:

"You're going *where*?" Aunt Gwen said with a touch of drama. "What's in Venezuela that you need to see? The capital, Caracas, is one of the murder capitals of the world!" Gwen then said that she had been on a cruise once that had to make a stop in Caracas. However, before docking, the ship's captain had announced over the loudspeaker that everybody should stay aboard the ship. Caracas was too dangerous for tourists to go out and wander about for the evening, the captain said. According to my aunt, when the ship did dock, it stayed in port only long enough to replenish water and restock, and then got out.

"*Be careful!*" she admonished.

Since it was my first time in Caracas, I didn't know anybody here. So, in a nod to Aunt Gwen's safety concerns, I chose to stay in a richer part of town, called Las Mercedes, which, according to my online research, was considered generally safe for visitors.

The cabbie took me to see a few hotels in Las Mercedes. One of them was a nice business-class hotel, where I negotiated a great bargain with the hotel manager. After checking in and stowing my stuff in my room, I set out to change money on the black market. I had read extensively about Venezuela's serious financial problems and hyperinflation and had no doubt that such a situation would have spawned a big black market in its currency. Currency black markets were one of the usual characteristics of seriously mismanaged economies.

I didn't have to look far. The enterprising receptionists at the front desk of my hotel had connections with the black market. With a little bargaining, I traded six U.S. hundred-dollar bills for the astronomical sum of 2.76 million Venezuelan bolívares—a rate of 4,600 bolívares to one dollar. The "official" rate at the time was 2,000 to one, so the black market was a screaming deal. I seemed to have gotten off to an auspicious start in this presumably dangerous country. Things have a way of changing, though, especially when you're traveling.

I was actually quite happy to be in Venezuela, mostly because I was eager to be getting on with my travels. After my recent journey in Indonesia, I had passed briefly through Thailand to see Achara and her family in Bangkok. I had then spent a month in southern California attending to some modest interests in a few real estate partnerships I held in the area. After the abrupt and painful financial loss I suffered earlier that year while being out of touch in Peru, I was determined to keep better tabs on my financial interests. I was interested in Venezuela because of its abundant wildlife and because I wanted to get a firsthand view of the political situation. Its government, led by the bombastic strongman Hugo Chávez, seemed a caricature of past failed systems in Latin America.

I spent my first two days in Caracas wandering the city, as I usually did in a new place. It appeared to me that the better-off parts were very Westernized and drew much influence from the United States. For instance, my first evening in town, a Friday, I visited a huge, popular shopping and entertainment center near Las Mercedes. The mall had several different levels, with names such as "Uptown Manhattan," "Hollywood," and "Las Vegas." Its many hopping bars and clubs, which seemed to draw the city's beautiful people and lots of foreigners, reminded me of nightspots in West Los Angeles. It was obvious, though, that this was a tiny minority of the city's populace, since Caracas appeared to have many very poor areas where the vast majority lived.

On my second night in the city, Saturday night, I went out for dinner at a chic Italian restaurant near my hotel. The restaurant was packed and festively noisy when I got there in mid evening. Waitresses and hostesses, all of whom looked like models, ran around nonstop delivering drinks and food. It was another island of beautiful people in a poor, dangerous city.

Since no table was immediately available, I grabbed a stool at the long, polished wood-and-brass bar. There, I struck up a conversation with a local man I'll call Reinaldo (not his real name). Reinaldo was in his early forties, with dark, slightly graying hair. He seemed a polished man and told me he directed a highly respected theater group in the playhouse next to my hotel. He spoke good English and had strong ties to the States—two brothers living in Houston, and a mother raised in Colorado—and I enjoyed talking with him. After we chatted for about fifteen minutes Reinaldo excused himself, explaining that he needed to return to a large dinner party he was with. So I invited him to join me for a drink at my table after his dinner party.

Later, as I was finishing dinner, Reinaldo came by my table and took me up on my drink offer. Although the restaurant and bar were still packed and boisterously noisy, we were soon discussing the national political situation.

"Venezuela has big problems under the Chávez regime. Things are going downhill fast," Reinaldo said bluntly. "He uses oil money to buy support from a poor, uneducated majority that don't know any better. We have galloping inflation. And Chávez is nationalizing and expropriating businesses and private property left and right, destroying investor confidence in the country."

This fit with everything I had read. Chávez's large public-program expenditures for his poor supporters depended on an ever-increasing revenue stream from the country's oil production and was no more sustainable than any other Ponzi scheme.

Reinaldo then argued that Chávez was not just a Venezuelan concern but should be one for the United States as well. Citing Chávez's strong ties with Cuba and Bolivia, his big military armament purchases from Russia, and his increasingly dictatorial rule, Reinaldo said he was a security threat to the United States and that the States should do something to remove him from power. He also added that Chávez had been very influential on Ecuadoran and Bolivian politics, where similar leftist policies were now being implemented—which should be an additional worry for the United States.

I agreed with my new friend that Chávez seemed to be leading Venezuela down a dark path of ruinous authoritarian rule. But I countered that he was a Venezuelan problem that the people of Venezuela, not the United States, must deal with. I pointed out that Venezuela posed no real military, terrorist, or WMD threat to the United States and that the so-called oil weapon Chávez barked about was nonsense because Venezuela needed the U.S. oil market at least as much as we needed its oil.

"I'm telling you, Gary," Reinaldo said, "with the continued erosion of our freedoms, the nationalizing of many components of the energy industries, price freezes on many commodities, land expropriations, and other lousy economic policies, it is really scary here."

After a few drinks and this discussion of the dismal situation in Venezuela, it was a bit past midnight. Reinaldo asked me where I'd like to go in Caracas. He had a car, knew the city well, and was glad to show me any aspect of the nightlife that I was interested in.

"Nightlife in Caracas really cranks up after midnight," he said. "Girls, strip clubs, discos, hookers—what are you into?"

I nixed all these, saying I'd rather see something unique to Caracas and its culture.

"I know just the place," Reinaldo said. "There's a salsa bar that will show you the real flavor of Caracas. But it's in a rather bad area of the city. I'll take you there, as long as you don't mind."

"Sure," I said, figuring I was in good hands with this pleasant and intelligent local.

So off we went. While driving to the salsa bar in his late-model black Fiat, to my surprise, Reinaldo casually lit up a marijuana joint and started puffing away. There was a lot of traffic on the roads, but the area of town we were passing through appeared to be getting rougher.

"Care to join me?" he asked while holding the sweet, pungent smoke in his lungs for a moment. "Venezuela has really high-quality weed."

"Oh, no, thanks," I said politely. Actually, I thought it was nuts to be getting loaded while driving in what appeared to be a rough slum. But then again, I supposed, this was probably just what bohemian artistic types did.

Reinaldo then reached behind his seat and grabbed a bottle of Solara, a popular Venezuelan beer. While holding the steering wheel with his knee, he used an opener to pop the top off the bottle. This would be the first of three that he ended up drinking on the way. All along the approximately forty-minute drive, as he smoked the marijuana and drank the beers, we continued our political discussion.

Finally, we arrived at our destination, and Reinaldo parked up a slight hill a long city block from the salsa bar. It was a dingy, dimly lit street lined with dilapidated apartments and some straggly-looking trees. We got out of the car.

"¡Deténganse!" (Halt!) a stern voice commanded from the darkness. Two Venezuelan policemen seemed to materialize in front of our car.

"We would like to investigate," the lead policeman said (everything they said was in Spanish). He was an older man with a mustache and a slight paunch. The other officer was pudgy, with a doughy white face, and appeared to be in his late twenties.

"Your identity card," the lead officer crisply asked Reinaldo. Looking at me, he said, "Your passport, please."

"These guys just want a bribe," I said in English to Reinaldo. "I don't have my passport on me," I replied to the cops in bad Spanish. "I left it in my hotel safe. We're just going to the bar down the street," I politely told the cops. "There is nothing for you to investigate." Turning to Reinaldo, I said in English, "Let's go."

Not surprisingly, these two examples of Caracas's finest were not to be so easily brushed off.

"Put your hands on the car," they commanded Reinaldo. The cops searched Reinaldo, taking everything out of his pockets and placing it on the car's hood.

Finishing with Reinaldo, they turned to me and said they would search me, too. I was wearing only a pair of thin slacks suitable for the tropics, and a dressy T-shirt. So I politely but firmly pointed out that there was nothing to search and told them they could plainly see that I was not carrying a weapon.

"This is our job!" they both exclaimed. "Put your hands on the trunk!" the lead officer insisted.

"Do it, Gary," Reinaldo said. He looked intimidated and uneasy.

I reluctantly put my hands on the trunk of the car. The pudgy officer came up behind me and started to pat me down. Then he put his hand in my right front pocket and grabbed my money. That was too much.

Reacting instinctively, I clamped on to his hand and wrist with my right hand and held his hand in my pocket. I didn't want to yank it out of my pocket, because then my money would come out, too.

"*¡No le doy dinero!*" I said (I do not give you money.)

"Reinaldo, translate for me—I don't know how to say it in Spanish," I said. "Tell Fat Boy to let go of my money!"

Reinaldo said something to them in a shaky voice. The lead officer commanded me in a raised voice to let go of his partner's hand, saying that his partner was only doing his job.

"It is not his job to take my money," I said evenly in my rudimentary Spanish. The lead cop and the pudgy cop behind me both insisted that I let go of the pudgy cop's hand clutching the money in my pocket.

"First he must let go of my money," I insisted, struggling to say this in Spanish. I dug my fingers into the pudgy cop's wrist and levered his hand slightly downward. It was caught in my pocket, which meant my weight was bearing down on his wrist joint.

This standoff continued for a solid minute, which seemed like a really long time. The lead officer stared at me. Reinaldo looked scared. Both cops, with increasing vehemence, insisted that I let go of the officer's hand clutching the money in my pocket.

"Let go of his hand, Gary! *Do you know what these guys can do to us?*" an openly panicked Reinaldo pleaded. "They can take us to *jail.* We DO NOT want to go there under any circumstances. Just let him have the money."

Perhaps foolishly, I wouldn't let go. I had noticed that the pudgy cop with his hand in my pocket carried his gun holstered on his right side, the same side as the hand I was gripping. I figured I was safe from him since he couldn't go for his gun. I calculated that if the older cop did not escalate by drawing his gun, I would "win"—that is, avoid being fleeced. But if the lead cop did move to draw his gun, then I'd stand down and pay my way out.

Fortunately, I figured correctly. The sticky-handed cop finally released my money. I slowly drew his hand out of my pocket and deliberately delivered it to his side, away from me, where it belonged.

Looking at Reinaldo, I said forcefully, "Screw these guys. Start walking with me down the hill to the bar."

"*¡Deténganse!*" the lead cop commanded in an angry voice as Reinaldo and I turned our backs and started walking downhill.

"We need to investigate your car," the lead officer told Reinaldo, "Unlock it and give us your registration."

Oh, no! I thought. Half of Reinaldo's joint was still in the ashtray, and the fumes of the marijuana would be obvious. I knew that this was real grounds for arrest, and the three empty beer bottles on the back floor of his car wouldn't help. I had to draw the cops' attention away from the car at all costs.

So, acting with more bluster than I felt, I grabbed Reinaldo's arm and started pulling him down the hill.

"We are done wasting our time with these guys!" I said angrily in my poor Spanish. "They obviously just want a bribe!" (I used the word "*corrupción*" because I did not know "*mordida*," the Spanish word for "bribe.")

Thank God, my bluster worked. The cops forgot the car and started moving down the hill after us. Commanding us yet again to halt, they insisted that they were not finished investigating.

Luckily, three women dressed in provocative clothing, one wearing thigh-high tight black leather boots, came walking up the street. I figured they were prostitutes working the bar we were headed for. I disdainfully pointed my thumb over my shoulder at the two police and, in a loud voice dripping with disgust, said they were looking for a bribe.

Despite the tense situation, I almost burst out laughing at the women's response. They seemed to embody a pent-up, volcanic hatred engendered by the police among the populace. The women blew up. Leaning forward with pure, disdainful hate flashing in their eyes, they yelled at the cops at full pitch. I caught some of the words, and it sounded as if they were calling the two cops every vile expletive in the Spanish language. I was blown away by their vitriol. They yelled and taunted the cops, accusing them of corruption, jabbing their fingers in the air, spittle flying, their faces scrunched with fury.

The two increasingly agitated officers started yelling back at the angry women. Finally, they threatened to arrest them if they didn't leave. Fearing this, two of the women dashed up the street, got their truck, and came back for the third one, who was still yelling at the cops. The two women in the truck got out and pulled the third woman, still swearing at the top of her lungs, into the truck.

"Good luck!" the two called to me in English, while the third continued to shout profanities at the cops through the truck's open window as they sped off into the night.

I grabbed Reinaldo by the arm and half dragged him farther down the street. "Just keep going," I said. "The bar's not that far away now."

The cops followed us and started yelling for us to halt. Reinaldo stopped, so I had to, also. Now, though, the cops changed their strategy. The lead officer took Reinaldo aside and spoke with him in a low voice for a moment.

Reinaldo then turned to me. "He says he must call an ambulance for his partner," Reinaldo explained. "His partner thinks you broke his thumb from the pressure you put on his hand. He said his partner needs to go to the hospital to check his hand. They are asking that you pay compensation of a hundred fifty thousand bolívares for the ambulance and medical treatment" (about seventy-five dollars at the official exchange rate, thirty-five at the black-market rate).

"Tell them that is idiotic," I replied. "I'm not paying them anything." Looking at the lead officer, I said in my poor Spanish, "Any problem with your partner's thumb was his fault. It is not the job of the police to try to steal a person's money."

The cops continued demanding compensation before letting us go. Again Reinaldo was no help. "Just pay them off! I'd pay, but I have no money—only credit cards," he said. "These guys can take us to jail, Gary, where *anything* could happen to us."

At this time, two young men walked up. I explained in English what was going on and that the pudgy cop was claiming I broke his thumb and demanding "compensation." Like the three women before, they started vehemently yelling at the flabbergasted cops. The two young men both turned their focus to the pudgy cop with the supposedly broken thumb. A shouting match ensued for perhaps five minutes.

During this time, I moved next to the lead officer and tried a new tack. "You know," I said in a low voice, in my basic Spanish, "your partner is just looking for money. What about your integrity and sense of duty! I am a guest in your country. As a guest, you should treat me with appropriate hospitality."

The older officer just looked at me, expressionless.

I then pointed out, "We are both men. What would you do if I put my hand in your pocket and grabbed your money?" Then I took hold of his wrist and gave a demonstration squeeze.

"I have a solid grip," I said. The lead cop looked surprised as he limply held his hand while I squeezed his wrist. "But do you really think I am strong enough to break your partner's thumb?"

The lead officer stared at me, flabbergasted, and pulled his hand away.

Turning to the two guys shouting at his partner, the lead cop threatened to arrest them if they did not leave. So the two guys left, wishing us good luck. Again I grabbed Reinaldo and we continued on our way to the bar. Then a very spirited old black man—a thin, wiry guy—came up.

"What's going on?" the old man asked energetically in English. "I do 'security' for cars parked on this street by the bar. I heard all this shouting."

I explained what was going on. The old guy got angry and poured yet more verbal abuse on the two comically hapless cops.

Latching on to him, I sensed a way to finally escape.

"Walk with us," I implored the old man. "Stick with me and my friend here and walk with us all the way right into the bar." The bar was now very close.

"We won't stop or pay any more attention to the cops," I said to the old man and Reinaldo. The old man obliged. All of us turned our backs on the two now checkmated examples of Caracas's finest and marched without hesitation the rest of the way to the bar's entrance. We walked past the two burly bouncers in black sport jackets at the door, into the bar, and never looked back.

The two police officers went away, the ugly, menacing potential they represented vanishing back into the night as suddenly as it had appeared.

———

Inside the dark, smoky, noisy salsa club, I bought a double shot for the old man who had escorted us into the club, and beers for Reinaldo and me. Even though I felt a wave of relief in the festive, fun atmosphere in the bar, I had a hard time letting go of the totally clear and focused emergency mind-set that I had kept during the drama with the police.

"Don't say a word to anybody here about what just happened," I said to Reinaldo in a low voice. It was far-fetched, but I was concerned that word might somehow get back to the police and lead to another confrontation when we left the club later that morning. (By now it was past two a.m.)

Disregarding my request, Reinaldo immediately blabbed the story to some friends of his we met in the club. This attracted attention I didn't really want, and we became surrounded by a growing crowd, many of whom spoke English. Several people bought, or offered to buy, drinks for Reinaldo and me. All applauded the fact that someone, at least in this small instance, had stood up to the hated, horribly corrupt police.

"It is so cool how you Americans stick up for your rights!" a young man in a long-sleeved white shirt proclaimed, handing me a shot of tequila. He seemed to be summing up what everyone around us was saying. Others scornfully commented on how terrible the police were and how much worse they had gotten in the past few years. All I could think was how relieved I was to be in the bar, having drinks with friendly people, and not in jail, where anything could have happened.

———

The next day, I called Achara in Bangkok, using Skype from my hotel, and mentioned what had happened. She got quite angry.

"Were you really willing to risk your life for the hundred and fifty bucks you were carrying?" she scolded. "Where is your sense of perspective!"

I guess she had a point.

"Our families strongly encourage us to establish ourselves outside Venezuela," said Javier, a handsome, well-educated 24-year-old. I was talking with him and his two equally earnest young friends early one evening in the large dining room of Hato el Cedral, a well-known tourist wildlife ranch in Los Llanos, the savanna heartland of Venezuela.

While talking with Javier and his friends, I enjoyed the staggeringly brilliant sunset unfolding over the vast wetland plains. Several big buff-necked ibises, with gray feathers on their sleek oval bodies, white feathers on their longish necks, and long, curved black beaks, wandered the grasses outside the mosquito-screen walls of the dining hall. A tiger heron, tall and skinny with a gray-feathered body and a long, thick neck with rust-colored plumage, peered curiously at us through the screens into the dining room. The wonders of nature surrounding us were a stark contrast to the gloom expressed by my new companions.

I had come to Los Llanos to see its renowned abundance of wildlife. But my conversations with these three young men encapsulated the overriding theme of my journey through Venezuela: that of a dysfunctional country with dangerous social and political schisms.

"The preferred country to settle sons or daughters into is the U.S. But Argentina, Canada, or Europe would also do. This is a common strategy of the middle and affluent classes of Venezuela under the Chávez regime," Javier explained. An athletic, very European-looking 24-year-old, he had recently graduated from a top business university in the States and was in Venezuela vacationing with his two best friends. After this, he was bound for New York, where he would begin work in private banking. He should be here, of course, using his talents to build the future of his own country, but under the current populist kleptocracy there was no future. He and his two friends, Hernán and José, were explaining why so many of Venezuela's best and brightest were bound for lives outside their home country.

"Having a son or daughter in one of these countries is a hedge in case the rest of the family eventually has to leave Venezuela to escape upcoming 'revolutionary' changes," said José, who, at 22, was beginning his senior year of university in Venezuela, studying premed. "After graduation, I am leaving Venezuela for the U.S., to go to medical school."

"It is a lousy situation," added Hernán, a serious young man with dark, piercing eyes and a three-day beard. Also 22 years old, he was entering his senior year of university in Venezuela, where he studied industrial engineering. "We all have what should be a bright future and our whole lives ahead of us. Instead, we have to contemplate living our lives outside our homeland."

"I am not planning to leave Venezuela, though," Hernán said. "They wish I would, but I want to make my home here in Venezuela, for better or worse."

The families of the three young men were affluent by any standards. Javier's father was a highly placed executive of a large international pharmaceutical conglomerate, Hernán's father was a cardiac surgeon, and José's father was a dentist. Each of the young men told of friends, colleagues of their fathers, and acquaintances who had sent large amounts of money out of Venezuela to protect their capital. I thought about how strange it would seem to someone in the States to feel the need to settle their children in a foreign land just to protect their property rights and secure their future.

During the five days I stayed at the wildlife ranch, the young men gave me a detailed view of the societal divide the Chávez regime was fostering and then using to consolidate its grip on power. All three men explained how Chávez and his movement had deliberately orchestrated a class war in Venezuela. They were using a militant populism against anyone with any sort of wealth to systematically erode civil liberties and centralize power into Chávez's hands. There was a "revolutionary view," they explained, fostered by Chávez and his camp, that one was either for or against Chávez. There was no in-between, and both sides hated each other. For those of the professional, middle, or upper classes, a general fear of reprisal had taken hold, with one obvious fear being that of outright property expropriation. For example, if someone owned a vacation home, it could become a target to be taken away and given to the "poor."

The reality, though, was that the expropriation threat did not apply to those who were good supporters of Chávez, and the recipients of expropriated properties were not necessarily poor.

This situation applied to the wildlife ranch where I was staying in Los Llanos. According to the people who ran the ranch, they were under current threat of expropriation by the government. Their ranch, with its wealth of capybaras (the largest rodents in the world), tapirs, anteaters, jaguars, raccoons, caimans, lizards, and birds, served a vital national purpose as wildlife reserve and was a good tourist business. This didn't seem to matter: their large landholdings were deemed to be well "in excess" of what the owners needed to make a living. Not only could they lose their lands, but with the deep corruption of the thuggish regime, the land's use as a vital wildlife refuge would be doomed.

On the day I left the ranch, my three new young friends were also leaving, and they gave me a lift to the bus station in their rental car. During the drive, the three young men told me of another insidious threat feared by the middle and affluent classes. It sounded like a sick mind-control tactic befitting totalitarian states such as the old Stalinist USSR and present-day North Korea.

"Many middle- and upper-class parents worry about the increasing politicization of schools," Javier said. "Public schools are under rules to teach a curriculum stressing the 'revolutionary socialism' of the Chávez movement. Private schools would soon be required to 'voluntarily' adopt such curriculum requirements. Otherwise, they would risk losing their charters as private schools."

"It gets worse," said Hernán. "There is a proposed plan, which has already been implemented in some places, where children must attend schools while living apart from their families. The goal, of course, is to increase the effectiveness of the Chávez movement's indoctrination on the children through total immersion."

As my friends dropped me off at the bus station, I wished them and their country good luck, though it was hard to see any good outcome for Venezuela under Hugo Chávez.

From Los Llanos, my bus journey continued northward for three days to the coast. The first day brought me through several dusty towns and some arid mountains on buses that were pretty basic (but at least there were no goats or chickens on board). Along the way, I saw signs advertising an upcoming change in money denominations. The advertisements were so flagrantly dishonest that even I, a foreigner, was offended.

The signs advertised that new money would soon be issued, in which the last three zeroes from each denomination of currency were to be removed. For example, a thousand-bolívar note would become a one-bolívar note. This policy was necessitated by the hyperinflation created under the regime's incompetent fiscal policies. The runaway inflation in Venezuela meant that prices for inexpensive items, such as groceries or a meal in a moderately priced restaurant, were quoted in thousands and tens of thousands of bolívares. More expensive purchases, such as household appliances, a meal in a nice restaurant, or any other purchase running more than fifty U.S. dollars, saw prices into the hundreds of thousands and even millions of bolívares. (This situation was not new in Latin America. It was a common outcome of the statist, inflationary policies of many Latin American governments during the 1970s and 1980s.)

To counter the inconvenience of dealing in such large figures, the government was moving to do what other Latin American countries did when failed fiscal policies produced hyperinflation: remove three zeroes from the currency, as the signs were advertising. This would actually not change the value of the currency in any real way, since all prices would also be reduced by three zeroes. For example, a pint of milk cost costing 1,800 bolívares would be repriced at 1.8 bolívares. Everything would remain the same, though the numbers would be easier to deal with.

But this was not how the government propaganda put it. As Javier had mentioned in one of our conversations at the wildlife ranch, the government played on the poor masses' ignorance in financial matters. The ads for the redenomination, rather than being a frank admission that the government's policies were failing, cynically depicted the redenomination as making the currency more "valuable" and as a way to help the poor "get more" for their money.

Javier had told me about one widely shown government ad for the coming redenomination. In it, a father was shown giving his daughter her twenty-bolívar allowance. The message with the advertisement was that now her twenty-bolívar allowance will "mean something" by being more valuable. This was nonsense, of course, since the money would not be more valuable. That ad, like the ones I was seeing, showed the hypocrisy of a regime that purported to care about the peasants and poor people while merely playing cynically on their ignorance.[4]

As the bus rattled northward across Venezuela, I saw government-sponsored billboards everywhere. Most illustrated the fears of the

---

[4] The reality, as case histories on actual situations of currency redenominations show, is actually worse than if the currency had stayed the same value. Rather than being neutral, prices actually *increase* in real terms. Sellers can take advantage of the fact that the nominal stated price is so much lower (ten bolívares instead of ten thousand, for example). So it's easy enough to fudge a bit by adding slightly more to the price, and it will still seem like a screaming bargain (something costing 10,000 bolívares, instead of being cut to 10, would be repriced at 11, for instance—a 10 percent increase in real terms).

three young men I had met in Los Llanos. Some posters promoted the recent government takeover of the oil industry. Others extolled constitutional changes giving Chávez the right to decree various laws. Many posters trumpeted the ongoing "revolution." As in Cuba, everything was of and for the revolution—a revolution that never ends.

I had first seen this constant barrage of government propaganda when in Caracas. Along with the "revolutionary" banners seen around the city, television played a big role. One station, VTV, served as the government propaganda station. VTV ran "news" stories and continuous programming of Chávez propaganda, with nonstop pieces on various government programs that help the poor, flattering news about the government and Chávez, and negative portrayals of the government's opponents. Along with its chilling Orwellian overtones, it was dreadfully boring.

During my bus journey, I saw some predictable results from Venezuela's economic mismanagement. For instance, in several towns I visited (both on the way to Los Llanos and then on the way north after I left the wildlife refuge), I tried finding milk and yogurt in stores but noticed that most stores were out of these products. Finally, miffed at the constant lack of such basic foods, I asked a store owner about this. He informed me that dairy products, as well as cooking oil, sugar, rice, and a few other things, were under government price controls. The government set what it deemed a "fair" price, which was much lower than what the producers felt was a proper price. So, in a classic response that anyone with even a rudimentary grasp of economic history would expect, producers refused to produce.

Chávez was reinflicting the same economic policies that dependably failed in the past, and somehow expecting a better outcome this time around—a classic definition of insanity or, at least, cynicism.

A few months after my Venezuela journey, I finished the first full year of my travel project in a charming, romantic bed-and-breakfast in Prague, on New Year's Eve 2007. It was a beautiful night, cold and with a dusting of snow. Prague's huge Old Town section was quite atmospheric in winter, and it should have been a perfect place to unwind and celebrate after the past year's travels. But the main part of my reason for being here was missing. Achara, who was supposed to join me, had an unexpected last-minute assignment arise at her new job with the Thai Ministry and had to cancel joining me in Prague.

Normally, though disappointing, this wouldn't have caused me much unease, since I understood that things can arise unexpectedly. And though I had traveled with little pause since Venezuela, I had arranged a few nice opportunities to see Achara in that time. Just after Venezuela, I had flown her out to join me for a week at a nice countryside B and B outside Washington, D.C., near the historic Civil War battlefield of Manassas. Then, in November, I took my mother for a two-week visit to Thailand. Achara's family had really rolled out an even bigger red carpet than usual for her, and she had a great time as we all did a fun whirlwind tour of Thailand together.

But during the trip with my mother, Achara had seemed somewhat distant from me. She was very polite and went way out of her way to make my mother feel at home and, as always, was thoughtful and considerate with me. Now, though, looking back on it as I sat alone in the Prague B and B, I realized that she had not been her usual bright, fun self, and that had we interacted almost as dear old friends rather than as spouses. At the time, I figured it was just the stress of her new pattern of life as she adjusted to her growing new workload with the Thai government. So, I didn't pay it much mind. But now in Prague, I began to worry that maybe I should have.

So, with no one to celebrate the snowy beauty and festive atmosphere of New Year's Eve in Prague, I retired early to my charming room, originally reserved with two in mind, and was asleep before midnight.

CHAPTER 7

Into the Flooded Forest

At first, I thought I was fighting to save rubber trees;
then I thought was fighting to save the Amazon rain forest.
Now I realize I am fighting for humanity.
—Chico Mendes, Brazilian rain forest environmentalist,
human rights advocate (assassinated 1988)

Destroying rain forest for economic gain is like burning
a Renaissance painting to cook a meal.
—Edward O. Wilson, biologist, Harvard University,
two-time Pulitzer Prize winner

Late January 2008
Fortaleza, Brazil

It was a bright, sunny early afternoon when I arrived in Fortaleza, a sprawling industrial city on Brazil's northeast coast. I was tired after a long night that had involved three connecting flights from Quito, Ecuador, where I had gone shortly after my solo New Year's Eve in Prague. So as the taxi took me toward town, I was looking forward to an afternoon nap before getting down to business in Fortaleza.

My main objective for this trip to Brazil was to travel into the heart of the Amazon. First, though, I wanted to spend a couple of weeks in Fortaleza, intensively studying Portuguese, so I could get around more easily while in country. I had learned the hard way on previous trips into the Brazilian interior that it is often hard to find anyone who speaks much English or even Spanish. So I planned to hire a private tutor for two-hour daily sessions for two weeks and study intensively the rest of each day. My goal was to achieve a "survival" level in Portuguese before setting off into Amazonia.

My taxi from the airport brought me straight to a nice budget hotel in a glass-and-steel high-rise near the beach in Beira Mar, Fortaleza's upscale oceanfront area. Beira Mar is emblematic of the new rising affluence of Brazil. But not far inland, the buildings get older and the neighborhoods poorer, with dodgy sections where the wise think twice before venturing out at night.

When I checked into the hotel, the receptionist was very friendly and talkative. So I asked her where I might find a Portuguese tutor. The young woman, who was full figured and slightly plump but attractive, said she would contact me later that day with some suggestions.

Later, after my nap, I passed by the front desk on my way out to run errands. The friendly receptionist, whom I'll call Larissa, took me aside.

"I have good training myself in English," she said. "I went to a good university and have a four-year degree. I can be your tutor," she offered, beaming a big smile.

"Oh, this sounds great!" I said, surprised at how easily my tutor search had gone. "What would be a fair hourly fee for your time? I would like to be tutored two hours a day for the next two weeks."

"I'll do it for free, Gary," Larissa replied.

"Well, I do appreciate your generous spirit, but that wouldn't be fair," I said. "Tutoring is a lot of work, and I'm serious about studying. To get around in the Amazon, I really need a survival level of Portuguese. What's a fair rate for me to pay you that makes it worth your time and effort?"

"Hmm . . . okay, I'll think about it and talk to you later this evening," she said.

That evening, I had just walked back into my fifteenth-story hotel room and was standing on the balcony, looking out at the oceanfront a block away. It was a balmy, clear night, and I was wondering what to do. I had turned on the television and flipped through the stations, many of them music channels. Brazil is a country of music, which seems to pervade the fabric of daily life.

Larissa called on my room telephone, so I turned down the music to hear her. She said she had decided on a price for her services.

"Great! What is it?" I asked, planning to go to the ATM in the morning to draw her first week's pay.

"You," she answered simply.

At first, I didn't know what she meant. "I'm sorry, I don't understand," I said.

"I'd like you to be my payment," she said in a low, friendly voice. "I want to sleep with you."

Well, that sounded funny in a way, though also flattering, and I thought she was joking. So I laughed and said it would be better if I just paid her in cash.

"No, I'm serious," she said, sounding a bit taken aback at my response. "I don't need money. I have a job. I like you."

"Well, *that is* a compliment," I said, now realizing that she was serious and not wanting to hurt her feelings. "But I'm married and not available. And I really need a serious tutor."

"You are not married! You're not even wearing a ring," she said, sounding hurt and angry. (This was true. I didn't wear my ring on my travels, because I didn't want to risk losing it.)

"If you don't like me, fine!" Larissa continued angrily. "But don't lie to me like I am a stupid child."

I tried to salvage the situation. For one thing, she worked at the front desk of the hotel where I planned to stay for the next two weeks. But Larissa abruptly said good-bye.

Well, that didn't go well, I thought as I turned the volume back up again on the TV music channel. On the screen, one of those tall, leggy, impossibly sexy Brazilian pop singers was on a glittering stage. She had long, wavy hair and was wearing a slinky, in-your-face-provocative short gown with long, white thigh-high boots. Theater spotlights flashed around her against a hazy blue background. Young pretty boys in dark suits stood below her, doing a standing dance where they continuously bowed to her as she belted out an angry tune. I couldn't understand the Portuguese lyrics, but it was clear from the images being flashed on the screen that she was angry at a lover who had spurned her.

I turned off the television and walked back out onto my balcony, wondering where I would find a Portuguese tutor.

The next morning, Larissa called to apologize. We agreed on an hourly fee, and I had my first Portuguese lesson that morning since she was working the afternoon shift at the hotel that day. I was relieved that the awkward situation had turned out okay.

After my Portuguese lesson, I walked along the beachfront avenue. It was hot, sunny, and beautiful, with many people out jogging or exercising at the recreation area along the beach. I stopped for lunch at a bustling café and was seated next to two college-age women, one of whom was tall and athletic looking. They were speaking in Portuguese, but I happened to overhear and understand the tall woman saying something about swimming. So I leaned over and asked her in English if she knew the city and could recommend a beach with clean water where I might swim. I explained that I liked distance swimming as a workout but that the waters around Beira Mar looked dirty. The tall woman, who happened to be a beach volleyball player at a local university, spoke good English and knew the beaches around Fortaleza well. Both women were friendly and ended up joining me at my table. I enjoyed their company, and they invited me to meet them for dinner the next evening at a popular entertainment area called Dragão do Mar.

The next evening, I met the two young women for dinner at the Dragão do Mar, a large outdoor promenade area with many restaurants and bars. Dinner was fun, and we had a couple of drinks of a winelike Brazilian beer called *chopp de vinho*. They invited me to go dancing afterward, but I had to be up early the next day for my Portuguese lesson and wasn't into the loud club scene. So I left them and started the long walk back to my hotel.

Not far from the Dragão do Mar, I came to a long stretch of unlit street, lined with dark buildings and completely deserted. Not liking this, I altered my route home and started walking through a bustling area of loud nightclubs and open-air bars. As I walked along, a few girls on the sidewalk or inside the open-air bars called out "hello" or gave me an inviting smile. The area seemed to be some sort of red-light district, but, it was lively, well lit, and safe enough to walk through late at night.

Halfway through this bar district, I needed to find a bathroom. So, I picked what appeared to be a decent-looking "normal" nightclub. Five or six beefy security guys were standing on the walkway outside the club's front door. All had on white knit short-sleeve shirts and blue pants. Using my rudimentary Portuguese, I asked one of them if I could go in and use their toilet, then come right back out. The bouncer said "sure" and pointed me to the restroom area. He also handed me a little piece of paper, which I tossed onto a table on my way to the restroom.

Mistake. When I tried to leave the nightclub a few minutes later, one of the bouncers at the door asked me, in English, for my receipt.

"Receipt?" I said. "I don't have any receipt. I just came in a few moments ago and used the toilet."

"We can't let you leave without your receipt," the huge bouncer said. He stood well over six feet and had biceps bigger than my leg.

"Didn't you see me?" I asked. I looked around but didn't see the same bouncer who had let me into the club a few moments earlier. The place was huge, and he must have gone somewhere inside.

"You were given a receipt when you entered the club, like all clubs around here," the bouncer said. "I can't let you leave without your receipt. Otherwise, we have to charge you a minimum of sixty reais [about US$35]. The receipt tells us what you had to drink. You must then pay the cashier for your drinks." He motioned to the cashier.

"Oh, *that's* what that piece of paper was," I said. "I didn't know. I just tossed it on a table somewhere."

I continued to protest politely, but my explanations were getting me nowhere. "We need your receipt to be marked 'paid' before you can leave," the bouncer insisted.

All five bouncers moved a bit closer, all looking as though they were calmly relishing the opportunity to use a fellow human being as a heavy bag. Forcing my way out was probably not the answer, so I went back inside to look for the piece of paper I had casually tossed somewhere on my way to the restroom. I couldn't find it or the bouncer who had originally let me into the club.

Returning to the front, I insisted that they find the bouncer who had let me in. And they insisted they didn't know which one I was referring to; perhaps I could describe him. But "big and muscular with white knit shirt, blue pants, and short black hair" basically described all of them.

A tall, slim guy with sandy-colored hair and a light brown suit jacket came out and said was the bar manager. He spoke in Portuguese to the bouncer for a moment.

"We found your bill," the giant bouncer said, sounding less friendly than before. "You owe a hundred and fifty reais [about ninety dollars]. If you refuse to pay, we'll call the police and press charges against you for trying to skip out on your bill without paying."

Looking at me in an intimidating manner, the giant bouncer warned, "You do NOT want to deal with the police. You should just pay the bill."

"That's nonsense," I said. "Take me to the bartender who said I bought 150 reais' worth of drinks. He won't recognize me!"

"You must pay the bill if you want to leave," the bar manager insisted. "The bartender is in the back bar and busy. He described a tall foreigner that could barely speak Portuguese and looked exactly like you. Pay the bill now or we call the police."

Three bouncers then escorted me through the crowded, dark club and the pulsating music, to an isolated spot in back, with no obvious exit. I refused to pay. The idiotic standoff continued, with several bouncers watching me.

Then a young very pretty girl with café au lait skin, wearing a skimpy dark top and a very short red skirt, came over to the isolated spot. She looked all of 19 years old, but she spoke good English. She asked me what had happened. I explained, and she said maybe she could help. After talking in Portuguese with the bouncers, she came to me with an offer.

"I'll pay your bill," she said, looking up at me. "In return, maybe you can spend the night with me and pay me whatever you feel is fair." I told her I appreciated her help and that her offer was tempting. But I was married, and it was not my way to pay women to spend the night with me.

"There is no other good choice," she replied. "If you don't take my offer, the police will come and arrest you. Then you will have to pay them a big 'fine' and *still* pay the bar bill. Better to have a fun night with a beautiful girl who will take care of all your needs!" she concluded with a smile.

"I'll take police," I bluffed. "Call them NOW!" I demanded, looking at the bouncers.

The young girl walked angrily away. It was now well past midnight, and I had been detained for over two hours. The bouncers supposedly called the police. Another hour and a half went by, and when I inquired where the police were, the bouncers said the police were busy and I would have to wait. By this time, I knew I had been set up, and sensed that they hadn't really called the police. So I figured out how to call the police myself.

I was carrying my cell phone on this trip and had gotten a Brazilian SIM card for it. I didn't know the number for the police and didn't know enough Portuguese to speak with them anyhow. So I called the customer service number for my SIM card phone service. They had an English-speaker option. I explained my situation and the name of the bar to the customer service representative and asked him to call the police. He said he would. Sure enough, within twenty minutes, two police officers showed up.

The two cops were neatly groomed young men, smartly outfitted in black Kevlar upper vests and new-looking black boots. After talking with the bouncers and bar manager for about ten minutes, they brought me outside. Since they spoke little English, communicating was difficult, but I told them my story in my simple Portuguese with some Spanish thrown in. They explained that I would have to go down to the police station. The nightclub manager would come later to the station to fill out a complaint against me. So I reluctantly climbed into the back of their dark compact police SUV, and we left the bar.

As soon as we left, though, one of the officers asked me where I was staying. I told him the name of my hotel. He then said they would take me there. The other cop explained that they knew I was telling the truth.

"We see you are respectable, professional man," the officer explained in basic English. "We are sorry for your trouble."

However, a few moments into the drive, a call came over their radio. The officer driving the vehicle gunned the accelerator, and we tore off down the street at high speed.

"There is drug deal now in alley near here," the officer on the passenger side explained. "Please, don't mind. We must go there and make arrest. We don't want to leave you on street here. Not safe for you to walk to your hotel. Few taxis now at this hour."

With their high beams on, the officers zoomed down a dark backstreet and made several turns through a maze of narrow alleys. Coming to an abrupt halt, they trained their guns on two scruffy-looking men lying spread-eagled and facedown on the pavement. After cuffing the suspects, they shoved them in beside me in the backseat.

The friendly police officers then dropped me off at my hotel at four thirty a.m., six hours after I stopped to use the bathroom at the nightclub.

"Good night," they said. "We hope you enjoy your stay in Fortaleza."

February 2008
Manaus, Brazil

I gazed in awe through my window at one of nature's truly jaw-dropping displays. My flight from the central Amazonian city of Manaus to the small town of Tefé had just taken off, and the Brazilian-built Embraer twin turboprop thundered upward, its big propellers slicing through the steamy air. Below was the confluence of the Rio Negro and the Solimões, two gigantic highways of water.

I stood up in the plane and looked out the window facing east, across the aisle. The two giant rivers, one the color of black tea, the other café au lait, seemed unwilling to mix, each keeping to its own half of the watercourse. Perhaps a mile later, the Negro's acidic, tannin-rich black waters and those of the light-brown, sediment-laden Solimões eddied together in great, bicolored whorls and ribbons before finally blending into one, miles downriver.

The best part of coming to Manaus, it seemed, was leaving it and gazing at this awesome spectacle. The Amazon's largest city, itself, was not a big draw. Big and noisy, chaotic, and dirty, Manaus had not held my interest any longer than it took to make arrangements and move on toward my destination in the heart of the rain forest.

Though it looked a little down at the heels now, Manaus would have been fun to visit in the late nineteenth century, when it was the center of the world's rubber boom. At the time, the newly rich population, mostly of European descent, went to extraordinary lengths to re-create their European homelands, building vast domes and gilded balconies of marble and glass imported all the way from Europe.

One opulent relic from the rubber boom is the pink-and-white opera house, called the Teatro Amazonas, still in use today as a venue for performing arts. The structure sticks out, loudly incongruous with the city's tropical jungle setting.

In true Brazilian style, Manaus was a very social place, and I met lots of nice people during my extended weekend there. Surprisingly, it seemed that few of the city's dwellers had ever visited the Amazon forest, even though they lived smack in the middle of this great wilderness. Except for guides and others in the tourist business, most people I met in Manaus had never ventured into a spot any wilder than the several parks and resort areas at the city's edges.

This lack of familiarity with the Amazon seemed typical of most Brazilians I met. For most of them, who are still relatively poor, cost is probably the barrier. But even among the growing class of affluent people who can afford to visit the Amazon, it seems that few do.

"It is a vast, mysterious, even dangerous place," said one business-man I met in Fortaleza, summing up what I think many Brazilians feel about the immense wilderness.

"We don't want to deal with all the inconvenience, expense, bugs, and heat of the wilderness," two young professional women told me over drinks at a bar in Manaus.

"I really want to go to the Amazonas," a young building contractor had told me on my flight into Brazil a couple of weeks before. "But I prefer to vacation in other countries and have no time to go there."

My impression was that many Brazilians see the Amazon the way Americans in the 1800s saw the West: as vast, mysterious, dangerous, and costly to get to.

My flight to the isolated river town of Tefé loosely followed the great, brown Solimões as it snaked through the dense, endless carpet of green that stretched to infinity in all directions. I planned to spend only one night there before catching a speedboat for the two-hour ride to Mamirauá, a vast and remote wetland in the heart of the rain forest.

Deep in Amazonia

After landing at Tefé's tiny airport, I met Elizabeth, a young, blonde Brazilian who was my host from Mamirauá. She spoke passable English. We hopped into an old tan jeep for the short ride to town. Driving past rough huts set amid skinny trees and low jungle growth, I noticed a jarring phenomenon.

There were vultures everywhere. The sinister-looking creatures resembled enormous bald, pimply-headed crows with white, pasty legs and hooked beaks. They milled in the green brush along the sides of the road into town or sat on fence posts and the tin roofs of the shacks. They eyed our jeep as we rolled by.

"Was this place hit by a plague?" I asked Elizabeth, half expecting to see piles of animal carcasses, or human bodies, littering the landscape. "Why so many vultures?"

Laughing, Elizabeth said, "Tefé has very poor public sanitation services. Everywhere in town, people dispose of food, garbage, and sewage carelessly or not at all. So the job that the public services and the residents don't do falls to the vultures."

I joked that this presented the town with certain advantages, since the vultures worked at no cost and were not apt to form unions and go on strike.

As we arrived in the moderate-size frontier town, the vultures were even more concentrated, presumably because the pickings were also more concentrated there. Tefé was a shabby place, mostly low-rise and single-story buildings and wood-frame houses. Garbage, including scraps of meat, fat, and bone, lay everywhere. An old colonial church, one of the few outwardly appealing sights, stood in the town's center.

Elizabeth let me off near the church, at the least dismal-looking hotel in town.

After stashing my things, I walked to the river. A bunch of small wooden boats, with peeling paint and rusty metal fittings, stood docked along the shore. Evening darkness was setting in, and storm clouds were boiling up overhead. From the riverfront, I looked inland at the black vultures huddled atop the old buildings lining the wharf. It looked like the perfect setting for an Alfred Hitchcock film. I was glad I would be here only one night.

Early the next morning, I happily said good-bye to the vultures and garbage of Tefé. Elizabeth and I took a speedboat up the Solimões River, turning up into the Mamirauá, a tributary. Our speedboat blasted through gorgeous virgin jungle with large green lily pads, many adorned with equally large and striking white flowers, lining the riversides. The air was fresh and slightly sweet. Howler monkeys occasionally appeared in the trees overhead, white egrets fished along the shorelines, and a few pink dolphins surfaced along our route.

After two hours, we came around a bend in the river and into a small bay surrounded by dense primeval forest. At the back of the bay, a few small, neat wooden houses, with thatched roofs and large screened window openings, stood on a permanently floating wooden platform tethered to the river floor. The calm waters of the bay were dotted with many pairs of eyes that appeared to float on the water, serving as periscopes for submerged black caimans. A tawny-bellied screech owl—a small tan bird with round orange eyes—sat quietly on a branch in the forest understory along the bayside. A couple of scarlet macaws flew high overhead. But for the bugs, the heat, and the stifling humidity, it was an Edenic setting.

Elizabeth explained that the floating housing structure was the Uakari Lodge, where I would stay while in Mamirauá. The lodge was named after a rare monkey, the white bald-headed uakari, found only in the vicinity of the Mamirauá Reserve. It was quiet my first day at the lodge, since I was the only guest there. (Spring is the rainy season at Mamirauá, and a slow time for the Uakari Lodge.)

I admired the whole idea of a floating lodge. By building it on the water and tethering it only to the river floor, the operators made its footprint much less intrusive to the surroundings than a conventional land structure would be. And the lodge's low environmental impact clearly showed. Lunch was served in a large common room with very large sections of screened window openings. I watched as small, colorful birds fluttered around or walked lazily along the outdoor wood-plank walkways surrounding the common room. A loud cackle—the raucous yelling of macaws—rang out occasionally in the distance. A couple of times, a *whoosh* came from the surrounding waters as a large fish or caiman submerged after surfacing. I imagined that except for the lodge, this was probably how the bay had been for thousands of years.

While I enjoyed the amazing nature all around me, Elizabeth briefed me on the area. Mamirauá encompasses a huge area of the Amazon forest that floods annually, she explained. In this type of ecosystem, called *várzea* forest, water levels during the rainy season rise as much as forty to sixty-five feet each year. The entire ecosystem of the várzea forest is quite different from the rest of the Amazon since all its plant, animal, and insect life has adapted to this annual rising and falling water level.

From what I had read and from what Elizabeth explained, the Mamirauá Reserve, with the Uakari ecotourist lodge where I was staying, was one of those rare huge wins for the environment. It was all part of a pioneering conservation project begun in the 1990s by a man named Dr. José Ayres. His idea was to form a reserve to protect the unique ecosystem of the flooded forest and create ways for local people already inhabiting the protected lands to remain there, living from the forest in a sustainable manner.

This made eminent sense compared to previous attempts at conservation in the Brazilian Amazon. Past practices would have the Brazilian government decreeing a reserve and requiring all inhabitants to clear out of their forest homes. Or the government would make it illegal for the inhabitants to do any of the things they did to sustain their lives, like fishing, hunting, logging, and clearing lands for farming. Under Dr. Ayres's plan, the existing inhabitants could adapt their lifestyles to exploit the forest in a sustainable manner. If this proved successful in the newly created forest reserve, the inhabitants would become strong advocates for protecting their forest homes.

All this tallied with other conceptually similar projects I had seen or learned about in different parts of the Amazon. Through the creation of interest groups and advocates whose interests lie in preserving the forest, the forest has a much better chance of surviving the huge onslaughts from countless interests that would exploit it for short-term gain. On a personal level, it was gratifying to believe that these commonsense approaches might actually succeed in preserving some of these natural wonders that, as a child, I had despaired of ever seeing before they disappeared.[5]

That afternoon, I went with Elizabeth on a motorized canoe trip along the waterways near the lodge. We started in what seemed like a living minefield—the lagoon around the lodge was teeming with huge black caimans. These monsters, now a highly threatened species, can grow to sixteen feet and weigh over eight hundred pounds. They are the largest predators in the Western Hemisphere. I joked with Elizabeth that the lodge guests were probably discouraged from swimming.

"It might be the guest's last swim," she said, laughing, though it was no doubt true enough.

---

[5] The creation of Mamirauá led to an even greater ecological achievement. After being formally designated a sustainable reserve in 1996, it was the model for two adjoining sustainable reserves. The two additional reserves, the Amana Reserve (a dry-land forest) and Jaú National Park, together with Mamirauá, now form the Central Amazon Ecological Corridor, the largest continuous area of protected rain forest in the world.

Along the shore, howler monkeys swung in the trees, and parrots and parakeets fluttered about the canopy, seeking out whatever fruits were in season. Sitting in a bare tree branch high overhead, a kingfisher with a punk-rocker Mohawk looked down, watching the shallows for prey. Practically all the nonaquatic wildlife we saw was tree or canopy dwelling since the forest had no dry land during the high-water season.

Our boatman, a young indigenous man, brought us into a narrow waterway off the river and pointed to what looked like a hanging nest high on a branch near the upper canopy. Looking through my binoculars, I saw that it was a sloth, hanging upside down from a high tree branch.

As if hanging upside down from high tree branches were not weird enough, the sloth's lifestyle is even weirder. As Elizabeth explained, they spend 80 percent of their life sleeping, and they do this—and almost everything else—while hanging high above the forest floor. When a sloth moves it has one speed: very slow. Indeed, it moves so little and so slowly that its long hair is greenish from the algae growing there. They almost always stay in the trees, though they can swim well to escape predators. The big event in a sloth's life happens once a week, when it inches its way down to the ground to defecate. Then it buries its poop and inches its way back up into the high canopy again.

As we continued down the dark waters of the river, we saw a splash ahead of us, and something huge shimmered for a moment under the water's surface. It was another one of the spectacular gems of the Amazon, a giant pirarucu, the biggest freshwater fish in the world. The pirarucu, which can grow to over 6.5 feet long (2 meters) and weigh more than 220 lbs. (100 kilos), is unusual for a fish in that it is a lung breather. Elizabeth said that the reserve had a good population of them.

After our canoe ride, Elizabeth explained how different the flooded forest is from the rest of the rain forest. For one thing, the life cycles of low-lying plants are very quick. When the waters rise during the rainy season, low-lying plants drown, but they grow back again fast during the "dry" season. Much stranger was the fact that certain trees actually "hibernate" when the water rises over them.

The next morning, I met two new lodge guests: young Brazilian university students named Aldemar and Rondinelle, who, like the Mamirauá Project, represented hopeful prospects for at least some of the Amazon. Along with his university studies, Aldemar hosted and produced a half-hour weekly documentary on the Amazon, and Rondinelle was his cameraman. They were at the Uakari Lodge to make a feature episode on the positive role of ecotourism in helping fund the worthwhile activities of the Mamirauá Reserve.

"Each Friday evening, our show is broadcast throughout the Brazilian Amazon region on the Amazon Cable Television Network," Aldemar explained. "Each episode tells of some aspect of the Amazon. "Our mission is to raise people's knowledge of their unique habitat (the Amazon) and show how to sustain it through more prudent exploitation, conservation, and ecotourism measures."

It was encouraging to see young people from the Amazon make shows aimed specifically at people living in the region. And it made total sense. The biggest threats to the rain forest came from outsiders, of course, through clearing of land for grazing, mining, and timber extraction. But the growing populations of people living in the forest itself also add to the pressures on it. Turning more of these people into advocates for sustainable use and protection of the great forest would help alleviate some of these pressures from within and add resistance to the onslaught of outside pressures.

Our activity for the day was a canoe ride to visit two villages inhabited by "river people," or *ribeirinhos*—forest inhabitants who are a main focal point of Mamirauá's mandate. The ribeirinhos, Elizabeth explained during breakfast, were not indigenous. Rather, they were descendants of outside settlers who came into the Amazon region several generations ago, who have long since adapted their lifestyles to the rain forest. Some ribeirinhos have traces of European ancestry—from colonialists and settlers who intermingled with local indigenous people long ago.

As on previous sojourns among nonindigenous Amazonian forest dwellers, I marveled at how difficult life in Brazil must have been for the settlers *before* they moved to the forest. After all, living in the forest was a hard subsistence lifestyle that involved fishing and hunting for food and gathering or cultivating certain crops that grow well in the rain forest. And it was a harsh, bug- and parasite-infested environment of high humidity and heat. The very existence of the river people attested to the harshness and poverty that so many in Brazil have faced through much of its modern history.

Getting to Caburini, the first village, meant a lovely two-hour motorboat ride from the lodge through the dense forest, under densely clouded skies. The length of the ride, though, demonstrated another challenging aspect of the river people's lives: the extreme remoteness of where they lived, and the need to be truly self-sufficient. This distance was great enough that we covered quite a variety of microenvironments along the way.

Our journey started in a river several hundred yards wide, where we startled a huge flock of white egrets lazing on the waters ahead of us. The tall, elegantly slender birds took flight en masse as we approached. Farther along, we passed bright-green lily pads and patches of tall river grasses, and at another point we cut through a large section of forest only partly submerged in water. There, huge old trees, whose finlike trunk buttresses made them look almost like rockets on their launching pads, jutted boldly out of the tea-colored water. Our boatman cut the engine, and we glided silently through what felt like a low-lit outdoor cathedral of giant buttressed trees, twisting vines, and hanging aerial roots.

Upon our arrival at Caburini, we were greeted at the village dock by Raymundo, the "guest relations" host for visitors to the village. Raymundo was a fatherly-looking older figure, short with deep-brown skin, kind eyes, and receding white hair. He wore once-red shorts and a faded aqua T-shirt. His story and what he told us about the village demonstrated both the extreme remoteness of his home and the wisdom of the Mamirauá mandate in winning the cooperation of the river people.

I spent perhaps an hour walking through the village and talking with Raymundo while Elizabeth stayed by our boat and Aldemar and Rondinelle went off to shoot video of the village. Raymundo took me down the main dirt road, which was lined with small, simple wooden houses on stilts. Large upright wooden poles running along one side of the main road held power lines that brought electricity, supplied by the village's diesel generator, to the village homes for four hours a night. The entire village was built on a high embankment along the riverfront—protection against waters that can rise up to fifty feet during the annual rainy season. Small kids ran up, smiling and waving at me.

In surprisingly good English, Raymundo explained that his village had 105 people belonging to seventeen families. They lived a simple life in the forest, farming, fishing, making handicrafts, and harvesting "ornamental" fish that were sold for aquarium use—one of Mamirauá's many sustainable activity projects. They also did some ecotourism activities—mainly, supplying labor to the Uakari Lodge. Raymundo also told me about the village's work on an important environmental recovery project, acting as a turtle hatchery. This was urgent work, he explained, since turtle populations in many parts of the Amazon have crashed from centuries of overexploitation.

"This past year, we have released over four hundred turtles into the river," Raymundo said with obvious pride.

I liked Raymundo. He was friendly and open and seemed to enjoy having visitors to his village. We continued walking slowly along the main village road, at one point passing several black vultures that peered down at us from a roadside tree, and a gaudy red and green parrot sitting in a tree near them. I asked Raymundo about schooling for the village children. His answer was another reflection of Caburini's extreme isolation.

The village had a small primary school with twenty-eight children, Raymundo said, but it was temporarily closed because it had no teacher. They expected a new teacher to come and live here in a few months' time. High school age children attended school in a nearby village.

I remarked that it sounded pretty inconvenient not to have a teacher, and then asked how many young people from his village had gone on to university.

Raymundo explained that no one from Caburini had ever gone to university and that most people from the river stayed in the villages after growing up. Only three young people that he could remember had ever left the village to reside elsewhere. All three now lived in Manaus.

I was a little surprised by this answer. In my travels around the world so far, the pattern I saw was one of young people leaving the poor, isolated villages for the modern cities. All too often, they trade slow, dull lives set in remote natural splendor for a bleak existence in the appalling slums and shantytowns mushrooming around the major cities.

While we walked, I noted that even in this terribly remote place, several satellite TV dishes were on prominent display. So, curious about what people actually got on television, I asked Raymundo what they watched. I also asked about how images from the outside world might affect the young people of the village.

"People usually watch soap operas," he said with a slight laugh. For the most part, he said, people realized that the drug use, fighting, and immoral behavior depicted on television were bad.

At one point during our talk, Raymundo showed me a little house that served as the village church. Inside was a spare wooden room with a cross and a picture of St. Lazarus, Caburini's patron saint. He then explained his other role in the village, which showed something of the self-sufficiency needed to live in such a place.

"My other duty is the role of substitute priest for the village," Raymundo said. "Although almost all the ribeirinhos are Catholic, we lack a resident ordained priest. Because our village is so remote, the few priests in this region of the Amazon only visit on special occasions, such as funerals, baptisms, and confirmations. So I perform the day-to-day functions of the priest and conduct weekly mass."

Near the end of my village tour, Raymundo took me to a small hut near the town's center. Inside, he proudly showed us a display of many big golden trophy cups that Caburini had won in intervillage soccer competition. He then finished the tour by taking me and also Aldemar and Rondinelle, who by this time had joined us, to the village soccer field. There, many of the village's boys enthusiastically ran onto the field and did a playful demonstration of their soccer prowess.

Watching the kids play soccer for us reminded me of the soccer tournament that my wife, Achara, and I had seen while in the Sepik River region of Papua New Guinea a few years earlier. Two constants of the outside world had penetrated into the lives of even the most remote and simply living peoples: television (when those people have a way to get satellite television antennas and a source of programming) and the almost universal passion for the sport of soccer.

The second village we visited was called Villa Alancar. Here we were greeted by Francisca das Chagas. Dona Chagas was a plump, gray-haired, grandmotherly woman in her mid-fifties, and despite her sun-bronzed complexion, she had Portuguese facial features.

Her grandfather was one of the founders of the village, Dona Chagas explained with pride. He had been one of only a handful of settlers in this area over sixty years ago. Since then, the village had grown to its present population of over 180 and growing.

Villa Alancar was a small-scale example of another problem facing Amazonia: a rapidly growing population.

Villa Alancar had many similarities to Caburini. The twenty-five village families' simple wooden houses were lined up in a neat row facing a lagoon. Dona Chagas was the village substitute priest, filling the same functions as Raymundo in Caburini. There were satellite TV dishes as at Caburini, and electricity for the village was supplied by a small diesel generator station and available during the early evening hours.

Villa Alancar had one thing that Caburini didn't. At the end of the neat row of houses, and looking out of place in the middle of a rain forest, a public telephone was set up under a covered wooden platform.

"The telephone is part of a government plan to bring improvement to the lives of people living in the Amazon region," Dona Chagas explained when I asked her about it.

How incongruous, I thought, to be able to make calls to faraway places from this simple wooden platform, while the forest buzzed with the noise of insects, birds, and frogs, howler monkeys hooted and swung in the treetops nearby, and caimans peered up out of the nearby lagoon.

———

I spent eight days at Mamirauá, canoeing and hiking some mosquito-infested dry ground. I also visited a research center that specialized in research on the threatened pink and white river dolphins, and studied ways to create sustainable livelihoods from the rain forest. The sheer, mind-boggling abundance of life in every niche of this luxuriant forest was hard to fathom.

It was equally hard to fathom that much of this amazing natural wonderland faced real threats to its very existence.

From Mamirauá, I journeyed two days back to Manaus, where I caught a commuter flight to the remote Amazonian town of São Gabriel da Cachoeira. Founded in the sixteenth century, São Gabriel was originally a Portuguese slaving town. Today it is a smallish town of around 13,000 people, almost all of them indigenous. It is the last Brazilian town in the northwestern Brazilian Amazon, near the Venezuelan border on the Rio Negro. My main objective was to visit some Yanomami tribal villages in the region.

I arrived in late morning and grabbed a taxi from the airport to the town's main street. It was lined with a motley collection of older low-rise wood-and-stucco buildings and very quiet. The taxi let me off at a small but surprisingly pleasant hotel.

My first goal was to seek a jungle guide I had heard about. His name was Vald, and apparently, he was the only real English-speaker in the city. I had no other information on Vald, though—no address, phone number, or possible business name. I would have to search him down.

I asked my hotel's receptionist if he knew how to find Vald, the jungle guide. He suggested that I ask around at a general store a mile down the main street, where many people shopped. Since it was noon and São Gabriel is near the equator, my walk to the general store was in blast-furnace heat. I arrived at the store completely soaked in sweat.

No one in the small general store knew of Vald the jungle guide. So I pressed on since my plan to visit the Yanomami tribespeople depended on my finding the man. I asked around at any place that looked as though it attracted people. I was glad I had learned a bit of Portuguese, since almost no one spoke any English. I walked the city for hours in the blazing sun, going into small restaurants, an Internet café, a community center, and more shops. São Gabriel was a poor and dusty city that felt very isolated, but its people seemed friendly and open to me everywhere I went.

In midafternoon, on a side street with broken sidewalks, I met a man tending his garden. After I told him what I was looking for, he pointed me to an engine repair shop that happened to rent two engines used on canoes. It was a hole-in-the-wall place with greasy engine parts lying about, whose owner appeared to be alcoholic and had a face badly scarred with rosacea. He directed me to an area of town where he thought a jungle guide, a customer of his, lived. Finally, my first real lead!

I found him. Vald lived in a tiny but neat house set among fields of cassava, plantains, and corn on the edge of town. A short, very fit, wiry man in his sixties with graying hair and dark sun-bronzed skin, he was on his shaded back patio when I walked up in the late afternoon. After introducing myself, I told Vald of my desire to visit some Yanomami tribal villages. He needed to go into town on some errands and asked me to walk with him. While walking, he gave some background on himself.

Vald said he was born in an Amazonian forest village a few days east of São Gabriel by motorized canoe and had lived his entire life in the North Brazilian Amazon. Over the years, he had guided numerous groups of biologists, ethnologists, researchers, and mountain climbers into the lands of the Yanomami and other indigenous groups. (Mountain climbers went to Pico da Neblina, the tallest peak in the Amazon Basin, a four-day journey from São Gabriel.)

I liked Vald. He was funny and open and seemed to have a good attitude about life. As we walked around the town in the still blazing late afternoon sun, I was drenched in sweat. Even my pants were wet. Vald, however, who wore an old blue long-sleeved cotton shirt and beat-up heavy, dark cotton long pants, was not sweating in the least.

"I am surprised to meet a traveler like you," Vald said at one point. "The jungle here is a sort of lawless area. The only people who usually come visit the Yanomami tribal people are researchers, scientists, or NGO types. I can't remember the last time I actually had a customer like you."

At one point, we passed an old whitewashed Catholic church. "I assume most people here are nominally Catholic?" I asked.

"Yes," Vald replied. "Almost everybody is Catholic. It is much better being Catholic, you know, because if you're Protestant, you can't do anything or have any fun. Being Catholic, you can drink, smoke, dance, poke your neighbor's wife, and it's okay. But if you are Protestant, you can't do any of these things!"

I got a good laugh out of that.

At another point, I told him that my interest in the Yanomami was due to their relative isolation from the modern world. I had read that this isolation had allowed them to keep many aspects of their traditional lives intact.

From my readings, I had learned that the Yanomami always resisted assimilation into the outside world. The first major European invaders, the Portuguese, had little success in bringing these fierce people into their colonial and slaving activities. The missionaries didn't get far with them, either.

Vald said dealing with the Yanomami people was a challenge. They were not very open or friendly with outside visitors, because they had a dark history with outsiders. Starting with the Portuguese invasion in the sixteenth century, the Yanomami population had dropped from an estimated population of over a hundred thousand to perhaps twenty thousand today.

I mentioned that I had read about some of that dark history, which lasted into very recent times. When gold was discovered on Yanomami lands in the northwest Brazilian Amazon during the 1980s, the rush brought many outsiders—and new diseases that killed maybe a tenth of their remaining population in this region.

Vald said this was true and that many had also died from conflicts and violence as the Yanomami tried to defend their lands against the interlopers (losing perhaps fifteen hundred more tribespeople) and from pollution of their rivers and streams by the mercury used in gold prospecting. The gold rush also wreaked cultural destruction.

It was no surprise that the Yanomami didn't want much to do with outsiders.

After Vald finished his errands, we agreed to do a five-day expedition up the Rio Negro to several Yanomami villages. The first step to doing the expedition, Vald explained, was to get the necessary permission to enter Yanomami lands, since they now had a semiautonomous relationship with the government. This meant my getting permission from the Brazilian government and from the Yanomami chief. So we planned to meet the next morning at the Brazilian government office dealing with indigenous affairs, called FUNAI.

Despite their unwelcoming attitude to outsiders, I was eager to see some Yanomami villages. I had read that they were a historically martial people and that, as with the tribal people of the New Guinea highlands, this meant periodic warfare with neighboring tribes, and occasional infighting among themselves. They have good botanical knowledge, using a large variety of plants for food, medicines, and housing construction, and believe that all things of nature, whether animals, insects, trees, mountains, or rocks, have spirits. Shamanism is still a major part of tribal life. I figured that just as in New Guinea, I could get a glimpse into the primal mind of humanity from its deep past and perhaps even have another sort of time-travel experience into humanity's long-ago nature.

It was already a Turkish bath outside under sunny, clear skies when Vald and I met at the FUNAI office early the next morning. The office was spartan, with a few metal desks and a large shortwave radio sitting on the main desk in the room. Several friendly security officers in blue short-sleeved uniforms, none of them English-speakers, worked there. Vald spoke for me, telling the lead officer, a burly indigenous man, my story while I filled in a few forms.

The lead officer then used the shortwave radio to contact the Yanomami chief's assistant in a village I wanted to visit. He received verbal permission to issue a permit for me to visit their villages. By Yanomami custom, there would be a request for a "gift" from me in return for allowing my visit. I was more than happy to bring a gift, I said. When we left the office, it was my understanding that we would pick up the permit the next morning.

"Wow, that worked pretty well!" I said excitedly after Vald and I left the office. "We got the permission so fast! Let's get to work getting everything we need for a five-day expedition!"

"Maybe we should take it slow," Vald said. "It is the usual custom for the Yanomami to demand gifts in return for the right to visit or cross their lands and waters. We don't know what their 'gift' demand will be yet."

"Well, what are they going to ask for?" I said. "A carton of cigarettes or a basket of fruit?" I was a lone tourist, not a researcher, journalist, or documentary filmmaker. My motives were not profit oriented, so the tribal leaders should be lenient in their gift demands.

Vald then told me that before we left the FUNAI office, the officer mentioned that the chief of all the Yanomami in the region just happened to be passing through São Gabriel the very next morning. He was on his way by river to a big conference on indigenous people's affairs, being held in the Brazilian capital. Vald said we should go meet him before he caught his boat to Manaus. Then we could negotiate good "gift" terms and he could personally sign my permit.

"Great," I said. "Let's do it. Once the chief sees that I'm just an ordinary single tourist, we should be able to bargain a reasonable gift."

Early the next morning, it was cloudy as Vald and I went to a house by the town docks, near the river. The Yanomami chief had spent the night there and was preparing to catch his boat to Manaus when we walked up the porch steps to the modest wood-shingle house. The chief, a young, short man with his hair cut short in a modern style, was drinking coffee at a round wooden table in the home's front room. One of his aides invited Vald and me to sit on some folding chairs at the table while he and another aide got things ready to load onto the boat. My first thoughts on seeing the chief were that he looked like a normal guy and should be reasonable.

He wasn't. The chief, speaking to Vald in the local language, demanded a thousand U.S. dollars and two hundred gallons of diesel fuel in exchange for the short series of village visits. He then handed

Vald the permission letter, which stated these terms. The chief would sign the permission letter if I agreed to the demands. Vald told me the demands.

"That's ridiculous!" I said, making no effort to hide my disdain. Vald indignantly protested this unreasonable demand to the chief. So the chief lowered the request to just the diesel fuel. This was still a big demand since fuel was expensive—the equivalent of over four hundred dollars.

"That is still a big demand just to visit a couple of villages," I said. "But I'll pay it."

Unfortunately, the chief then made another unreasonable demand. First, he insisted that we buy the fuel that very day and give it to one of his aides. The aide would then bring the fuel into the jungle to the villages rather than let Vald and me take it ourselves. It also appeared that the chief was being devious with us. He would not take the time to alter the permission letter, which still stated the original, higher gift demands, to reflect the new, lowered requirement of only the diesel fuel. The document had just been printed a few moments earlier with a printer and computer sitting on a nearby desk.

I pointed out that the document with the revised demands could quickly be printed out or that the chief could even scratch out the old terms and write in the new ones by hand.

But instead, the chief just got up and walked away, claiming he had no time to change the agreement. Vald and I were left sitting alone by the table as the chief went into a bedroom and closed the door.

"I know you came a long way to do this expedition, Gary," Vald said, "but this is no good and the chief is not playing fair. The Yanomami can be dangerous. Ten years ago, I was leading a group of Swiss mountain climbers upriver to Pico da Neblina. On the way, as we passed a Yanomami village, we were stopped by several drunk male villagers waving shotguns at us. They demand all the possessions my customers had with them in their canoes. The hostile, drunk

Yanomami took *everything* we all had, including all our food, supplies, and gear."

"We were left with nothing in the remote wilderness," Vald concluded.

I didn't say anything. I was trying to see a way to salvage the situation and my expedition plan.

"We should forget this expedition, Gary," Vald said gently, knowing I was determined to go. "The permission letter is our passport to the Yanomami lands, and we have to carry the one with the original high demands. The chief did say he would communicate to the villages about the gift terms being changed and that his assistant would be carrying the diesel fuel, but what if these facts weren't communicated properly? If we show up at a village empty handed, with a permission letter saying we should have two hundred gallons of diesel fuel and a thousand dollars, we just might get a violent response. This is no good."

And that was that. My time and money spent getting to São Gabriel da Cachoeira were wasted. So without seeing the Yanomami, I flew back to Manaus a few days later, frustrated.

After wasting my time in São Gabriel, I traveled for seven weeks in other parts of South America and then flew to Los Angeles in mid-April. While in L.A., I would briefly see Achara before flying to Bangkok and then China, my next travel destination. Achara happened to be in Hawaii at the time, doing a month-long training program for her Thai government job, and was able to get away from it for a weekend and see me in L.A. I hadn't seen her for almost four months and was looking forward to the brief reunion. I booked us into a nice hotel near the airport, and we went out to a couple of good restaurants during our short rendezvous. But our time together was awkward, and we both seemed overly formal with each other.

My flight to Bangkok was late on our second evening together. I said good-bye to Achara in our hotel room around midnight. While pulling my rental car out of the hotel parking lot, I called her on my cell phone.

"I just wanted to say good-bye again," I said, feeling a strange loneliness, as if I had not really seen her at all that weekend. "I wish we had had more time together," I added, feeling awful about being off again and away from her for another long stretch of time.

"I hope you will not be gone too long from Thailand this time, Gary," Achara replied, sounding sad on the phone. "I think maybe you are away from me too much. So much is happening in between times that I see you." She paused, then continued in a low, somber voice, "I am worried that I don't really know you anymore."

CHAPTER 8

China

When I was growing up, my parents told me,
"Finish your dinner. People in China and India are starving."
I tell my daughters, "Finish your homework.
People in India and China are starving for your job."
—Thomas Friedman, American author, journalist,
and three-time Pulitzer Prize winner

Late April 2008
Guilin, Guangxi province, China

I scored pretty well here, I thought while walking through the charming main lobby of the three-star business hotel I had just checked into. The floors were marble, and two terra-cotta statues of demons, each about the size of a 5-year-old kid, stood along the wall by the walkway. Three large red velvet chaise longues were set facing a white porcelain fountain bowl in the middle of the room, and stylized dragons snarled on large plush tapestries that lined the tops of two of the walls.

All this for only 270 yuan (about US$37). I had bargained hard on my room price with the hotel reception person. This was done mainly by writing figures on a piece of paper, since the reception person spoke no English, and I no Chinese. The rack room rates displayed on the board behind the reception desk showed the price of the cheapest room: a "deluxe room" at 700 yuan (US$100).

I had been in China only a week, but I was already learning that capitalism can be very raw in this country. Local hotels that are Chinese owned, like this one, are run very differently from foreign-owned hotels. For example, the prices advertised have little to do with what one will actually pay. But as I also learned, a nice outward appearance of a Chinese-owned hotel often belied badly deferred maintenance on the actual rooms.

This was my first real trip in China, other than the ten days Achara and I had spent in Beijing at the end of 2006. I had just arrived in Guilin, a city of around 4.5 million—only moderate in size by Chinese standards. I had eagerly looked forward to this trip, wanting both to get a feel for the massive modernization going on in many parts of the country and to see some of its still-colorful ethnic minority cultures. I came to Guilin because of the famous natural beauty of its surroundings. The city is on the Li River, which cuts through one of the most sublimely scenic areas on earth. Before coming to Guilin, I had spent a few days in Hangzhou, renowned for its big lake with many old temples and palaces, before going to Shanghai, China's huge financial powerhouse. From there, I had flown into Guilin earlier in the afternoon.

After taking the elevator up from the main lobby, I found my room and went in. It was early evening, and I switched on the main light, planning to relax, read, and catch up on e-mail. As seems to be the case almost everywhere in China, the smell of stale cigarette smoke permeated the air. I sat on my bed. It was hard—also the norm in China. "Hard bed good for back," several Chinese people had told me. I wasn't convinced, since I sometimes woke up with sore hips, as if I had been camping on hard ground.

I reached over and flipped on the switch for the lamp next to my bed, but nothing happened. The bulb was missing. Oh, well. I plugged my laptop's power cord into the outlet by the nightstand to recharge the battery. I could still work by my bedside without the useless lamp. (Calling downstairs for housekeeping to bring up a lightbulb would mean getting someone on the phone who spoke English.) I then noticed that my laptop battery was not recharging—the outlet by the bed didn't work, either.

Since my laptop was out of power and I didn't want to get up and plug it in at the desk, I decided to be nonproductive and watch news on the television. But I couldn't find any English-language news programming, since every news channel was in Chinese and seemed to be of the government stage-managed kind. So I reluctantly gave up the dubious comfort of my board-hard bed, went to the desk, and plugged in my laptop—I could at least take advantage of the hotel's free Internet service. Unfortunately, the Internet didn't work, either. My "score" on the room price wasn't looking so good now.

Muttering to myself, I stepped into the bathroom to take a shower. The tile flooring and pretty white counters looked nice. The lighting was dim, though—of the bathroom's three light fixtures, two had burned-out bulbs. Still, I could see well enough to shave.

I had just lathered up when the telephone rang. Surprised that it actually worked, I dashed out to answer it.

"Hullo. You . . . want . . . massagee?" a soft female voice on the phone asked.

"Huh? Oh, you have a massage studio?" I said slowly, enunciating clearly. Since I couldn't do much else, a nice massage would be relaxing.

"Okay. Two . . . two . . . three . . . come soon . . . one girl," the soft voice on the phone said.

I thought, *two two three, hm-m, that's my room number.*

"No, no, that's okay. I don't want a girl," I said, realizing that the offer was for an in-room "massage"—that is, prostitution. "Thank you," I said, about to hang up the phone.

"Oh, you want two girl? Okay, okay," the soft voice replied.

"Ah, no, that's okay, thank you, *sheh sheh*," I said—my rough attempt at the Chinese word for "thank you"—and politely but hurriedly hung up the phone, ending the conversation.

I sat on my bed for a moment, surprised at how up-front prostitution was in this hotel. (I would come to learn that it was actually quite typical for single males to get this sort of solicitation in moderately priced business hotels in China.) While in Shanghai, I had heard that both Beijing and Shanghai were cracking down on their prolific prostitution scenes to "clean up" those showpiece cities in preparation for the upcoming 2008 Summer Olympics. Well, maybe the hookers from Shanghai had moved their business down here to Guilin. I went back into the bathroom to finish shaving and start my shower.

Unsurprisingly, the shower control didn't work correctly. It would adjust to only two water temperature settings: very hot and very cold. I settled for cold and plunged in, and in that moment, I heard a light knock on the door. Apparently, the caller had missed the "Do Not Disturb" sign I had hung on the knob. So I quickly wrapped a towel around myself to answer, wondering who it could be.

"Who is it?" I called out. A female voice answered in Chinese, which, of course, I didn't understand.

Opening the door slightly, I looked out. Standing there were two young, beautiful women who looked dressed to go out to a nightclub. One was tall and slender, with a light complexion, dark eyeliner, red lipstick, and long, wavy hair that fell halfway down her back. She wore red heart-shaped earrings, a tight red vest showing off small but firm cleavage, a short blue miniskirt displaying perfect legs, and high heels. She looked like a beautiful, perfectly made-up mannequin. Her friend was slim but shorter, with olive skin and wearing a dark open-shouldered purple dress and red miniskirt. If a guy were single and into prostitutes, he could certainly do worse than this hotel.

"I don't want massage," I said politely. Apparently, the soft voice on the phone earlier must have thought that declining the massage meant I wanted not one but two "masseuses" to service me.

"Thank you, *sheh sheh*," I then said while smiling politely, starting to close my door.

Both girls said something in Chinese, sounding confused. So, not wanting them to think I had ordered a service and was then stiffing them, I motioned to wait a moment and I went back into the room for my English-to-Chinese pocket dictionary. Returning, I fumbled through it a few moments. Finally, I managed to convey that I had not ordered a massage.

The girls gently took my dictionary, crowding up next to me. I felt funny standing in my half-open doorway, going through this while wearing only a towel. An older European couple happened to walk by us in the hallway and flashed a disdainful expression. After a moment, the girls looked at me. They both smelled like flowers.

"You no like?" the tall, beautiful mannequin asked, pointing to herself and her friend. "Okay, wait . . . Two new girl come."

At this, I got exasperated.

"No, no girl for me! Bye-bye," I said firmly, waving my hand. I took back my dictionary, waved good-bye, and gently but authoritatively closed the door on them.

———————

The next morning, I was up early for a four-hour boat ride south on the Li River, to the city of Yangshuo. I stood on the upper deck, enjoying the heavy mist and the cool, sweet-scented air. A short way downstream, we passed several water buffaloes grazing on a rocky spit of land that jutted out into the dark river waters. The pastoral setting seemed emblematic of much of tropical and subtropical Asia since time immemorial.

Soon, as the day's heat set in, the mists along the river rose to reveal some of the most stunning scenery I have ever seen. Countless hills, shaped like gigantic eyeteeth covered in lush green vegetation, jutted up along the riverside.

The formations are limestone karst hills, an unusual geological phenomenon found in only a few places on the planet. This famous scenic stretch of the Li River was sometimes referred to as "the hundred-mile natural art gallery," and its sublime otherworldliness seemed the perfect antidote to the crass, jarring, hyperactive commercialism of the big Chinese cities I had visited so far.

The picturesque boat trip ended too soon at Yangshuo, a pleasant (though perhaps a little overdone) tourist city. The bustling main streets were paved with stone and lined with old-style low-rise buildings of dark wood and white stucco. Big red-and-gold-trimmed cloth lanterns, shaped like half-squashed soccer balls, hung prominently from buildings along some of the main streets. The picturesque city was set against the verdant backdrop of karst hills. If I looked past the tourist signs and advertisements, Yangshuo appeared to be what many Chinese towns might have looked like at some point in the past.

My plan was to stay in Yangshuo a short while and then trek among the ethnic villages to the north, past Guilin. While in Yangshuo, I looked for someone to help me learn some basic Mandarin phrases. I could see from my experience in Guilin that once I got out of the main international cities, it would be tough trying to get by speaking only English.

I also wanted to make a stack of small index cards with the characters for useful Chinese phrases such as "Where is the bus station?" and "Where is a food market?" and even basic words such as "toilet," "vegetables," and "milk." Pronunciations for Chinese words can be difficult for foreigners, and dialects vary considerably from one area to another, whereas the characters remain much the same. The English translation for the word or phrase would also be written on the card so that I knew what the pictographs said. I could then show these cards to people I needed to communicate with.

While searching for someone to help with my Mandarin project, I met a nice young woman who worked a small tourist booth in the town center. Her "Western" name was Joanie. She was 25 years old, attractive, and lean but strong looking. Joanie had gone to "tourist college" and spoke good English. She agreed to help me in exchange for my helping her with questions she had about English. Over the next few days, she and I got together on her off hours, and she filled out my little cards with Mandarin words and phrases while I tutored her on some points of English.

The day before I was to leave, Joanie asked if she could join me as I traveled around China. She was switching jobs and moving to the big eastern city of Guangzhou in a month, so she had time to travel. Joanie had never traveled anywhere in China, because she didn't want to travel alone. I was a bit surprised, but it would be wonderfully convenient to have my very own interpreter with me. Moreover, Joanie knew I was married, and she had a long-term boyfriend from Europe, so our arrangement would have no misunderstandings regarding romantic intentions.

The next morning, Joanie and I caught a local bus going back through Guilin. We were heading to the town of Jinkeng, in a rural area with huge ancient terraces carved into its mountainsides. The bus rides would take the next day and a half, so we had lots of time to talk.

That afternoon, after passing through Guilin, our route took us through rugged forested hills, occasionally running alongside a river that cut through the mountains.

"I can't believe I am doing this," Joanie remarked, gazing out the window. "I have never been on vacation in my life. I sell people tours and airline tickets to places all over China, but I have never really been anywhere."

I could understand why. In Yangshuo, after one of my Chinese lessons, I had tagged along with Joanie as she ran errands around town and stopped by her home. Like many young Asian women, she bore huge responsibilities taking care of her elders.

She lived with her parents and her mother's parents, as well as her uncle, she explained while we were out running her errands. Her parents were older now and didn't make much money at the small noodle shop they owned. So she helped support them and her grandparents as well as her retired uncle. Her brother had died, so there was no one else to help.

As I went around with Joanie and saw all the burden of responsibility that she just seemed to accept and handle in stride, I developed a deep respect for her. Despite the "economic miracle" that China was now performing before the world's eyes, the truth was that the vast majority of its people barely got by. In a society with so little in the way of a social welfare safety net, the labors of the young women were often the only lifeline for the survival of dependent older relatives. I could hardly imagine a Western woman in her early twenties extending herself so for her older family members.

The next morning, after spending the night in the small city of Longsheng, we caught a shabby bus to Jinkeng. It ran along poor roads through gorgeous green hills and mountains. In the tiny hamlet of Jinkeng, we caught a minibus to Dazhai, a village of ethnic Yao people. The mountain-dwelling Yao are one of China's many ethnic minorities. Historically, they have been rebellious against central Chinese authority, and over the past two centuries, many have had to leave China to resettle in the highlands of Thailand, Vietnam, and Laos.

As our minibus plodded through the forested hills from Jinkeng toward Dazhai, an astonishing landscape opened before us. In a vision from some fantasy novel, terraced rice paddies climbed high up the mountainsides. Rising like bench seats in a steep, curving stadium for giants, row after row of narrow rice fields was etched into the steep terrain, from the bottom almost to the peaks, covering most of the entire mountainsides for as far as we could see. Channels of muddy irrigation water curled like brown ribbons around the outer rims of the narrow fields. Some of the hillsides went pretty high, with terraces rising up a vertical distance of almost half a mile. Almost as amazing as the visual spectacle itself was the fact that these agricultural wonders had their beginnings in the late thirteenth century. They are sometimes referred to as the "Eighth Wonder of the World."

Gaping in awe, I wondered how many people in the new and modern China, in their rush for the trappings of ever greater consumption, had even seen this wonderland where some of their daily rice may have grown. Even Joanie, who grew up as a farmer, had seen these sights only in photos.

Our minibus dropped us off in the center of Dazhai village, surrounded by these magnificent green terraced mountainsides. Long, sturdy two- and three-story wooden residential buildings with wood-shake roofs crawled up the village's steep hillsides. The place was surrounded by lush, impossibly clean-looking greenery, and along some of the roads hung the familiar Chinese red-and-gold-trimmed cloth lanterns. The whole place seemed taken from a fairy tale in some faraway magical setting.

Dazhai didn't get many outsiders and had no real facilities for them. So Joanie asked around and learned of a woman who ran a small homestay for the occasional visitor, at her farmhouse on the outskirts of the village near the top of a hill. After lugging our baggage up steeply winding roads to the little farmhouse, we were greeted by our hostess, an energetic middle-aged woman with her hair rolled and pinned up in the traditional Yao style. She wore a black flannel jacket with pink sleeves and pink trim along the shoulders, a pink waist sash, and a black midcalf skirt. She brought us into her neat, spare wooden house. The simple dwelling in this idyllic setting all felt very romantic, and it made me think of Achara, who would have loved it.

Our amiable hostess killed a chicken and cooked up a mix of fresh vegetables and herbs from her garden for a wonderful dinner. Afterward, she told Joanie that she wanted to show us an interesting local Yao women's style. She then undid her hair bun, which had not seemed especially notable, and started unraveling . . . and unraveling what seemed an endless amount of hair. When she was finished, her long black hair flowed all the way to the floor. She gave Joanie a wink, as if immensely proud of this prodigious local feat. Joanie's hair, which was merely waist length, seemed short by comparison.

Over the next few days, Joanie and I trekked among the huge, lush terraced mountainsides around Dazhai and another nearby Yao village. On these rambles, we ate in local villagers' homes since no formal restaurants were available.

Here was a place where time had stood still, and this was another of those time-travel experiences that I often felt when journeying in remote, traditional regions. The way of life for the Yao villagers seemed in many ways unchanged since the days when Europe languished in the Middle Ages. Traditional religious practices based on Taoism and Buddhism were still widely practiced. The terraced fields were largely tilled and worked by hand, with only a few gasoline-powered implements—mainly light chain saws—to be seen. Women wearing dark, heavy clothing, with their hair under black scarf turbans or wide-brimmed rattan hats, walked back and forth from terraced field to terraced field, carrying out their daily labors. Men did the heavier tasks, such as herding water buffalo, digging and repairing terraces, or using the few power tools for other chores. This was a part of the "other China," perhaps reflective in some ways of a still-large proportion of the country's population, whose simple lifestyles and poverty stood in contradiction to the newly minted image that the central government was so intent on presenting to the world.

From the Yao villages near Dazhai and Jinkeng, Joanie and I continued our journey into this "other China" of minority ethnic cultures. We took local buses northeast through thickly wooded mountainous areas, staying in more small villages along the way and visiting the Dong, another important ethnic minority in the region. They live mostly in southeast China, in lower elevations than the Yao.

The Dong are also known for their outstanding carpentry skills and rich performing-arts tradition.

In one village where we stayed, called Chengyang, we saw one of the most famous examples of Dong carpentry skills. A local guide took Joanie and me down to the river, which was spanned by a beautiful wooden bridge. Five wood-shingled pagodas had been built and spaced evenly along the bridge, and a shingled roof pavilion provided shelter in between the pagodas. The exquisite bridge was supported by three sturdy square stone columns built into the waters. Behind the bridge, Chengyang's multistory wood homes were tucked into a valley hemmed on three sides by forested hills and mountains. In front of the bridge, brilliant green rice paddies ran along the riverbank.

Our guide told us that the bridge was a traditional Dong type called a wind-and-rain bridge. This one, the most famous in the region, was a UNESCO World Heritage Site. Built over a century ago without using any nails, it was around sixty-five meters long.

Looking at the beautiful structure, I admired the exquisite attention to detail, design, and harmony that went into it. Though this bridge was a specialty of the Dong ethnic minority, these design traits seemed a characteristic of past Chinese cultures in general. But as I would see firsthand in my further China travels, these special Chinese craftsmanship traits of design, detail, and harmony were lacking in the hurriedly mass-produced cities being thrown up almost overnight in the new, modern China.

One of the benefits of travel to far-flung places and cultures, which I have grown to value immensely, is the ongoing experience of just how universal human nature is. In Zhaoxing, another Dong village where Joanie and I stayed, we experienced this benefit of travel in a fun way.

Zhaoxing is set in a gorgeous valley surrounded by rolling green hills, some of them terraced. It's a charming place with sturdy wooden two- and three-story buildings lining the concrete main street, and several wind-and-rain bridges spanning the two rivers that flow through it. Our first night in town, Joanie and I went to one of the drum towers along the main road to watch a performance. The drum tower, a wooden house with a many-layered pagoda roof structure, is integral to Dong villages. Usually set in an open space or court-yard, it is a place where the village people gather, socialize, and hold religious or other events. Zhaoxing, being a large village, has five drum towers.

The performance in the large courtyard in front of the drum tower featured several short plays or skits. Though neither of us could understand the language, several of the skits were easy to figure out. In one, five young men in white, flowing shirts, burnt-gold vests, dark baggy pants, and turbans go out in the village one night, drinking and merrymaking, in search of eligible women. Finding a house with four attractive single women, they are invited in. The four women are wearing shiny burnt-gold tops and shimmering rust-colored knee-length skirts. They have their hair pinned in a bun adorned with an open red rose and topped by a delicate silver wire, shaped into ivy with small, delicate leaves.

In the house with the four available women, a pairing off of couples gradually takes place. But with five men and four women, there is an odd man out. So the skit, a farcical comedy, shows the odd man out cunningly trying to interpose himself in the place of each of his comrades who have successfully paired off with a girl. Ultimately, he is foiled in his efforts. At the end of the show, the poor guy has to slink off into the night by himself, lonely and depressed. What struck me was how the skit (probably coincidentally) depicts the gross imbalance between the sexes in China, where marriageable young men greatly outnumber young women—a sad and potentially explosive demographic reality.

Another play that evening was a Dong version of a theme as old as human society: that of Romeo and Juliet. The plot involves two young lovers entwined in a hopeless and forbidden love affair. But the play doesn't end in a mutual suicide as in Shakespeare's play. Instead, the Dong Romeo is murdered by a male family member of the "proper" husband for Juliet. So Juliet gets her revenge. She tricks the killer into dropping his guard while working in a field and bashes his head in with a shovel. Though I assumed the play to be one with a plot that was quite traditional for the Dong, I liked its modern twist of casting the aggrieved young woman as the heroic avenger of her slain lover.

———

From Zhaoxing, Joanie and I continued our journeys into the "other China," but our ways parted. I headed to Zhongdian, now officially called "Shangri-la," a heavily Tibetan-influenced city in Northwestern Yunnan province, while Joanie went to Lijiang, a popular tourist city. She had sent many people there on package tours and wanted to see it for herself.

The long journey to Shangri-la involved several days' travel in smoky trains and, sometimes, equally smoke-filled buses. Chinese people smoke a lot and seem to do so wherever they are, even in "non-smoking" areas such as public transportation. The final part of this journey, after Joanie split off, was lonely for me. It had been fun having a travel partner for much of my time in China. Although Joanie tried to be "one of the guys," keeping up on the hikes and roughing it without complaint, she still brought a feminine touch and was a sharp reminder of how much I missed Achara and a woman's presence in my life.

As if to ease my loneliness, the final stretch of the journey to Zhongdian was full of glorious scenery. Majestic snowcapped mountains with white cumulus clouds hovering above them were an almost constant backdrop. The bus passed many quaint Tibetan villages of stone-and-plaster houses trimmed with dark hardwood. In one large green field near Shangri-la, a line of eight squat, white bell-shaped structures about the height of a two-story house, each topped with a cylindrical spire, stood before a steep mountain covered in white-flowered bushes. The structures, which reminded me of the white queen from some ornate chess set, were Tibetan *chortens*—stupas that often house ancient holy relics.

As we drew closer to Shangri-la, I began to notice a curious thing. Set up in the backyards of many Tibetan houses were structures that looked like huge wood-plank benches. Some backyards had a long row of several of these huge structures. They looked like benches for a race of mythical giants. Unfortunately, I spoke no Tibetan, so I never learned what they were. But this was a small complaint indeed—the majestic panorama and the mysterious, exotic sights along the way more than made up for the hassle, effort, and loneliness of the journey.

Shangri-la (Zhongdian) was a big town with a frontier feeling. Near the border with Tibet, it sits at an altitude of around ten thousand feet and has so far escaped the rampant ugly high-rise overdevelopment so common in much of China. Though much of the city is "new" town—meaning built within the past generation—the structures retain a regional rustic flavor, and many show a strong Tibetan influence. Tibetan women, wearing heavy woolen dark shawls and long skirts and red, blue, or pink wrapped-scarf turbans, were always about the streets. The old-town section, though a touristy place, was still inhabited mostly by Tibetan and other local ethnic peoples.

The city officially changed its name from Zhongdian to Shangri-la in the early 2000s after some enterprising Chinese officials determined that the famous Shangri-la of the James Hilton novel *Lost Horizon* was in the same spot as the region around Zhongdian. I could see the argument for this. In Hilton's novel, Shangri-la is a lovely, remote, harmonious valley surrounded by a high mountain range and given guidance by a monastery of Tibetan lamas—an apt description of the stunningly beautiful area where I now stood. The city is surrounded on all sides by snowcapped mountains, dense primeval forests, alpine lakes, and lush grassland. An elaborate Tibetan monastery, built by the fifth Dalai Lama, sits in the nearby hills amid a countryside dotted with picturesque Tibetan villages.

My main goal in the Shangri-la area was to trek in the nearby Meiji Snow Mountains at the eastern edge of the Himalayas, on the border with Tibet. This is part of a huge national park complex called the Three Parallel Rivers Park. The park covers a unique geographical accident: The upper reaches of three major rivers of China—the Yangtze, Mekong, and Salween rivers—run side-by-side courses in close proximity for 170 kilometers. Their paths run in deep valleys separated by high mountain ranges, creating zones of significant biological diversity due to the isolating nature of the terrain. Well-known endangered species such as the snow leopard, Bengal Tiger, Yunnan golden monkey, and black-necked crane live in the park, which is now a UNESCO Biosphere. It is one of the most biodiverse places in China that is still relatively unspoiled. In a country that has seen environmental degradation on a massive scale, the Three Parallel Rivers Park represents hope that at least some of China's natural jewels can escape being bulldozed, polluted, or given over to hordes of tourists and tacky souvenir shops.

After several days in Shangri-la, I was ready to leave on my trek. But the day before I left I got a nice surprise: Joanie showed up. She had recommended the guesthouse where I stayed while in Shangri-la, so she knew where to find me. It seemed she had gotten bored in Lijiang and came to join me on my trek. I was delighted to have her company.

The next evening, after trekking all day through pristine alpine forests with gorgeous vistas of rugged, glacier-covered mountain peaks bounded by deep ravines and canyons, Joanie and I arrived at our next destination in the "other China." It was a place of breath-taking grandeur.

As we walked down a steep, rocky trail that emerged from the forest cover near the end of the day's trek, the idyllic mountain hamlets of Upper and Lower Yubeng appeared below us. Upper Yubeng sat in a lush, green bowl-shaped valley. A couple of dozen mostly two-story white stone, plaster, and wood houses with shake roofs stood clustered together in the middle of the bowl. Flat green fields surrounded the village, and a white stupa with a gold spire stood at the far end of one of the fields. Forested mountainsides rose on two sides of the village, and a dramatic white glacier-covered mountain towered over the entire valley. Lower Yubeng, where we would be staying, was similar in appearance and setting. This was how I imagined that a real Shangri-la would look.

As we entered Lower Yubeng after shuffling through the dense grass that had begun to overgrow the main path, we heard an arrhythmic jangling and clanging. This only heightened the dreamlike feel of the place, since neither of us could determine the source of the sounds. I mentioned to Joanie that perhaps villagers were doing some sort of Tibetan Buddhist ritual, which would explain the cacophonous music.

But after walking through an opening in the village gate and along muddy paths between some buildings, we saw the source of the music. A dozen shaggy black-haired yaks, each wearing a small bell, were coming toward us from the opposite direction. And as we walked into the large dirt common ground of the village center, I noticed that the horses and cows wandering about the village grounds also had bells attached to their necks. It seemed so quaint and appropriate for Shangri-la to have animals that made such music.

A few moments later, at a homestay for trekkers who visited the village, we learned about the bells. A young Tibetan girl with full, pink cheeks offered us chairs on the front porch of the wooden house. While she checked us in I asked her about the bells on the animals.

"Our animals like to walk away from the village, into the fields, to graze," the young girl said in passable English. "We put bell on our animals to scare off other animals that want to eat our animals." She then explained that each animal had a bell of a different size, to make a distinct sound. This way, the owner could recognize and find that specific animal. At dusk, which it now was, the animals were brought back to the village, which explained why we heard so much noise.

Looking out from the rustic wooden porch, I saw colorful prayer pennants attached to many of the roofs. There, fluttering in the light breeze, they sent the villagers' block-printed blessings out into the world. Even the mountain stream that gurgled through the center of the village sent out the people's blessings to the world, by turning a water-driven prayer wheel inside a little wooden shelter.

I could happily have stayed a month in Lower Yubeng. I imagined that if it were to experience the dire fate of commercialization, as so many of China's rustic treasures seem destined for, it would become a place where stressed type-A refugees from the country's frenzied, polluted industrial centers could come and decompress.

The next morning, when Joanie and I hiked to the top of the steep, rocky mountain behind the village, we came to a glacier-covered plateau backed by magnificent white peaks and strewn with yet more colorful prayer flags. Beside two ribbons of water that wisped down from a high rocky ledge stood a metal sign that read, "Mountain Is Sacred. Do Not Speak Loudly." It all seemed wonderfully, naively serene.

Each evening, some young local people from the village gathered in the village common area inside the inn where Joanie and I stayed. We would join them there as they drank home-brewed liquor and sang by a fireplace. Someone always played an erhu, a folk-music fiddle common in this part of China. The villagers would do a traditional dance, moving in a circular motion around the center of the room. The whole setting seemed perfect for a wayfaring pilgrim seeking inner peace.

Sadly, though, I noticed something completely incongruous amid this Edenic setting. The beautiful gurgling stream that ran through the village and turned the prayer wheel in its little streamside house was strewn with discarded modern trash. Plastic bottles, caps, and rusting cans were marooned along the stream bank—an ugly intrusion from the modern world into this fairy-tale scene.

It reminded me of what I had seen in Central Borneo a year ago, along the train tracks in Peru, and on the otherwise unspoiled beach in Easter Island. There seemed no way for people in these remote places to dispose of modern trash properly. And, as with the chief in Tumbong Anoi in Central Borneo, the people here in Lower Yubeng probably weren't even conscious of it. Until recent times, they probably had never had to deal with refuse that basically lasted forever. I hated to think that even the mystical Shangri-la was on the verge of taking its place in the Disappearing World, swamped by tons of nonbiodegradable modern garbage.

My exit from the Yubeng villages—and China—had to be quick. On my last night in Yubeng, I had only three days left on my China visa. So, two days later, Joanie and I were back at our guesthouse in Shangri-la, and it was time to say good-bye. I had a bus to catch to a city down south, where I would take an airplane out of China that evening.

Joanie was strangely sad and quiet when I said good-bye, and her uncharacteristic behavior mystified me. A moment later, stopping by the guesthouse front desk on my way out, I learned the reason. I spoke with a friendly young Tibetan woman, a university student who spoke good English and worked as receptionist for the guesthouse.

"Will Joanie be okay?" the young woman asked.

"What do you mean?" I replied, perplexed.

"Oh, you don't know," she said. Then, in a quiet voice, she explained. "Joanie was here earlier, frantically trying to call her family in the east from my front desk phone. Her bank ATM card does not work at any of the local bank machines, and she has no money to get home."

So I went back to the room to ask Joanie about this. She was in a sweatshirt and long wool pants, sitting on the edge of her bed, looking as if she was about to cry.

Yes, this is true," she said. "I am so ashamed. You have been so generous with me on this trip already that I didn't want to tell you I was out of money." (Although she had never asked or expected it, I had covered most of Joanie's expenses on the trip. Even roughing it as we had been doing would be a major expense for her.)

"I spent too much when I went to Lijiang," she said. "Now my bank card won't work in any of the ATMs here, and I can't get any money to go home. I didn't want to ask you."

"That's silly," I said. "We've been travel partners for almost a month now. I wouldn't just leave you stranded here." So, I gave her five hundred yuan (about US$70), which she said was enough for the buses, lodging, and food to get her home comfortably.

Then Joanie burst into tears.

"What's wrong now?" I asked, totally mystified again.

Still crying, Joanie said, "I didn't realize that you cared that much for me."

"That seems strange. Why would you think that way?" I asked.

"Most of the time we traveled together, you were well mannered, polite, and nice to be with," she said, still sobbing but not looking so miserable now. "But you were always *so formal and proper* with me."

This was true. Perhaps because I was married, I had made an extra effort to keep my guard up. After all, Joanie was young, attractive, strong minded, and good natured and had proved to be a spunky, can-do travel partner. She was a city girl, yet she had kept up with me on the treks in the terraced fields and the Meiji Snow Mountains. I respected her spirit.

"Now," she said, drying her eyes with a tissue, "I know that being formal is just how you are. I am so happy to know that you really do care."

From China, I routed myself through the Philippines for a short visit before going back to Bangkok. There I met my brother and his wife and son, who had just arrived from America. They would travel with Achara's family and me for twelve days in Thailand. As always, Achara's family rolled out the red carpet and made sure everyone had a great time.

While the trip with my brother's family went well, things with Achara and me didn't. Between us, everything seemed more distant than ever. We didn't get along at all, arguing about petty things, and ended up sleeping separately the whole time. I saw a troubling pattern develop, whereby things didn't work well between us whenever I came to Thailand. Achara seemed almost a completely different person while in Thailand compared to how she had been in Los Angeles. So I asked her why at one point.

"In L.A., I had only you," Achara replied. "Here in Thailand, I have my whole family. So I don't need you as much. And also, with all my family activities and work now, I don't have the time for you like before."

This explanation certainly didn't help.

Achara's whole family remained unwavering in their welcoming attitude toward me, however. They were inclusive regardless of the strained relationship I was having with Achara. Achara's mother, especially, made it clear that I was to feel at home there. Partly due to the wonderful warmth I felt from Achara's family and maybe also out of pride, I carried on as if everything were fine.

After the tour we gave my brother and his family, Achara had to go on a trip for work. And so, with nothing to do in Bangkok, I set off for Myanmar (Burma), my next destination.

CHAPTER 9

Myanmar (Burma): Dreaming of Guantánamo

Within a system which denies the existence of basic human rights, fear tends to be the order of the day. Fear of imprisonment, fear of torture, fear of death, fear of losing friends, family, property or means of livelihood, fear of poverty, fear of isolation, fear of failure. . . . Yet even under the most crushing state machinery courage rises up again and again, for fear is not the natural state of civilized man.
—Aung San Suu Kyi, Myanmar pro-democracy activist, winner of Nobel Peace Prize, Sakharov Prize for Freedom of Thought

July 2008
Kalaw, Central Myanmar highlands

"How can I get into Mr. Bush's jail?" Jason, a talented, university-educated 29-year-old trail guide asked me. He looked completely serious. I had hired Jason to lead me on a two-day trek to some Palaung villages in the beautiful, cool hills surrounding the small central Myanmar city of Kalaw. We had been hiking in the heavily forested hills for about forty-five minutes.

"Come again?" I asked. "What do you mean when you say "'Mr. Bush's jail'?"

It was early in the day, and the broad leaves of the lush jungle vegetation we passed through were so wet with the morning mist that
my pants were soaked from brushing against them.

"The one in Guatemala," he replied.

"Oh," I said, "you mean Guantánamo Bay Naval Station in Cuba,
where the U.S. locks up captured terrorists?"

"Yes, that is the one," Jason replied. He then went on to say—half
seriously, I believe—that it was his and his wife's dream to get put into
Guantánamo along with their young son.

Astonished, I asked him why, and he explained that living there
would be a much better and easier life than here in his home country,
Myanmar.

"I and my family would be given three meals every day," he said.
"I would have a clean, warm place to live on a nice island." (In the
hills where Jason lives, the clime is quite cool.)

"Since there is nothing to look forward to in Myanmar as long as
the current government is in power," he continued, "my wife and I
have been trying to think up a plan that would get us put into Mr.
Bush's jail. Can you give me suggestions on how to do this?"

I decided to play along with what I assumed was a rhetorical
question about how to get thrown into Guantánamo.

"Well, your best bet is to pretend you are a Muslim fanatic and go
to Afghanistan," I said, trying to sound serious. "There, you could get
caught by American troops. Or perhaps you could just go somewhere
out of Myanmar with your family and make threats against the U.S.
You should do this from an area where you can be tracked down and
captured easily. Otherwise, you might just get shot, and you can't go
to Guantánamo if you're dead."

I had been in Myanmar for a week by now and had run into a
number of young people who had little hope for themselves in
Myanmar. Instead, these young people saw their best prospects as
lying outside their country. As Jason discussed the difficulties of life

in Myanmar, we continued to trek up and down rolling hills through lush, wet highland jungle.

"There is no hope as long as the current military junta is in power," Jason said ruefully. As he gave this dismal prognosis for his country, we were passing through gorgeous patches of wildflowers. A variety of colorful birds flew about, calling in the near distance. The air was scented from so many flowers.

Periodically, we passed through cleared areas planted with small plots of taro, grain, and orange and tea trees. In a field with young green corn plants, a scarecrow made from sticks and dressed in a brown checkered long-sleeved shirt, with a potato wrapped in white cloth for its head, hung by a rope from a long stick stuck in the ground.

Even though we were in deep forest far from town, Jason was reserved and worried about being overheard by someone.

"They can hear us using satellites," he quietly informed me.

I mentioned that this was not possible—not yet, anyway—and that there was no way anybody could be hearing us at this moment.

"But I heard that satellite cameras can see things from the sky as detailed as a license plate on a car and as small as a pen," Jason countered.

"That is true," I replied. "But this is very different from being able to listen to conversations on the ground from outer space."

With some hesitation, Jason began to relax and not worry about satellites being able to eavesdrop on our conversation. During our trek, he elaborated on the many difficulties of life in Myanmar. These included the rampant corruption of the clique of elites associated with the government, the abysmally low wages for most working people, the lack of opportunity unless you knew the "right" person, the lack of general freedoms such as those of speech and press, and the suppression of all opposition political parties. It was an oppressive situation with little hope for any type of fulfilling future, which most people from the richer world could never imagine.

At a little past noon, after trekking for over four hours, we were approaching our trek's first big objective, the Palaung ethnic minority village of Pein Ne Bin. As we walked uphill along a dirt path through the forest, Jason explained that the Palaung practiced a syncretic Buddhism with strong animist beliefs and made periodic sacrifices to various spirits.

As I would see during my trek, the Palaung villages we visited were all fairly isolated from the outside world. I had learned from my research that shamans and sorcerers played an important role in Palaung village life. This was especially so when a perceived evil spirit was making someone ill or creating distress in general. I always found places like these, where traditional beliefs still existed undisturbed by foreign missionaries, to be an enlightening firsthand view of the colorful spirit worlds that the human mind has conjured up since time immemorial.

At the top of the hill, we walked through the entrance to Pein Ne Bin and past a small wooden house on high stilts. Four small kids on the porch looked down at us with big smiles. A boy in a blue sweater gave us a wai greeting (customary in many parts of South and Southeast Asia, in which the palms are pressed together, fingertips up, with a slight bow of the head). We continued into the village, passing houses of mixed wood and brick construction, most with rusting corrugated metal roofs. The village had a casual feel, with tall, untended grasses, bushes, and flowering plants growing in front of some of the homes. A few young women, all with light-brown skin and roundish faces, high cheekbones, and dark hair, walked by, smiling at my local guide and me, the big, white intruder.

At an intersection of narrow dirt paths, a large cast-iron pan, like a deep-fry skillet with no handle, hung from a length of vine tied to a wooden structure shaped like a football goalpost. This was the town bell, Jason explained.

A little past the frying-pan town bell, we came upon a group of mothers with their small children, all sitting on some firewood stacked alongside the path. As we approached, two of the children burst out crying at the sight of my white face and skin—something they had never seen. One of them covered his face with his small hands.

We ended up at a dark wooden longhouse on stilts, where Jason said we would stay while here in Pein Ne Bin. It was a lively place inside. Several families lived in the longhouse, and rambunctious young children were always running about. My hostess was an attractive young woman who wore a long, purple sarong and a darker purple light topcoat with bright pink trim—the traditional dress for Palaung women. Her light honey-colored skin and high cheekbones, accented by a special golden sawdust makeup popular with women in Myanmar, gave her a beauty that was at once exotic and innocent.

Jason and I happened to come to Pein Ne Bin on festival day for a special full moon. During the afternoon, most of the villagers gathered in the large common room in the village Buddhist temple and monastery. Jason had explained that the temple for this village, as for most villages in the area, was the social focal point.

We joined the villagers in the temple. It was a colorful gathering. Nuns with shaved heads, wearing light pink sarongs, sat on floor mats in one section of the room. Next to them sat monks in deep-red flowing robes. Large groups of women dressed much like my longhouse hostess and wearing pastel head scarfs sat on mats here and there, intermixed with groups of village males, many wearing dark, low-profile turbans. As we first walked into the temple I felt like an alien intruding on their intimate festival. But immediately, many in the crowd looked up and smiled, inviting me to sit with them, which made me feel welcome. Almost everyone, it seemed, wanted their picture taken. (Later, through Jason, I sent fifty printed photos to the village.)

As the afternoon went on, a group of very friendly women invited me to sit with them for tea. Several giggled when I joined them, and all wanted photos of themselves taken with the white foreigner. But several of the women appeared worried.

"Won't these pictures of you with all these young women cause problems with your wife?" one woman asked with Jason interpreting.

Smiling, I assured them that my wife trusted me and that it was okay. Her question typified how considerate and friendly the villagers had been with me.

The women also had a special request. There was an elderly woman with them, whose age they estimated to be around eighty years. She was a mother of twelve and had many grandchildren. Several of her older middle-aged daughters were part of the group around her.

"Can you please take a portrait photo of our mother and send us a very large print?" one of the daughters asked. "She feels she may die soon, and wants a nice portrait of herself to leave for her descendants. This way, her grandchildren and great-grandchildren will know where they came from."

Of course I was happy to do so, I told her. Later, I would send back to the village the highest-quality large photo I was capable of producing.

The next morning, Jason and I trekked through the forest and crop fields to more Palaung villages. At one point, he asked me what I did in the United States.

"I oversaw the creation of, and then managed, a software-based service for a major bank," I explained.

"Oh, really!" Jason said in response. "How much do you know about computer and network security? Maybe you can tell me how much danger there is of the government intercepting an e-mail I send."

"I'm sorry," I said. "This is outside my expertise."

"The reason I ask," Jason explained, "is because I have a great desire to send a message to a journalist outside Myanmar. In my e-mail, I want to share with the outside world my views, opinions, and observations of the terrible government we live under."

"Well, perhaps your message could be sent in an encrypted form," I said, "You could use one of the government-blocked e-mail services like Yahoo."

Jason pressed me for my opinion on how to accomplish this. Since it was out of my area of expertise, I said he should consult with one of the talented young IT guys at an Internet café.

"After all," I said, "these guys at Internet cafés have figured out ways to get around the government censors and were accessing blocked sites."

"You really need to be careful on this," I cautioned. "You must make sure you consult someone who really is an expert. Your very life and liberty could be at stake if the government intercepted what they considered a subversive e-mail."

"But what I say here doesn't carry any real stamp of authority," I added. "I don't have the proper technical background in these issues."

As we were having this discussion, we came upon what looked like a shrine to a tree at an apex in the trail. The shrine consisted of a simple little wooden table. On the table sat two shallow teacups and an old ceramic vase holding a bouquet of yellow and peach-colored flowers.

Interrupting our discussion, I asked Jason if the shrine was someone's grave.

No, he said, the shrine was to the spirits of the forest. Many local villagers believed that the various aspects of nature each had their own spirit. There were thirty-seven spirits altogether, he explained. Some included the spirits of the water, fire, ground, banyan tree (a holy tree in Buddhism), and air.

After this brief diversion into the local animistic superstitions, we returned to our discussion of twenty-first-century totalitarianism and Internet censorship as we pressed on to the next village.

The next day, back in Kalaw, Jason invited me to his home for lunch and to meet his wife. He lived in a small house on the outskirts of town. Inside Jason's small, cramped house was a wooden bookcase with a few old pieces of stereo equipment, a shortwave radio, and equipment to receive foreign television stations, which was illegal for him to have.

During our lunch of chicken soup and vegetables, we watched an illicit BBC News broadcast on his small color television. Jason, with his cheerful, pretty wife corroborating their intent, once again brought up their hope to go to Mr. Bush's jail.

Later, while walking back to my hotel after visiting his home, I still wasn't sure whether Jason was joking about his Guantánamo ambitions.

———————

To be one of the vast majority of people born into modern-day Myanmar is to be one of those who got shafted in the birth lottery. These hapless souls were born into a country whose regime rivals such dictatorships as North Korea and Zimbabwe in its repressive, venal, selfish, incompetent, and disastrously ruinous rule.

When I first entered Myanmar a week before my trek with Jason, the country was reeling from a huge disaster. Cyclone Nargis had struck the south of the country two months earlier, in May 2008. The death toll from this horrific cyclone was almost 140,000 people when the government stopped reporting the count. Tens of thousands more were missing, and an enormous number of survivors had their homes and everything they owned wiped out.

In its response to this terrible cyclone, Myanmar's government showed its awful, callous ineptness to the world. The government stalled, put up roadblocks, and often refused outright the outpouring of aid from the outside world to the unfortunate victims. Its behavior seemed hideously irrational to many, as if the regime was perpetrating a kind of genocide against the victims. France even warned at one point that Myanmar's leaders could face potential charges of crimes against humanity for their obstruction of relief efforts. At times, it looked as though the government was holding its own people hostage in a grotesque shakedown of the international community and in fear of being found out to be the powerless wizard behind the curtain.

Myanmar, formerly known as Burma, is a country slightly smaller than Texas.[6] It is in Southeast Asia, northwest of Thailand and south of China, on the Bay of Bengal. This location puts it in the most dynamic, economically growing region in the world. And yet, the overall impression I would have while there was one of stagnation. From my research, Myanmar shares some similarity to North Korea. Like North Korea's regime, Myanmar's ruling military junta has, over many years, disastrously mismanaged and isolated the country from the rest of the world. The predictable result is a country that is among the world's poorest.

I entered Myanmar late one morning on a flight from Bangkok into Yangon. Yangon was the country's capital until a few years earlier and is its largest and most important city. From the airport, I caught a ride into town in a beat-up, rusty taxi. My cabbie, to earn a little more money, gave me a quick driving tour of the city.

The taxi vibrated, bounced, and shuddered over the city's potholed, cracked, and crumbling streets. When I tried to roll down my window at one point the handle came off in my hand. My cabbie, a gaunt-looking older man with long hair and wearing a jean jacket, was embarrassed by this and apologized, saying the roads were so rough on vehicles that it was difficult just trying to keep these old cars from falling apart.

---

[6] I use the terms "Myanmar" and "Yangon" here because, according to people I met, those are the real names of the country and city respectively. Well-meaning outsiders, naturally opposed to the repugnant regime running the country, use the old terms "Burma" and "Rangoon" as a small protest against the regime. But these were artificial names imposed by the British during their long colonial rule. The renaming of the country as "Myanmar," and "Rangoon" as "Yangon," may be the only thing that the military regime ever got right.

"Well, one advantage to riding over these roads is that with all the vibration, you don't have to worry about ever getting kidney stones," I joked.

"It is hard on my back, doing this all day," he said.

I realized how inconsiderate my joke was to this man stuck in the open-air prison that is Myanmar. His lot in life was to endure these terrible roads every day of his existence.

The sprawling city we drove through appeared old and dilapidated, like its roads. My cabbie showed me the city center, which sits on the Yangon River. It was mostly old low- to medium-rise buildings and, here and there, a taller, more modern building of glass and steel. It felt like being in a time warp since most of the cars were quite old and the billboard signs advertised styles that appeared awkward, out of date, and a little strange.

Moving away from the river and the city center, we came to some very nice neighborhoods with elegant, stylish houses behind high fences. Near these nicer areas were a few sections of modern development with some sleek restaurants, spas, and boutiques.

"Government and military and their friends and families are most of the people in these rich areas," the cabbie said with disgust. "They take everything and leave us with crumbs."

Much of the sprawl away from the city center, though, appeared to be much like the center: poor, old, and crumbling. The time-warp aspect and the shabby, dilapidated feel of Yangon, combined with its contrasting pockets of wealth for the few in the privileged classes, reminded me of my time a few years earlier in Cuba, another of the world's open prisons. It was what one should expect to find, I supposed, in a country so poor, repressed, and shut off from the outside world.

My driver brought me to a Chinese family-run budget hotel in an old colonial building. It was on a road so potholed, it looked as if it had undergone a sustained mortar barrage. I checked into the hotel and went out to change money.

Since Myanmar is an economic basket case, changing money, naturally, meant seeking a reputable black-market money changer. My hotel's proprietress, an older Chinese woman with dyed-black hair, helped me do this by bringing me to a black-market money changer who worked out of an office building near downtown. There, in a smoky little room with white linoleum tile flooring and a couple of sturdy metal desks, I changed four hundred U.S. dollars into Myanmar currency. To my surprise, in exchange I got back a small plastic bag of neatly stacked and rubber-banded bundles of thousand-kyat bills.

As I would soon learn, carrying money—a modern necessity for most inhabitants of the planet and usually done with little thought— is a chore in Myanmar. The largest bills in print at the time were thousand-kyat (pronounced "chet") notes. Each thousand-kyat note was worth about eighty-three cents. Since credit cards were of no use in Myanmar, this meant carrying big stacks of money for simple things.

For example, after changing money, I went to buy groceries from a local supermarket (I had a refrigerator in my hotel room, and I like to eat cereal, milk, and fruit for breakfast.) I bought groceries that cost US$35. To pay this modest sum, I had to peel off and count 42 thousand-kyat bills. Being inexperienced at this, I held up the long line at the store's cashier station for a while. With Myanmar's rapid inflation rate, the wad of paper currency that one must carry will only get bigger.

That evening, I went out to experience the nightlife of Yangon. I left my hotel room, my pockets bulging with money. Just to have the equivalent of a hundred dollars, I had to carry stacks of bills forty thick in three of my four pockets.

For most of Myanmar's citizens, the inconvenience of carrying around a large wad of cash is not an issue, though, because most people in Myanmar don't make much money. The per capita income is quite low, with World Bank estimates of under $935 for 2007, and UNData putting it as low as $281 for 2006. This should never have happened. The tragic misrule of Myanmar under the military was so totally inept that it turned this country of industrious people from one of Asia's wealthiest, during its time under British colonial rule, into the poorest country in Asia.

The next morning, a Saturday, I visited an Internet café downtown. With its rows of computers and mostly high school and university students surfing the Web, the place seemed almost like a sanctuary of modern normality. That illusion of normality dissipated, though, when I typed the address for my Yahoo e-mail account into the computer I was assigned. Rather than Yahoo Mail appearing on my screen, I received the following message in bold letters: "REQUESTED URL ADDRESS BLOCKED, ACCESS DENIED."

It was my first experience of the government oppression that the people of this country endured daily. I had seen this sort of thing in other repressive countries before, though, including the Internet cafés in Syria I had visited a few years earlier. So I called over one of the café's young and friendly attendants to take care of it. The attendant, a slim, intelligent-looking guy dressed in a white knit shirt, came over.

"Government, you know," he said in a low voice, as if the government were just a nasty inconvenience to work around.

The young man then proceeded to open one of the two programs the café used to evade government blocks. He typed a few numbers into the appropriate field of a pop-up screen that appeared. I was then able get into my e-mail account and access other blocked sites.

"Where do you get these programs to go around the government blocks?" I asked the young man helping me.

"China," he answered.

"Of course," I replied. "Chinese Internet operators have good experience dealing with government censorship." Sure enough, with typical Chinese industriousness, its clever Internet geeks had not only come up with programs to go around the official nuisance but were exporting their much sought-after product to those under even worse government oppression.

That evening, I went to the famous Shwedagon Golden Pagoda, the iconic site of the city. It was just starting to get dark, and being Saturday night, the grounds of the pagoda complex were still busy with hundreds of people there to pray or just hang around. The pagoda, a gigantic gilded structure topped by a smooth golden stupa rising 330 feet, glittered brilliantly under the spotlights in the night sky. Countless smaller golden stupas, as well as many shrines and temples containing numerous statues and images of the Buddha, surrounded the giant structure. It was an impressive, majestic site.

As I made my way around the crowds, I met and hired a guide to take me around and tell me about the pagoda complex. Kim was an amiable guy with a sensitive, serious demeanor. I liked him right away.

Walking with me through the complex, Kim explained that the central golden pagoda dated back to the eighteenth century, although, according to legend, the original pagoda on the site dates back over two thousand years. He also told me how the Shwedagon Golden Pagoda was an extremely holy site for Myanmar's heavily Buddhist population. "It is considered a duty of each Buddhist person in Myanmar to make at least one pilgrimage to the Shwedagon Pagoda during their life," he said. "This obligation for Myanmar's Buddhist people is similar to a Muslim person's obligation to make the hajj to Mecca."

Since it was late in the day, I was Kim's last customer. As he started to relax with the finish of his day we got to talking.

"What have you done so far on your visit to Yangon, and where did you fly from?" he asked.

I told him I had flown in yesterday, Friday morning, from Bangkok. I had just gotten into Yangon and so had little to tell. I did mention, though, that I had gone out last evening to a couple of the city's popular nightspots. I explained that I had met some younger guys in Yangon's Chinatown, who had invited me to join them as they went out.

"Ah Bangkok," Kim mused. "I hear there are a lot of very pretty prostitutes available there. Is this true?"

"Yes," I told him, "but, it is not so different from what I saw last night here in Yangon."

This last piece of information took Kim completely by surprise. "What do you mean? We have prostitutes here in Yangon?" he asked, sounding as though he didn't believe me.

"Of course," I answered. "They're all over."

I went on to explain that when I went into a well-known Irish bar in one of the nicer hotels of the city, I was greeted by a bevy of young and friendly Filipinas and local Myanmar women. The young women did entertainment in the bar and, for a fee, "personal entertainment" outside the bar. Later, in the nightclubs I visited with the younger locals I had met, there were dozens of "working" girls on offer.

Kim was still incredulous. "I find this hard to believe," he said, sounding as excited as if he had just won the lottery. "We have young and pretty prostitutes available here, in Yangon?"

Kim eagerly pressed me for more details. I was surprised by his reaction.

"Why are you so interested in prostitutes?" I asked. "And how come you don't know about these obvious things in your own city? Are you Muslim? Perhaps you can't go out to drinking establishments."

"Oh, no," he said. "I am Buddhist and I like women. I don't have any hang-ups about them, religious or otherwise. But I am thirty-one years old and I haven't been with a woman for eight years," he explained.

To me, Kim appeared healthy, normal, and pleasant looking, so I asked, "Why have you deprived yourself of women for so long?"

"I am terrified of AIDS," Kim answered. (The disease was spreading rapidly in Myanmar, according to articles I had read on the Internet.)

"I am so afraid of AIDS that I have not been with anyone since my last serious girlfriend, almost a decade ago."

Sounding more than ready to end his long dry spell, he pressed me for further details.

"What were the names of the clubs you went to?" Kim asked. "How did you know what the girls were doing? How could I find a prostitute, and how much do they cost?" he continued, not even trying to mask his eagerness.

Then Kim paused and looked at me with a strange curiosity and asked, "And how is it that you, a foreign visitor with only one day in my city, managed to know all about these places? I live here and don't know anything about them!"

I explained that I was an experienced traveler. When in places that were new to me and where foreigners tended to stand out, I often asked around about the most popular nightspots or bars. My experience had been that as a foreigner, it was usually pretty easy to meet and get information from people in the popular drinking spots.

Feeling a bit sorry for Kim, I took him out to dinner after my visit to the pagoda. He directed me to a nice open-air restaurant along the Yangon River—a fairly busy place that had several rows of rectangular tables covered with white tablecloths. We sat at a table next to the river. The restaurant had very bright lighting, making the emptiness over the river next to us very dark, so that it was like sitting at the edge of a great, black void.

During dinner, we continued our discussion about his situation and lack of female companionship.

"I never have the time or money to go out," Kim said. "I make only around two hundred U.S. dollars in the good months of the year for tourism but barely get by on around fifty during the slow periods. I don't really have anywhere to take a girlfriend, either," he added. "I live in a ten-by-sixteen-foot shared dormitory room in a hostel near the pagoda."

Kim told me he was a university graduate. But there were two tiers of higher education available to young people, he explained. There was "regular university," where a student attended campus classes full-time for three years to complete a degree, and "distance university," similar to correspondence schooling in the West. In distance university, the student did one year full-time on campus and the remaining two years mostly off campus.

"I attended a distance university, like most people here, because it was the most affordable option," Kim said. "Unfortunately, a degree from distance university does not carry much weight outside Myanmar."

Kim then elaborated on his plans and hopes for a better future. For many young people, the best opportunity to get ahead in life was as a migrant worker, he said. The best destinations were Dubai, Malaysia, and Singapore. For example, he could go to Dubai as a laborer and save, after covering living expenses, as much as US$200 a month. He could send this home to his family or put it away for a house and the future. (Other people I met later told me that with better-paying jobs in Dubai, one could save as much as US$400 a month.)

"For those with professional or technical backgrounds, such as in computers or other areas in IT," Kim continued, "Singapore is the best destination. In Singapore, a person could earn over a hundred thousand U.S. dollars a year, which is a fortune for the average Myanmar person."

"I see, I said. "Why, then, don't you go to one of these countries to work?"

"Well, to get to Dubai," he said, "a person needs an agent, who arranges the job, visa, and other formalities. This costs around six hundred to seven hundred dollars, which is a lot for someone like me making less than two hundred a month on average."

For jobs in Singapore, though, the fee was much higher—over US$3,000 for the agent.

"How long do these jobs last, and what is the arrangement?" I asked.

"In Dubai, the usual deal is for two or three years," he replied. "The person must work twenty-six days a month, nine hours a day."

After our dinner, Kim scouted around for a pay telephone from which to call his hostel. He wanted to let them know he would be getting home late this evening. He explained that the hostel wanted its tenants to be in by ten at night or else call and let them know when he would be home.

As Kim looked for a pay phone, I realized that I had not seen many cell phones in use in my short time so far in Yangon. I asked him about it.

"All cell phones are imported, and this trade is controlled by government interests," Kim explained. "The government then adds a tremendous markup to the actual cost. So cell phones here in Myanmar, on average, sell for around two thousand U.S. dollars. This is too much money for almost any citizen of Myanmar."

"Sometimes, to get a cell phone, family members will pool their funds together to buy one," he added. (Later, a pearl merchant I met in Yangon's huge Aung San Market told me the same thing.)

During my travels in Myanmar, I met several people who told me similar stories of their own barely sustainable incomes. Many in the country scrape by on between fifty and two hundred dollars a month. Jason, the Guantánamo-aspiring guide I hired in Kalaw, told me, for example, that he managed to sustain himself and his wife and child on about fifty dollars a month. I would also meet or hear about several young people working toward the goal of leaving Myanmar for opportunities such as those Kim described in Dubai, Malaysia, and Singapore.

Because of low overall wages and lack of opportunity in general, I often encountered highly educated people from professional backgrounds who ended up doing relatively menial work. These underemployed professionals drove taxis, waited tables, did janitorial work, ran small roadside food stands, or acted as guides to Myanmar's many tourist attractions. This type of situation again reminded me of Cuba, where highly educated professional talent was similarly squandered.

After five days in Yangon, I flew to Kalaw, the small hill town in Central Myanmar where I would meet Jason and trek in the nearby ethnic Palaung villages. Riding up into the hills in another beat-up taxi, I felt relief from Yangon's stifling tropical heat and humidity.

On the early afternoon when I arrived, the streets of Kalaw were bustling with life. Its few short main streets of dirt and crumbling pavement were lined with old wooden buildings and houses with tin or red tile roofs. As my taxi came to the town center, several horse-drawn covered buggies sat about waiting for customers. A few canvas-covered old work trucks rumbled about, spewing thick clouds of black smoke. We passed the town's main Buddhist temple, which consisted of a small golden pagoda topped by a stupa, with several little golden stupas surrounding it, in a dirt yard. Next to the temple, I was dropped off at a small guesthouse in a two-story wooden building.

On my first night at the guesthouse, I met Olivia, an Australian woman who was using the computer at the Internet café in the lobby. We struck up a conversation, and she told me that she was doing a seven-week cycling trip around Myanmar. (Curiously, Olivia was given a much longer time to stay on her visa than the two weeks that I got.) I enjoyed talking to this adventurous woman and invited her to join me at a local restaurant that evening. While at dinner, Olivia told me a strange story.

"They have been following me for the past couple of weeks," she said in a low voice. Olivia and I were sitting on the dimly lit wooden porch of a small rustic restaurant off a dirt side road. Our little table was covered by a white lace cloth, and we were sipping gin and tonics while waiting for our dinner.

"They have been watching me almost the entire time I have been in Myanmar," she continued. "I'll be in one village in the morning and see two men. Then, later that day in another town, I again see the same two men. The next day, I will see the same two men yet again, in another town. When I confront them, which I have done a couple of times, they don't even deny that they're following me!"

Thirty-three years old and married, Olivia was direct and matter-of-fact. She struck me as a no-nonsense woman with a resilient inner strength. She explained that she was traveling alone on this journey because her husband was too involved in the construction of their new house back in Australia to get away.

Three weeks before we met, Olivia had started her bike trip in Myanmar by riding out of Yangon toward the Southern Delta. She was trying to go to the area that had been hit by the recent, devastating Cyclone Nargis.

"I wanted to volunteer to help with the reconstruction during part of my time here in Myanmar," she explained. "But shortly after leaving Yangon, I was turned away at a roadblock. Foreign tourists and other unauthorized visitors were not allowed anywhere in the cyclone-hit areas. So, I cycled to a nearby town, where foreigners were generally not allowed to stay, either, because there were no hotels with government approval to host foreigners. Once I got into that town, the police chief drove up and stopped me. He ordered me to leave and return to Yangon or go to another town some distance away."

"After pedaling most of that day, I was too tired to go to another town, though. So instead, I pedaled to the edge of town while a police car followed at a distance. Then I dashed around a corner onto a side road, out of sight of the police car. I pedaled fast down the side road a ways, then into a barn near the roadside.

"I lay down inside the barn and peered through a window," Olivia continued matter-of-factly. "I watched the police car pass by, unable to find me. I then took a nap for several hours in the barn."

From that point forward, Olivia explained, she was a marked woman. Various agents would follow her, often quite conspicuously.

"I even threatened to report them and lodge a formal complaint," she said, "but they didn't seem to care."

At this, I asked her, "Who did you think you were going to complain to: their bosses who had sent them to follow you in the first place?"

Laughing, Olivia agreed that there was really no one to complain to. Then she continued with her story.

"More than once, the agents even went into a hotel where I was staying, and asked the reception people about me. They would ask questions: Did they know where I was from? What kind of activities had they seen me doing? And did they know where I was heading next?"

It was a strange blend of comical and sinister.

Two days after I met Olivia, she left Kalaw in the early morning, pedaling toward Inle Lake. This was about fifty miles away and just happened to be the next stop on my itinerary a few days later. That same morning, after she left, I went to the café at the hotel where she had stayed, to grab breakfast. I happened to sit next to a middle-aged Myanmar woman who was vacationing in Kalaw and staying at the same hotel as the Australian woman. She recognized me as a friend of Olivia's and told me about some excitement at the hotel earlier in the morning.

Apparently, Olivia's early departure had really spooked the agents who were following her in Kalaw. According to the vacationing Myanmar woman, the agents came into the hotel not long after Olivia had left for Inle Lake.

"They became very agitated and upset about this," the woman explained, laughing. "One of the agents sternly questioned the hotel receptionist, 'Why did the Australian woman leave so early, and where is she going?'" (She had left town about seven thirty a.m.—not really all that early for a cyclist.)

"The receptionist didn't know where Olivia was going," the Myanmar woman continued. "So the agents got on the telephone and began to call the police chiefs of each of the surrounding villages outside Kalaw. They gave a description of Olivia to each chief, along with orders to report any appearance by her.

"The agents became even more agitated when they got a call from their office informing them that Olivia had left some luggage behind with a hotel in a town she had passed through a week ago," the woman added. "To the agents, this behavior seemed incomprehensible!" (I assumed that the agents did not realize that it is common for bicycle tourists and other travelers to lighten their load as they travel in an area, and return later to retrieve their things.)

"I couldn't believe how angry the agents became," the vacationing woman continued, laughing gleefully. "They really vented their frustrations. They used the hotel phone here and called the manager in the hotel in the town where Olivia left her things. They *demanded* that the poor manager on the other line explain why the woman (Olivia) would do such a thing."

Hearing this story, I almost felt sorry for the agents. I figured it was going to be embarrassing for them to explain to their commander what had happened, making them look comically inept for letting her get away.

A few days later, after my trek with Jason in the Palaung villages near Kalaw, I took a bus east through the forested hills to Inle Lake. I wanted to see the various ethnic groups such as the Intha, Shan, Pa-O, Taungyo, Bamar, Danu, and others living along the shores and in the lake itself, on reclaimed land or in houses on stilts.

Though the distance wasn't great, the bus ride took several hours. Road conditions, as expected, were poor. Also, the roads were almost barricaded by a seemingly endless convoy of big flatbed trucks carrying huge, freshly cut old-growth logs. I had read that Myanmar has one of the fastest rates of deforestation in the world. Now I was seeing it happen.

I stayed in the tiny tourist town of Nyaung Shwe, near Inle Lake. It is a touristy town but still charming and friendly, with one main road of shops, eateries, and cheap guesthouses catering to budget tourists who come to see the lake.

On my first evening there, sure enough, I ran into Olivia again and told her about the stink that the agents following her had raised over her "early" departure from Kalaw. She was shocked.

"I cannot believe what I am hearing," she said, flabbergasted at the silliness of it all. "It is so surreal! Why were they following me? For God's sake, what did they think I could possibly be doing?"

After she got over her initial shock, though, we both got a good laugh out of it.

"I have to say," I told her, "I'm a little jealous that you're getting followed and I'm not." She would have a great story to tell at the next party she went to back in Australia.

Inle Lake is joined to two other lakes by a long canal that runs in a line between them and serves as a highway for the local communities. The lakes sit at an elevation of about three thousand feet, so temperatures are pleasant. The day after I arrived, I hired a private boat for the day. Olivia joined me, and we took a jaunt through Inle Lake onto adjoining Sankar Lake.

It was early morning, cool and overcast, as our motorized canoe puttered into the broad, shallow waters of northern Inle Lake. Wooden stilt houses, dwarfed by the forested mountains behind them, rose up through the tall grasses of the lakeside wetlands. A lone fisherman in a conical rattan hat, holding a fine white net in both hands, stood on one leg at the stern of his dugout boat, his other leg wrapped around an oar with which he sculled silently through the bright-green floating mat.

When I expressed admiration for such an adroit balancing act, our boatman explained in halting English, "This is way of Intha fisherman. He cannot see the plants if he sit down, so he stand and paddle with leg and keep hands free for fishing."

We continued through the main lake to the southern end, where we passed through a village of simple woven-bamboo houses standing on high stilts over the shallow lake waters. Small rectangular patches of leafy plants and grasses fronted each house, like little floating yards. A woman in an orange-patterned sarong crouched on a boardwalk under her house, brushing her teeth in the lake waters. Other villagers were getting into their canoes or doing various chores on the board supports under their homes.

After passing through the village on stilts, we came to a floating market. The waterway entrance to the market's dry grounds was jammed with the long wooden canoes of shoppers and people with produce and other goods to sell.

We parked our canoe and walked toward the market. It had a festive air as crowds of shoppers and vendors bustled about rows of cinder-block stalls covered by rusted tin roofs. In the clear areas by the water's edge, water buffaloes lumbered by, pulling wagons or carts piled with goods for various shops. A young man in a blue shirt waved to me and pointed to his table laden with dozens of metal and carved-wood Buddhas. I smiled back but shook my head.

Olivia, our boatman, and I walked down a busy aisle between rows of stalls. Women wearing bright reddish-orange scarf turbans squatted or sat on the ground beside plastic sheets holding small piles of potatoes, green vegetables, and other produce. Our boatman explained that the women in the orange scarfs were Pa'O people and that their headpieces symbolized the crest of a dragon. According to Pa'O legend, mothers were descended from the dragon.

The market was a kaleidoscope of colorful ethnic dress. A tall, olive-skinned young man came up and began bargaining in earnest with one of the Pa'O. He wore a baggy bright blue woolen skirt and a white cotton long-sleeve shirt, with a magenta sash slung over one shoulder and across his body. Farther down the aisle, women in wide conical hats, pastel shirts, and purple sarongs stood over the various mats, inspecting the produce. A man in a white shirt and purple-patterned sarong passed by carrying a basket full of small yellow fruit he had bought. Two women, each with a green scarf tied into a small turban and wearing a thick, baggy dark-gray woolen jacket and skirt, hovered over a pile of potatoes.

Incongruously among this gathering of traditionally dressed ethnic groups, heavy-metal music blared out from big speakers at several points on the market grounds—a sign of the outside world's influence relentlessly pressing in.

From the market, we proceeded down a canal, past a field of giant yellow sunflowers, to Sankar Lake, where Olivia and I strolled through a couple of dusty villages. As I had seen almost everywhere during my short time in Myanmar, several old stupa ruins stood here and there amid the lightly wooded landscape.

In the center of one village, we came to the town "cinema." This was a rectangular bamboo-thatched building with a television screen and a DVD player. Inside, villagers watched various movies and other productions for an entrance fee of about a nickel.

We happened to pass by the village cinema fifteen minutes before the next show was to start. Some kids in bare feet or sandals were milling around. Our boatman pointed to some little holes in one of the building's walls.

"This is for the kids who do not have any money to go in and see the shows," our boatman said.

I felt sorry for the kids having to stand in the hot sun, peering through little holes and cracks in the wall to see the show. So I asked our guide to tell the children in front of us to put out the word for all the kids in the village to come to the cinema and that I would pay the entrance fee for all comers. Within ten minutes, some twenty children were lining up at the admission table and getting their tickets. They were giddy with excitement at actually getting to go inside the "cinema."

After our lake tour, I spent a few days in Nyaung Shwe near the lake. During that time, the power was cut twice to the section of the town where I stayed. A friendly receptionist at the guesthouse explained about the power.

Beginning at dusk on alternate nights and running till five the next morning, the power was diverted from various sections or quadrants of cities and towns in Central Myanmar, she explained. This was done to supply electricity to Napyitaw, the government's new capital. From what I read, the new capital was a lavish place, tucked away in a remote location that was off limits to most visitors.

I had seen the same diversion of electricity while in I was in Kalaw—yet another bit of selfishness from a grotesquely selfish government.

CHAPTER 10

Uganda and Zambia:
Gorillas, Pickpockets,
and Suffering in Silence

When the missionaries came to Africa they had the Bible
and we had the land. They said, "Let us pray." We closed our eyes.
When we opened them we had the Bible and they had the land.
—Bishop Desmond Tutu, South African antiapartheid activist
and winner of Nobel Peace Prize

August 1, 2008
Johannesburg

"Miss, can you please pass me a customs form?" I asked the flight attendant. My flight aboard the South African Airways Boeing 747 had just landed at Tambo International Airport in Johannesburg. It had been a long eleven-hour overnight flight from Bangkok, and most of the restless passengers on the plane were piling into the aisle and gathering their things, eager to go. But I noticed that I had never received a customs declaration form during the flight. This was strange because passengers on international flights are usually given a form so they can declare items subject to possible tariffs.

"There is no customs form," said the young man in a tan suit standing behind me. "I am from South Africa and was in Asia on business. South Africa stopped doing customs procedures a few years ago due to the crime wave."

"Really," I said. "What kind of crime?"

The young man explained that corrupt customs officers or staff would note passengers who had declared a large amount of cash or other items of value. The corrupt official would then transmit a description of the target passenger to criminal accomplices waiting outside the arrivals exit area. These criminals would follow the unsuspecting victims to their hotel room, where they would rob them of whatever valuables they had declared on their customs form.

"In some cases, the unfortunate victims were also murdered," he said. "So the South African authorities just stopped customs procedures altogether."

This was only the first of several spectacular, high-profile crime waves that I would learn about in my short stay in Johannesburg.

South Africa was my entry point to Africa for my next set of journeys, which would take me to Uganda, Zambia, and Madagascar. After leaving Myanmar in the middle of July, I had spent two uneventful weeks in Thailand. Achara was busy or gone most of my time there, so I busied myself preparing and studying for this trip to Africa. I had gotten lucky and procured a permit to see the mountain gorillas at the famous Bwindi Impenetrable National Park in Uganda, so that would be my first stop after a short stay in South Africa.

I was greeted at the Johannesburg airport by Lood, a tall, lean Afrikaner with an angular face and longish dark hair. He was the son of the owner of the guesthouse where I would stay while in Johannesburg. As we drove toward their place in the city, our conversation turned to local crime. I got the feeling that in Johannesburg, crime was a more common topic than the weather.

"The current crime fad," Lood explained, "involves gangs using powerful explosives to blast open ATMs in bank branches around the city. This type of crime is usually done after midnight. They will place explosive against the outside wall of the bank, under the ATM. Then, after they blow it up, they simply pick up the money that is scattered on the sidewalk and street, and make their getaway before the police arrive."

"Wow! Is this a common occurrence?" I asked.

"Yes. So far this year (it was August 1) there have been hundreds of banks with their ATMs blown up. One reason for the problem is that many young ex-soldiers from neighboring Mozambique are now here in South Africa. These young men fought in that country's long civil war and don't know how to do anything but blow things up. So they get hold of the large amounts of military-grade dynamite available on the black market and blow up ATMs."

Lood brought me to his father's guesthouse, a single-story ranch house in a suburb near the chic shopping and café area called Melville Arch. The prosperous middle-class suburban neighborhood streets were lined with houses and lawns set behind locked metal gates and walls topped with barbed wire. Security signs, many warning of "armed response," were prominently displayed. The neighborhood had the feel of a place under permanent siege.

After entering the guesthouse through its heavy metal security door, I got a hospitable welcome from Lood's father, Pieter, a lean older man with graying hair. He invited me to breakfast at a rectangular wooden dining room table by the family room, and poured me some corn flakes and milk. As I started to eat, I glanced at the local news broadcast on the television in the adjoining living room. It was showing a murder crime scene. Yellow police ribbons marked the scene of violence.

During my breakfast, I mentioned to Pieter my conversation with Lood. Pieter then told me of a recent crime fad that sounded to me like something only Hollywood could dream up.

"Criminal gangs get insider tips on the routes of armored cars," Pieter said. "Using the tips and armed with automatic weapons, they ram the targeted armored car along its route with a heavy car—often hijacked. This causes the armored car to roll over. When the dazed occupants of the armored vehicle emerge, the heavily armed gang loots the vehicle of its valuables. If the armored car's occupants refuse to emerge from the rammed vehicle, then the criminals could threaten to pour gasoline over the vehicle and set it afire. There were a lot of these happening a few years ago in Johannesburg," he continued. "Once in a while, we hear of a new one."

I was both awed and horrified by these criminals' audacity.

That first day in Johannesburg, I took a taxi to a shopping area. After I settled into the front seat, the driver, a man of mixed Indian and African descent, asked me where I was from.

"California," I replied.

"Obama-a-a," he replied with a smile, stretching the pronunciation of the then-U.S. presidential candidate's last name as if savoring the pleasure of saying it.

A few moments later, the taxi came to a stoplight at a big intersection near the guesthouse where I was staying. A huge billboard there depicted three internationally famous leaders of African heritage: Nelson Mandela, Jomo Kenyatta (independent Kenya's first president), and Barack Obama. I was quite surprised to see that Obama was already being viewed with the same level of esteem as Nelson Mandela. Though I had previously learned from the news about the phenomenal adulation for Obama that had swept the world, the taxi ride that day in Johannesburg was the first time I personally experienced "Obamania."

This popularity bordering on hero worship would show up in many ways as I continued my African travels. Taxi drivers almost everywhere, it seemed, after confirming that I was from the United States, would simply say "Obama-a-a" in a knowing tone, as if repeating something that everyone universally knew and agreed on. It would be the same when I walked past people on side streets in dusty villages. They would say "USA," assuming by my appearance that this was where I was from, or they would ask. Either way, once they confirmed that I was from the States I would get the familiar, knowing one-word response of "Obama-a-a." Although I found the whole Obamania fad amazing, I would also be saddened to know that it must ultimately end in disappointment. No one man could possibly live up to all the hope, hype, and promise that Obama seemed to be representing at the time.

After a few days in Johannesburg, I left the city under siege behind and flew to Uganda. The date on my mountain gorilla viewing permit was approaching.

Just outside Kampala, Uganda

"You just have to smile and suffer in silence," said Precious, a young engineering student. Precious was a passenger sitting next to me at the front of a terribly overloaded bus. The beat-up old rattletrap was bouncing and hurtling along the dusty stretch of ground that passes for a main highway in Uganda, heading from the capital, Kampala, to Bwindi, in the southwest corner of the country. The famous Bwindi Impenetrable National Park, a UNESCO World Heritage Site, is home to half the world's remaining mountain gorillas.

The reason to suffer in silence was the ratio of five bodies for every three seats. People were standing in the aisle or, more accurately, on top of their luggage, which was piled in the aisle. Yet more people were hanging over the driver and smashed into the exit stairwells. I was sitting beside Precious, in what was supposed to be the most coveted seat on the bus: the frontmost seat, with plenty of legroom. But my coveted seat ended up being surrounded by a crush of bodies, all crammed together behind the driver and around the engine well.

Added to the intolerable crowding was the oppressive smell. Smoke and steam, from leaking water and burning engine oil, came out of the engine well and combined with the noxious odors of unwashed bodies and God knows what else, to form a rancid bouquet that pervaded everything. As I found to be the norm with Ugandan public transportation, the bus broke down and needed fixing en route. So everyone had to stand outside in the steamy tropic heat while the driver did his best to nurse the old rattletrap back to life.

"You would think people would eventually rebel against a service that treats its customers in such a lousy way," I said in frustration to Precious, knowing even as I said it that this was a ridiculously naive comment.

She dismissed such thinking. "The general population of my country doesn't know any better," she said. "Everyone just accepts such terrible service as what's expected."

She was probably right. For so many of the world's poor—those who had drawn the short straw in the birth lottery—this crummy transportation system was all they knew. Nevertheless, as these situations always do, it struck me how dehumanizing and degrading poverty is to a person's dignity.

Getting onto the bus in Kampala hours earlier, at daybreak, had provided a sobering show. The big, muddy bus yard was bedlam. Passengers streamed onto the yard, scurrying about, looking for the bus going to their destination. Many dragged ancient-looking suitcases, some held together by duct tape or wire, or cardboard boxes kept together by masking tape. White, smoky exhaust was everywhere from the jam of rickety, wheezing cars and small trucks trying to get on or off the yard. "Brokers," typically dirty, scrawny men in tattered old shirts who hang around the bus yard, glommed on to passengers looking for buses, prodding and sometimes lightly shoving them toward a bus of the broker's choice, in hopes of a commission for "referring" the hapless passenger to the correct bus for their destination.

Already familiar with this game, I strode directly toward the first bus with a driver standing outside it. Walking up to the driver, I asked him which bus made the eight-to-twelve-hour trek to Bwindi. The driver pointed to the correct bus, a little way into the lot. I then shrugged off the pesky brokers and slogged through the mud. Along the way, I weaved around the noisy, dirty masses till I got to my bus. Once aboard, I watched the drama below for about an hour before departing.

In several instances, fights broke out between brokers arguing over some poor customer who didn't want anything to do with either of them. Usually, the fight consisted of a few shoves between the brokers. A couple of times, a punch or two was thrown. The contestants were sorry, filthy, and desperate, struggling to get a few coins for their unneeded and unwanted efforts.

As I waited for the bus to fill up and get going, I thought, with a brief twinge of envy, of the *other* way that people can travel in Uganda, as in much of Africa. This *other* way completely removes the visitor from day-to-day dealings with the common people.

That is what happens, for example, when you spend ten thousand dollars for a two-week safari. You are greeted at the airport by a nice-looking, well-dressed young man who then leads you through the heaving, sweating, great unwashed crowd waiting outside customs, to a late-model four-by-four. Getting in, you cruise past the slums and over the bumpy, cratered roads to your oasis of the rich world, such as a Sheraton, Hyatt, or Serena Hotel.

Safely ensconced in your four- or five-star lodgings, sealed off from the reality outside, you dine on sumptuous fare accompanied by fine imported wines and cognac. The next day, upon leaving the gleaming oasis of rich-world comfort set among the chaos and poverty, you breeze along again in air-conditioned comfort through the countryside, to your game park, where a "rustic" luxury hotel—another sanctuary of the faraway modern world—awaits you. You then go home and tell all your friends about wonderful and exotic Africa as you put them to sleep with endless pictures of lions, buffaloes, zebras, rhinos, and elephants.

I was rudely awakened from my reverie about the *other* way to travel Africa when the greasy-smelling bus, stuffed to the gills with passengers, lurched into motion.

I accepted that as an independent long-term traveler going it alone in Africa, I often found it best to endure public transport. Other forms, such as hiring out a private SUV and driver, can be very expensive in much of Africa. One of the ironies of this situation is the fact that in much of Africa, encompassing some of the poorest places in the world, prices for gasoline are among the highest in the world. For example, in areas of Africa I traveled in the summer and fall of 2008, gasoline prices ranged from six dollars a gallon in some areas, to a whopping ten dollars a gallon in Zambia. Meanwhile, in my homeland of the United States, people scream larceny when gas goes over four dollars a gallon.

Of course, the main benefit of putting up with the hassle of public transport and suffering in silence is that one meets local people and learns ever so much more about the society and situation on the ground than would ever be possible in the sterile comfort of the other way.

This was my first trip in Uganda. It is a wrenchingly poor country with an estimated per capita annual income, at the time, of just over US$1000, and about thirty-five percent of its population living in extreme poverty (CIA estimates). Life expectancy at birth, according to the Uganda National NGO Forum, is a mere forty-two years. (The CIA-estimated life expectancy is around fifty-two years, however.) This low life expectancy is partly due to high mortality from malaria, AIDS, crime and civil strife, limited access to potable water, and low immunization coverage.

During my research before the trip, I also read that Uganda was seen as something of a hopeful model for sub-Saharan Africa. Economic growth over the past decade had been good at from five to seven percent while maintaining single-digit inflation, and the country had been recognized as making good progress in the Millennium Development Goals of Primary Education Enrollment, with more than ninety percent of school-age children attending classes.

It was hard for me to buy this optimistic note about Uganda, though. Daunting factors that had held the country back were still in full play. Pervasive corruption was one of these, with Uganda at the time ranking 143 out of 180 countries according to Transparency International (with the country rated at 180 being the most corrupt). And the man who had led the government that presided over this corruption for the past twenty-two years, Yoweri Museveni, though loudly criticized for not allowing truly fair and honest elections, was still in power. The country also suffered from a long-running insurgency in its north, by the Lord's Resistance Army—a conflict that has spilled over into neighboring, chronically unstable Democratic Republic of the Congo (DRC). None of this pointed to a country on the rise.

My destination, Bwindi, was a picturesque, richly biodiverse mountain forest area near Uganda's border with Rwanda and DRC. The nearby Bwindi Impenetrable National Park, with its 340 mountain gorillas, is one of Africa's tourist industry crown jewels.

I stayed in a tiny community lodge in the village of Buhoma, at the edge of the park. Buhoma is a small, dusty, friendly place with one main road and a few small restaurants, guesthouses, and lodges to serve visitors to the park. The six-thousand-foot elevation makes it refreshingly cool. I didn't do much on my first night in Bwindi. I was pretty excited, though—the big day for my mountain gorilla viewing in the national park would start early in the morning.

It was cool, overcast, and misty the next morning after breakfast when I walked over to the visitor area near the park entrance, where the twenty-four eager tourists who held gorilla permits for the day were gathering. Park rangers in olive uniforms and caps divided us into three teams of eight and briefed us about the mountain gorillas and the rules for viewing them.

A tall, husky ranger said that three gorilla groups in Bwindi were habituated to people. Getting gorillas habituated to people was vitally important because, otherwise, it would be nearly impossible for most visitors to get close enough to observe them in any meaningful way. A gorilla group is like a family, he explained. The family head is the alpha male, who has a number of females that are his mates, and the offspring that result. The gorilla groups can range in size. The smallest habituated group in Bwindi during my visit was eight gorillas, and the largest had seventeen.

The ranger explained that the mountain gorillas were highly endangered, with only about seven hundred remaining in the world. Half were found in Bwindi, the other half in adjoining national parks over the borders with Rwanda and DRC. The biggest threat to the remaining mountain gorillas is habitat loss and destruction caused by man. It was sobering to learn that mountain gorillas have never been successfully bred in captivity. These few remaining in the wild were all that remained.

After the briefing, each tourist team was assigned a guide ranger and a habituated gorilla group to track. The ranger then told how, earlier this morning, scout rangers had begun tracking the three gorilla groups. They did this by picking up each group's trail from where it was seen last night. Once a group was spotted, the scouts tracking it would radio the guide of the tourist team assigned to that group and give him the location. The guide would then lead his team through the forest to that location.

The most important rule was to keep at least twenty-three feet away from the gorillas at all times. This was to prevent disease transference from human to gorilla or vice versa. Other instructions were to stay very still when viewing the gorillas and never to make any type of aggressive motion toward them.

"If a gorilla were to approach any of you too closely, you must hold your ground and show no fear," the ranger instructed sternly.

After the rules review, the three teams were off. My team was assigned to track a small "family" of eight gorillas. We followed our park ranger, an amiable middle-aged Ugandan, uphill along a dirt path for about a mile. We then came to a grass and bush clearing with a nice view of a forested canyon below, where another ranger, with a rifle slung over his shoulder, was waiting. Our team hiked toward him, along a path into the dense forest.

I asked our guide ranger, whose name was Simon, how they habituated a group of gorillas and how long this took.

"The process of getting a group of gorillas accustomed to people is a long and patient process, taking up to three years," Simon replied. "Park rangers do this by working in teams. While always wearing their customary green park uniforms, they approach a gorilla group regularly, for an extended time. At first, the gorillas will greet the rangers with hostility. They make a lot of aggressive noises and threatening postures. This aggressive display is usually then followed by the gorillas making a wary retreat away from the rangers."

As Simon talked, we walked along a leaf-strewn ridge through dense brush, vines, and trees, shaded by the forest canopy.

"After a long period of continual visits, with the rangers just viewing the gorillas passively, the gorillas become accustomed to the ranger's presence," Simon explained. "Eventually, they become indifferent to the rangers, paying no attention them. With even more time, the gorillas begin to acknowledge the rangers."

"Do the gorillas ever become 'friendly' with the rangers?" I asked.

"Well, in one way," Simon answered. "After a prolonged time, some gorillas might seek the rangers' aid or protection. For example, gorilla group alpha males that feel they cannot win a fight against an aggressing alpha male have been known to 'hide' behind a ranger for protection. He'll do this until the aggressing alpha male goes away." (The aggressing alpha male is seeking to poach a female from the threatened group.)

After about two hours, we were hiking around a small knoll in the forest when, all of a sudden, the whole gorilla family was right in front of us. We all stopped and fell silent.

A mother gorilla was sitting on the twigs and leaves of the forest floor, playing with her baby. The baby was cute, looking like a fuzzy black plush toy in its mother's arms. A big silverback male, the alpha male of the group, was lying facedown on the dried leaf-covered ground.

We all stood in quiet excitement as the gorillas lounged about in the bush, lazily munching on leaves. They moved around a bit over a short range but were indifferent to our presence. Though the gorillas seemed harmless, it was humbling to know that we were there on their terms. The silverback could easily have pulverized even the strongest of us tourists in an eyeblink.

Near the end of our viewing time, a small drama occurred. A maturing male in the group made advances toward one of the females, provoking a rapid and aggressive response from the alpha male.

"Stand perfectly still," Simon instructed in a low voice. "We don't want to attract the alpha male's attention."

The alpha male charged the offending adolescent menacingly, almost running over us tourists in the process. Knowing he was in trouble, the offending adolescent male made a fast retreat and managed to get away unharmed.

The alpha male then calmed down and walked over the leaves and brush toward us.

"Stay still," Simon whispered. "Don't move or show fear."

The big primate walked up to one of the male tourists in our group. Looking curiously at the man's bald head, the huge silverback began rubbing his hand over the smooth, shiny pate. The tourist stood completely still, scarcely breathing. When the big gorilla made a motion for the camera the tourist was holding, Simon pushed the camera out of the gorilla's hand and gently shooed him away.

Eventually, the gorilla family moved on and our viewing session was over. Though the whole experience with these highly endangered wonders of our primal world was brief, I felt deeply privileged to be here. At the same time, it was deeply disturbing to think that there might soon come a day when these amazing creatures exist only in photos, videos, and travelers' accounts from a bygone era.

After the gorilla-viewing day, I spent a couple more days in the Bwindi area. In the area surrounding Buhoma are a number of small, very poor rural villages. A local guide I hired to take me around the area explained that some of the villages were populated by Batwa Pygmy people. These were a traditional forest-dwelling people who once lived in the Bwindi Impenetrable Forest, my guide explained. They were the losers in the mountain gorilla tourist business. All of them were removed from their forest homes in the park area, resettled into villages in the surrounding area, and given the tools to make a new type of life without having to exploit the forest.

This was one of the recurring tragic ironies of the disappearing world. To save one special treasure—in this case, the mountain gorillas and their remaining forest habitat—another treasure, the traditional culture and lifestyles of these Batwa Pygmies, was being destroyed.

One morning, after visiting a few local villages, I spent some time at the Bwindi Community Hospital. In the developing world, the societally traumatizing foreign colonialists are gone, replaced by international corporate-style charities that are laughably naive and ineffective at best, and enablers and abettors to terrible, malignant outcomes at worst. I had seen this many times and was beginning to look with disdain on many foreigners' efforts at "doing good" in poorer lands. But the Bwindi Community Hospital appeared to be an exception.

At the hospital, I met an attractive young woman in the administrative office area. Pauline worked as a PR and marketing person doing fund-raising for the hospital. She generously spent two hours showing me around and explaining what the hospital did.

A U.S. missionary couple working with the Batwa Pygmies had started the hospital in 2003. The much-needed facility had grown to provide many essential health services and outreach programs to the hundreds of thousands of people in the surrounding hillside communities, many of whom were hours away by vehicle, or days away by foot along forest trails. She told me the hospital was funded by donations and an active fund-raising effort, which was a major focus of her work. Large funding came from a family in Nevada and some families in California.

"Many of our hospital's services are basic," Pauline said. "We work with the traditional midwives in the communities to provide modern maternity services, and we also do dental and eye services, AIDS prevention education, and treatment for the HIV positive."

A big focus of the hospital was treatment for children suffering from malnutrition, a very common problem in the area. This included an ongoing education effort teaching parents how to give their children better and more balanced diets.

This last service was critical. Typical of people living in deep poverty, diets were starch intensive, consisting mostly of white rice, cassava, and potatoes. The hospital program taught people how to create and tend micro gardens around their huts, where they could grow various vegetables and fruits that children needed to supplement their mostly starch-laden diets.

Another major program of the hospital dealt with HIV. To the Westerner, the mind-boggling numbers of HIV-positive people in Africa can seem quite abstract. But in the area around Bwindi, these hard facts were very tangible.

"Fifteen percent of all children die of various causes before the age of five," Pauline grimly pointed out. "Many of these children started life HIV positive—never even had a real chance."

This was one of the more horrific abominations of the birth lottery: damning babies not only to be born into a poverty-stricken backwater, but also to be afflicted with HIV. But Pauline proceeded to tell me about what sounded like a modern medical miracle.

The Bwindi Community Hospital had brought to the region a modern medical procedure for baby delivery that, in most cases, prevented the transmission of HIV from the mother to her newborn baby. This effort required the hospital to gain the cooperation of the local midwife community (since midwives still perform most baby deliveries in the villages) and encourage midwives to see that all expectant mothers get tested for HIV. If the mother is HIV positive, the hospital then encourages the midwife to have the mother give birth in the hospital.

"Before they give birth, the HIV-positive mothers can then be given certain drugs that help prevent HIV transmission to their offspring," Pauline said.

I left the hospital respecting the effectiveness of its commonsense approaches, based on local circumstances and realities.

Since Pauline had spent half the morning with me, I offered to treat her to lunch in the village. But she had another appointment, so she suggested meeting the next day, her day off, to watch a children's play at a local elementary school.

———

The next day at the elementary school, I asked Pauline how she became involved at the hospital, and got an unexpected answer.

"My work at the hospital is a repayment, you could say, for a miracle that I experienced myself as a child," Pauline explained. "I was born really poor in a village near Kampala. Even going to elementary school would have been an impossible dream because of the cost. But an international aid group, World Vision, started a program in my village. Thanks to World Vision, I got sponsored and went to primary, secondary, and high school. I was a good student and eventually finished university as a business major. World Vision was instrumental in creating the life path I have taken."

I found this personally meaningful because I had been sponsoring a number of children myself through World Vision since finishing university in 1990. It was heartwarming to hear a firsthand account of how the program had helped someone.

"One challenge I have with World Vision, though," I said, "is responding to the many letters I received from the children I sponsored over the years." (Children typically will write their sponsors several short notes during the year, especially around Easter and Christmas).

"Did your sponsor write back much when you wrote?" I asked.

At this, Pauline's face darkened. "My sponsor almost never sent any replies to my letters," she replied. "This is the one sad memory of my sponsorship."

Upon hearing this, I sheepishly admitted that I, too, had been remiss in replying to my sponsored children. I just never knew what to say to kids who were very far away and had life conditions and challenges so different from anything I knew.

"That is no excuse!" Pauline said. Then she practically *ordered* me to begin replying regularly to my sponsored children.

I determined right then that once I finished my travel project and was again in a position to receive mail I would write back without fail.

From Bwindi, I hired a private car heading north. My next destination was another famous primate trekking destination: Kibale National Park, a day's drive north of Bwindi. Kibale is well known for its abundant chimpanzees, other primates, and diverse birdlife.

After a dusty but pleasant six-hour ride, my driver dropped me off at a convenient spot to catch a regional bus going toward the park (the bus was much cheaper than going all the way by private car).

After riding a few hours, the regional bus arrived in Fort Portal, a city near Kibale, where I got off. As always in Uganda, a heaving crowd of people was waiting to get aboard. I had to squeeze and jostle to get down the steps as hordes of people frantically shoved their way up, threatening to push me back inside. This was yet another example of the ways that gnawing poverty degrades human dignity.

Relieved to have made it off the bus with my bag and small backpack intact, I walked into town and went in a small store to find something to eat. When I went pay for my milk, small bag of almonds, and candy bar, I reached down into my cargo pant pocket and found it open. My money was gone.

I knew at once what had happened. When getting into the private car earlier that morning, I had carelessly stuffed my Ugandan cash, equivalent to about US$160, into the front zip pocket above the knee of my cargo pants. I then forgot that the cash was there when I transferred to the regional bus. Apparently, one of those desperate, struggling wretches getting onto the bus as I was getting off took advantage of my being pinned by the horde on the steps, and helped himself to my money. I left the store still hungry, since I now had no Ugandan cash to pay for my food, while cursing myself for being so foolish as to leave my cash in such a vulnerable pocket.

And as if being pickpocketed weren't enough, my visit to Kibale National Park was a dud. The place was so tightly regulated, and all visitor activities so heavily structured, that it killed my interest in being there. I saw a few chimpanzees and some colorful birds, including a great blue turaco, a majestic creature with aqua wing feathers, a yellow beak and underbelly, and a deep blue "Mohawk" tuft on its crown. Then I cut my time short there and moved on after a few days.

I finished my Uganda travels in the southwest of the country, staying a week by Lake Victoria in the pleasant town of Jinja. Lake Victoria is one of the African Great Lakes, the primary source of the White Nile (which eventually joins the Blue Nile to become the Nile River of Sudan and Egypt). It is also Africa's largest inland fishery.

Victoria is a very troubled lake. Its shoreline runs through Uganda, Tanzania, and Kenya and is dotted with towns and cities, making the region all around the lake one of the most densely populated rural areas in the world. Raw sewage and factory waste, farm fertilizer runoff, and the taking of too much water from the lake have greatly damaged the ecosystem and lowered water levels. The lake can also be dangerous to poor fishermen who work its shallow waters and surrounding wetlands. I had heard several stories of crocodile attacks: fishermen losing a limb or even having their entrails snapped out as they bent over their nets in the shallows.

I stayed in a homey lodge complex that was popular with long-term expats. The place had several small stucco-and-wood buildings with simple but comfortable rooms, with nicely groomed lawns, flowering garden beds, and palm trees. It was just what I needed after the very basic accommodations I had taken in Uganda.

On my first night in Jinja, I went to the lodge's popular open-air restaurant. The high stools around the semicircular bar were full with patrons, including several middle-aged Western expats. Several women in form-fitting, short evening dresses and high heels lounged about hoping for "work." The bar had a nightclub vibe, with red-hued lighting and loud Western dance music.

Since I didn't want to go into town for dinner, I pulled up the only empty stool at the bar. Next to me sat a Western expat with his receding hair slicked back à la Gordon Gekko. Dave from Dallas was one of the lodge's longer-term residents. An engineer in his mid-fifties, he worked on large power projects in East Africa—yet another of many expats I have met in Africa who were hooked on the alternative lifestyles offered to foreigners on the continent.

"It gets in your blood," Dave said over a cold Nile Special lager. "Many expats are drawn to life in East Africa because it's still got that free-for-all Wild West atmosphere," he explained. "These people find it hard to ever fit in again to life in the rich, safe, predictable modern world."

At that moment, a tall, friendly young woman with glistening coal black skin, wearing a short, skin-tight gray body dress that set off a pair of long, shapely legs, sauntered over. I wasn't interested but politely said hello, then returned to my conversation with Dave. I asked him how long he had been here.

"I have a home in Nairobi, where I've lived over ten years," he replied. "My current job in Uganda has brought me here for the last three years. I don't think now that I could ever go back to living in the West again. So many people here, in the various power and extraction industries, go home for a few years to France, Germany, the States, and can't fit in." He shook his head ruefully. "The rules, the restrictions, all the safety devices, and everything so bloody predictable—it's too boring. Here, with all the corruption, all the rules are bendable. Life's possibilities are wide open, and every day is different from the day before."

"And it's fun for a single man, of course," he added, nodding appreciatively toward the young woman who had approached me earlier. "Especially here in East Africa. As a white male making good money, you *never* have to be alone."

After my dinner and conversation with Dave, I got to thinking about myself. By now I had been traveling over a year and a half straight, mostly in places similar to what Dave described. I had a nagging inner worry that I, too, might have trouble returning to "normal" life in the rich world.

From Jinja, I crammed into yet another dirty, ramshackle minibus taxi for the ride to Entebbe, where I would catch a flight to Zambia. This time, I would bypass Kampala, Uganda's capital.

I had already stayed in Kampala my first five days in country, before catching the bus to Bwindi. It was a sprawling, dusty city, though not a bad place by sub-Saharan African standards. Some of the city's roads were reasonably well paved, and toward the city center, a number of the intersections had stoplights, some of which actually worked. There were several high-rise buildings of modern construction, and a few chic cafés and restaurants. I could feel the city's hustle, as indicated by an almost uncontrolled proliferation of advertising billboards everywhere, touting everything from bands playing at downtown bars, to antacid tablets, to cell phones, to condoms. One advertising banner that I saw hanging all around downtown read "Male Enlargement, No Side Effects" and listed a phone number to call.

Getting around in Kampala involved a learning curve. The most prolific form of transport is the *boda-boda* motorcycle taxis. These are rolling deathtraps. The boda-boda drivers, often drunk, are notorious for using their cell phones while weaving between cars at high speed in heavy traffic. Almost every day while in Kampala, I read stories in the local press about horrible accidents involving boda-bodas. In many of these accidents, the drivers had been known to abandon their injured fares right there in the street and make their getaway.

The main form of transport for most citizens of modest means is by *matatu*. Common in the undeveloped world, these are minibuses, usually older looking and in shabby condition, that run regular routes. They are a sort of group taxi, with people getting on or hopping off as the vehicle goes along a preset route, and riding them can be a cultural experience, as I discovered.

One night, on the way to my hotel, I took a matatu. A woman with a baby got on and sat in the seat ahead of me. As always with public transport in Uganda, the matatu was overfilled. It was a balmy evening, and darkness was settling in.

A few stops later, the woman got out of the matatu and left her baby on the seat. I pointed to the baby and called after the woman. Others in the minibus also noticed that she had left her baby. Several passengers got out and started scolding the woman. There was much arm waving and excited jabbering while the women slumped in shame onto the sidewalk. She ended up back on the minibus with her baby. I felt sorry for the baby.

Another form of transport is a "special hire" taxi—the Ugandan term for what people in the developed world people consider a regular taxi. As with most vehicles in Uganda, the taxis can be quite dilapidated. One night, my special-hire taxi ride started with me actually having to get out and push-start the car. Local people sitting in front of little eateries or walking along the street watched with bemusement the spectacle of the rich white foreigner pushing the taxi that he was paying for, down the muddy road.

Again, Kampala is not a bad place at all by sub-Saharan African standards.

From Uganda, I flew to Lusaka, the capital of Zambia, where I caught a small twin-prop plane to a tiny airstrip on the edge of South Luangwa National Park. One of the world's great national parks, South Luangwa is considered perhaps the best game-viewing park in all Africa.

Late August 2008
South Luangwa National Park, Zambia

The lions fanned out, breaking off into two groups, moving quickly but silently in the half-moonlight. Several dozen impalas—medium-size African antelope with reddish-brown upper coats, white belly and flanks, and black stripes forming an "M" on the rump—grazed on an open field of dry grass, oblivious of the coming attack. The warm night was quiet but for an occasional rustle of leaves in the slight breeze.

"See the three over there," said Allan, our guide, pointing to three lionesses that had crept to spots in the thickets behind the impalas. Allan, a young Australian couple, and I were sitting in an open-top Toyota Land Cruiser, under a low acacia tree at the edge of the field. We had a front-row seat to the timeless drama unfolding before us.

"Now look over there," Allan whispered, pointing to four more lionesses and two cubs that were ghosting through the field, in front of the impalas.

"Once they get close enough, they will charge the impalas, trying to get some to panic and run back toward the lions waiting in ambush behind those bushes," Allan explained. A fortyish Shona man with a pugnacious face, Allan was uncanny in his ability to find dramatic things to watch on our safaris. As we watched, I found it curious, as I always did on safaris like this, that the animals paid no attention whatever to the people in the vehicles that followed them around. The animals just went about the business of living (and, sometimes, dying) as if the strange beings observing them were just moving plants.

The four of us watched as the lions appeared poised to spring their trap on the impalas. Two juvenile impalas—cute Bambi-looking creatures in the direct path of the impending lion charge—perked up as if sensing something amiss. The four lionesses and two cubs continued creeping slowly but steadily toward the herd, on a broad front, flattening themselves as low as possible against the ground as they advanced.

Then one of the cubs, which looked like a big rust-brown spotted housecat, raced precociously ahead of its elders, running headlong toward the impalas. The cub ran around several of the antelope, which at first paid little attention to the little scampering pest. Then, as if a silent alarm had gone off, the herd raised their heads. An instant later, the graceful creatures took flight, making long, flowing bounds as if on pogo sticks, toward a clear spot at one end of the field. In a matter of moments, the entire herd of perhaps forty had galloped far away from the threat, settling into another open field a quarter mile away.

The lionesses appeared to regain control of the cub, and soon, some of the adults were again slowly but conspicuously approaching several of the impalas. They appeared to be coaxing the antelope into retreating in a direction away from the main herd and toward a group of lions that had moved to some nearby tall grasses and brush. But we didn't get to see the endgame. The park closing time of ten p.m. was approaching, and it was time to leave.

It was my second day at the Flatdogs Safari Camp, at the edge of South Luangwa National Park. The park, which has some of Africa's biggest concentrations of animals, is on the Luangwa River, a major tributary of the mighty Zambezi. The Luangwa supports many crocodiles and the biggest concentrations of hippos in Africa. It is still a true wilderness area—quite remote and difficult to access, so it doesn't get the crush of visitors seen in other famous game parks, such as Kruger in South Africa, or parks in the Serengeti. Thus, it fit right into my quest to experience the planet's last great wilderness areas.

I had been in Zambia almost a week since leaving Uganda. Zambia, a landlocked country the size of Texas, is mostly high plateau with a tropical climate. Dirt poor like Uganda, it, too, has a low life expectancy, estimated at less than 50 years. HIV and AIDS are rampant, and the illiteracy rate is high, with much of the population mired in deep poverty. On a more optimistic note, Zambia has rich copper reserves, which generate some revenue for the country, and—perhaps most important—unlike many of its neighbors, it has had a run of decent governance for the past decade.

The next morning, our small group was in the Land Cruiser and off again for more wildlife viewing. It was hot and sunny under dazzling blue skies. We drove along paths through scrub, small wetlands, dried brush, and low, flat-topped acacia and mopane trees. Lions lazed along sandy riverbanks. Saddle-billed storks, whose spindly legs seemed scarcely able to support their massive red bill, hunted in the wetlands while hippos lazed in the muddy waters. Cape buffalo, looking like huge black bulls with wickedly curved horns, grazed in the brush.

At one point, we came to a small pride of lions lounging by their kill: a cape buffalo carcass that lay half eaten in the dried grass. Two cubs goofed around on the carcass, as if playing on a jungle gym in a school playground. Brownish-gray vultures loitered on the ground nearby, at a suitable distance from the lions, and on high branches above the kill. When the lions looked away or dozed for a moment, a few of the more intrepid vultures would jump in and grab a morsel or two from the carcass.

At another point, we came to a shallow pool in a grassy clearing. Five giraffes—two adults and three smaller ones—emerged from the scrubby forest behind the pond and warily approached the water's edge.

"They want to take a drink—a simple act that can be life threatening to them," Allan said as we stopped nearby to watch.

Standing by the edge of the water, none of the giraffes would take the first drink. Instead, they looked all around them for several moments.

"When a giraffe's head is down sipping the water, it is most vulnerable to attack," Allan said. "It has a very strong kick, flicking the front hoof forward, which can kill even a lion. So predators try to attack when a giraffe isn't looking."

Appearing satisfied that no predators lurked in the thickets behind them or in the trees on their right flank, the giraffes tentatively, one by one, lowered their head to grab a quick drink. It seemed a nerve-racking process to go through every day, just to get a drink of water.

Later that afternoon, we came to a vast plain that looked like a war zone. In all directions, the dried grasses in large swaths appeared trampled, dotted with countless shattered tree stumps sticking up forlornly from the parched earth. It looked as if the area had been blasted by heavy artillery. Our little group got out of the Land Cruiser and walked amid the devastation.

"What happened here?" I asked Allan. "This place looks as if a massive tornado swept through."

"It is the elephants," Allan said, laughing. "They are like gigantic eating and waste-producing machines. A big herd will go into an area and literally eat it out, knocking down the trees and trampling everything underneath."

I mentioned that it seemed amazing that such an Armageddon-like scene was created by an endangered species.

"It is natural," Allan continued. "Over time, this huge field will regenerate, and the elephants will return to start the process over again."

That evening, we were out again on a night safari. Early after dusk, we quietly followed a leopard as it hunted, though we eventually lost it. Allan then found another group of lions on a hunt. This time, the pride—six of them—was perched on a low hill looking down on a small herd of puku, a medium-size antelope. They were grazing in a field of tuft grasses, which backed from the bottom of the hill into the rushing waters of a wide creek. Allan parked our jeep at a good vantage point nearby, on the same low hilltop. We all watched quietly in anticipation of the drama about to unfold.

The lions charged down the hill in an all-out frontal attack on the puku, but the puku reacted quickly. With long, graceful bounds, they launched themselves away, jumping so high they seemed almost to take flight. The puku ran straight into the creek. The attacking lions chased them only to the creek's edge and abruptly stopped—they had no chance at keeping up with the graceful antelope in the water.

"One didn't get away!" Allan said quietly, pointing to a spot on the field below.

A tiny puku fawn had gotten left behind. The terrified baby lay flat on the ground, motionless but quivering in a shallow depression toward the center of the field. The lions, turning back from the creek bank, appeared to realize that one of the antelope was behind them. Since it was dark, they couldn't see it. (We saw it briefly in our spotlight, though Allan couldn't keep it on the puku, or the lions would also see it.)

The lions fanned out in a wide circle around the helpless creature. It appeared that they still couldn't actually see it, though. They slowly closed in until they were almost in a huddle on top of the puku. One of the lions finally saw it and pounced. The puku shot practically straight up, as if on a spring. Somehow, it dodged and weaved through the oncoming lions like an expert runningback evading tacklers. It then made the same long, graceful bounds that its older comrades had done, and somehow made it to the safety of the creek, with all six lions charging frantically after it.

"Oh, my God, he got away!" the young Australian woman exclaimed in relief, from her seat behind me. "I'm so glad that cute little thing wasn't caught!"

I turned, pretending to look sad, and said, "Really? I was rooting for the lions."

———

I finished my travels in Zambia a week later and flew on to beautiful Cape Town, at the southwest tip of South Africa. While there, I studied my next big destination: Madagascar. After enjoying the good food and wine that Cape Town is known for, I took an evening flight back to Johannesburg, to catch my flight to Madagascar.

I had to stay overnight in Johannesburg since my flight to Antananarivo, Madagascar, was early the next morning. It was about eleven at night when I was taking my taxi, a several-year-old black Mercedes sedan, from the Johannesburg Tambo airport to a nearby airport hotel.

On the way, in the middle of the major four-lane road ahead of us, an ambulance was stopped and turned at right angles to the road. It was surrounded on three sides by other vehicles. My taxi driver hurriedly pushed the buttons to close off the front windows, which had been open on this pleasantly cool late evening. Gunning the engine, he raced past the stopped cars and ambulance.

"The situation does not look good," my driver said as we shot past. No explanation was needed. It appeared that a robbery of the ambulance was in progress.

I agreed with the taxi driver's response: best not to stick around and find out for sure.

CHAPTER 11

Partying with the Dead in Madagascar, and Off to West Papua

Mid-September 2008
Antsirabe, Central Highlands, Madagascar

Everybody likes a good party, and some people can always come up with a reason to party. I was in Madagascar's central highlands, where they take this idea a big step further. There, it is customary to throw a party whose guest of honor is a deceased ancestor, exhumed from the crypt for this special event. Called a *famadihana*, this unique custom has managed to survive meddling missionaries' attempts to stamp it out, and it looks likely to stay on for a while longer yet. Unfortunately, this cannot be said of Madagascar's natural treasures, which make the country such an amazingly diverse wonderland.

I was riding with my local guide to a famadihana in a rickshaw, called a *pouse-pouse*. It was a bit after eight a.m. as we rolled down a red clay road between large fields of lettuce, tomatoes, and rice. My driver—or, more accurately, my human draft horse—was breathing heavily from the exertion as his bare feet slapped the ground with each running step. I marveled at the strength and endurance of this skinny middle-aged man in a dirty wine-red sweatshirt and faded blue shorts. He didn't look that strong, but his thick, leathery hands held the two wooden poles that pulled the wooden cart on which my local guide rode and I rode, and he never faltered a step the whole journey.

"There are two guests of honor at today's famadihana party," said Herman, my guide. "They are brothers who both died in the past five years. One of the men was the former headman of the village. He died five years ago. The other man, his brother, died three years ago. Both lived long lives, more than ninety years each."

Approaching the place where the famadihana would be held, we passed through a small, neat village. White stucco shops with corrugated metal roofs lined the red clay road. Villagers wearing small caps or round sun hats, and several pouse-pouses were on the road, going about their business. The village was obviously a deeply impoverished place but seemed pleasant in its lush agricultural setting. The bounty from the area was on display at the end of the stucco shacks, where a row of women vendors sat by the roadside, selling small piles of bananas, potatoes, carrots, lettuce, green onions, tomatoes, and squash.

I had been in Madagascar for six days. It is a desperately poor island country in the Indian Ocean, 250 miles off the southeast coast of Africa. The world's fourth largest island, Madagascar has an astonishing bio-diversity and is a cultural melting pot of many waves of immigrants from the Indian Ocean region, the African mainland, and the South Pacific. As early as 2,500 years ago, people from the island of Borneo are believed to have settled in Madagascar. These various peoples brought to the island their cultural traditions and beliefs, including a veneration for the spirits of dead ancestors.

I had met Herman the day before the famadihana, in Antsirabe, a large town in Madagascar's central highlands, near the village where the celebration was taking place. I had just arrived by bus from Antananarivo, Madagascar's capital, earlier in the day. Shortly after getting into town, I took a walk to Antsirabe's local market near the town center. There, I hoped to learn of a possible famadihana that might be happening soon. Here and in much of sub-Saharan Africa, I quickly learned that it is impossible to stay alone if you are "white," because you stand out as a foreigner. People want to talk to you, help you, sell you stuff, and take you places. In markets, this is especially the case, and sometimes a visit actually turns up something interesting. In this case, it did.

As I slowly walked among the small vendor stalls selling small boxed foods, tea, wood carvings, and cheap costume jewelry, Herman, a local fixer and guide, came up and introduced himself to me. After I told him of my interest in a famadihana, Herman told me of one that was happening the very next morning.

"I will bring you to the famadihana," Herman said. My newly met fixer was a tall, skinny fellow with an ebony complexion and a scraggly beard. He appeared to be in his late twenties. "Can you pay me a fee of ten dollars for this?" he said. "I know that the family of the dead persons will welcome you, especially since you want to come for the whole event and not just the part where the bodies are removed from their graves."

When I agreed to his more than reasonable fee, Herman suggested that I also donate ten or fifteen dollars to the family of the deceased to help cover costs. This I was also happy to do.

After our pouse-pouse passed through the small village, we continued a short way before pulling up behind a small pink stucco house. It had an unglazed window opening on the side, an old clay tile roof that was noticeably sagging, and a wood-frame porch on the front. The house, which was surrounded by large fields of dry weeds and some trees, had a large tented area to its side with walls of tattered plastic sheeting. Many people from the local village were walking up to the house as the sun broke through a heavily overcast sky. The famadihana was just beginning.

I was invited inside the tent with the tattered plastic sheet walls. The celebration had begun with a big feast of freshly slaughtered and boiled pig served with white rice. As I walked into the tent, some villagers eating at a benchlike wooden table looked up and waved to me to join them.

"Welcome . . . you America?" asked a young athletic man with a military haircut, wearing a blue, red, and white striped rain jacket.

When I nodded with a smile, two women sitting on the other side of the bench both grinned and said, "Obama!"

As Herman walked away, someone handed me a dish of pork and rice. I was quite hungry since I hadn't yet eaten breakfast. But the pork was awful. It was rubbery and tasteless because there was little seasoning. But I gamely slogged through my meal, grinning and smiling at everyone in the tent and not betraying my dislike of the food. Since the main language of Madagascar is French, it was hard for me to talk with the villagers. But everyone was very welcoming to me, the only foreigner there. I felt as if the party had three guests of honor: two dead and one—so far, anyway—very much alive.

After eating, everyone gathered behind the main house, in a yard of clay dirt surrounded by weeds and high brush. The attendees to the party included the large extended family of the deceased brothers, family friends, and people from the local village. Some musicians appeared and started playing trumpets, clarinets, and flutes while people started dancing. The dancing crowd held aloft a big tube of woven rattan and passed it around.

"That is the shroud that we will wrap my grandfather's mummy in after we remove him from his grave," a clean-cut young man standing next to me explained in English, pointing to the woven rattan tube. "I am Patrick. My grandfather is one of the two people this party is honoring. I am glad you are here with us today."

Patrick, one of many grandsons of the older deceased guest of honor, was a friendly guy wearing a black baseball cap and white knit shirt. He introduced me to his cousin, Mahefa, standing next to him. Mahefa, wearing dreadlocks and a faded jean shirt and pants, came across as a gregarious party type. Patrick and Mahefa became my mentors during the celebration and would tell me what was going on since most of the guests spoke little English. They also introduced me to members of the large extended family in attendance, including the sons of the deceased, one of whom was the village sheriff. Every family member welcomed me and expressed their pleasure that I was attending the celebration.

The dancing in the backyard continued until midday, when everyone paused for a brief lunch. Then, as the skies darkened from storm clouds moving overhead, the musicians' horns started blaring again. The gathering of perhaps seventy-five people began moving toward a big field of weeds and grasses in a most festive procession. People danced, sang, and laughed as they walked into the field behind the house.

"Come up to the front with me," Patrick said. "We are now going to my grandfather's and great uncle's crypts. We will dig them up and then prepare their mummies for a big party in their honor tonight."

I then noticed that two teams of people in the procession were carrying ceremonial wooden litters above their heads, while others were carrying a couple of tubes of the rolled woven rattan cloth. Somebody also carried a flag of Madagascar on a stick, its two wide horizontal stripes, one red and the other green, flapping in the breeze.

"We will put the mummies in those baskets to carry back to the house," Mahefa said, referring to the wooden litters.

About a hundred yards out in the weed-filled field, we came to a couple of concrete grave markers in the red clay ground, marking the crypts of the deceased brothers. The musicians stopped playing, and everyone paused. One by one, some of the grandsons got up on an adjacent elevated concrete platform mound and gave speeches and testimonials. Some of the speeches sounded quite moving. I couldn't understand them, though, since they were all in French or the local language.

After the speeches, the music started up again and everybody resumed dancing and began to gather around the underground crypts. As the music again tapered off, several grandsons of the deceased took some spades, and each made a symbolic thrust into the ground above the crypt. The spades were then passed around. I was surprised when a spade came almost immediately to me.

"You are our special guest today, like family," Patrick said as I received the spade. "Not many foreign people come to these events and stay all day like you."

"Yes, sometimes foreign people come only to see the bodies after they are dug up," Mahefa interjected. "They take photos and then leave."

Now, truly feeling like a part of the celebration, I made my ceremonial spade thrust. After many people made their symbolic dig into the ground above the crypt, the real digging began in earnest. For about twenty minutes, the spades were passed back and forth between the grandsons, some other able-bodied men, and me as we took turns digging.

Then we hit the crypts. More digging revealed the openings. A call went out to halt and get some alcohol.

"Can you buy us some rum from one of the vendors over there?" another grandson of the deceased asked me (since I was the "rich" foreigner). He pointed to some local vendors who had set up tables nearby with snack foods and bottles of rum, moonshine, whisky, and beer to sell to party participants.

I happily obliged by buying a bottle of local rum for a few dollars from one of the vendors and bringing it back to the now unearthed crypts.

"Go ahead, please pour a small amount of rum into each grave," Patrick instructed. After I did this, he passed the bottle to several other family members, and each ceremoniously poured a tiny splash of rum into the graves of the deceased. Mostly, though, to my amusement, the rum went into the grandsons and their friends.

After the bottle of rum was finished, a tall, thin bearded man came to me and demanded that I buy more liquor. Wearing a rumpled, dirty brown long-sleeve shirt and looking older than his probable mid-thirties, he appeared not to have slept in several days. Not sure what to do, I tried graciously and good-naturedly to brush him off. It was the first time all day that anyone had been less than friendly to me. I was relieved when my dreadlocked new friend Mahefa came to my rescue and fended off the grumpy guy.

As the digging into the crypt continued, the two dead men's caskets were soon exposed and then removed from the crypts. Each casket was picked up by six or eight people and hoisted up into the air as everyone again started dancing. The musicians' horns blared again and played festive music as the party sprang back into full gear.

The caskets were then laid down and opened, revealing a mummy inside each one. Once again the music stopped as relatives came to the caskets and said some private words, with a couple of them weeping. The mummies were then carefully wrapped in the new woven rattan shrouds. Several people then hoisted the mummies into the air, holding them aloft. The music resumed, and everyone began dancing anew.

The procession slowly headed back to the main house, with participants holding the two mummies high in the air, and others holding the ceremonial wooden litters up high. Most of the people in the procession dance-walked on the way back, shaking their arms in the air and swaying their hips as the musicians blared away on their horns.

About halfway back to the main house, the procession stopped and the mummies were placed inside the ceremonial litter. The procession then continued toward the main house as a thin, cool drizzle began to fall. I was helping at times to carry one of the litters, and a pretty young woman in her mid-twenties, with a nice wavy hairstyle and a small diamond pin in her nose, walked next to me. As the rain grew a little stronger, she eyed the safari hat that I was wearing.

"Can I borrow your nice hat to keep my hair dry?" the pretty woman asked me, giving me a damsel-in-distress look. "The rain will ruin my hair."

"Of course," I said, offering it to her.

This became a problem, however, because the woman apparently never intended to return my hat. After the bodies of the deceased were brought to the tented area by the house, she tried to slip away from the party with my hat. Seeing this, I went over and asked her for it back.

"Oh, I just want it for the night. It goes so well with my outfit," the young woman said, trying to edge away. If she had just asked me for the hat, I probably would have given it to her. But since she was just trying to steal it, I politely but firmly suggested she return it.

Fortunately, Patrick came by. He knew, of course, that the young woman intended just to keep the hat of the rich white foreigner, so he unceremoniously snatched it off her head. Looking angry and embarrassed, the young woman turned abruptly and stalked off.

"Here," Patrick said, returning my hat to me. "I am sorry for this behavior."

The party lasted all night long. The two mummies were placed in a position of honor at the head of a long table in the main ceremonial tent while everyone ate, drank, and danced. About an hour before midnight, I wore out and reluctantly bade everyone good-bye. A friend of Patrick and Mahefa, with whom I had shared a few drinks—a young man in his late teens wearing a yellow and black sweatshirt with "Steelers" emblazoned on it—walked me through the darkened streets of the nearby village to a main road. There he flagged down a pouse-pouse to take me back to my hotel.

Before saying good-bye, he explained how the famadihana would end.

"The next morning, the mummies will be carefully unwrapped by some specialists in attendance," the teenager explained. "They will then be rewrapped in a fresh set of cloth and shrouds and reburied for the final time."

"Since you have taken many pictures of this event," he said, "can you please send me and my brother a CD with copies of the pictures?" I agreed, of course, and got the address of his brother's work at the local airport, where I could mail the CD.

Overall, I thought the whole event was quite a remarkable show of love and respect by the extended family and surrounding community for the two once-important dead loved ones.

———————

After the famadihana, I spent a few more days in Antsirabe, the large town near the village where the event was held. A very poor but pleasant town, it has a mild climate since it sits at an elevation of around 4,900 feet. The town has wide palm-lined boulevards, brightly colored colonial-era houses, several stately old colonial buildings, and a huge fleet of colorful wooden pouse-pouses. I found it a nice, friendly place to linger for a short while. After several days in Antsirabe, I started my journey to one of Madagascar's most famous national parks, the amazingly biodiverse Ranomafana.

Madagascar is one of the most biologically distinct places in the world, with some bizarre fauna and flora that can almost seem as if they evolved on another planet. Scientists estimate that 5 percent of all animal and plant species in the world are found in Madagascar, and most of them nowhere else in the world.

This amazing diversity is attributed to long geographical isolation. Around 165 million years ago, the landmass containing Madagascar broke away from Gondwanaland, the larger landmass that would eventually separate into Africa and South America. Around 65 million years ago, Madagascar then broke off from the Indian subcontinent. And ever since, the flora and fauna of Madagascar evolved in geographical isolation.

The cute and cuddly lemurs are the most famous of the many uniquely Madagascan life forms. Lemurs evolved from the forerunners of modern primates. After Madagascar separated from the mainland that became Africa, the many varieties of modern primates found on the African continent—baboons and other Old World monkeys, gorillas, and chimpanzees (and, eventually, humans)—evolved into being. But in Madagascar's very different ecosystem, lemurs evolved and thrived in isolation from all that was developing on the huge African continent. Today there are an estimated thirty-nine distinct lemur species and ninety-nine subspecies—all of them found only in Madagascar.

Tragically, Madagascar is a starring poster child for Our Disappearing World. At one time, much of the island was covered in forest. Today, though, over 90 percent of this primeval forest is gone. A growing population; slash-and-burn agriculture; the use of charcoal derived from forest trees for cooking and heating; and mining, timber extraction, and bad, unstable governance do not bode well for the future of this biological wonderland.

Getting to Ranomafana National Park was no picnic. Starting at dawn, I found myself yet again crammed into an overstuffed, dilapidated old minivan with balding tires. These are Madagascar's main form of intercity bus transport. If I didn't expire from the heat and smell inside the old, filthy minivan—or from shock from the periodic near accidents that are part and parcel of a journey in these vehicles—I figured on arriving at the Ranomafana National Park late in the afternoon.

After I endured two hours of this misery, sitting with my knees shoved into the metal seat in front of me, and beside a mother holding a baby who periodically drooled on my shirt, the minivan stopped for a break at a small roadside store. There, I saw three middle-aged English travelers getting into a nice red SUV parked facing in the same direction I was going. Walking up to them, I asked if I could hitch a ride toward Ranomafana. To my relief, they were going right by the park and welcomed me aboard. This made the journey much more fun.

On the way, we stopped at a small hilltop village above a long, winding road. The village offered a beautiful view of large flooded rice fields in the valley below. Neat, narrow furrows of dirt segmented the rice "lakes" into different sections. The village consisted of simple A-frame one- and two-story concrete or brick houses with tile roofs and paneless windows, dotting the hills above the rice fields. A patch of forest stood on a hill behind the rural village.

While I was at the village, a barefoot middle-aged woman in a shabby red coat, and a skinny boy, wearing a green cap turned at an angle on his head and also barefoot, were pushing a crude, rickety wooden wagon along a flat area on the road. The wagon, whose left front wheel was precariously crooked, looked like something from *The Flintstones* cartoon show.

"That is a 'Madagascar bobsled,'" explained Didier, the driver and guide for the three English travelers. "These are a common form of small transport vehicle here."

The middle-aged women and her son pushed the wagon, which had a large woven twine basket of eggs on it, to the crest of the hill. They both then sat aboard the contraption and started rolling downhill. Gradually at first but slowly gathering speed, they were soon careening precariously along the winding downhill grade until out of sight. Riding that rolling deathtrap seemed an exercise in faith. The only braking system is a big stick, dragged along the ground to slow the vehicle down. There appeared to be no actual steering mechanism.

My new English friends dropped me off in the center of Ranomafana, a small village near Ranomafana National Park. Hauling my luggage along rocky dirt paths surrounded by forested hills, I looked for a decent place to stay. Soon, I found a nice, clean though spartan room at a missionary residence staffed by nuns. In Africa and Madagascar, it is common for missionary compounds to offer rooms for rent to help with the overhead. These are often great deals as well as clean, pleasant, and—very important—secure.

I was really excited about my upcoming chance to see Ranomafana National Park. Reading about it, the park sounded like a wonderland of strange and interesting creatures. A World Heritage Site, the park is a rain forest and one of the most important parks in Madagascar. It was originally established to protect its golden bamboo lemurs, which are found only in that general area, though it has eleven other lemur species.

Along with the lemurs, Ranomafana has a huge smorgasbord of wildlife, including civets, mongooses, all kinds of bats, well over a hundred different bird species, and many other interesting animals, along with an equally impressive assortment of reptiles and aquatic life. The park is home to some truly odd creatures. One is the rare nocturnal lemur known as the aye-aye, which has rodentlike teeth and searches for food by tapping on trees to find grubs hiding under the bark, then fishes them out with a specialized elongated finger. Then there are the park's eight different species of tenrecs. Some of these little insectivores have quills and a long snout and look like a bizarre hybrid of a shrew and a hedgehog. Some of the animals I read about sounded impossibly cute, like the tiny brown mouse lemur—a highly endangered nocturnal lemur small enough to sit on a man's hand. I couldn't wait to see one. It was sad to think, though, that this amazing trove of natural oddities is one of the few remaining scraps of Madagascar's original treasures—and is at acute risk of being lost forever.

On my first full day in Ranomafana, I went hiking in the thick, lush forest with a French couple I had met, and a hired local guide. We were richly rewarded for our efforts. Typically, a hiker in rain forest doesn't see much in the way of wildlife, other than a glimpse of birds in flight among the treetops. But on this hike, as we walked along the muddy, often slippery trails, our guide stopped the group several times to point out lemurs that we would never have noticed in the nearby trees.

At one point, Michael, our young Madagascan guide, pointed to several brown lemurs crawling on tree branches overhead, just a few feet in front of us. Two or three feet long, with a tail half their body length, and dense, short fur and short necks, but with raccoon-shaped snouts and orange eyes, they looked like plush teddy bear toys.

In the evening, we finally came upon some of the park's famous golden bamboo lemurs, crawling among some vines in trees along the trail. The fluffy little creatures were maybe a foot to a foot and half long, with a tail the same length, dark, pointy snouts, and orange eyes. Michael explained that golden bamboo lemurs eat a diet of bamboo leaves. They have developed a resistance to the cyanide in the leaves, which is strong enough to kill other animals. Unfortunately, like almost all of Madagascar's lemurs, they are highly endangered, with only about a thousand remaining, due to continual destruction of their habitat.

In one section of the park, we came across an old burial ground. The site consisted of a series of rectangular rocks, each of a different height. It was the graveyard for a family of Tanala, a forest-dwelling people. The height of each rock indicated the life span of the person buried there: the longer the person lived, the taller the stone that was placed above the grave.

One of the more amazing wildlife sightings of the day occurred when we started to hike away from the burial grounds. As we walked past some rocks half buried in brush off to the side of the path we were on, Michael pointed to something on the ground, a few feet off the path. At first, I was puzzled—he wanted me to see what looked like a couple of brown pinecones lying against each other.

"Look very closely," Michael whispered.

On closer inspection, I realized, to my amazement, that the "pinecones" were actually a pair of wonderfully camouflaged birds sleeping together.

Michael said they were collared nightjars, so effectively camouflaged that they could sleep the day through on the open ground, and their predators wouldn't see them.

Another impressive example of camouflage was a leaf frog, which looked like nothing more than a leaf sitting on the ground. Michael had to spend quite a while pointing at it before I or the French couple could actually see it. And yet, the frog was less than three feet away!

Ranomafana is one of the last best hopes for the fragile biological treasures of Madagascar. It is also a prime example of how even these priceless biological jewels of the world are under serious threat. On my second day of hiking there, our small group stopped by the research station in the park. It was staffed by several mostly young European graduate students doing various forms of research. The students spent some time talking with us during our visit.

It was not a fun conversation, because the research students were very pessimistic about the future of Madagascar's rapidly dwindling biological treasures. One of the researchers, a Frenchwoman in her mid-twenties, explained that the park was only a small rump of the larger surrounding wilderness, created specifically to preserve the endangered golden bamboo lemur. And yet, the park was too small for this, and the surrounding primary forestlands were rapidly being destroyed by logging and mining. Another researcher, a tall, slender Frenchman, then told us how the destruction of the forest surrounding the park was causing an overconcentration of predators of the golden bamboo lemur in the park. These predators were mainly fossas, a small catlike carnivore, that were being forced into the national park area as their other forest hunting grounds were destroyed. Therefore, the golden lemurs were not only losing habitat critical to their survival but were also being killed off at an accelerating rate due to unnaturally growing numbers of their predators in the park.

Another destructive force in the park—and a common one all over Madagascar—was mining. The researchers explained to us that mining actually took place inside the borders of the park. In making the charters for the 'protected' National Parks, mining interests were so strong, and corruption so pervasive, that mining was still allowed in these designated protected areas. It was a story that applied in many other parts of Madagascar as well, the research students glumly pointed out. Even though the island was suffering terrible environmental destruction, the small patches of unique wilderness that remained were under serious threat. While the theme was certainly not new, it was a depressing conversation all the same.

After a few more days in Ranomafana, I almost reluctantly left the area, knowing that if I ever returned, the park would probably be in much worse shape that it was now. But it was time to get back into one of the hot, uncomfortable, grimy minivans and head toward my next major destination: another famous national park called Isalo. This required a full day and a half's slog. I broke up the discomfort by staying a few days in Fianarantsoa, a city along the way, known for its charming colonial section.

Isalo National Park is in the island's central high plateau. This is an arid region of low mountains and large sandstone canyons with colorful rock formations of layered sandstone. Though Isalo is a drier area vegetated mostly by various types of scrub, it still is home to over a dozen species of lemur and a wide variety of other wildlife.

I enjoyed hiking in the arid mountain plateaus of Isalo, which were a nice change from the dark, wet rain forests of Ranomafana. The most common lemur in the park is the ring-tailed. They are large and slender, weighing almost five pounds, about a foot and a half long, with gray and sandy-colored bodies, narrow faces, and foxlike muzzles. Their most striking feature is their tails, which are much longer than their bodies and ringed with black and white stripes. Some, apparently, have gotten accustomed to the small but steady flow of hikers through the area. While I took a pause during a hike along a streamside trail in a narrow canyon, a baby ring-tailed lemur sitting in a tree overhead actually crawled down onto my back when I wasn't looking.

Isalo also features quite a large variety of other types of life, including some strange but very pretty insect life. My favorite insects were the flatid leaf bugs, which look like little soft, creamy-white seeds with thick, hairy white strands. I was also interested in the culture of the Barra people who live in the park. The Barra practice another type of famadihana, different from that of the people near Antsirabe.

The Barra, I had learned, bury their dead in sturdy wood-and-metal caskets without mummifying the bodies. The casket with the deceased is then set into a small cave in a mountain. After three to five years, there is a famadihana ceremony, in which the casket is removed from the cave. The only remains of the deceased, which are the bones (since the flesh has long since rotted away), are removed from the casket in a touchingly respectful way. Each bone is distributed to one of the extended family members or friends in attendance, who washes the bone thoroughly in a nearby creek. The bones of the deceased are then reburied forever. Unlike in Antsirabe, I didn't have the good fortune to see a Barra famadihana.

The grinding poverty of the country was readily apparent in Isalo. Shortly after I arrived at the isolated village of Ranohira near the Isalo National Park, I went to the park entrance to pay my US$25 fee for the entrance permit to the park for the next few days. While there, I started talking with one of the two armed park officers manning the small office. A middle-aged man with an open, friendly face, he told me that he and his partner were new there.

Just last week, the two park officers who had been working this office were murdered, he said. "They were attacked in broad daylight. One guard was killed with a spear thrust through his chest, and the other was hacked to death with a machete. The two officers were killed by robbers stealing the relatively small amount of money they collected from foreigners visiting the park."

Hearing about this horrible tragedy made my excitement at getting to see the adorable lemurs seem frivolous. The story was also another of many jarring reminders of the steep uphill battle Madagascar has in preserving the remaining scraps of its amazing natural legacy. The desperate poverty in Madagascar, which cheapens and degrades human dignity there just as everywhere else it exists, doesn't spare those whose work is to help manage the last sanctuaries of the island's biological wonders.

I spent my final two weeks in Madagascar in the southeast and then the extreme southwest of the country. I saw more lemurs and marveled at more strange insects and forms of plant life found only in Madagascar. It was a wondrous but sad experience, for it was only too obvious that the island's inhabitants were on a headlong rush toward destroying their amazing natural treasures.

———

From Madagascar, I caught a flight to South Africa and then on to Jakarta, Indonesia, via Singapore. My plan in Indonesia was for a short visit to West Papua, another land with one foot in the Neolithic age, and still a place of clan wars and some exotic dress styles.

Like Papua New Guinea on the eastern half of the island of New Guinea, West Papua, or Irian Jaya, is a cornucopia of different tribal groups speaking hundreds of different languages. Unlike Papua New Guinea, though, West Papua is not a separate nation but, rather, a part of Indonesia. In the early 1960s, Indonesia forcibly annexed the lands of West Papua, which had been under the control of Indonesia's former Dutch colonial masters.

After annexation, vicious, long-running guerilla warfare against Indonesian rule ensued for decades and continues at a low level today. Some observers have described the actions of the Indonesian government in West Papua as a "slow genocide." Indonesian troops have been accused of indiscriminately shelling villages, even using naval ships to do so, committing massacres, and "disappearing" people. But the Free Papua Movement (OPM), the movement behind the guerilla war, has been known to target outside Indonesian civilian settlers into the region with violence. More than 150,000 people (over 1 percent of the population), many of them civilians, are estimated to have been killed in the long-running guerilla war.

Because of the protracted conflict in West Papua, the Indonesian government kept outsiders from entering the province for years. Only in the past decade or two has the area started opening up to visitors and tourism. To get into many parts of the island still requires a government-issued permit. Now that it was possible to travel legally in West Papua, I was looking forward to my short visit. It would be another chance to do some time travel, visiting peoples whose life patterns, beliefs, and day-to-day activities still harked back to the Stone Age.

After flying into West Papua, I got my government permit and soon was trekking in an area called the Baliem Valley, located in the Central Highlands. This is an area so remote that until just before the Second World War, it was believed to be uninhabited. Just before the war, reconnaissance flights saw tribal people in the valley, and the peoples of the Baliem Valley were "discovered."

The Baliem Valley is home to villages of mainly Dani, Lani, and Yali tribal people. Many of the tribal people in the region live a fair distance from the main town of the valley, Wamena, and have had only limited contact with outsiders. This is partly because there are no roads from Wamena to much of the surrounding valley. Until recently, the Dani were considered fearsome warriors and headhunters. Along with the Lani and Yali, they still live lifestyles rooted in their deep traditions. Today, it is estimated that around 100,000 Dani live in the valley, along with lesser numbers of the other tribes.

My trek started on a dirt path a few miles out of Wamena, and my main destinations would be villages of the Dani tribespeople. I was with a grubby-looking man named Janus, whom I had met in Wamena and who acted as my guide. I hadn't much time to get to know Janus before we started, though. Like many of the men in the area, he had badly stained teeth from incessantly chewing betel nut. He also smelled as though he hadn't bathed in many days. But he spoke very good English, was friendly, and seemed knowledgeable.

We hiked under bright, sunny skies along the path through grassy fields with low scrub and patches of forest, often passing neatly tended fields of taro and sweet potatoes. Here and there along the path stood wooden houses, each with a small food garden behind it. At times, the going was challenging on muddy, slippery paths that sometimes ran along the tops of high, narrow ridges.

Soon after our trek started, I saw that the ecosystem of the Baliem Valley appeared much like that of the Tari Highlands. This was not surprising since the Baliem Valley lies in a system of mountain ranges that extend into the Central Highlands of the Papua New Guinea side of the island. The Baliem Valley is set in forested highlands ranging from around 5,000 feet to 7,000 feet, with some peaks over 10,000 feet, as in the area around Tari.

After a couple of hours of hiking, while walking along a narrow dirt path, Janus and I saw a naked man approaching us on the pathway ahead. He was carrying a long spear and had what appeared to be a smaller spear protruding from his lower midsection.

The naked man had seen me, the white foreigner, from afar. Curious, he came up to us and greeted Janus in the local language. I noticed that the man was tall for the area, appeared to be of early middle age, with a very strong, well-defined musculature and a friendly face. Unusual for the area, he had very good and clean teeth. He was naked but for a small thong around his buttocks, which held a long, narrow penis gourd sticking perhaps eighteen inches straight up from his crotch. In one hand, he was carrying a long stick that looked like a spear, which, I learned, was for tending the small crop garden behind his house.

The man spoke to Janus.

"He wants to invite you to his house," Janus explained. "It is down the road, in the same direction we are going."

All three of us walked together down the path. The man courteously took hold of the backpack I was carrying and lugged it to his house, which had small crop fields next to it and was surrounded by grassy fields full of brush. There, we sat on the small, clean wooden porch on the side of his house and talked.

"This man is from the Dani tribe," Janus said, interpreting for me. "He is from the village down the road, where we are going. He prefers living alone in his house by this path, though, rather than behind the walls of the village. His wife died unexpectedly, and he has no children."

"He asked me where you were from and how many children you have," Janus continued. "I told him you were from America and had a wife but no children."

It was no surprise to me that one of the first questions I should hear from a local villager concerned the number of children I had. The people I had met from more traditional cultures almost invariably placed a high priority on the number of children a man had. Compare this, for example, with the usual initial question from someone in the modern world: "What do you do?" It was just one of those many recurring simple things I noted every time I did this sort of time travel in my journeys.

The conversation went on for a while, with the man and me both asking each other questions while Janus interpreted. The man seemed lonely to me, and a bit sad. I didn't ask directly but gathered that his wife had died recently and that perhaps the man was still quietly grieving.

Reluctantly after about three quarters of an hour, Janus and I got up to continue to the nearby village. The man once again hoisted my pack and lugged it down the road. He went with us for about a quarter hour, then returned my pack, said good-bye, and turned back toward his house.

Shortly after, Janus and I came to the village. It was set behind sturdy six-foot wooden board walls. A row of simple round thatch-roofed wood huts stood along the walls inside the village, and small pigs wandered around the dirt grounds.

Janus pointed out that here in the Baliem Valley, pigs were a major form of wealth and almost the sole source of protein. He also explained that the walls around the village had been built for protection from warring enemies in the past, as well as to keep the pigs inside. This was all familiar to me from my experiences in the Tari Highlands of Papua New Guinea. Like many highland cultures of New Guinea in general, the Dani at one time lived in a state of chronic warfare with the neighboring villages.

During my trek, I noted many similarities between the Dani with the Huli people in Papua New Guinea. Similar to the Huli and other tribes of the Central Highlands, the Dani had a diet heavy in root starch plants, including taro and many varieties of sweet potatoes, as well other vegetables, greens, and bananas. Also like the Huli, Dani men and women lived separately, though in the Dani villages, women and men lived in separate houses but in the same actual village.

Near the walls of another village I visited on the same day, a high wooden tower stood in a field. It was a simple structure that looked almost like a long, narrow funnel. Long, skinny wooden poles were bunched together to form a tall, narrow base. Near the top, the poles were splayed out in a circular arrangement, with a round platform in the middle. Janus explained that the platform had been used in the past for a man to stand lookout on, watching for approaching enemies. The lookout tower, which did not look that old to me, was a sign of how recently constant conflict had been a part of daily life.

In each Dani village we visited, the style of dress was simple. Many women were mostly naked from the waist up and wore knee-length skirts of thick dried grass. Another type of skirt was made of strands of thin vines, either plain or dyed, wrapped around the waist. Children I saw wore mixes of simple, ragged modern short pants and shirts, and small children wore nothing.

The defining characteristic of male attire in the Baliem Valley region, especially for older men, was the penis gourd. Often a man was totally naked except for this outlandish, almost comical-looking adornment. The Dani penis gourd, or *koteka*, is made from a long, skinny gourd that is hollow at the bottom. The bottom, hollow portion of the gourd is set over the man's penis and sticks straight up. It can be as long as several feet and is held up in place by a thin string wrapped around the man's waist or back (for really long ones). Men of other tribes in the area also wore penis gourds. Some used a thicker gourd, or a thin gourd that stuck straight outward, to the front of the body, rather than upward like the Dani gourds.

The men and women in the villages generally also wore various other adornments, including shells, feathers, flowers, and leaves. For a more ceremonial look, men often wore a white sash about six inches wide, which dropped from the throat down to the waist and appeared to be made of pieces of shiny shell or bone.

A few times, I saw men wearing a headpiece shaped like an upside-down bowl, which appeared to be made from thick strands of woven hair. To carry things, women often wore colorful woven bilum bags, secured by a tumpline from the forehead. The bilum bags in the Baliem Valley were similar to those I had seen in other parts of the New Guinea highlands, including the Tari Highlands.

Each night during my trek, I stayed in a male hut of the village I was visiting. Though the accommodations were perhaps not the most comfortable for a Western visitor, the warm welcome and hospitality were something I was becoming accustomed to in traditional cultures. The hut on my first night was typical: round, with a thatch roof, and a dirt floor covered with a light layer of grass. Simple tools of wood and twine, along with other gear, hung neatly arranged along the walls. A few paper boxes and large plastic liquid containers, artifacts of the modern world, lay haphazardly on the ground along the walls. If the night was cold, the Dani sometimes built fires inside their huts, which meant it could get ridiculously smoky inside since there was no ventilation.

For several days, we trekked through other Dani villages. Though I was essentially an uninvited intruder everywhere I went, almost all the people I met were friendly and welcoming. Along the way, I noticed a strange thing about Dani women, as well as women of the closely related Lani tribe. Some of the older women were missing parts of one or more fingers. Some older women had many fingers missing. I asked Janus about this.

He explained that this was due to a mourning custom. When a male relative dies, a Dani woman colors her hair, face, and body and also has one of her fingers chopped off at the second joint as a sign of mourning.

But this custom was dying out, Janus said, and that was fine by me. Along with other abhorrent practices that women are subjected to in some parts of the world, such as genital mutilation and honor killings among certain ultraconservative Muslim peoples, the custom of removing finger parts from women's hands belongs in the dustbin of history.

On the third and last full day of our trek, we had circled back toward Wamena and visited a small village only a few hours' walk from the town. There, Janus explained, the village elders kept the mummy of a powerful chief who had died around 250 years ago.

As we walked into the village, a short older man who, I assumed, was one of the village elders came out to greet us. He then went back into a hut and carried out the mummy of a man sitting on his haunches. The mummy, which was not wrapped, had been preserved by being smoked and totally dried out. It looked like a whole human smoked jerky.

The village elder invited me to take a photo of it—for a few dollars. It was pretty cheesy, I thought, and a sign that I was near Wamena, where a regular flow of visitors came. But I paid my three-dollar fee and took the requisite photos of the mummy. I also had a photo taken with me standing next to the elder, with the mummy sitting in front of us on the ground, on a block of wood.

Later, back in my fairly modern hotel room in Wamena, I marveled at the resulting photo. In it, I towered over the short, old naked man wearing only feathers and a penis gourd, standing next to his village's moneymaking mummy. I appeared to be a modern giant who had traveled in a time machine back to a bygone era. The image clearly showed the amazing possibility of time travel that is still available to those who venture into the Disappearing World.

CHAPTER 12

Transition and Tragedy

The sun is always behind the clouds.
—Truism

Mid-November 2008
Bangkok

It was a dreary, humid, overcast day in Bangkok when I deplaned into the huge new Suvarnabhumi International Airport. This seemed to reflect exactly how I was feeling as I returned to Bangkok. Dragging badly after my African journey and short trip to West Papua, I felt tired, lonely, worried, and generally disconnected from everyone.

An e-mail I had sent to a friend in California while waiting for my flight from Indonesia back to Thailand captures something of what I felt:

"I am two years into my travel project. My travels for the past 18 months, since May 2007, when I last traveled with Achara, have been almost nonstop and mostly solo. Being alone much of the time can wear on a person, more than I expected. I meet a lot of people in my travels and often socialize with new and interesting people. But hit-and-run encounters with new people, most of whom you'll never see again, is no replacement for the normal healthy interactivity one has with loved ones, friends, and close colleagues."

My relationship with Achara was also a concern. She had sent me happy e-mails when I was gone somewhere, asking when I'd be back in Bangkok and saying she looked forward to seeing me. But when I periodically returned "home" to Bangkok, she was a different person from the one who had sent the e-mails. She would be distant, irritable, and mostly not around. Even though I had been in and out of Thailand regularly for the past year and a half, Achara and I had not been together in any real way for almost a year by this point. Time had gone so fast, and somehow, each opportunity to reconnect had slipped by. I missed her.

Also, I was a long way from completing my objectives in the originally planned three years. This was despite traveling almost nonstop for two years. I wondered if I would even be able to complete my travel project. One reason for doubt was that the Great Recession had hit me hard. Along with the big loss with the mortgage company that I suffered in spring 2007 while in Peru, my investments had taken some other hard hits.

By November 2008, my personal assets were barely half what they had been when my long journey started. The monies set aside for my travel project were gone, and my personal financial situation was badly compromised. I had planned that upon completing my travel project, I would have resources to buy a home and finance some kind of new business venture. After my absence from the workforce for so long, my career path would probably not be so viable. So starting my own endeavor of some sort seemed the logical choice. Now that possibility was in serious jeopardy.

Also, I was suffering from chronic sharp pain in my left shoulder. I had hurt my shoulder doing one of my improvised travel exercise regimens earlier in the year. Rather than healing, though, the pain got progressively worse, to the point that I could hardly even hold anything with my left hand. I hoped that rest would help.

Sorting out my situation with Achara was my first priority for this time. I had planned a family gathering in Florida over the Thanksgiving holiday period. My brother and his wife, who lived there, and I were taking our mother on a Caribbean cruise (not my kind of deal, but I figured my mother would love it). Achara, her aunt and uncle, and my aunt Gwen would all be going, too. It seemed a perfect way to make my mother happy and have a romantic reconnection time with Achara.

I had five days in Bangkok before my flight back to Florida. Achara was out of town, in training in the north of Thailand, so I would reunite with her when she flew to Florida. Along with having some fun dinners with Achara's mother, aunt, and cousins, I used my short downtime in Bangkok to come up with solutions to my challenges.

First, I reaffirmed my commitment to continue with my travels despite the challenges. Quitting was not really in my nature. My whole life had come to a screeching halt for this project. Everything I owned was in storage, and this opportunity would never appear again. And waiting to travel long-term in "retirement" someday was out of the question since much of what I wanted to see would be gone, no longer recognizable, or no longer genuine.

I also decided to extend my travel time for another half year, envisioning completion in summer 2010. It made no sense to do a project halfway. At that point, in late 2008, I would have laughed at the idea of actually extending my travel project all the way to the end of January 2012, which was what I ultimately would do.

After reaffirming my commitment to press forward, I had to deal with the wreckage of my finances. For this, I needed time to concentrate and focus. So I opted to spend the first quarter of 2009 in Bangkok and use the time to deal with my financial challenges. I also figured that the time in Bangkok would be good for Achara and me. And I would study French intensively at the Alliance Française in Bangkok—a basic command of French would be invaluable on my upcoming travels in Central Africa.

After this brief five days in Bangkok strategizing how to complete my travel project, I flew to Florida, reinvigorated and ready for a nice reconnection with Achara on the cruise.

But the family gathering in Florida and the cruise turned out dismally for me. My mother had a great time, which was good. And everybody else—Achara and her aunt and uncle, my aunt, my brother Paul, and his wife—all seemed to enjoy it, too. But Achara and I did not get along well, and she became even more distant. At nights, rather than joining me, she would stay out until late with her aunt and my aunt in the casino. We had a comfortable, nice-size cabin, where I basically spent the nights alone. The gulf between us was growing ever wider.

The night after we returned from the cruise, we all had a farewell Thanksgiving feast at my brother's house near Fort Lauderdale. After our turkey dinner, I asked Achara to take a walk with me in the neighborhood. It was a warm evening with clear skies and lots of stars. As we strolled past the neatly manicured lawns of my brother's gated community, Achara and I had what seemed our first honest conversation since our time together in Papua New Guinea, back in May 2007.

It's amazing how so many relatively unimportant issues can become real irritants when two people in a relationship don't communicate well over a long time. We had a number of these petty grievances, but all were things we could agree to put aside or move on from. The real challenge, though, was different.

"It is true that I resented your selling our home in L.A. for a long time," Achara said matter-of-factly. "I don't like being without a home, as I had said before we left L.A. I got over it, though. But now I'm at home in Bangkok, and I'm happy there."

We were walking around a small, grassy park area where some people were walking their dogs. It seemed such a thoroughly American neighborhood.

"I love being with my family, and I don't want to be without them again," she said. "And I'm really happy with my job. I am finally getting my career started. What I do makes me feel as if I matter."

I mentioned that I liked Bangkok and Thailand and loved her family but that Thailand could not be my home.

"Yes, of course. You are American, and Los Angeles is your home," Achara replied quietly, knowing that this simple logic pointed to an irresolvable situation. "I'll always love you, Gary. But Thailand is my home."

And that was how we left it. We both kept an imaginary door open to somehow finding a solution to the obvious dilemma. Neither of us brought up the logical end result of what our dilemma meant. It was as if not talking about it made the intractable problem go away.

Achara and her aunt and uncle flew back to Thailand the next day. I would return to Bangkok a week later.

———

Suvarnabhumi International Airport in Bangkok was eerily dark, like a ghost town. It was late evening, and I had just arrived on an almost empty Thai Airways 747 jumbo jet on my return from the States. The handful of other passengers and I were shepherded down long, unlit walkways. The cavernous international terminal, normally an ordered pandemonium of bustling passengers scrambling toward the immigration stands, was empty and unnaturally silent.

Thailand was roiling in crisis yet again. The highway to the international airport had been blockaded, and the airport occupied for the past couple of weeks by huge crowds of antigovernment protestors referred to as the Yellow Shirts. The Yellow Shirts, so called for the yellow knit shirts they all wore, were stepping up their campaign to topple the government by paralyzing key functions of the government and capital. The week before, when Achara and her aunt and uncle had returned to

Thailand, their flight came into an alternate airport on a military base, which was being used to take some passenger flights.

Since Thailand was like a second home for me, it was sad to see the land of smiles in such a state. The crisis had been triggered back in the fall of 2006, with a military overthrow of then prime minister Thaksin Shinawatra. One of Thailand's richest men, Thaksin made his power base with populist policies aimed at the poor majority of Thai people, who had been left out of the country's great economic gains of the past two decades.

Many of Thaksin's policies did help alleviate poverty, and the government's finances improved on his watch. But his administration faced allegations of serious corruption and electoral fraud, and Thaksin was personally involved in high-profile suspect transactions as well as possible large-scale tax evasion. After his overthrow, Thaksin financed his supporters' party from exile. His supporters became known as the Red Shirts for the red knit shirts they wore at mass protest rallies. The inept military junta that ran Thailand was pressured to allow elections, and Thaksin's party won. The opposition to Thaksin's party, including the Yellow Shirts, then took up mass protest tactics, including the blockade of Bangkok's international airport, to try to bring down this new Thaksin-backed government.

During December in unsettled Thailand, I spent most of my time on the pretty southern Thai island of Koh Samui. There, I planned how to take advantage of an opportunity to deal with my financial challenges. The U.S. stock market had tanked big time over the previous year. It was hitting lows that I had assumed I would never again see in my lifetime, and presented a huge opportunity. So I called a friend of mine, the trading room manager at the bank where I used to work, and asked him about the situation.

"This is the opportunity of a lifetime," my friend Todd said emphatically. Todd had been in the professional trading game for most of his twenty-five years with the bank. He also traded stocks very seriously on his own account and had done very well for himself.

"It is unbelievable how low the prices are right now on many of America's best companies," Todd continued. "Some, like Deere and Company, Caterpillar, Dow Chemical, DuPont, Eaton, Merck, Pfizer, Textron, Harley Davidson, GE, Ford, and many more are at prices half or even a third of where they were. I'm buying all I can at these prices and will continue to do so."

So I did the same. I started putting all the money I had received from the equity out of the sale of my home when I started this travel project into blue-chip stocks like the above-named companies. I made these purchases through December, January, and February. I was making a long-term bet on my belief that America would eventually come roaring back, as it always had done in times of deep adversity. I also subscribed to the logic that the best time to buy things is during panics, when everyone else is selling. It was actually the only way I could see to salvage my financial situation adequately to continue my travels and be in a reasonable position upon completion of my travel project.

In hindsight, I bought a bit early. The stock market actually hit rock bottom on March 2, 2009, when the S&P 500 index briefly touched 683. But my timing was good enough. Anybody who bought during those times ended up doing very well over the ensuing years as the stock market staged a powerful recovery. Prices of countless beaten-up but solid companies doubled or even tripled over the next three years. Although I picked some turkeys (such as Bank of America, which continued to drop like a rock after I bought), my overall bet worked well enough to let me continue traveling, recover much of what I had lost, and gain some peace of mind.

I returned to Bangkok shortly before the New Year. My intensive French courses would be starting soon. Since I would be staying in Bangkok for at least three or four months, I mentioned to Achara's mother the first night I was back that maybe I should rent my own apartment in the city. This didn't go very well.

"You don't like it here in my home?" Achara's mother asked in surprise. When I tried to explain that I didn't want to take advantage of her always wonderful hospitality toward me, she interjected decisively. "When I come to America, you take care of me. When you are in Thailand, I take care of you. No problem. You are family."

I didn't press it with her further. Instead, I brought it up with Achara the next evening. I figured it was only fair to give her some space since we were effectively apart anyhow, staying in separate rooms even at her mother's home. This didn't go over well, either.

"Why do you want to go rent a place here in Bangkok when you have a nice home right here?" Achara said. "Plus, how would that look to the rest of the family if you rent a place here in the city? It is okay if you buy a place, as my family believes in buying property. But if you rent, it would appear as if we put you out and did not give you the proper hospitality as part of our family. You are family, Gary. My home will always be your home, no matter what."

So I dropped the issue, and in the long run, I was glad I did. I loved Achara's mother, aunt, and family in general. All of them, Achara's mother in particular, provided a stable, wonderful, warm place of welcome for me to look forward to as I traveled. This helped me complete my travel project in more ways than they could imagine.

Shortly after these conversations about my (not) getting my own place in Bangkok, I decided to buy a New Year's gift for Achara's mother. I wanted to do something to express my appreciation to her for the wonderful hospitality. Usually, since Achara's mother enjoyed good food, I did this by taking the family out to a nice dinner. But this time, I opted for a fun surprise. Achara's mother had a passion for cooking, so I went to one of the most fashionable malls in Bangkok and bought her an expensive high-quality German knife set for her kitchen. This simple gift, though, became an object lesson in the minefield of cultural differences.

The evening I bought the knife set, I discreetly brought it into my mother-in-law's house. During the night, I placed it in a prominent location in the kitchen. I figured Achara's mother would see it the next morning and have a really happy surprise. But the next morning, I was the one to be surprised. Arising shortly after dawn, I came out of my room and walked into the family den. The morning light was shining pleasantly through the big window, lighting up the hardwood floors.

The knife set was sitting on a table in the den. Achara and her mother, in their bathrobes, were standing next to it. Both looked as if someone had just died.

"*Why* did you give my mom a *knife set*?" Achara asked angrily as I walked out of my room. She pronouncing the words "knife set" as if this were something unsavory or dirty.

"Well, I thought your mom would like it, of course," I said, dumfounded at their reaction. "I thought it would be a nice addition to her kitchenware. She loves to cook, and I noticed that all her present cooking knives were an ad hoc collection and some were getting old."

"Is there something wrong with it?" I asked. "These are very high-quality knives, from what I could tell. The salesperson in the store where I bought them told me they were from one of the top knife makers in the world."

Achara and her mother just stood there and looked at me for a moment in silence. The air was so thick, you could cut it with one of those fine, sharp knives I had bought.

"You shouldn't have gotten such a thing for my mother," Achara hissed. "Don't you realize that that giving a Thai person a sharp object as a gift is believed to bring bad luck onto the recipient and their household?" She was incredulous, as if any village idiot knew this.

"These are standard household cooking utensils," I explained. "And no, how could I possibly even remotely *imagine* that such a thing would be considered bad luck?"

Achara and her mother then quietly, almost mournfully, walked away from me. They left the damning knife set, all set up with the gleaming new knives in a beautiful wood block, on the table in the den. Crestfallen, I went back into my room.

About an hour later, Achara and her mother came back into the den and called me.

"There is a solution to this problem," Achara said, with evident relief. "My mom will buy the knife set from you for a small price of ten baht" (about thirty U.S. cents).

"If we buy knife set," Achara's mother explained, "then it not bring bad luck on my household."

Relieved that the situation was resolved, I happily accepted the tiny ten-baht coin from Achara's mother.

Unfortunately, another problem that had arisen would not have such a good resolution. The Great Recession in America and much of the West had its tales of tragedy. Stories had even been in the news over the past year of prominent financiers committing suicide after presiding over large losses. The day after the knife gift drama, the evening before New Year's Eve, I called to check on a good friend of mine in Los Angeles who was having serious difficulties.

"I'm not good, Gary," my friend Jake (not his real name) replied when I asked him how he was doing. His voice was haunted and distant—this was not the hard-nosed, no-nonsense guy I knew. Jake was a senior vice president and attorney at one of the major motion picture studios in Los Angeles. He lived in a nice neighborhood in West Los Angeles, on the edge of Beverly Hills.

Jake was extremely analytical, almost Spock-like. We had done a few investments in some real estate partnerships where he had analyzed every angle to death, and he was similarly careful and conservative in almost everything he did. His consistency and judicious investing over the years, and the high income from his law career had made him modestly wealthy, and he was aiming for early retirement in his late fifties.

Jake had seen huge opportunity in the Great Recession. Banks had essentially stopped lending money, even to highly qualified home and property owners with good credit and lots of equity. So Jake implemented an investment scheme that involved him personally borrowing money at rock bottom rates and lending at double-digit rates to these types of property owners. He put most of his assets on the line as collateral for a US$2 million personal line of credit, through a banker I had originally referred to him for an earlier transaction. Jake even tried to get me to put up my home sale money and partic-ipate in his deal (which did seem brilliant), even calling me a coward for refusing. But his scheme didn't fit my situation. I was always away traveling, often completely out of touch. Also, I took a more cautious view of his plan and stayed out of this deal.

This was a good move for me because his project backfired dramatically on him. Within the past four months of 2008, Jake went from a comfortable, almost debt-free position with close to US$5 million net worth to facing bankruptcy. My bulldog attorney friend had just folded like a house of cards and fallen apart.

"There's no hope now. . . . I don't know what to do," Jake continued. "I can't sleep and have not slept, it seems, for almost three months. I can't even go the store now to buy food, because I feel paralyzed. I'm looking at bankruptcy, and there's no way out."

I tried to get him to calm down, saying maybe we could analyze his situation rationally together. I had already tried to do this with him on several previous phone calls, the last one being about three weeks earlier. I also asked him if he had tried exercising and running to help relieve his stress. (He was a regular jogger.)

"There's nothing to analyze, Gary," Jake replied. "And I've stopped running. I can't even *move* anymore. I'm even having bizarre thoughts about killing myself. *Me!* I could never have imagined thinking such a thing before."

Jake and I had been friends for over fifteen years. He was a bachelor, older than me and with quite a different personality type, but we had strong ties. Jake had acted as my attorney in fact, for instance, when I sold my home at the start of my travel project. The home was put up for sale before Achara and I started traveling, but didn't sell until late April 2007, when I was going to be in Papua New Guinea. He also was storing some of my most personal papers at his home for me. These included a copy of my will, my birth certificate, banking, stock, and other financial records. I had been storing much of this stuff in a safety-deposit box, but for various reasons, Jake had said I should just keep them in storage in his home while I did my long travels.

"There is something you can do, Gary," Jake said, perking up a bit. "Do you know anybody who might know a good psychiatrist? I never told you, but I've been seeing two for several months. They have me on all kinds of powerful pharmaceutical antidepressants and sleeping pills. They're fucking me up, and I want to get off them. I believe they are making me think about killing myself. I'm certainly not going to kill myself, but I don't trust the two shrinks I'm seeing now."

"Just stop taking those drugs," I urged. "You don't need that garbage!"

"I want to stop, but it's actually more dangerous to stop cold turkey," he explained. "Do you know anybody who might be competent in these pharmaceuticals?"

"My aunt would probably know someone," I told him. "But she's on a two-week cruise, so I'll have to wait till she gets back to contact her. Just sit tight. This will all work out."

I called my friend again the next day, December 31, New Year's Eve. I didn't want him to feel alone on the holiday. But he didn't answer his phone. Nor did he answer when I called on New Year's Day and several times that next week.

On January 9, I got an e-mail from Jake's brother-in-law in Pasadena, California, informing me that on January 3, 2009, Jake had put a gun to his head and shot himself.

It was morning in Bangkok when I got the news of Jake's suicide. After getting over my initial shock, I called his brother-in-law, Peter, in Pasadena, where it was evening. We talked about our mutual shock for a while, and Peter described to me what he knew about Jake's death. Then I asked him if he could pick-up the boxes with my personal papers at Jake's house and keep them safe for me.

"I'd be glad to, but this isn't possible," Peter replied. "Just before Jake shot himself, he scribbled out a one-line will naming his four-year-old son, Brandon, the sole inheritor of his estate. The day after Jake's body was discovered, a court appointed Eunice, Brandon's mother, executor of Jake's estate. She won't even let me or Jake's sister onto the property!"

This news represented a direct threat to my security. Jake was not as analytical in his sexual exploits as he was in everything else. Five years before, he had met an apparently very sexy woman at a party and taken her home for a one-night stand. This resulted in a baby boy. While Jake accepted responsibility for the child, including stiff child support payments and shared custody, the situation was a horrible nightmare for him.

Eunice was, to put it charitably, an unhinged human being—"a crack whore" was how Jake put it—who did drugs and was always in trouble, having auto accidents, and getting fired from her various jobs as a nurse's aide. I had never met Eunice in person, though I had heard her screaming irrationally on the telephone at Jake many times when I was at Jake's home over the four years before his suicide. She worked the court system and jerked Jake around, squeezing extra money from him at every turn.

I got Eunice's telephone number from Peter and called her. I introduced myself and explained that I had some boxes at Jake's home with some personal travel gear and a few things of personal importance. Since I was in Thailand at the moment, I asked if I could have a friend stop by to pick them up. I did not let on exactly what was in the boxes, though.

Perhaps sensing an opportunity, or perhaps just because she was plain mean or greedy, she blew me off and hung up.

This was a serious problem. This nasty woman could have access to all my most intimate financial records and even a copy of my birth certificate. She seemed the type who might sell it to criminals who could then use the stuff for identity theft. That night (morning in L.A.), I called an attorney friend of Jake's who specialized in probate law. I explained to him my situation and asked him how to get my stuff back.

"The probate courts could take a year or more to handle the final disposition of all things involved in Jake's estate," the attorney explained. "The child's mother will have plenty of time to go through your papers and do damage if she is so inclined."

I then had Jake's attorney friend refer me to a criminal lawyer. I reached the lawyer an hour later, well after midnight in Bangkok, and explained my situation.

"What charges could I face for breaking into and entering Jake's home and taking my own possessions?" I asked.

"If you were arrested in the act, it might be hard for a prosecutor to make a serious charge stick, other than trespassing," the attorney opined. "After all, you are merely stealing your own things." He then added, "However, I strongly suggest that you not get caught by the police."

While I appreciated this last piece of sage advice, I presumably would have guessed this much on my own.

I then bought a ticket on the next Thai Airways flight from Bangkok to L.A. It left around eight a.m.—six hours later. The air ticket was expensive to buy at the last minute. But no matter—I had to break into Jake's home right away to recover my goods.

I arrived in Los Angeles at midmorning, rented a car, and went straight to the house of Jake's next-door neighbor. A nice, relatively young retired man lived there. I had gotten his name and number from

Jake's sister and called him just before my flight. After I introduced myself and explained my situation, he agreed to help me.

When I got to Jake's neighbor's house, we spent a few moments in his kitchen, talking about the tragedy. He then showed me out to his backyard. It was a cool, overcast day outside. Birds were chirping in the jacaranda trees. Everything seemed so calm and peaceful—a stark contrast to the inner tension I felt over what I was about to do. I created a small hole through the tall, thick hedges that separated the neighbor's home from Jake's, using rope to tie off the lowest branches. I then crawled through the hole onto Jake's property.

Silently, I made my way through Jake's backyard, passing behind hedges and the high wood fence that, I hoped, was shielding me from the eyes of any curious neighbors. I went to where Jake kept a hidden key to a second-story back door that led directly to his master bedroom—the room where he had shot himself. I had an attaché case with a few personal papers and a supply of antibiotics and malarial medications stored in his bedroom closet. I figured that once I was inside, I could retrieve a key, which hung in his kitchen closet, to the storage garage under his house. My most important things were in several boxes in that storage garage. But if I couldn't find the hidden key(s), I had some tools with me to break into the house and storage garage.

To my relief, the key to Jake's second-story back door was still in its hiding place. I took it and, to keep a low profile, crawled up some steps to the second-floor back door and let myself in.

Jake's master bedroom was eerily quiet. It was creepy being in the room where my friend had shot himself only a few days ago. I could tell that the room had been cleaned by a professional service that dealt in such things. But the room still showed obvious signs of the tragedy. A big corner section of the headboard of Jake's king-size bed had been cut away. It was obvious to me that this was where my friend had sat when he shot himself. The wall behind his bed, where debris from his head had splattered, had been meticulously whitewashed. Blood splotches and stains were still evident all over, though. It must have been a hideous mess.

I hunted around in Jake's closet but couldn't find my attaché case. I then rummaged through his entire house, searching anywhere it might have been moved. Perhaps ridiculously, I used my shirt to wipe every surface I touched, to avoid leaving fingerprints. It felt strangely intrusive to be going through my friend's place in such a way. I also searched at the same time for the key to the storage garage. This, too, had been moved.

I never found my attaché case. But I did find the key to the storage garage, saving me the hassle (and added risk) of breaking into it. Thankfully, my boxes in Jake's storage area were still there and intact. I could tell by the undisturbed dust layer on each box that they had not been opened for a long time. These boxes contained my most critically important things. Quickly and quietly, I brought them, one by one, to the small hole I had made in the hedges. Shoving them through, I made my exit. I then removed the rope that had held the branches of the hedges open for me.

Later that same evening, I was on a Thai Airways flight back to Bangkok.

———

Back in Bangkok, I pursued my daily intensive French-language classes at the Alliance Française organization located there. One of my classmates at the Alliance Française, a powerful bodybuilder type named Ross, was also a long-term traveler from the States. A competitive judo practitioner who sported a military-style buzz cut, Ross was thirty years old and had been traveling for three years by this time. He was the first person I met in my travels who had been in the wind for so long.

Ross had lived in New York City and had done well in a small IT-related business. This allowed him to save some money and travel. Although he was very much a budget-oriented traveler, which kept him on more mainstream destinations, mostly in Asia, I quickly grew to appreciate his sharp mind and keen insights into the societies that he visited. He was very studious, researching in depth the various countries he planned to visit. More often than not, he also tried to learn the nation's language. At the time we met at the Alliance Française, Ross could get around in as many as thirteen different languages, including Mandarin, Japanese, Korean, Malay, and Thai. I found this amazing.

We got on very well almost immediately. Ross and I both had strong personalities, were serious travelers and voracious readers on international matters, and were exercise buffs. I would join him regularly at his apartment gym to exercise, and we often went out in Bangkok, where he introduced me to several of his friends. We made a good bond, and I knew that we would end up meeting several times in various places over the coming two years. The first such place would be Mongolia in July, for the country's big national Naadam Festival holiday, which centers on a set of competitive tournaments in wrestling, horsemanship, and archery. Even though it wasn't on my travel plan, Ross had convinced me to change my plans and join him there. I welcomed this chance to have a new travel friend and saw it as part of a more social dimension that I could really use in my travels going forward.

During this "settled" period for me in Bangkok, a big life change took place—at least on paper. Achara and I had to become officially divorced, thanks to the bizarrely twisted rules of the U.S. Citizenship and Immigration Service, or USCIS (which everyone, including our immigration attorney, still called the Immigration and Naturalization Service, or INS).

Achara's work with the Thai Ministry required her to travel quite often, including to the United States. Being married to me and having lived in the States for years, she had a green card, of course. (A green card is officially an *Alien Permanent Residence Identification Card* and shows that the foreign national has the right to reside and work in the United States). But since Achara had been out of the country for a couple of years, she no longer qualified for her green card. Her entry into the United States for the Florida cruise was the last time she would be allowed to use her green card.

Even though Achara was married to me, I learned, during a long telephone conversation with our immigration attorney in L.A., that she would not actually be able to enter the country *under any quickly obtainable visa.*

"The INS does not just allow a foreigner that is married to a U.S. national to enter the U.S.," the attorney said. "Nor will the INS usually grant any normal traveler's-entry visa, such as a tourist or business visa, to a foreigner married to a U.S. national. Instead, the foreigner needs to obtain a 'marriage visa' first, applying from outside the U.S., before being allowed back into the U.S. This process can take up to two years."

I explained to our attorney that this would not work. Achara had an important training assignment coming up that summer in Hawaii and, moreover, needed to be able to get back into the country in general—her work duties sometimes meant she could be called on unexpectedly to go to the States. If a visa issue kept her from fulfilling her duties, it would be a serious problem for her career.

I asked why she couldn't apply for a business visa, since it was official Thai government business that she would be coming to the States to transact.

"I'm sorry, Gary," the lawyer said. "But Achara would most likely be denied a request for any type of visa other than the marriage visa." He explained that the INS's logic was that if a foreign national who is married to a U.S. citizen were allowed to enter the country on another type of visa, the foreign national could then stay in the United States. Once the foreign national—in this case, Achara—was Stateside, she could then file a change-of-status form to apply for a marriage visa. Doing this while in the United States would immediately grant her the right to reside here temporarily while the paperwork was in process and until the marriage visa was issued.

"To prevent this situation, the INS forces a foreign national who is not already in the U.S. to apply for the change-of-status and marriage visa while outside the country, and will almost for sure deny any application for any other type of visa," the attorney said. He went on to point out that since Achara was, in fact, working for the Thai government, she would be presumed to be a resident of Thailand. That meant that under most circumstances, she was not qualified for a green card anyway.

Responding to what seemed some pretty twisted logic, I said, "If I understand you correctly, in essence, even though Achara is married to me, a U.S. citizen, but is a resident of another country, she really has no effective way to gain entry to the U.S. in the short run if she stays married to me? And that even in the long run, she may not be able to gain entry to the U.S. if she intends to maintain her foreign residency?"

"That is not exactly what the law says, Gary, but in effect, that's how it works," the attorney answered. "I'm sorry. As long as Achara is married to you, a U.S. citizen, and continues her present employment situation, she probably has no way to get back into the U.S."

This possibility of Achara's being denied a normal visa to come to the States was a serious problem. It posed a real threat to her new but promising career with the Thai government ministry. She was proving very capable and had quickly been gaining more responsibilities. The scope of many of her responsibilities would have her working with counterparts in the U.S. government and require regular travel to the United States. Of imminent concern was her scheduled month of training for the coming summer, 2009, in Hawaii.

When I later explained to Achara what the attorney had told me, she became quite worried. For the next two weeks, she periodically asked me if I had learned of some type of solution. Each time, she expressed concern about getting a task at work that could require her to go to the United States quickly. She would be unable to fulfill that task. Achara also expressed that it would be very embarrassing for her—and a big career setback, to say the least—if she couldn't attend the summer training in Hawaii, because her request for a U.S. visa had been denied.

To me, the answer was obvious even during my conversation with the immigration attorney: just divorce. Once Achara was unmarried to me, a U.S. citizen, she would then have no problem getting into the country. It would be easy enough at some future time to fill out the forms in the United States and once again become married. But for two weeks, I didn't mention this simple solution to Achara. I knew inside that if we took this step, the following step—filling out the forms to become married again in the United States—would never happen.

When I finally mentioned this simple solution to Achara, she didn't respond. For the entire week, she stopped asking me about the issue when I saw her. Then one night, she brought the issue up.

"Maybe we should just go ahead and put in the divorce papers," Achara said matter-of-factly. "We can always just fill out marriage forms later to marry again."

And that was it. Our marriage, fittingly, was ended to ensure that no obstacles would occur to Achara's budding career—the same career path that had played a major role in effectively ending our marriage in the first place. In true Thai-Asian fashion, there was no conflict involved, no fighting, no uncomfortable discussion about the relationship needing to end, no settlement fight—nothing. I filled out some forms online for an attorney who specialized in quick, inexpensive divorces. Ten days later, in late February, a package of forms for the divorce arrived for me in Bangkok via airmail from the United States. Achara and I filled out the forms and notarized them at the

U.S. consulate in Bangkok. I then mailed the stack back. It was done.

I knew, though, that it really was done. I had to let Achara go. I knew, of course, that we would never fill out forms to remarry. Nor, I suspect, did Achara really think we ever would.

We never talked about it.

———

I stayed in Bangkok until late April, finishing the introductory intensive French-language course and doing various therapies for my shoulder. I had seen an orthopedic specialist about it in January at Bumrungrad Hospital, a very highly regarded facility. After some tests and an X-ray, the specialist told me I needed surgery to correct the problem. This process could take six months, with a month of pre-op therapy and several months of post-op therapy, which would really set back my travel plans. I got a second opinion at another reputable Bangkok hospital and was told the same thing.

I didn't want surgery. So I did online research about therapies for my problem and devised an exercise program based on what I found. Also, Achara's mother really pitched in to help. Being a strong believer in a holistic approach to health, she had me see a special "Thai chiropractic masseuse" who had been getting good results for her mother (Achara's grandmother) and the family in general. Over the next two months, I underwent twenty hour-long (and rather painful) full-body sessions with this special chiropractic masseuse. Also, every morning for breakfast, Achara's mother religiously made me a juice shake, consisting of lots of organic greens and herbs.

Miraculously, over a two-month span, between the special massages, juices, and my self-directed exercise therapy, my shoulder returned to full strength and use, and the pains went away.

So, despite the turbulence and my sadness about the effective end of my marriage with Achara, my time in Bangkok had at least one favorable result. By late April, it was time to resume my travels. My first stop would be Japan. It was the beginning of new chapters in both my long travel project and my life.

I plunged back into my travels, first with a nineteen-day trip in Japan, then followed by a long road trip across northern Vietnam, and across China, eventually going all the way to China's westernmost major city, Kashgar. From there, I went on to Mongolia in early July to meet Ross for the Naadam Festival. This next round of travels would be virtually nonstop till mid-January 2011. I figured that the constant excitement of new experiences and places would help me forget the recent bumps that had occurred in my life's road. And making the most of this opportunity to carry on in my journeys would justify—mostly—the personal and financial challenges that had come my way during the travel project.

CHAPTER 13

A Rocky Time in Mongolia

Early July 2009
Mongolia

G reen fields of grass stretched forever in all directions, with rolling hills and low mountains in the background. Small cumulus clouds floated in brilliant blue skies above the distant highlands. It was a bouncy, dusty ride as the bus followed the only break in this view: an unevenly paved two-way road that cut through the endless fields. At times, the bus passed small herds of grazing yaks. With their fluffy black hair and long white tails, they looked like the product of an accidental mating of bovines with some sort of gigantic sheep. In other places, brown or white goats with small white horns moved about in the fields.

Riding through this timeless Mongolian landscape, I looked out at a high meadow dotted with perhaps fifteen big, round white tents, known as *gers*. It seemed almost incongruous that seven centuries ago, from this peaceful-looking, sparsely populated land had sprung one of the most ferocious and successful militaries the world has ever known. Under the leadership of Genghis Khan, who ranks among history's greatest mass killers, one of the world's largest empires ever was assembled in an amazingly short time.

Sandwiched between China to the south and Russia to the north, sprawling landlocked Mongolia has historically been populated mainly with nomadic peoples, and even today around 30 percent of its population is still seminomadic. With less than three million people spread over 600,000 square miles, this is the world's most sparsely populated nation. It is also one of the world's poorer nations.

With mountains to the north and the Gobi Desert to the south, Mongolia's heartland is mostly nonarable steppes subject to long, bitter winters. This harsh landscape and climate and the sparse population have led to a strong tradition of hospitality toward any travelers who arrive at a nomadic settlement or ger camp. So although it is difficult to get around, when a traveler arrives at a ger camp he can be assured of a warm welcome with food, shelter, and strong drink.

Three days earlier, I had flown from China into the country's capital, Ulaanbaatar ("UB" for short). UB is a sprawling, tumbledown city of about 1.3 million people—almost half the country's population. From UB, I set out on a short six-day road trip to the country's heartland. Although it is a huge country, I had dedicated only thirteen days on this trip, so there wasn't much time to explore. After this brief jaunt, I would return to UB to meet Ross, the friend and fellow traveler I met in Bangkok. In UB, we planned to enjoy the festivities for Mongolia's biggest national holiday, the Naadam Festival—a series of tournaments in the country's "manly sports" of wrestling, archery, and riding.

My road trip had started early this morning when I caught the bus from a dirty, dusty terminal field at the edge of UB. Getting onto the bus, I sat beside two Western female backpackers, who were among the few non-Mongolians on the bus. As the bus got going, one of the backpackers, a tall Canadian woman with freckles and frizzy blond hair, introduced herself as Gail and asked me where I was headed.

I told her I was off to Karakorum. I had only six days for my road trip, and seeing this ancient capital of the Mongol Empire, an eight-hour ride southwest from UB, would be a good start.

"Maybe you should join us and go to Tsetserleg instead," suggested the other backpacker, a petite but rough-looking young Frenchwoman named Francine. "It's just another two hours on this bus past Karakorum." Pointing to her Lonely Planet guidebook, she said that Tsetserleg, in a beautiful valley surrounded by majestic mountains, was supposed to be the most picturesque of the Mongolian provincial capitals. By contrast, Karakorum was an old, dusty city and not so interesting.

Gail was energetically agreeing with Francine, and it would be nice to have some company, so I decided to join them as far as Tsetserleg. This became a problem, though.

When the bus stopped at Karakorum I told the driver I would pay the difference in fare to continue to Tsetserleg. The driver, whose English was about as nonexistent as my Mongolian, said he wanted double the extra fare. The extra money wasn't much—around four dollars, which I knew he would just pocket himself. But a Mongolian woman sitting in the front of the bus, who spoke decent English, heard him trying to take advantage of my being a foreigner.

"He is cheating you," the woman said to me. She then proceeded to rebuke the driver sharply in Mongolian. At first, the driver shouted back at her. Then several other passengers in the front of the bus, picking up on what was happening, started in on the bus driver. Embarrassed and red faced, the driver motioned for me to pay the proper fare and waved me back to my seat.

The bus rolled on into some jaw-droppingly beautiful green mountains. Two hours later, it came to a stop at a sizeable settlement on a rocky plateau.

"I think this is Tsetserleg," Gail said. There was no sign to indicate the name of the town—not unusual, since none of the small towns along the way had name signs. The passengers who had raised the commotion when the driver tried to cheat me had long since gotten off at earlier village stops, so to make sure we were in the right place, I walked up the aisle to the driver and asked, "Tsetserleg?"

The driver, still obviously angry and embarrassed from the over-charging incident, turned around and gave me a grudging nod. So the two women and I grabbed our things and got off, with the driver glowering after us. The moment we stepped down, the door closed and the bus roared off, leaving us on a rocky turnout under the hot late afternoon sun, engulfed in a cloud of dust and exhaust fumes.

"I can't figure this out," Francine said, scrutinizing the simple map of Tsetserleg in their guidebook. "There's supposed to be an inn run by an Englishman, next to a town landmark on a road parallel to the main drag. But the layout of this town doesn't match the map."

We all looked out at the village. It wasn't a promising sight: a stretch of shabby old one- and two-story wood buildings and shacks on the other side of the rocky open ground where we stood. The map, on the other hand, showed a neatly laid-out town of several roads running in a grid, with a small green park area in the middle. There was nothing like that here. So we wandered around the barren, windswept village under the beating sun, trying to find the inn. Absolutely no one spoke English or could make sense of the guidebook map, so our search for the inn was fruitless.

"This is not Tsetserleg," I said after an hour. "I think the bus driver let us get off here as payback for not being able to cheat me. What a complete asshole, since he also did this to you guys, who had nothing to do with it."

My two companions realized that I was right. Now our challenge was to figure out how to get to Tsetserleg. But since none of us could actually pronounce "Tsetserleg" correctly, none of the locals we met could understand where we wanted to go.

Finally, I went into a convenience store near the town's center, hoping it would carry a map of Mongolia. There, after a few moments of my comical miming attempts to describe a map of Mongolia, the woman working there figured it out and produced a map. Of course, all the writing on it was in Mongolian, so I couldn't read it, but with more comical hand motions, I managed to convey to her to show me Tsetserleg. The woman pointed it out on the map and then showed me where we were: about an hour from Tsetserleg.

Gail and Francine managed to hitchhike with someone who passed by on the main road. There was not enough room for me in the car, though. And since not many cars were passing through this remote, bleak village as evening approached, I ended up having to hire a local guy to drive me to Tsetserleg. I was relieved—I didn't want to be stuck for the night in this dismal place.

An hour later, my driver dropped me off in the center of Tsetserleg. Though obviously poor, it was a neatly laid-out village in a beautiful valley amid rolling green hills and low mountains. The people were very friendly, though almost no one spoke English.

Visiting the Zayain Khuree Monastery, I got a glimpse of what had been a dark time for Mongolian culture, during its days as a Soviet satellite. This old Buddhist temple complex, set in the rolling green hills surrounding Tsetserleg, had been turned into a Communist propaganda museum in the 1930s. Mongolia had become a "socialist republic" in 1924 and remained so until the fall of the Soviet Union in the early 1990s. Starting in 1928, the new leader of Mongolia, as part of a general campaign of Stalinist repression, began systematically destroying Buddhist monasteries and murdering monks. In 1932, Communists killed the head of the monastery and turned the place into a museum.

The museum had several old-fashioned Communist propaganda banners and pennants from Mongolia's Soviet days, with their bold red color, white star, and promise of a better social order. They looked so out of place in this raw, wild, sparsely populated land with its traditions of shamanism and Buddhism. They also seemed quaint reminders of the futility and arrogance of trying to abolish a people's deeply ingrained religious practices and replace them with a belief in rationality, leaving essentially a spiritual void (except, perhaps, for the worship of an all-powerful state). Not surprisingly, after the fall of Communism, Buddhism had a resurgence and is once again Mongolia's majority religion.

Along with seeing the museum, I visited a herders' ger camp not far from Tsetserleg. Gers are essentially collapsible wooden frames covered by heavy layers of felt, with an outer shell of white cotton cloth. They are the traditional homes of Mongolia's nomadic people, and probably what most people picture when thinking of the country. While at the camp, I learned that some of Mongolia's large nomadic population live in conventional houses in towns or villages during the summer, then move to camps and live in gers for the winter to save on heating costs. The reason for this seemed ironic. These traditional tents, a part of life on these steppes for thousands of years, were easier and cheaper to heat through the long, frigid Mongolian winters than modern insulated homes.

During my stay in Tsetserleg, I met two friendly Germans in the restaurant of the lodge where I was staying. Both were athletic-looking men who appeared to be in their early thirties. They explained that they were doing a four-month motorcycle journey that had started in Germany and taken them across Russia and into Mongolia. From Mongolia, they would continue to Manchuria. The two had been sponsored in part by a German sportswear company and were wearing special helmets with built-in video cameras to record their journey. Since they were heading toward UB and would be there when I returned to the city, we agreed to meet again in UB a few days later. I had enjoyed the company of these two adventurous fellows and looked forward to seeing them again.

After six days in Tsetserleg, I took the long, dusty bus ride back to UB and arrived in the late afternoon, dirty and tired. I was looking forward to my comfortable private room in a place called the Happy Guesthouse, which I had reserved online a few weeks earlier.

The instructions on my reservation for the Happy Guesthouse were to go to a restaurant on UB's main road—a wide boulevard called

Peace Avenue. There, according to the online reservation instructions, someone would bring me to the guesthouse. Getting to the restaurant required a short taxi ride from the bus station, which turned into an unexpected hassle. When we got to the restaurant the taxi driver who brought me tried to cheat me by claiming I had to pay an extra fare for my bag. After what became a heated argument, I grabbed my bag and simply walked away, dropping our agreed fare onto the front passenger seat, without any extra for a tip. I was now dirty, tired, and irritable.

The restaurant was a large, airy German-style beer tavern, and its manager, a tall, rough-looking mustachioed German, greeted me. He informed me that the Happy Guesthouse was closed and had been for several months, but if I waited for a while, he would have the guesthouse's owner come to see me. I had to wonder why I was able to make a reservation only weeks ago for a hotel that had been closed for several months.

At about the same time I arrived at the tavern, a young British backpacking couple showed up, also with reservations for the Happy Guesthouse. So I joined them for a couple of beers while we waited.

After about forty-five minutes, the owner of the Happy Guesthouse strolled in. She was a plumpish middle-aged woman, apparently of Chinese descent, who introduced herself as Ochmaa. Plopping down in an empty chair at the table where my new companions and I were sitting, she casually mentioned that her online ad for the Happy Guesthouse was out of date.

"The Happy Guesthouse is now closed," Ochmaa blithely said. "But since each of you has a prepaid reservation, I can offer you one of two other places. One is a small room in an apartment building with a young woman and her child. It is not the nicest place—a little dirty—and the building is old and not so clean, but it is comfortable. Or there is a two-bedroom recently refurbished apartment available."

Ochmaa's bait-and-switch deal was insultingly obvious. But the British couple and I didn't see a lot of choices. It was Naadam Festival time in UB, and finding decent lodgings at anything close to a reasonable price would be tough. So the couple and I decided to share the two-bedroom apartment.

Following Ochmaa's directions, we hauled our luggage down Peace Avenue and through a side alley off of the main boulevard, not far from the city center. We arrived at a slum building with graffitied walls and with bars on the ground-floor windows. We looked at one another and shrugged—it was a pit, but it would do for the night. Our "two-bedroom apartment" was on the second floor of the building and turned out to be a small one-bedroom with a foldout couch in the living room. Naturally, since I was solo, I got stuck with the foldout couch.

I took a quick shower and left the apartment to meet the German motorcycle travelers I had met in Tsetserleg. We had made plans in Tsetserleg to meet this evening at a popular live-music restaurant and nightclub called Strings. It was dusk, but darkness had not yet fallen, so I decided to walk there.

Strings was a bit of a haul down Peace Avenue, away from the city center and then onto a lesser street. Peace Avenue, like the center of UB in general, exuded an ambience of shabby, rundown modernity. It had wide sidewalks, lined mostly with low-rise buildings and a few more modern high-rise buildings. There was a steady traffic flow of old beaters, and the smell of exhaust was pervasive.

Once I turned off Peace Avenue I had to watch my step since sidewalks in UB are often broken or wildly uneven. Also, it's common to see live wires dangling down over the sidewalk from the power lines above. Adding to the hazards of walking in the city, manhole covers are often missing, ankle-breaking potholes can lurk anywhere, and crossing the street is an adventure sport, since drivers can be both drunk and very aggressive.

After about a half hour's walk, I arrived at Strings. It was a large two-story place with a long oval bar and large square dance floor. While a Filipino band played current hits on the little stage behind the dance floor, I took a bar stool next to the German motorcyclists. At first, I just drank bottled water since my new friends were eating and had a bottle of wine for themselves. Then, around eleven p.m., I got a text message from the British couple I was sharing the apartment with.

"We are locked out of the apartment," the text read. "There is a digital security lock at the front entrance to the building. After 10 pm, you need a security code to get in. Ochmaa did not give us the code."

Since there was no way to reach Ochmaa at this late hour, the three of us were effectively locked out of our apartment for the night.

"We will sleep tonight on the floor at a friend's apartment in town," the text concluded.

I sat there digesting this unwelcome piece of news and thought through my options for the night. It was too late to schlep around town hunting for accommodations. UB at night can be a dangerous place for a foreigner on foot. Robberies, muggings, and other assaults on foreigners are not uncommon. Also, the sidewalks, with their potholes and open manholes, are dark in most places. Taking a taxi was not a good option, either, since UB cabbies cheat foreigners obscenely at night. Also, trying to tell a taxi driver where to go, when you yourself don't actually know, is next to impossible without a bit of a common spoken language. Finally, any place I might find that was open and actually had a vacancy would be a terribly expensive proposition.

Trying to keep a good humor in a bad situation, I decided just to stay out all night. I could stay at Strings till closing time at two a.m. and then figure out how to get to an after-hours nightclub I heard about— perhaps by tagging along with some other patrons in Strings who might be heading there. In the morning, I could retrieve my luggage from the apartment and set about finding new accommodations.

I talked with the German motorcyclists until about half past eleven and shared with them a bottle of wine that I bought. I then moved on to talk with a Danish expat, a businessman I had happened to meet when I first came into UB the week before. While I was talking with the Dane a couple of young working girls who had seen me earlier came over to say hello. They seemed nice enough. One was slim and petite, with Eurasian features and tastefully dressed in a rather short skirt. Her friend, also Eurasian looking, had long dark hair and wore a red bodysuit.

I was not interested in their services but suspected that the two German motorcyclists might be. So, to help them find work, I brought the two working ladies across the bar and introduced them to the German guys. I figured that after riding for three weeks in the Mongolian hinterlands, they would probably welcome the female company. They did, and left with the two girls shortly thereafter.

With nowhere to go, I hung out at the bar, talking with some expats and drinking bottled water to pass the time. At closing time, I went to pay my bill for the bottle of wine and two waters I had drunk. As it turned out, the German motorcyclists had skipped on their bill.

"You must pay your friends' bill," the tall, lanky bartender said in halting English. Their bill included a pricy bottle of wine, two full dinners, and several beers, as well as drinks they had with the girls I had introduced them to.

"This is not my bill," I told the bartender. "Yes, I was talking with those two German guys, but I don't know them well."

The bartender then adamantly insisted that I pay the German guys' bill since I had been talking with them for a while.

"Their bill is not my responsibility," I replied. "I have a separate bill for the things I ordered, which I will pay. Nothing more."

This created a very uncomfortable situation for me. Almost everyone who worked there came by and strongly suggested that I pay the two motorcyclists' bill. Although I was soon surrounded by some very hefty, cross-looking bouncers who could have pulverized me in no time, I held my ground.

"Those two were merely acquaintances of mine that I recently met," I said to one of the bouncers, who spoke English. "I am not responsible for the bill of everyone I may have talked to or shared a drink with. I have a bill for the items I did order, and that is all I am paying for."

Finally, the bouncers agreed with me. I paid my own bill and left. (Later that week, I learned that the German motorcyclists were consistent in cheating people. While in UB's central square during the Naadam festivities, I happened to run into the two working girls who had left with the German guys. They had cheated the girls, too—brought them home for the night and then didn't pay them.)

By now all the club's other patrons had left, and I had no one to try to tag along with to the after-hours club. So I just sat on the steps out front of the now-closed nightclub, thinking about what to do until daybreak. While I sat there, a couple of young Mongolian women who were at the other end of the parking lot, waiting to flag a taxi, came over to me.

"Why are you just sitting here, mister?" one of the women asked in the darkness of the empty parking lot. Wearing a slinky short blue dress, she was pretty and perhaps all of 18 years old. Her friend was maybe a year or two older and also attractive. They had bumped into me inside the club earlier that evening and were rather flirtatious. I hadn't paid much attention to them, though, since they basically looked like high-school kids.

I explained my predicament of being locked out of my place for the night. "I was thinking of passing the night in the after-hours club," I said. "Are you two going there now?"

"No, we are tired," the pretty young woman in the blue dress said. "We came to UB from out of town today. It has been a long day, and we want to go to our hotel. You can stay with us in our room tonight if you'd like. It is not a very nice hotel where we stay, but we can make a bed for you from some extra sheets if you don't mind sleeping on the floor."

This sounded good, and I gladly took them up on their offer. Eventually, they flagged a taxi, which took us to their hotel. Once again I had a heated dispute with the taxi driver. Dropping us off at the girls' hotel, barely a third of a mile from Strings, he asked for an outrageous amount—perhaps six times the proper fare. (The girls had forgotten to bargain with the cabbie when we first got in.) This time, I dropped an amount equal to double the normal fare onto the front seat and hustled the girls out of the car and into their hotel while the taxi driver threatened and swore at me.

The next morning, around seven thirty, I quietly got up from my makeshift bed in the corner of the room. Without waking the two sleeping young women, I wrote a note thanking them for their hospitality and left US$22, to pay the cost of the room for the night, on a little table by the door before leaving.

In a couple of hours, I had retrieved my luggage from the unused apartment I had been locked out of the night before, and managed to find a room at a nice guesthouse just off the main boulevard. I then took a walk down Peace Avenue toward the central square, which featured a huge statue of Genghis Khan. Traffic on the wide boulevard was fairly brisk, and lots of people were out on the sidewalks. It was a lovely, sunny morning, and my luck in Mongolia seemed to have changed for the better.

At the corner of a main intersection, about a quarter mile from the central square, I stood on the corner among a growing group of local people, waiting at the light to cross the street. While waiting for the stoplight to turn, a tall man in an old jean jacket who was standing directly in front of me backed very gently into me. Instinctively, I felt a warning jolt of adrenaline. I then had the faintest sensation of a hand in my right side pocket being quickly withdrawn.

I was being pickpocketed!

Instantly recognizing the attack, I looked over to the man on my right. He was of medium height and build, with the weathered look of someone who worked outdoors. I stared down into his eyes and saw a hint of panic as he knew he had been made.

Without delay or even conscious thought, I stepped behind him, grabbing his left hand with mine while putting a choke hold on him with my right arm. He seemed completely shocked by my immediate and violent reaction and made no movement to resist.

"Thief! Thief!" I shouted at the top of my lungs, hoping to draw the attention of the two policemen I had passed earlier just down the street.

I got lucky and somehow managed to trip/flip the pickpocket onto the sidewalk. He landed flat on his back. I then pinned him down, my knee in his neck, and forced open his left hand to retrieve my money. The pickpocket looked terrified and made no attempt to resist. His hand was empty, though—he had apparently withdrawn it from my pocket before getting my money. I double-checked my pocket with my free hand and ascertained that my money was indeed still there.

While I was yelling and pinning the pickpocket, the surrounding pedestrians looked on in surprise but with understanding. Pickpocketing of foreigners is a common scourge in UB.

Still kneeling on the pickpocket's neck, I then looked over to my left at his accomplice, the tallish man who had backed into me a couple of seconds earlier.

I could not believe what I was seeing. The tall thief was punching a short little old woman in a long grey coat! He smacked the woman in the ear and then punched her again in the side of the neck, *and no one did anything to stop him!* I figured that she must have seen what the two guys were doing, since she appeared to be cursing profusely at the pickpocket's tall accomplice.

Reluctantly letting up on the pickpocket I had pinned on the sidewalk, I jumped in front of the old woman to shield her and shoved the accomplice into the street. (Happily, there was no oncoming traffic.) Realizing now that I was very exposed, with one assailant behind me getting up off the sidewalk, another in front of me, and possibly more that I was unaware of, I didn't push it any further. The two pickpockets then quickly crossed the street and dashed off in different directions.

To my astonishment, not one of the dozen people who had witnessed this little drama on the street corner said a thing to me. Maybe this kind of thing was so commonplace that no one gave it a second thought.

Continuing on my way toward the central square to visit Genghis Khan's statue, I was glad to know that my friend Ross, a strong, well-trained judo practitioner, would be in town later in the day.

I didn't actually see Ross until the following evening. The train he took to Mongolia from Beijing was held up at the border crossing for over eighteen hours under temporary quarantine because of the bird flu pandemic plaguing China at the time. So I used the rest of Thursday and most of Friday to poke around Ulaanbaatar before the Naadam Festival's official start on Saturday.

My first sightseeing stop was at Sukhbaatar Square, UB's expansive central square. On the north end stands the imposing white marble and glass Parliament and Government Building. Fronting this is a large monument, also of marble, with tall, round support pillars. In the center of this monument is a huge bronze statue of a seated Genghis Khan, flanked on his left and right by bronze statues, one of his son Ogedei and the other of his grandson Kublai, both mounted on horses set on raised blocks of marble.

On the streets around Peace Avenue near the city center are a few other main boulevards, lined mostly with low-rise and some higher-rise modern buildings. To serve a small but growing modern middle class, a number of newer restaurants, cafés, and even a few chic international-style eateries were doing a brisk trade. I was surprised to find that UB even had a touch of modern nightlife with a couple of nice discotheques.

Venturing away from UB's semimodern core, I started seeing what looked to be a more authentic Mongolian city of mostly older, rougher-looking buildings. Farther out, vast ger camps dotted big sections of the city's periphery, crawling up some of the surrounding hillsides.

As I walked about UB, the country's martial attitude toward life seemed quite evident. Along with the museum and monuments to the country's glorious past, I routinely would see young kids playing wrestling games along the sidewalks.

My friend Ross was with me when the Naadam Festival started Saturday morning. It opened with a grand ceremony that began at the parliament building. Mongolian soldiers marched down the building's steps holding tall horsetail standards—small golden canopies with long, whitish hairs of horsetail hanging from them, held up by a long pole. The horsetail standards were then handed off to mounted soldiers, who paraded them down the street and into the grass field of UB's large main sports stadium. As the horsetail standards were brought into the stadium, a huge orchestra of predominantly female musicians played celebratory music using the *morin khuur*, Mongolia's traditional musical instrument. The morin khuur looks like a squarish violin and is held upright between the musician's legs as the musician bows the strings.

After the horsetail standards were brought into the now very full stadium, the traditional Mongolian *khoomei*, or throat singing, began. An eerie, deep primal-sounding buzz filled the stadium, rising at times to a very high pitch. It was astonishingly loud. Following the throat singing were speeches by the Mongolian president and a host of famous national athletes. The ceremony lasted for a couple of hours, with more colorful pageantry and celebratory music, depicting a mix of both modernity and the ancient traditions soon to be seen in the upcoming sport competitions.

During part of the opening ceremonies, Ross and I went back out of the stadium to the muddy grounds fronting the huge structure. It was like a big family street fair and neighborhood carnival. As we each walked around with a plastic cup of beer, kids played various games in tented stands set up around the stadium.

When the competitive Naadam sports of wrestling and archery started, we headed back into the stadium. The third "manly" sport, the horse-racing competition—actually performed mostly by young boy jockeys—was held in an area outside town.

For me, the games themselves, while demonstrating the remarkable skills of most of the participants, were anticlimactic after the color of the opening ceremonies. I found it hard to get too excited watching people shoot arrows at a target. The wrestling competition—perhaps the main event, was also a surprisingly slow spectacle. Each contest featured two very muscular men inside a relatively small circular area. They would lock together in a standing crouched position, and the match was over when one of the contestants maneuvered his opponent to touch one of his feet outside the circle.

For me, the most fun part of the wrestling came when a winner was announced after each match. The victorious fighter would do a dance in a ritualistic depiction of a great mythical bird taking flight. To a Western observer, these performances by brawny men, doing a sort of slow-motion ballet, moving in large semicircles and flapping their arms gracefully like flying birds, looked a little comical.

The Monday following the weekend of games was a national holiday, and the streets of central UB were very lively. In the afternoon, Ross and I visited Sukhbaatar Square, which was jammed full of people attending outdoor concerts. Later that afternoon, we went to a popular beer pub called Ik Mongol, where we ran into a group of people, including a couple of judo competitors in the Naadam games, whom we had met a couple of days earlier. After a beer or two, I decided to take off from the bar on my own and walk to a popular Western-style restaurant called California, about a half mile down a secondary main street that ran parallel to Peace Avenue. One of the young Mongolian women with the group, who also wanted to eat there, joined me.

It was a sunny early evening when the young woman and I left Ik Mongol. Several people were on the sidewalk, and street traffic was light. As we stepped out of the beer pub onto the sidewalk, a man leaning against the wall of the next building started throwing catcalls my way. He was a tall, weathered, rough-looking guy around 40 years old. Noticeably drunk, the man started following the young woman and me down the sidewalk. As he closed the distance between us, his catcalling grew louder and more belligerent.

"What is his problem?" I asked the young woman next to me, a petite university student named Oyuun.

"He is angry about a foreigner appearing to be with a local lady," Oyuun answered.

The belligerent man kept getting closer and more bellicose.

"Fuck you Americans! Fuck Bush! Fuck Obama!" he called out, along with what sounded like other obscenities in Mongolian.

After a bit more of this nonsense, I turned around and yelled back at him to get lost. He then went into a wrestler's crouching stance, hands up and out, ready to fight.

Before I reacted, though, Oyuun jumped in front of me. "Just ignore this idiot!" she said. "Come, let's go." And grabbing my hand, she urged me to keep walking. We turned and started off again toward the restaurant.

"Let's get a taxi to get away from that louse," Oyuun then suggested.

"No," I said. "It's a beautiful, sunny afternoon, and I'm not going to let some drunken asshole spoil it."

In truth, I also didn't want the hassle of negotiating the fare with a taxi driver. As I had already learned, this silly exercise is obligatory every time a foreigner takes a taxi in UB. At this particular moment, it would have involved clarifying all the fine details of the tiny one-third-mile ride: the total price, that this price would be the total for *both* of us, not per person, that there would be no surcharges, and so on. Negotiating all this with the taxi driver could make me vulnerable since my back would be turned toward the belligerent drunk, who might then attack.

We continued down the street, passing in front of another bar. The drunk persisted, getting very close to us now and screaming obscenities practically into the back of my head.

We were only a hundred yards from the California restaurant when the guy just got too close for comfort. In an instant, I mentally reviewed my options. If I continued walking, he could hit me hard from behind. But if I faced him, signaling a desire to fight, I'd be squaring off against a guy who looked dangerous and was likely trained in wrestling, a fighting skill I had never trained in and that most men here seem to know. Or I could go for a preemptive strike and use the element of surprise to alleviate the threat.

I chose the preemptive strike: go at him immediately and try to put him down.

Turning fast with no warning, I caught the aggressor by surprise, shoving him upward hard into a short flight of four concrete steps that led into a low-rise office building. I was aiming to bash his back into the edges of the concrete stairs, disabling him enough to make him no longer a threat. He toppled backward, crashing on his back near the top of the steps. Adrenaline pumping through me, I leaped onto the steps over him, trying to hit him hard while I had the advantage. I *did not* want him to get up again anytime soon.

But this didn't turn out so well. The drunk did exactly what a fighter on the ground should do: he kicked up and out with his feet and kept moving around to keep his feet aimed toward me. Parrying his kicks as best I could—and they were dangerous because he was wearing heavy, hard shoes—I managed to duck in and downward on him and make a few ineffectual punches to the side of his head.

Unfortunately, while doing this, I was moving around on the steps, and I slipped and fell backward, bashing my right arm on the concrete wall and then whacking my hip and knee as my body slammed into the short flight of stairs on the way down. Not yet noticing the pain from the fall, I popped up, ready to go back at him. By now a bemused group of onlookers had gathered around. Perhaps for the better, the drunk, who had gotten up, decided he had had enough, and limped off in the opposite direction.

Then I noticed the pain. I tried to keep my dignity after my pratfall down the stairs, hiding any sign of the jarring pain in both my hip and my knee. I turned and continued toward California restaurant, doing my best not to limp or otherwise betray that I had sustained any damage.

"Are you okay?" Oyuun asked.

"I'm fine," I managed to say, still breathing heavily and wincing with each step. "Damn it! I wish I'd done a better job at hurting that stupid drunk!" I blurted out, partly in anger at myself for my embarrassing performance.

Oyuun didn't say anything else about the incident. It seemed that what had just happened was an almost normal occurrence in Ulaanbaatar.

To add insult to my embarrassing performance, I realized hours later that I had dropped my high-quality Maui Jim sunglasses. They had been clipped onto my belt and must have flown off during the fight. (The next day I searched the scene of the incident but didn't find them.)

Later that evening, back in my hotel, I was talking with Ross on my cell phone. I told him what had happened and that I was feeling a little glum.

"Like a complete dope," I said ruefully, "I beat myself up worse than anything I did to the drunken idiot!"

Ever the optimist, Ross assured me that I should feel proud of myself for hanging tough in the situation.

"You should just think of it as good practice and experience," he argued. "After all, this was probably the first time you ever fought someone who was trained in wrestling and ground fighting!"

I wasn't convinced.

CHAPTER 14

Staggering Drunk in the Caucasus

September 2009
Pankisi Valley, Georgia

"To Gary, whom we welcome to our homes, and to the deep friendship of Georgia with America!" Saleem Khan proclaimed in a toast as we all held up our shot glasses of vodka. "We all pray that this friendship will result in a stable and secure Georgia that might one day regain territory lost in last year's war with Russia!"

Everyone made hearty sounds of agreement and downed their shots. Saleem was referring to two provinces that Georgia had lost in a disastrous five-day war with Russia last year.

"Everyone in this room will be moving to America if we can join NATO. Indeed, everyone in Georgia will move to America. Do you think America will want us?" inquired Saleem, a big, bald, heavily muscled man with a protruding belly and bear-paw hands.

Saleem was the chief of a village in the hills of the Pankisi Valley in the Caucasus Mountains, at Georgia's northernmost point, on the Chechen (Russian) border. Pankisi is settled mostly by Kist people—Chechens who were born and raised in Georgia. The area gained international notoriety from the wars in Chechnya in the late 1990s and early 2000s, when it was a reputed refuge for Chechen fighters and terrorists battling the Russian army. The Pankisi region had become quite ungovernable for much of that time.

I was sitting in the position of honor at a table of middle-aged and older men. We were waiting for the groom to arrive in a traditional Pankisi-style wedding celebration. Our group was in the groom's living room, in a modern home with wood flooring and red Turkish-looking carpets.

"I am sure that America would welcome such excellent fighters and workers as you in this room," I half lied in reply. In response to this, everyone at the table broke into an excited and frenzied chatter in a language unintelligible to me. They all then held up one hand, with the palm facing toward me. Each man then pointed with the other hand at the upheld hand. This behavior, which I found baffling, was accompanied by more highly animated chatter, this time directed at me.

"They are showing you what hard workers they are," Saleem said. "Notice the deep calluses each one of us has?"

I nodded in agreement. "Yes, these are hardworking men indeed," I said. I did not have the heart to point out that America would not suddenly fling open its doors to all these admittedly hardworking people, whose work consisted of tending their grapevines, goats, sheep, and cattle in the hills of a hardscrabble land in a dangerous part of the world.

The importance of the United States' friendship with Georgia, as expressed by Saleem, was an overriding theme that would come up many times during my travels in the country. This was easy to understand in light of Georgia's precarious position. It had been badly beaten up in the disastrous short, lopsided war with Russia, suffering a humiliating defeat and effective loss of sovereignty over two chunks of its territory. It was a blow that the country had no obvious way of correcting at the time, so the quixotic hope that Georgia's friendship with America would somehow make things right found fertile ground in the national psyche.

While reading about Georgia's history before my travels there, I was struck by its long past of fairly constant warfare to survive as a national entity. Georgia is a small country that historically has always found itself between large, covetous empires. The Greeks, Romans, Persians, Mongols, Persians again, Ottomans (Turkey), Russians, and Soviets were among the highest-profile aggressors. Each of these adversaries dwarfed little Georgia, creating an almost impossible situation for it to prevail against the onslaught.

Perhaps because of its perennially insecure circumstances, Georgia seems to breed men like Saleem Khan—big, sturdy men with big hands and big appetites. Fittingly, considering the country's martial history, fighting, judo, and wrestling are key national sports. And as I had seen on my trip to Mongolia earlier in the year, the practitioners of these martial arts are held in high esteem.

The wedding was held in a banquet room with several long tables and a live band. I enjoyed the mix of modern life, with young women texting or taking photos on their cell phones, and Georgian tradition, with its energetic, romantic wedding dances. In keeping with Pankisi's conservative Muslim traditions, men and women sat at separate tables. But in a sharp departure from traditional Muslim gatherings, the vodka and wine flowed like water, and there was an endless succession of boisterous toasts. As the honored visitor from America, I had to give a short speech after getting snockered from the interminable toasting.

Along with drinking, one of the main activities was people doing the traditional wedding dance called the *kartuli*. In the kartuli, the male and his female dance partner do their movements in tandem, each shadowing the other's movements. The two dancers never touch. Instead, the man maneuvers respectfully around the woman while focusing his eyes exclusively on her. As he does so he holds his upper body motionless while moving his arms in dramatic upward and outward reaching motions, expressing his love and desire for the woman. The man may accompany his dramatic arm motions with stamping his feet several times. The woman, for her part, keeps her eyes looking shyly downward. She moves gracefully, like a beautiful swan, gliding around in sync with the man. The kartuli is difficult, but I loved watching the more skillful examples of this energetic, romantic, stylized pantomime.

The wedding did have one unfortunate incident. During the celebration, the late-model minivan I had ridden to the wedding in was burglarized while parked in the lot outside the banquet hall. I had left my cell phone inside. I had already had a cell phone stolen in the capital, Tbilisi, just a few days earlier, so this was my second one stolen in my first week in Georgia.

My route here since Mongolia had taken me through South Korea and Taiwan, then back to Bangkok for a few days in late August before flying on to Kerala, India. After a fast road trip north along that country's scenic coastline, I made brief visits to Dubai, Cairo, and Istanbul, then flew to Tbilisi.

After five days in Tbilisi, the owner of the guesthouse where I stayed had arranged a ride for me to the Pankisi Valley with his friend, a man I'll call Bakhar, who worked with the UN refugee resettlement project in the Pankisi region. (I managed somehow to forget this wonderful man's name after neglecting to write it in my travel notes at the time.)

During the three-hour drive in Bakhar's UN truck, he talked about the changing refugee situation in Pankisi. He explained that during the terrible Chechen-Russian wars of the late 1990s, many Chechens—ethnic cousins of the Kist people of Pankisi—naturally fled the conflict through the mountain passes between Chechnya and Georgia's Pankisi Valley.

"At the time of the wars, and for a few years after, the Pankisi Valley and Pankisi Gorge probably had some al-Qaeda types and other fighters from Chechnya," Bakhar said at one point. "But today, there are less than a thousand Chechen refugees in Pankisi, and I feel that al-Qaeda no longer operates out of the area anymore.

Bakhar brought me to Duisi, a village on the Alazani River, about a hundred miles from the Russian-Chechen border. The road was hard dirt and rock, and five- to six-foot stone fences lined many stretches. The houses, too, were of stone, with roofs of slate, tile, or corrugated metal. Many of the homes had grape trellises.

Bakhar pulled his truck up to a tall rock fence, behind which stood a big two-story house of stone and mortar. The yard was a riot of greenery, with tall berry bushes, various fruit trees, and what was already becoming familiar: two rows of high trellises supporting many grapevines. A very old woman came over to welcome us. She wore a long, dark wool dress and a headscarf.

"Come in, come in. I Badi," the old woman said. I could tell that she was a warm and hospitable person, and liked her immediately. Badi was also quite energetic and upright, without the stoop that the very old often have. Bakhar left, and she brought me upstairs to a huge, well-worn but nonetheless elegant and warmly furnished room. Though she spoke only a few words of English, she managed to communicate with me well enough.

After settling into my large room, I went downstairs to the courtyard patio for an early dinner that Badi had prepared. She first brought me potato soup with tomatoes in it. Then she brought a small, thick cocktail glass and a dark-brown glass bottle. She poured into the cocktail glass some of the dark-brown liquid, which was her own homemade wine.

"*Paye!*" she said. The youthful, mischievous twinkle in her eyes belied her advanced age. She then gestured with her hand that I was to drink the entire glass in one big gulp.

I thanked her and, raising my glass to her, downed it.

I almost gagged. The wine tasted like how I would imagine a mixture of gasoline and rancid cooking oil would taste. A kinder description might liken it to really awful sake. But I kept a brave face and even attempted a smile. Then, to my dismay, the old woman proceeded to pour me another brimming cup.

"I am okay," I protested, doing my best to convey that I had thoroughly slaked my thirst with the first drink.

"*Paye! Paye!*" Badi said again, with the same mischievous twinkle in her eyes. Again she raised her hand, commanding me to toss back the entire drink at one go.

Not wanting to insult my animated ancient hostess, I again steeled myself and drank the vile liquid.

And again, ignoring my good-natured protests, she poured yet another draft of the nasty stuff. Fortunately for me, she then had to go back to her outdoor kitchen and attend to the dinner she was cooking for me. So I left the glass of awful wine untouched.

Badi soon delivered my dinner: lamb in a dark savory broth, and potatoes. Again she commanded me to "*Paye! Paye!*" but then went back to her kitchen before I actually complied. Upon finishing my dinner, I discreetly poured the stuff into a large planter near my chair.

The next morning, I awoke early to the smell of smoke from the open-hearth kitchen. Its pleasant aroma, promising a tasty, hearty breakfast, wafted throughout the guesthouse grounds. Going down to the outdoor table to eat, I met three young men who lived in Pankisi and were sitting there waiting for me to join them for breakfast.

A burly young man got up and shook my hand, introducing himself as Lasha. He said he worked with Bakhar and heard that I was staying at Badi's guesthouse. He and his two friends had come over to welcome me to Pankisi. Sitting on the ground next to him was a box with several ten-liter white plastic bottles of liquid. After Lasha introduced me to his friends I found out what was in the jugs.

"What would you like to start with for breakfast?" Lasha asked. "Beer, vodka, or wine? This wine comes from my father's vineyards and is very good."

I was hoping he was kidding. Alcohol at seven was not exactly the breakfast of champions.

"Oh, I'm okay," I said as I took my seat at the round metal patio table. "Water is good for me. I never start my drinking before eleven in the morning."

"Oh, you must honor us with a drink," Lasha replied, with his other two friends grunting assent. From one of the plastic jugs, he filled the thick cocktail glass in front of me with what appeared to be the same horrible stuff Badi had given me last night.

When I rather strongly suggested that I would drink only water, Lasha was undeterred.

"No, you must not refuse me!" he insisted seriously but with a smile. "Here in Pankisi, it is unmanly and an insult to refuse when someone offers you a drink."

"Okay," I said. "Well, in honor of meeting some new friends here," I said, "I'll drink this one glass of wine with you during breakfast." I then raised my cup to take a sip.

"Cheers!" Lasha said, and all three men downed the shots of vodka they had poured for themselves. I took a small drink of the nasty brownish moonshine wine.

"You must finish it in one gulp," Lasha chided. "You are a strong man. One glass of wine is nothing!"

So I finished the glass of wine and set it aside. One of the other men promptly refilled it. Just at that moment, our hostess cheerfully bustled up to the table with a platter full of fried eggs, mutton, and thick chunks of white bread. I got up and grabbed a clean glass from a nearby table and filled it with water.

All three men insisted that I join them for another toast. And then another and another. Finally, after several rounds of drinks, I just left the newly refilled glass of wine in front of me and raised my glassful of water for the next toast. This action met with some protest from my breakfast companions, but I held my ground.

I gobbled down my breakfast and excused myself from the table, saying that I was eager to get out and see the village. But the three men weren't done just yet, and remained at the table, drinking several more rounds before going off to work.

Walking up the stone stairway to my room to clean up after breakfast, I felt queasy. I knew that I had just learned the hard way that offers to drink in Pankisi were never for just one glass. I was also just starting to realize that drinking (or, in my case, drink avoidance), along with the importance to Georgia of its friendship with the United States, would be a big theme during my time here.

Georgians, especially the men, drink lots of alcohol daily. This was especially the case in the Pankisi Valley, despite the region's being overwhelmingly Muslim. The pressure on the visitor to drink can be really high, as I had just experienced. Once begun, the drinking generally stopped only when the wine, vodka, and beer ran out. That morning, I realized that if I took even one shot of wine, it would be hard not to end up consuming entire liters, or even gallons, of drink with my companions. Though the pressure to take the first drink might be relentless, I resolved, going forward, to stick to my guns in stopping the process from the start, before it could gather any momentum. This might be insulting, but it beat endlessly poisoning myself.

When I came back down a half hour later to start my walk around Duisi village, a new guest was standing by the now-abandoned patio table. He was a tall, skinny, ghostly pale European with unkempt curly blond hair. He introduced himself as Quentin, saying he was from Paris, and in Pankisi doing research for his master's thesis. He explained that this was his second time here and that his research was on Sufism (a mystical sect of Islam) in the Pankisi Valley.

I immediately liked Quentin and joined him at the table, having tea while he had breakfast. I told him of my Disappearing World travel project and said I was in the Pankisi area for a few days. Since Quentin had done a lot of solo travels himself, it appeared that we had a few things in common.

"You should stay here in Pankisi for a while," he suggested after we had talked for a while. "It's quite a unique place. I have been here and many other places in this wider region. You will find Pankisi fascinating and quite fitting for your Disappearing World project."

So I decided to stay longer and learn more about Pankisi. It would be fun to share the experience with a new friend who was an expert in the cultures of the area. The Pankisi Valley's mystique, remoteness, and lawless reputation had already piqued my sense of adventure. I also found it interesting that the valley was culturally different from the rest of Georgia, which is predominantly Christian. This despite the very un-Muslim drinking culture, which was common throughout the Caucasus region, Russia, and Central Asia. Also, as Quentin told me over breakfast, the Sufism of Pankisi was quite unlike the Sufism practiced anywhere else.

The predominant religious practices in Pankisi were of two similar types of Sufism called Naqsbandi and Quadiri, Quentin explained. Like Sufis in general, the Pankisi Sufis used meditation, chanting, and dancing as a means to know and feel closer to God. "The Naqsbandi and Quadiri do not have the whirling dervishes seen in the popular media," he said, referring to the spinning dance used to achieve a trancelike state in order to feel the presence of the divine. "Instead, the Naqsbandi and Quadiri use more meditative ways to reach similar states, usually involving lots of group chanting."

That afternoon, Badi took Quentin and me to a women's Naqsbandi Sufi *zikr* (ritual praying) session. The weather was bracing, with a light breeze, as we walked down a muddy pathway lined by stone walls. Ahead of us, thickly forested mountains with rugged snowcapped peaks rose up against a clear blue sky. We passed by many older women in conservative long dresses or light coats and head scarfs, walking slowly along the village paths. Eventually, we came to an old stone-and-wood house and went in the front door.

Inside the simple house was a room with wood flooring and bare of furniture. A group of older women, all veiled and dressed in dark, modest, heavy clothing, were sitting in a wide circle on the floor. Quentin and I sat on the floor, against a wall, slightly away from the women, as Badi joined the circle. One woman, who appeared to be the leader, began a repetitious chant. She had her hand to her ear, which made it appear as if she were talking on a telephone to God.

"*La ilah-ha illallah, la ilah-ha illallah,*" the women called out in a low, gentle monotone. The Arabic words meant roughly, "There is none worthy of worship except Allah." All the women had their eyes closed. At times, they all would chant or hum along with the leader, clapping their hands softly as they did so.

"Their goal is to enter a trancelike state so that they can better sense God," Quentin whispered in my ear.

Eventually, the women all got up and began walking around in a circle while doing a simple rhythmic dance. Most had their eyes closed and looked very relaxed. I assumed that the purpose of this dance was the same as that of the trance-inducing chant. Throughout the entire ritual, the women made Quentin and me feel quite welcome, graciously encouraging us to photograph their session as much as we liked.

Quentin and I would experience this Sufi ritual in Duisi village many times. Walking about any evening at dusk, it was common to hear a gentle, repetitive chant coming from some of the houses we passed. Inside would be a group of often older women, doing their ritual chant. It all felt peaceful and comforting and seemed nothing like the lawless reputed al-Qaeda haven that had recently been the image of Pankisi to the outside world.

Despite the warm hospitality and heavy-drinking ways of the Pankisi area, it was very conservative regarding women. Most women wore head scarfs, though none wore anything like a burka. In keeping with Muslim traditions, a man could have as many as four wives, whereas women faced heavy strictures. The day after watching the older women doing the Naqsbandi praying ritual, Quentin and I got a firsthand glimpse of some of the constraints that women in Pankisi faced.

We were having lunch in the modest but tidy little house of an older woman Quentin knew from last year's visit to the village. Her preteen granddaughter and the granddaughter's thirteen-year-old friend were serving us various dishes as we sat at the wooden table in the older woman's living room. While the woman was cooking in the kitchen, Quentin and I got to talking with the two girls. I asked them how old they were and what they wanted to do when they grew up.

"Oh, we sometimes don't have much choice about what we will do in life," the preteen girl said. (I will not use any names here.) She looked like a schoolgirl from anywhere in the modern world. She wore a modest Western blouse and longish skirt and had longish wavy brown hair, which she kept pinned back, and sunglasses perched on top of her head. "Many girls, even at very young ages, end up in arranged marriages," she said. "I hope that doesn't happen to me."

"Yes, of course, I can understand that you would want to pick your own husband when you are ready," I said. "Is this possible around here? Is there a way to get to know a boy if you wanted to?"

"This is very difficult," replied the other girl, who was thirteen. She appeared as if she could have grown up in America. She was very pretty, tall and slender, with dark brown hair, and wore a red pullover sweater, tight jeans, and aqua costume jewelry earrings. "If a young women has a boyfriend or even appears to have, let alone has sexual relations with the boy or man, the girl could possibly be *killed* by her family." The younger girl nodded in agreement.

"I am home on holiday now from a high school that I attend in Toronto, Canada," the thirteen-year-old explained. "My mother lives and works in Toronto, and I go and live with her during the school year. Even there, way off in faraway Canada, if I dared to have a boyfriend of any kind, word would get back to here in Pankisi, and I could still be killed for it."

What a strange world this young woman lived in! To see and partly grow up in the free, liberal society of North America, yet still be trapped by Dark Age strictures of the Pankisi Valley in the Caucasus Mountains! It was yet another example of a chunk of the world's population, in this case, many women born into strictly traditional

Islamic societies, getting a lousy draw in the birth lottery, with so many restrictions on their life possibilities and potential.

The strictures on women carry onward even later in life. From my casual observations, I noticed that Duisi had a lot of older widows. I had to wonder, was this because men died younger due to lifestyles of constant heavy drinking and smoking? So, later that day, I asked Badi if a woman had much opportunity to remarry if her husband died.

"This is not an option," Badi said. "A widow cannot remarry. If her husband dies, she stays celibate the rest of her life."

Another tradition in Pankisi exemplifying women's restricted freedom of choice showed in a strange courtship behavior practiced in the region. Several young men who lived in the area came by to meet Quentin and me that evening around dinnertime at Badi's home. After they all introduced themselves and poured drinks, we had a few moments to talk about courtship customs in Pankisi.

"If you don't want to be in an arranged marriage," I asked one of the young men who was unmarried, "and if it is not proper to date a girl, how do you get a marriage partner?"

"Sometimes a boy or a man will kidnap a girl he wants to marry," explained the young man, an amiable, scruffy-looking guy in his early twenties. "He can then use this situation to force the parents' consent to his marriage with the girl.

"Of course, sometimes the bride is a willing participant in this scheme," the young man said. "Even then, she must at all times appear to be resisting the kidnapping in order to keep up appearances."

Although Pankisi had a very Muslim conservative streak regarding women, its un-Islamic practice of drinking continued to be one of the major themes of my time there. My efforts to avoid drinking approached the level of slapstick comedy. One day, Quentin and I went with a few of Badi's male friends and her neighbor, who took us in their car to visit people in nearby villages. It was a mild, cool midmorning with partly overcast skies.

In about fifteen minutes, we reached the first village on our itinerary, where we stopped at the home of an ex-colonel in the Georgian military. The colonial lived in a large white wood and concrete house with an expansive backyard of tended lawn and lots of trees. As our group entered his backyard I noticed the familiar sight of high wooden trellises of twisting, hanging grapevines. Nearby, several men sat around a long rectangular table, awaiting our arrival. The women of the house—the colonel's wife, mother-in-law, and two daughters—all sprang into action as we took seats at the table. Big platters of various cheeses, nuts, and several vases of water appeared on the table. With our arrival, the drinking was about to begin. Gallon jugs of wine were at the ready, and thick glasses were laid out for all the men.

It was only midmorning, and getting staggering drunk by noon was not what I wanted. So I quickly removed the empty cocktail glass that had been placed in front of me, and put it over on a nearby serving table. I was hoping that with no glass in front of me to pour the wine into, I could escape the first round. I then discreetly poured myself a glass of water from one of the big vases on the table.

Not surprisingly, without anyone's saying a word, another glass was found and brought to me, full of wine. The toasting was about to begin. I then scooted the cup of wine away from me, trying to hide it behind a flower arrangement on the table. Someone good-naturedly moved it back in front of me. I picked up the glass of wine and raised it for the toast but quickly switched it to the water glass when I actually had to drink something.

My actions were greeted with protests and guffaws since Quentin and I were the honored guests. But I knew that if I humored my hosts by downing even one cup of wine, escape would be impossible before self-inflicted oblivion eventually set in. So I just steeled myself to being something of an outcast and continued to raise only my glass of water each time they all downed yet another cup of wine.

I had to do some version of this silly routine the entire day as my group visited several villages. In each village, all the men I met were very polite and hospitable to Quentin and me. But to a certain extent, I remained an outcast. Quentin, on the other hand, matched our hosts all day, drink for drink, and got on fine with everyone. He paid the price, though. When evening came, he threw up violently and repeatedly and couldn't eat dinner.

Of course, I didn't always refuse to drink. I joined in at the wedding party and a few other times. In my short time in Pankisi, I probably consumed more alcohol than I had in the previous three months. One of the people I did drink with was Elder, a prominent man in Duisi village who lived next door to Badi. Quentin and I met Elder through Mary, his wife, who invited us to her home one afternoon after I had been in Duisi a few days. Mary was Badi's close friend and had graciously taken Quentin and me around the village on several occasions.

Elder was a natural leader. A powerfully built man in his early fifties, he was the life of the party wherever he went. He was the one who told "manly" jokes to his male friends when the women were out of earshot, or who took the microphone at a party to give a rousing toast. Fittingly for a man of Elder's social talents, he was running for mayor of Duisi village at the time I was visiting. Elder and I hit it off immediately even though neither of us could speak the other's language. To communicate, Mary or Elder's son Arbi, both of whom spoke good English, patiently interpreted for us each time we got together.

It was late afternoon the first time I visited Elder's home. Like many others in the area, he had several grape trellises in his yard. He took pride in his wine, bragging to me that his actually tasted good and insisting that I try just one glass to see. Since Elder was so convincing, I relented in my usual refusal to have that first drink and downed a glass with Elder and Quentin. After that first drink, Elder was charming but relentless in persuading me to continue drinking with him. (His wine, though awful, was far more drinkable than the other local vintages I had sampled.) Our conversation was very enjoyable, though. Along with a knowledge of local and regional politics, he seemed to be quite an industrious man. At one point in the evening, he brought me out to his work shed to show me a spine-stretching table contraption that he built to help people with back pains. It resembled something that I had seen in a chiropractic office in the States. I was frankly impressed with his creation.

Four hours and four bottles of wine later, Quentin and I staggered out of Elder's home, back to Badi's, where I apparently passed out just as I reached my bed. I woke up the next morning flopped facedown across the bed, my head hanging slightly over the edge and still wearing the same clothes I had on the day before.

Along with spending a few more enjoyable times with Elder at his house, Quentin and I spent time with his son, Arbi. A ruggedly handsome, tall, powerfully built man in his early twenties, Arbi was smart, and surprisingly technology oriented considering the remoteness of where he grew up. He was also a very different person from his father. Unlike Elder, who could drink copiously, Arbi had almost never tasted alcohol in his life. Serious and introverted, he seemed to embody a generational divide regarding religion, which I had started to notice in Pankisi. Arbi practiced a type of Islam very different from the Sufism of his father.

A strong fundamentalist Sunni streak was taking hold in the younger generation of Pankisi. In this, they differed sharply from the middle-aged and older generations, who traditionally embraced Sufism, which is quite lively and colorful compared to the more fundamentalist Islamic practices. Since the Pankisi area was heavily cultivated with grapes, wine was something that many households made and consumed. But some younger men I met, like Arbi, did not subscribe to this drinking culture, instead adhering to the tenets of stricter forms of Islam.

"I am in the middle, between the young people, who believe in a really strict practice of Islam, and the Sufis," Arbi said. "Older people accuse younger people of being Wahhabis [adherents of an extremely fundamentalist Muslim doctrine originating in eighteenth-century Arabia]. But this is usually not the case. The younger and stricter Muslim believers feel that many of the Sufi traditions in Pankisi are not 'true' Islam. This is why I don't drink and why many younger people don't."

Arbi also explained that younger and stricter Islamic practitioners didn't agree with some other prominent Sufi traditions, such as that of a man kidnapping a prospective bride. They also rejected the long-standing ritual of vendetta killings in murder cases. (In this ritual, the murderer was brought to the cemetery where his victim was buried, and was then killed there in revenge.)

During my interactions with Elder and Arbi, I could plainly see that Elder was proud of his son. But he was openly worried about Arbi and his future. It was common, during my several visits to Elder's home, to hear Arbi express deep anger and frustration at the brutal treatment that Chechens on the other side of the border suffered under the Russian heel.

"My main life goal is to 'make a difference,'" Arbi said with conviction on a couple of occasions. "One way to do that is to go to the Chechen side, to fight against the Russians if another war breaks out. If I should die helping the Chechen cause, than my life would have meaning."

I privately understood Arbi's indignation at the raw deal the Chechens were getting from the Russian government. But I hoped he would be able to find his meaning in life without becoming a martyr.

Near the end of my time in Pankisi, I had another opportunity to see Bakhar, the UN refugee specialist, when he made a visit to Badi's guesthouse. Over a snack that Badi prepared, I asked him why this religious generational divide had arisen between the generations.

"The religious differences are partly the result of the social earthquake that came with the fall of the Soviet Union," Bakhar said. "After the collapse, the Sufis came out from underground. Their practices—and the Quran—had been banned under Soviet rule. Since they never had access to the Quran, their lifestyle and rituals were a blend of what they took to be those of Sufi Muslims. This was coupled with the lifestyles and traditions of the region."

In contrast, Bakhar explained, young people today had grown up in freer times, when they had unrestricted contact with the Quran as well as with Islamic teachings and doctrine from outside the region. Many young people adopted the usually far stricter interpretations of these outside Islamic influences. In particular, the Chechen wars in the mid- and late 1990s led to the introduction of Wahhabism and other radical Islamic influences into the region.

"Many people who know the region," Bakhar concluded, "worry that older Sufi lifestyles and traditional activities are in danger of being lost as their adherents diminish in numbers."

After nine days in the friendly, colorful Pankisi village that I had enjoyed so much, it was time for me to leave and continue my travels in Georgia. On my last evening in Duisi village, Badi took Quentin and me to the private home of one of her friends. In the small, cozy living room, a group of older women had gathered to do their ritual chanting and play some traditional songs for us. There were also several younger women, some in their late teens, and one young man in his early twenties. They spoke a smattering of English and helped interpret what the older women were doing and saying to us. These younger people participated in earnest with their elders by playing the traditional instruments and dancing for us.

I was sad to leave Duisi village after everyone had made me feel so welcome. But seeing the younger people participating with their elders in their traditional rituals, I felt hope that perhaps some of these colorful traditions would live on.

About a week after leaving Duisi village, I joined Quentin again in Tbilisi, Georgia's capital. He had stayed in Duisi another week after I left, and he was feeling a bit hungover from yesterday, his last day there.

"The group of guys that came for breakfast when you and I were there—they came again yesterday morning," Quentin said. "They had several containers of the usual booze. After they gave me lots and lots of pressure, I made the mistake and agreed to do just one teensy shot of vodka with them at breakfast. And, well, you know the rest. They wouldn't let me stop drinking with them till four in the afternoon. That's when I finally passed out."

CHAPTER 15

Togo: Romance, Glamour, Voodoo

He who has diarrhea knows the direction of the door
without being told.
−Togolese proverb

Mid-November 2009
Akodessewa voodoo fetish market
Lomé, Togo, West Africa

The skulls stared silently at us. The empty eye sockets of some were filled with dirt, and most had dirty teeth set in eerie frozen grins. As my small group walked through the Akodessewa fetish market in Lomé, I started to recognize the animals whose dried or decaying parts, stacked on tables or ground mats, filled the sandy lot.

There were heads and skulls of cats, crocodiles, hyenas, vultures, owls, chameleons, small antelopes, and monkeys. Skewers of mummified bats, heads of small rodentlike animals with short, furry hair and grinning teeth, dogs' heads, and, sadly, even some cheetah heads were stacked about the dusty grounds.

We walked past a skinny shirtless boy who looked bored sitting by his table stacked with fetishes. His wares looked like gigantic fishing lures made from long golden-brown hair, tied together and hanging by a narrow rope. Next to the hairy fetishes, a huge assortment of dried paws of all kinds of forest animals was laid out. Even though Akodessewa was an outdoor market, the place had a subtly putrid stench emanating from the huge collection of animal parts it sold.

"Maybe we can find a fetish to bring good luck for you so you don't have any more phones stolen," suggested Vanessa, a vibrantly beautiful young woman who had accompanied me to the market and was helping as an interpreter. I had mentioned to her earlier that I had had three cell phones stolen in the past few months. (In my two months of travel after leaving Georgia and before entering Togo, I had passed through Morocco, where I lost yet another cell phone—the third theft in three months!)

Vanessa and I were following our market "guide," who was showing us around and giving explanations in French. But he sometimes spoke too fast for my limited French, so Vanessa was a great help.

"This is the biggest fetish market in West Africa—probably the biggest in all of Africa," our guide explained. The tall, slender young man with coal black skin and a missing front tooth was wearing a red long-sleeved shirt unbuttoned halfway down his chest. "People come here to get cures and aids for many different things. Our voodoo market is like a huge pharmacy. We also have things which can give protection, bring good luck, and ward off evil."

We walked past a pile of blackened animal skulls, each with several thumbtack-looking things stuck all over it. As we wandered among the gruesome piles of animal parts, our guide continued to explain the huge variety of uses for voodoo and fetishes.

"Those bones are used to protect a person's home," he said, pointing to an assortment of bones lined up against some wooden crates on the ground. "If a person is sick and the Western medicine doctor can't help, they come here for a cure.

"We have things to help with impotence or a woman's inability to have a baby," the guide continued, pointing at two carved wooden sticks in the shape of penises. "You want someone to fall in love with you? No problem! Our voodoo priest can make a fetish for you to take home for this purpose."

The enthusiastic guide went on to show us fetishes and medicines for a huge variety of purposes, even for sportsmen. For example, to run faster in a marathon, a runner could put materials from horses sold at the market onto his body. Another medicine purportedly helped football goalkeepers have faster reaction times. For me, the voodoo market was a fascinating window into that deeply primeval part of the human mind in all of us, which has always needed to grasp on to some mysterious, complex world of hidden spirits, all in the vain hope for some control or understanding of those things in life that are beyond human control or understanding.

It was my third day in Togo, and the trip had started badly. I had flown into Lomé from Casablanca, Morocco. While checking in for my flight to Lomé with Royal Air Maroc at the Casablanca airport, I was told that a system error had invalidated my confirmed, fully paid air ticket. The obsequious red-uniformed customer service manager whom I then saw to fix the problem said that there was nothing she could do. With a plastic smile pasted on her face, the chubby blonde calmly said I would have to pay an additional US$250 for my ticket. I wanted to strangle her, if only to rid her of that phony smile. Instead, after heatedly venting my frustration over the lousy service, I coughed up the two hundred fifty dollars to the woman, whose smile remained frozen as if her face might otherwise crack. I figured this was better than being stranded in Casablanca for several days trying to fix the mess created by Royal Air Maroc. Damn!

Then, when I got into Lomé, my high-quality Nikon digital SLR camera quit working properly. That meant I would get very few quality photos while in Togo and none in Gabon, my next destination. Double damn!

I was visiting Togo because I was interested in the voodoo culture of the country and of West Africa in general. Also, Lomé was a good place for me to get my visa for the upcoming month-long journey in Gabon, since Gabon had an embassy in Lomé.

Togo is a very small country in tropical West Africa, on the Gulf of Guinea, sandwiched between Ghana to the west, Benin to the east, and Burkina Faso to the north. Like much of West Africa, Togo is dirt poor, with an agrarian population, low educational standards, and lousy governance. The country's recent history is colorful and sad. From the sixteenth to eighteenth centuries, the coastal region where modern Togo now sits was a major slave-trading center for Europeans. So much slave trafficking took place along this stretch of the Gulf of Guinea that it became known as the Slave Coast.

Lomé, Togo's capital, has a population of just under a million. It is a dusty, crumbling, decaying place with some wide boulevards and sizable squares. The city fronts on a wide, sandy beach area and sits near a big lagoon. The local fishermen usually go to sea early in the mornings, and their small, colorful boats lie about the beaches in the afternoons. Lomé features a large mixture of architectural styles, from turn-of-the-century German neo-Gothic to some bland modern buildings and a few nicer high-rises. All this is sprinkled among colorful and eclectic wood, stucco, and concrete-block buildings and houses.

I had met Vanessa my first night in Lomé, which was a Friday. Following my usual practice when arriving in less-settled places, I went to the city's popular gathering spot, where I hoped to meet some of the more interesting expats, NGO types, local businesspeople, and embassy workers who gather in such places. In Lomé, the only real choice was a place called Privilege, a large restaurant, sports bar, and nightclub near the beach. It was the place in the city where the young and affluent—Lomé's "pretty people"—and foreigners gathered. Not unexpectedly, a fair number of prostitutes in slinky dresses were working the place.

Almost immediately after I arrived, around 8:30 at night, I met two interesting Danish men. So I joined them upstairs at the nightclub's large, chic oval varnished-wood bar. One of the Danes was an ex-military bodybuilder in his mid-thirties. His friend, an aircraft dealer in West Africa, had a salesman's entertaining personality. The former soldier explained that he did security consulting in Nigeria and was just passing through Lomé on the way to Lagos (Nigeria's largest city). There, he was to take part in a hostage-rescue situation involving an oil company executive.

I asked him what this entailed.

"We'll do whatever we have to do to extract the victim," the Dane answered, "including an armed raid on the kidnappers if all else fails."

It sounded like dramatic stuff.

As I sat at the bar having drinks with the two Danes, a striking young woman came up to the bar where I was sitting, to get a bucket of ice. She was slender, elegant, and drop-dead gorgeous, and with her long, tightly braided hair and long, gold off-the-shoulder silk dress, she looked like a Hollywood movie starlet. The young woman happened to drop a small pouch as she took her bucket of ice from the bartender and turned to walk back to a nearby table. Seeing it fall, I picked it up and brought it to her where she was sitting with two friends.

"Oh, thank you, mister!" the young woman said. "I can't believe I dropped this! I'm Vanessa. Would you like to join us for a drink?"

I told her I was talking with some new friends at the bar but that I appreciated the offer.

Later that evening, Vanessa came over to the bar, where I was still in conversation with the two Danes.

"Excuse me, mister, would you like to join my friends and me dancing?" Vanessa asked with a warm smile. "It would be a big help to me. Those drunk guys out there keep bothering me." She pointed with her head toward a couple of tall backpacker types who looked Scandinavian and quite drunk. "A dance partner would really help to get rid of them," she said softly, looking up at me with mischievous brown eyes.

After I danced a while with Vanessa, she invited me to join her for a drink. My new Danish friends looked preoccupied with some local girlfriends, so I went over and sat with Vanessa at her table. She introduced me to her companions, who were her brother Samuel and his girlfriend, Sabine.

All three were in college. Samuel was studying IT in Germany, where their father worked for Lufthansa Airlines. On a two-week break from his studies, Samuel was visiting Vanessa and their older sister, who lived in Lomé. Both Sabine and Vanessa were doing their studies in the neighboring country of Ghana. Vanessa had done a two-year degree already and was currently doing a three-year fashion design course. She, too, was on school holiday for about a month, staying with her sister in Lomé.

I sat with them the rest of the evening. When the place closed around four a.m., Vanessa insisted that her brother drive me back to my hotel. "It could be dangerous for a foreigner to take a taxi so late at night," she explained. As they drove me to my guesthouse, I mentioned my interest in voodoo.

"I must take you to the big voodoo fetish market," she said.

I eagerly agreed. She must.

"I'll come by your hotel after lunch the day after tomorrow to pick you up," she promised.

Two days later, true to her word, Vanessa came by my hotel in the early afternoon to bring me to the Akodessewa Voodoo market. At first, I almost didn't recognize her. She had a completely different hairstyle with no braid extensions this time, wore a bit of makeup, and was casually but tastefully dressed in tight jeans.

The owner of the guesthouse where I was staying, an older French expat who had been in Lomé for over twenty years, took a liking to Vanessa, seeming almost bewitched by her presence. The three of us spent a short time talking, and then Vanessa and I left for the voodoo market. Before I left, though, the French guesthouse owner took me aside for a moment.

"I have been in Lomé a long time," he said in a hushed, earnest voice, in slow French so that I could understand.

"I know when I see a quality lady," he continued. "I think this is a good one."

That evening, when we came back from the voodoo market, the guesthouse owner invited Vanessa and me to join him and his girl-friend for dinner. He was also the cook for his guesthouse and made us an excellent French-Togolese style meal, served complete with quite decent French red wine. His little tent-covered outdoor patio restaurant, with a profusion of potted and garden tropical plants and low lighting, made a lovely setting for a long and pleasant dinner of the sort you want to last all evening.

My time in Togo became very relaxing. I met several people at the Frenchman's guesthouse and soon found myself doing a lot of socializing with new, friendly strangers. Within my first few days in Lomé, I had obtained my visa for Gabon and bought yet another throwaway cell phone to replace the one stolen in Morocco. I was ready to leave for Gabon.

But I decided to linger a while in Lomé. I was tired. Since starting in Northern Vietnam seven months earlier, I had been on a series of long, almost nonstop road trips. The guesthouse where I stayed, a big old colonial two-story, while not luxurious, was like an oasis with its friendly charm. Though my second-floor room didn't have much of a view beyond the wide dirt road with its few small shops and a fruit stand, it was huge, with a ceiling fan and floor-to-ceiling windows.

Lomé was not exactly the type of place one would initially pick to relax in. Before visiting Togo, I had read an online article about Lomé. It said that visitors could be excused for thinking they were in Southern California. But from what I had seen so far, the writer must have been on heavy hallucinogens at the time. Almost everything in Lomé had the appearance of long-deferred maintenance. It was as if the buildings, once up, were never again repaired or rehabilitated.

Just walking along the roads was hazardous. The walkways that passed for sidewalks often had large holes or gaps, which made walking an especially dicey proposition at night since Lomé had many large stretches with little or no lighting. A pedestrian could break an ankle, or worse.

My guesthouse was close to the beach. Almost every day, I walked there and did some distance swimming in the ocean. This was great exercise and had long been a passion of mine. I did my swims in late afternoon, when Vanessa could get away from her sister's clothing shop, where she was helping out. She was refreshing to be around, and I welcomed her company. We went to the beach together for the first time the day after visiting the voodoo market. Swimming parallel to the shore and about a quarter mile out, I noticed Vanessa walking along the beach, following me. I swam maybe a mile or so down and then back past my starting point, and she dutifully followed me along the shore the entire way.

"Why were you following me on the beach when I was swimming?" I asked her as we walked back to my guesthouse.

"I was worried that something might happen to you," she replied.

I found this cute but impractical. Vanessa was athletic, but she was afraid of swimming in the ocean, so she would be of little help if I had trouble. She did help in a practical way, though, since I didn't have to leave my sandals unattended on the beach while swimming. In such an impoverished area, anything left unwatched was apt to walk away. Moreover, the main street back to my guesthouse was littered with sharp rocks, rusted metal debris, and broken glass—not a great place to barefoot it.

On two occasions, Vanessa took a day off from her sister's shop and accompanied me on day trips out of town. One of these trips was to a village called Agbodrafo, on Lake Togo, about an hour's drive east from Lomé along the coast. As we reached Agbodrafo in our hired SUV, skinny, shirtless barefoot children ran up to the road, waving and shouting greetings to us.

"It is your welcoming committee, Gary," Vanessa joked. "They are excited to see you, a white person. They know you are from somewhere else."

We continued driving into the village, passing small houses intermittently lining the packed-dirt roads. Our driver explained in French, with Vanessa interpreting, that many voodoo ceremonies were commonly done in Agbodrafo.

We parked our SUV slightly away from the town center, near the lakeshore. Several women in brightly colored body wraps had large vats of water perched on their heads. They had drawn the water from a well nearby and were returning with it to their homes.

We walked down a dirt road and saw several voodoo shrines along the roadsides. One looked like an upside-down cone-shaped vase with a whitish powder finish. Another, more ornate, had a concrete base shaped like a large tree stump, and on this was a stone table with a huge carved stone arrowhead mounted on it. Seeing all the relics and altars around Agbodrafo and in the village of Togoville, across the lake, I was fascinated at how voodoo seemed just part of the villagers' daily life.

During the downtime I spent in Lomé, I had gotten accustomed to having Vanessa around. I didn't pay much attention to this at first. She was mature, polite, well-spoken, and well educated considering her circumstances.

Incongruously, she was like a movie star on a very low budget. Each time I saw her, she looked almost like a different person. One day, she would have really long braided hair and no makeup. The next day, she would be in a headscarf. Other times, she had elegant, wavy medium-length hair and makeup like a model's. And her outfit styles, always well coordinated, ranged from chic to casually sexy. She had managed a personal polish and glamour that stood in stark contrast to the grimy, run-down, poverty-stricken part of the world where she lived. She had a lot going for her, considering her lousy draw in the birth lottery: born in one of the world's poorest countries.

I tried to suppress the feeling, but I found her quite attractive. *She's just too young!* I reminded myself at times. The world she came from was too different from anything I could relate to—I told myself this despite all my travel experience. I also did not like the asymmetry of our situations in life. I was quite aware of the fact that in Africa it was normal for women to deal with men on a transactional basis. That was just how life was in areas of such grinding want and poverty.

But Vanessa never took or asked for anything. I offered a couple of times to pay her for her time as my guide.

"Don't be silly," she told me the first time I offered. "My father sends me money from Germany, and my sister pays me to help at her shop. I enjoy your company and am happy to show you some of the interesting things about my country." The only money she would accept from me was the tiny sums for motorcycle taxis she took between her home and my guesthouse.

So instead of direct payment, I took her out to dinners. A couple of these occasions were with other new friends I had met in Lomé. One of these was Charles, a reasonably affluent and well-traveled businessman involved in information technology. We had met through the owner of the guesthouse where I stayed. We got along very well, and one evening Charles had Vanessa and me over at his family's housing compound for dinner so I could meet his family. After dinner, the men of the extended household family gathered outside on the rock-and-dirt compound grounds to drink shots of whisky. While there, Charles spoke to me about Vanessa.

"That is a quality woman, Gary," he said in a low voice. "I was watching her carefully all evening, just looking out for you as my friend. As a local person, it is easier for me to know what I am looking at. She is a very good woman, I think."

"Yes, I think she's great, and I have enjoyed having her show me around," I replied. "But she is just a friend I met here in Lomé. She's too young for me, anyhow, and we come from too different of worlds and life paths for it to be anything more."

"You shouldn't close your mind this way," Charles said. "You're not in America. Age doesn't make any difference here. Also people think differently in West Africa. Life is tough and uncertain for most people. So there is much more of a live-for-today mentality. Maybe you need to learn to think this way sometimes, too, Gary."

I changed the subject and raised my glass of whisky to toast the other men gathered around.

It wasn't only Charles who felt the need to let me know the virtues of my new female friend. Even the women who worked at my guest-house would remark on how special Vanessa was, how well raised she seemed, and so on. Despite all this unsolicited praise for my new friend, I still saw the huge gap between Vanessa's world and mine. I knew it was best for her that we not cross a certain line, and keep our nice friendship as it was.

One morning, my taxi driver took me to see a voodoo practitioner he knew. Driving down a dirt-and-rock road near the outskirts of Lomé, he dropped me off at a modest white stucco house, where I was greeted at the front door by a solidly built middle-aged man with a gold tooth.

"I am Kofi," the man said. He invited me into his front room, which was comfortably furnished with a few cushioned chairs, a couch, and a low hardwood table. Several hand-carved wooden masks hung on the walls, and a couple of large wooden sculptures of stylized female figures stood in the corners. I didn't see any humanlike dolls with pins sticking out of them, though. As I sat in his front room drinking tea, Kofi gave me an insight into his life's work.

"I learned my craft—voodoo—from my father, who had learned it at the instruction of his father," Kofi explained in unusually good English. "Passing the knowledge of this profession from one genera-tion to the next is how most voodoo practitioners gain their skills." Kofi went on to explain that voodoo is an old and organized religion, practiced widely in the area of West Africa that has become Ghana, Togo, Benin, and parts of Nigeria.

I asked Kofi about his practice, what he did specifically from day to day.

"People, my customers, come to me for a big variety of reasons," he explained. "They seek treatment for illnesses, deficiencies in sexual performance, to find love, to bring on good luck, to help with a particular business deal, and for protection from evil spirits or physical enemies." Other common examples of day-to-day voodoo practice, according to Kofi, involved people needing medical assistance. For some of these purposes, the voodoo practitioner would process various animal parts into powders or potions—by grinding and heating over a fire, for instance.

"What about those who want to hurt their enemies?" I asked at one point, once again picturing little dolls with pins sticking out of them.

Kofi explained that he practiced voodoo only for curative and defensive purposes, although there were certainly those with more malevolent intentions.

"Is this a religion that believes in a god or gods?" I asked.

He said that voodoo was similar to the widely practiced religions of Christianity and Islam, except that it had one main god and a large number of lesser spirits. These spirits ranged from all-powerful forces of nature and human society to the lesser spirits of individual aspects of the natural world, such as the spirit for each tree or creek. "Unlike Christianity or Islam, though, voodoo precepts are handed down orally," he noted. "There is no written equivalent of a Bible or Quran."

Kofi pointed out that the voodoo religion, like religious practices in many Asian societies, was big on ancestor worship. "The belief is that the spirits of ancestors abide next to humans in the living world."

According to Kofi, everything in nature had a spirit, and voodoo was essentially the art of manipulating, cajoling, or beseeching those spirits into helping achieve some desired goal. "For example, voodoo ceremonies, such as certain dances, are done to please lesser spirits, who can then intercede with the more powerful ones to solve a problem."

Another common voodoo practice involved fetishes.

"The fetish attempts to take the power of the spirit of the animal from which it was made, and use it to serve some purpose," Kofi said. "An example of this is a fetish made to protect a house. The fetish might be displayed prominently as a warning that anyone who violates the property will suffer severe internal disease."

Remembering the skulls of cheetahs and the huge piles of animal parts at the Akodessewa voodoo fetish market, I asked Kofi whether he ever worried that the use of so many animals for fetishes was making an already bad situation worse.

He reflected on this for a moment. Then he explained that the voodoo practices dated from time immemorial and that before modern times there had never been a problem with animals disappearing. The problems with animals today had many other causes, not just from their uses in voodoo. He also said that most of the animals used in the markets came from other countries, not Togo, and added, "There must be many animals in these other countries since so many are available for sale in the markets."

I decided not to challenge him on the circular logic he was using here.

Kofi also talked about spirit possession and a host of other things. But around noon, it was time for me to bid him good-bye. I left feeling that I had a much better understanding of this vast and mysterious subject. It was also sobering to consider how the use of animals in voodoo was yet another of so many ingrained practices that "had always been done" and were now hastening the precipitous decline of wildlife in many parts of Africa.

Around midafternoon, after I had done my exercise workout for about ninety minutes in my room, I needed to get ready for the evening. Vanessa would be coming to my guesthouse, and we planned to go out to dinner. So I stepped out of my room, into the common bathroom-shower next door. The shower was behind a high wood-framed wall covered in smooth stucco. The sun shone through the dusty window to one side of the shower.

I had finished lathering up with soap and was rinsing off when I thought I heard knock on the bathroom door. I had locked the door, naturally, since I was using the room. But I saw no harm in letting in whoever was knocking. (I presumed it was my neighbor from the room next door, and anyway, the shower section was walled off.) So, reaching around the high wall that backed the shower, I unlatched the door, called out that it was open, then quickly stepped back into the shower.

I didn't hear anybody come into the bathroom, though. This was strange, I mused while rinsing off. Then, perhaps a minute or two later, my senses instinctively and suddenly sharpened and I became very clear headed. Something felt amiss. *Something was moving to my right, at the opening of the shower.*

I spun to the right and caught my breath.

Vanessa was standing there, completely naked, with an impish grin on her face.

"Why do you lock the door, silly?" she asked. "Is there something you're afraid of?"

I just looked at her, not saying a thing, but suddenly feeling very alive though slightly stunned.

Vanessa stood there, tall and proud. Her lithe, dark body glistened in the sunlight as the shower's mist drifted onto her. She came up to me and gave me a hug. Pressing against me, she buried her face in my chest. I put my arms around her and squeezed back, and we just stood there a while, embracing under the warm shower.

For the moment, the grime, noise, and poverty of Lomé seemed infinitely far away.

At five the next morning, Vanessa's cell phone alarm went off. She wanted to get back to her sister's house before her sister awoke. It was one of those fig-leaf behaviors that women—and some men—sometimes do to keep up appearances of propriety. As she explained, it wouldn't look good for her to be openly sleeping with a foreigner. So I got up and quickly threw on some casual clothes to walk her out to the street and get a motorcycle taxi.

I wasn't sure what the protocol should be in this situation. This was West Africa, after all. I was a foreigner, noticeably older than she, and with people who have so little, nothing is really free. But I didn't want to do the wrong thing, so I hedged.

"I'd like to go shopping with you today and buy you a present—perhaps a new outfit," I said. "But I have some things to do, so what if I give you some money and you go shopping yourself?"

Vanessa laughed. "I don't need any money," she said. "I have more outfits than I know what to do with. Maybe we can go shopping another time. Today, though, I have to work at my sister's shop." And out the door she went.

I walked downstairs with Vanessa, out of the big house and into the rising sun. The night guard let us out the front gate of the compound and onto the wide, dusty street. Within a minute, a motorcycle taxi came by. Vanessa hopped on and was whisked away, blowing me a kiss as she rode off.

I returned to my room. I had been gone barely five minutes while walking Vanessa out for the motorcycle taxi. I hadn't locked my door when I left, since there was almost no one staying in the guesthouse except the American couple in the room next door. As soon as I reentered my room, I knew that something was amiss. A packing stuff sack, where I kept my clean underwear and socks and which I had placed on the side of my bed, was turned right side up. Inside the stuff sack, I had hidden my Togo currency, which was shoved inside one of my socks. When leaving the room five minutes earlier, I had set the stuff sack upside down after Vanessa said she didn't need any money to go shopping.

I checked, and sure enough, my Togo currency—90,000 CFAs (about US$180)—was gone. Mystified over who could have stolen it, I immediately went outside, into the large open den area that fronted against a balcony. There, I saw the only other person in the hotel: a thin young housekeeper with a pinched face, who always seemed to have a sour disposition.

"Who just went into my room?" I asked her. "Someone just went into my room in the last few minutes and took my money. Who could have done it? You are the only person here."

The woman pleaded ignorance and said she hadn't seen anybody. But she was so unconvincing that I knew for sure she had taken it.

"You have my money," I said evenly without anger or raising my voice. "Please empty your pockets right now or I'll have the security guard at the front door call the police."

The housekeeper put on a loud and indignant act, pretending to be deeply insulted. Nevertheless, I knew it was her. The whole guesthouse compound was surrounded and secured by high walls. A guard at the front allowed only authorized visitors into the place, and presumably, no one from outside had flown into my room and back out through the window. And I knew that the American couple, who had two kids with them and were the only other guests at the moment, would not have dashed into my room and stolen the money.

So I informed the front gate guard. He told the housekeeper to stay in the open area in the dining room downstairs until management arrived. A couple of hours later, the guesthouse owner came, heard the story, and immediately reimbursed me for the money. He then called the housekeeper into his office, whereupon she confessed and begged him not to fire her. So he gave her a second chance, and things returned to normal. But I didn't leave my room unlocked again, even for a moment, when I wasn't in it.

It seemed that all too soon it was getting time for me to leave for Gabon. The time window for me to travel in that country would soon start closing, and I wanted a full month there. Thus began an awkward, sad time dealing with Vanessa. Late afternoon on the day before I was to leave for Gabon, we were lying in my bed. The sun shone brightly through the sheer curtains drawn across the floor-to-ceiling windows, casting a soft radiance across the room.

"I love you," Vanessa said simply. "I'll wait for you to return from Gabon." (I was planning to pass back through Lomé for a few days in a month, before catching a flight to Europe for the New Year's holiday).

Once again, Vanessa had surprised me. I gently said that this could not work, that we were too different in age, culture, and life experience.

"Don't you love me?" she asked.

"It's just not something that can happen," I replied. "We come from different worlds in too many ways. It is a gap that cannot really be bridged. It has been wonderful knowing you. But this is not a situation where love can actually conquer all."

"None of this matters," Vanessa replied, perhaps trying to sound more practical and worldly than she could possibly be at her stage in life. "It's what's in your heart that counts."

She said she could see that I was a "real good man with a big heart," and she had never met anyone who had lived a life like mine.

The whole situation was deeply touching, and I had no good way to handle it. I tried to make it better by having as nice an experience with her as possible while I had the chance. The next evening was my last in Lomé—my flight to Gabon was early the next morning. I took Vanessa to my favorite restaurant in town: a little French country-style restaurant with small tables and white linens and candles. While we dined, a violinist came and played at our table. I mentioned to Vanessa that I would be back in town Christmas Eve and that I would like to take her to this place again before I flew on to Europe.

She smiled and said that would be great, but looked achingly sad saying it.

Later, we returned to my guesthouse and had drinks with the owner. I had to prepare for my flight, and it was time to say good-bye. I didn't show it, but a sad, sick feeling hit me in the gut when I had to say good-bye to Vanessa. Being around her had reawakened a part of me that had fallen dormant during the long denouement of my relationship with Achara.

I flagged down a motorcycle taxi outside the guesthouse gate to take Vanessa home. She blew me a kiss and flashed a warm smile as the taxi whisked her away. With her hair blowing in the late evening breeze, she still looked like a movie starlet.

I knew I would not see Vanessa again when I returned for my short pass through Lomé in December.

I flew back into Lomé on Christmas Eve. My plan was to fly to Paris with Royal Air Maroc on December 27. From there I would fly on to Krakow, Poland. But once again, Royal Air Maroc goofed up my flight, and I was stranded in Lomé for a couple of extra days, finally making it to beautiful, friendly Krakow late in the afternoon on New Year's Eve.

I did not see Vanessa during that second visit to Lomé. When I called her as I had promised, she said she would really like to see me but she couldn't, because it would be too hard to say good-bye yet again. I understood, of course.

Vanessa added that if I ever came back to Lomé to see her, I would see that I had been wrong: that the age difference, and any other "differences" that I felt were important, were not what mattered.

CHAPTER 16

Borneo: Valentine's Day in the Jungle

February 2010
Sekonyer River, Tanjung Puting National Park,
Southwest Kalimantan, Indonesia

The cumulus clouds piled high overhead, obscuring the blazing equatorial midday sun. As we chugged up the narrowing river, an endless string of palms lined the river's edges, shading the murky brown waters. The engine rattled and droned like an old lawnmower in the background. Even here on the moving boat, there was no relief from the stifling heat.

"Look, Gary! Over there," Indah called out softly, pointing to some rustling branches on the riverbank.

I looked over to where Indah, the young Dayak woman serving as my guide, was pointing. Two adult monkeys and a baby were sitting on some branches overhanging the riverbank, in a domestic tableau that looked strangely human. The adults were potbellied and had longish, pointy noses. A small baby clutched one of the adults, presumably its mother, burying its head in the hair of her stomach as if trying to hide from us. Its mother looked impassively over at us with a wise, patient expression.

"Proboscis monkeys," Indah said. "Some of them, the man ones, have very long noses. There are many here in the park. But people tell me they are in trouble in the other parts of Borneo because so many people cut down the forests where they live."

Pushing on upriver, we passed more monkeys, who made their presence known by their frantic rustling in the treetops as our boat droned past. Unlike on my first river trip in Kalimantan, up the Kahayan a few years earlier, the forest here was alive with wildlife. As always, I loved the cacophonous, mesmerizing sounds of the jungle. Its multifold layers of bird whistles, caws, and cackles, and the timeless droning of a billion unseen insects, overwhelmed us whenever the pilot throttled the engine back to idle. We passed some hornbills scuffling on a branch, identifiable even at a distance by the upswept yellow and orange casque atop their long, thick white beaks. Stork-billed kingfishers flitted about a crocodile masquerading as a half-submerged log.

I had chartered the double-decked wooden riverboat with its crew of two to take us up the Sekonyer River, into Tanjung Puting National Park. Tanjung Puting, on Borneo's southwest coast, is well known for its work in orangutan preservation and rehabilitation. At the forefront of this effort is the famous primate research center Camp Leakey, based in the park. Along with orangutans, Tanjung Puting is home to the endangered proboscis monkey and has high biodiversity in other primates as well.

As the sun emerged from behind the towering ziggurat of clouds, I looked over at Indah, relaxing on one of the two deck chairs set up on the observation deck in the bows. Unfathomably to me, she was wearing a light sweater against the faint breeze of the boat's movement.

Completely by accident, I had managed to end up on a boat in the middle of the jungle with only the crew of two and this gorgeous young woman accompanying me. Too bad I didn't really know her, I thought. It was Saturday, February 13, the eve of Valentine's Day. It would have been the perfect time to be here with someone I was close to.

I had met Indah a few days ago in Pangkalanbun, a pleasant backwater carved out of the jungle not far from Tanjung Puting. Her boss, a man named Budi, was the manager of operations for a transport company in Pangkalanbun. I had met him while catching my flight to Pangkalanbun from Jakarta. Budi was a pleasant, friendly young man, and during the several-hour flight to Pangkalanbun, we became fast friends. When we touched down in Pangkalanbun he had his driver bring me from the town's tiny airport to a decent budget guesthouse that he knew. He also invited me to join him, his wife, and their 7-year-old son for dinner.

Budi's family and I hit it off at dinner. His wife was amiable and talkative, and I enjoyed their energetic but well-behaved son. In fact, we got along so well that they all wanted to join me on the five-day trip to Tanjung Puting. Budi just asked that I wait till Saturday morning to leave (it was Tuesday night at the time), since the weekend was the best time for him to start a short vacation from work. Thinking what fun it would be to have this delightful family along for the trip, I decided to knock around Pangkalanbun for the rest of the week.

On my second day in Pangkalanbun, Budi invited me to his office in town so we could meet his family for lunch at a local Chinese restaurant. While at his office, he had introduced me to his assistant, Indah. Indah had done some guiding for visitors into Tanjung Puting in the past and would handle all the necessary arrangements for our boat trip. I was pleasantly surprised to find such an attractive young woman in the boondocks of Borneo. Reserved but obviously capable, she could have passed as a legal assistant in a large, high-end law firm.

I had ended up having several lunches and dinners with Budi and his family during the rest of the week, and Indah joined us a few times. During our Thursday evening dinner, she asked Budi and me if she could join us on our upcoming river trip. She offered to be our guide in exchange for her share of the trip costs. Budi and I readily agreed.

On Saturday morning, the big day for starting our trip, I got a call from Budi. He was rushing to the airport. Something had come up, and he had to fly out of town immediately to handle it. He sounded truly mortified at having to cancel, and offered to pay his share of the trip costs, which we had earlier set at two-thirds of the total expenses. I told Budi not to worry about it. Then Indah called to say she was renegotiating a better price for the trip, since now less than half as many people were going.

I had looked forward to Budi and his family's company, but as the trip got under way, I got over my disappointment. I had done quite a few jungle river trips over the years, and this was one of my favorite ways to journey. Traveling on a boat was an easy way to "rough it" in wild surroundings. The boat's movement created at least a bit of a breeze to offset the oppressive heat and humidity, and it kept most of the bugs off us. Also, the sheer mind-boggling diversity of rain forest life added to the tingle of excitement I had always felt since early childhood when venturing into unknown, exotic places. As our boat pushed farther up the river, I had that familiar sense of entering a parallel world while the "real" world drifted ever further away.

To my surprise, Indah, who had been almost silent each time I saw her during the few days before the trip, turned out to be talkative and animated once we got going. At least I would have someone to talk to over the next five days. She was fascinated by the far-flung travels I had done, and like most people, she found it hard to fathom traveling for so long.

"It is my dream to travel like you," Indah mentioned shortly after we got started. "I want to go everywhere, to see the great natural places, animals, and interesting people in the world. But I have never been off Borneo."

As we both sat in folding chairs on the front observation deck, passing alongside the river's endless fringe of palm trees and other jungle foliage, Indah was relentless with her questions. What was the

Amazon like? Did the indigenous people there still use spears and poisoned darts to hunt? What was California like? Had I ever seen a polar bear? On she pressed. Her curiosity was touching. It was also a reminder of how the lives of most people who lived in the Disappearing World—even "modernized" people such Indah—were quite remote and isolated.

About halfway through the afternoon, our boat stopped by a raised wooden walkway that led into the lush green forest. We had come to the great park's check-in point. Our captain, an amiable, gangling middle-aged Dayak, went to register us and pay our entrance fees. Meanwhile, Indah and I walked along the half-mile wooden platform.

The shallow waters below were surprisingly clear. Tiny fish darted around, and a couple of iridescent greenish-gold dragonflies skimmed the water. Wetland plants sprouted out of the shallow waters, with larger, thicker trees dangling their aerial roots down toward the surface. One area we walked by had a thick patch of Venus flytraps, their clusters of little leaf baskets awaiting some hapless insect's misstep. The mosquitoes and biting midges were relentless, though, and it was a relief to return to the boat.

Back on board, Indah and I continued our conversation as the boat sputtered back to life and pushed on upriver. She was also curious about the great cities of the world. For someone who had never been off the island of Borneo before, she seemed to know a lot about them. She had even already planned some imaginative itineraries for New York, Tokyo, and many of Europe's major cities. On a visit to Paris, for example, the Louvre would be near the top of her list, of course. But she was also definite about going to a certain chocolate shop in St. Germain. I was impressed—even though I had been in Paris twice and had stayed in St. Germain with Quentin only last year, I was not familiar with the famous chocolatier.

"How do you know so much about these cities?" I asked.

"The Internet, of course—and television," Indah replied matter-of-factly. "But I really learn a lot from Facebook. I have many friends around the world who tell me all about their homes."

"Really?" I said. "Tell me about Facebook"

She practically gasped in disbelief. "Don't you have a Facebook account?"

I felt a bit sheepish all of a sudden, as if we had switched roles and I had been the one living in the jungle all my life.

"Yes," I replied, "I actually just opened a Facebook account two months ago. I had some new friends I met in Africa recently insist that I do it. But I haven't used it yet and don't really know much about it. I am very tech literate, though," I added a little defensively, not wanting to sound like too much of a Luddite. As exhibit A, I explained how my former position at the bank in Los Angeles had involved creating a software system that used the Internet for data communications. I pointed out that I had been traveling without a break since November 2006—over three years—and so was a little out of touch. I also mentioned that Facebook had only just started catching on around the time I started my travel project.

"Just think of me as a sort of Rip Van Winkle," I joked. "When I finally stop traveling, I'll have to reacquaint myself with all the latest developments of modern society."

I suddenly felt quietly overwhelmed by the irony of it all. Here I was, on a boat chuffing up some remote river in the jungles of Borneo, learning about Facebook from a girl who had never been off the island and whose not-so-distant ancestors were headhunters.

"So, tell me about Facebook," I said.

Indah proceeded to explain the basics of the social network phenomenon. She had almost a thousand "friends" on Facebook. She posted on it, uploaded photos, and commented on other people's postings many times each day.

"I would be posting right now, but there is no signal here," she said as she snapped a picture of monkeys in the trees along the shore, using the camera on her pink smartphone.

"I'd also make you post some things on Facebook, and I'd be your first Facebook friend!" she said, with a tinge of pride at being able to teach me something.

As I would come to learn, Indah was part of a huge trend in Indonesia. Incongruously to me, this country had one of the largest numbers of Facebook users in the world. Like a giant tsunami, the social network had swept the archipelago nation, connecting people from its thousands of islands and hundreds of cultures to people around a world that was otherwise hopelessly out of reach.

As the afternoon mellowed into early evening, the stretch of river we were on narrowed. Looking straight ahead always gave me the sensation that we were riding a brown ribbon on a heading that would soon take us smack into a sheer escarpment of deep green. Also, the activity in the trees along the banks seemed to be increasing. More proboscis monkeys than ever clambered among the branches, the males looking ridiculous with their outsize Jimmy Durante schnozzes. In a small clearing by the shore, a couple of yard-long grayish monitor lizards slouched, looking like little dinosaurs. A thin green snake lay beautifully camouflaged on a leafy bough overhanging the water.

Soon, we came to a halt, and the crew moored the boat for the night. As always in the equatorial tropics, darkness came hard on the heels of sunset. Indah, I, and the two crewmen took quick showers in the little stall aft. This was the only time, day or night, when we could have temporary relief from the constant sticky sweat.

Afterward, as the crew set about making dinner for everyone, Indah and I sat amidships and continued our conversation. I couldn't imagine living here in a time before mosquito repellent.

As twilight faded fast, Indah told me about her business studies, which she pursued at the local university while working for Budi. Her aim after finishing at the local university was to go to a top business school for an advanced degree.

Indah came across as very earnest in her ambitions. Her main interests lay in issues of social justice. She wanted to make a difference in bringing change to her corruption-riddled country, and the best way to do this, she felt, was to become a leader of a large business or go into law. Since the law didn't really interest her, she was pursuing the business route. She felt that as a business leader, she could guide a company to be good to the environment, fair to the workers, and profitable to the owners.

"Business leaders naturally influence politicians," she said. "So this is a path of change for the better. But I may have to switch my course-work," she added ruefully. "My mother doesn't want me to study for an advanced business degree."

"Why not?" I asked. "She doesn't like businesspeople?"

Indah went on to explain how her mother was afraid that no one would want to marry her if she went into business. "It is not a feminine thing to do," she said. "My mother is afraid it will scare men off. She really wants me to get married and give her grandchildren soon."

Instead, her mother thought she should study literature or history—or even perhaps medicine, and be a nurse. Indah sounded very discouraged by this maternal pressure.

"But you're only twenty-two years old," I said. "You have lots of time to get married, and anyway, men admire women who are strong and successful."

"Not here in Borneo—or anywhere in Indonesia, for that matter. This is what my mother is afraid of, anyway."

"Why don't you just do it anyway?" I said. "It's your life and, ultimately, your choice. I'm sure your mom would accept this."

"It doesn't work that way in Asian families—at least here in Indonesia," Indah replied, sounding more discouraged than ever. She explained that her mother would not pay for her studies if she didn't do what her mother wanted, and that she didn't make enough at her job to pay for her studies herself. Also, if she went against her mother's wishes, her mother might push her out of her life.

I asked what her father thought. He was a science teacher at a local high school.

"My mother is the boss in our home," Indah said flatly. "I am the oldest daughter, and I am expected to set the example for my younger brother and sister in respecting her wishes."

She concluded by saying that she often felt as though her best option was to marry a foreign man, someone who would let her live the life she wanted, travel, and be herself.

Indah was expressing an all-too-common life dilemma for young and ambitious women in still very traditional Asian societies. In my travels in various parts of Asia, I had heard many stories with a similar theme. In too many places around the world, outside the small rich parts, women's life possibilities were still severely confined by cultural obstacles, beliefs, and taboos.

The captain's assistant interrupted our conversation to announce that dinner was ready. He served us grilled fish, rice, leafy green vegetables, and beans with onions and broth. Nothing fancy, but it was healthy—perfect for me. The longer I traveled, the finickier I got about keeping a healthy diet, no matter where I happened to be.

After dinner, I returned to the bow to sit for a while. It was a clear night, with lots of stars and a bright platinum sliver of moon, and the forest was humming, hooting, croaking, and crying at full volume. The crew had set up two small mosquito-net tents amidships for us, each with a small sleeping mat, a single sheet, and a pillow. They had also pulled down the boat's canvas rain canopy before retiring to the lower deck to drink and relax.

Indah came up to sit with me. She had brought chocolates, which I loved, and we just talked for the next couple of hours.

Indah told me about her ancestry. Her whole family was Dayak. Some of her ancestors came from central and eastern Borneo, and from the stories passed to her parents, it was a very different world from hers—a wild world of animals and spirits.

"For them, the forest was their whole world," she said. "There was nothing modern like we have now."

In the blackness of the jungle, the chorus of insects, frogs, and birds blared away with their raucous nightly din. Moonlight glinted off the river's smooth surface. I loved being on the water in the rain forest at night. All the world's great tropical forests seemed to evoke a certain feeling in me: the illusory stillness of the waters, the reptilian eyes peering above the surface like little periscopes, the cacophony of animal sounds, mixed with the smells of the dark surrounding forests—it all gave a false sense of peacefulness, belying the constant struggle for survival that was going on at every level, from the river bottom to the top of the canopy.

We were sitting on a blanket on the deck. Indah had pulled herself slightly behind me to avoid the almost imperceptible breeze coming over the bow. Amazingly, she was actually feeling cold and using me for a windbreak. I always found it surprising and a little humorous how people living in these hot, humid places could actually feel chilled by the slightest breeze—as if they could be comfortable only in a sauna. I, on the other hand, was still sweltering from the relentless humidity.

Indah, meanwhile, looked radiant, with moonlight glinting off her black hair and shining in her dark eyes.

Then she asked with a soft smile, "Do you know what tonight is?"

"Yes, of course. It's Valentine's eve," I replied. I paused for a moment, then said, "I have to admit, this is a pretty nice place to be: on a river in the middle of a beautiful starlit rain forest."

All of a sudden, I felt a strange combination of self-consciousness and nervous excitement.

I couldn't resist, though. I had to throw it out there. "I can't think of a more romantic place or situation than here in this moment."

Indah looked at me, the reflected starlight gleaming in her eyes. "Yes, it doesn't get more romantic then this," she said in a low, soft voice.

The incessant rattle and buzz of the enveloping jungle now seemed like soft background music. The moment was just too perfect an accident to let pass.

In the dead of night, Indah nudged me awake. We both had nodded off under her mosquito net. She asked if she could go over and sleep in mine. She was freezing, she said. The stultifying heat and humidity was making me sweat so much, the sleeping mat and sheet were soaked, and it was giving Indah a chill.

"It is better that I go over to the other bed anyway," she said, "so the crew will not see us together when daylight comes. It would not look good for me."

Later, when the sun started to rise, I saw that she had wrapped herself in my sheet, tight as a mummy. I was amazed. How could someone actually be cold in an equatorial rain forest?

That morning, we hiked inland along some forest paths to Camp Leakey, the famous orangutan research and rehabilitation station. The research station was set up in 1971 by the paleoanthropologist Louis Leakey, whose work in East Africa included many excavations of early hominid fossils from different points in the human evolutionary chain. His camp in the Tanjung Puting Wildlife Reserve was set up to support primate research in the big national park. Over the years, the camp had been the base for impressive research into the behavior of orangutans, gibbons, and proboscis monkeys—including orangutans' capacity to learn sign language and other advanced cognitive functions.

The camp guide met our boat captain, Indah, and me along the path near the camp's entrance. He led us into Camp Leakey, which looked like a pretty simple affair for such an important research center. Its half-dozen small, rustic buildings set in a forest clearing looked deserted, as if the place was closed.

The young camp guide explained that everything was temporarily closed for the rainy season. Most of the staff had gone away for vacation. There were not a lot of orangutans around, either, since they spread out and stayed deep in the forest during the rainy season.

Seeing our disappointment, the guide pointed to a padlocked building and said he could open the camp museum for us. It seemed that the only orangutans I was going to see would be in photos in the museum.

Although I had read that the rainy season was not the best time to see orangutans, my research had indicated that they could still be seen all year round at Tanjung Puting since they were fairly numerous here and habituated to people in the park. I couldn't come in the summer, though, because I was planning a trip to the Alaskan Arctic. So I had decided to take my chances on seeing orangutans during the slow rainy season.

Further deflating my hopes of seeing any orangutans, the camp guide told us that for some reason, the great apes had been unusually scarce this rainy season. He advised me to come back in the summer, then offered to lead us on a forest trek to an orangutan feeding station. I felt a spark of hope. We might be able to see some orangutans on this trip, if we were willing to hike around for a while.

So we took a day trek down a trail that would take us past an orangutan feeding station. This was a place where Camp Leakey personnel came to leave food for orangs they were rehabilitating toward a fully independent life in the wilderness. Some of the orangutans here in the park were from other areas of Borneo that had been deforested. Others had been orphaned at a young age, before they could fend for themselves. Many of the rehabilitating orangutans had been raised in captivity as pets after being poached from the wild when they were babies. They had been saved from one miserable fate only to face an uncertain future in their imperiled forest habitat.

The camp guide had two local helpers carry a large bucket of chopped-up sugarcane stalks, which looked more like firewood than food, and follow us on our trek. We hiked along a narrow forest trail through dense patches of slender trees. At several places along the trail, colorful little mushrooms popped out of the ground, looking like tiny bright orange, purple, or aqua umbrellas. At another spot, we moved quietly past two scarlet-rumped trogons sitting on low branches. Several shamas, a pretty little bird with a rust belly, white rump, and longish tail, were chirping and darting about in the undergrowth. The place seemed timeless, as if it had always been here and would surely be here forever.

Tanjung Puting National Park includes several distinct tropical forest ecosystems, which give it a huge biodiversity. A big part of the park is primarily peat swamp forest and heath forest, with acidic, sandy soils poor in nutrients. This type of forest is also found in certain large sections of the Amazon Basin, along the Rio Negro. It makes for a fragile type of ecosystem, and deforestation tends to permanently alter the environment, so that the forest does not regenerate in the same manner. Thus, the protected areas of Tanjung Puting are vitally important to preserving this imperiled ecosystem.

During our hike to the orangutan feeding area, I noticed that the forest canopy in the areas we passed through was not very thick or high, and the trees seemed fairly young. So I asked the camp guide whether the area had been logged.

Yes, the guide said, most of this was second-growth forest. He then explained that even though Tanjung Puting had been a national park since 1982, it had nonetheless seen several logging operations. It was a familiar and depressing tale: Indonesia has a terribly corrupt government whose officials often don't enforce the rules. Thus, illegal logging, mining, and hunting in protected areas, even in national parks, are a problem all over Kalimantan (Indonesian Borneo) and throughout the whole of Indonesia.

After a bit of a hike, we came to a small square clearing in the forest. This was one of the feeding areas for the orangutans. Baiting the orangs with sugarcane wasn't exactly what I had had in mind when I set out on this trip, but it would be better than nothing. The two helpers emptied their load of sugarcane stalks onto a big crude wooden table set up in the middle of the clearing, and we all just sat back and waited.

And waited. No orangutans came. But a large herd of wild pigs happened to wander into the feeding area. These were nothing like domestic hogs down on the farm. The adults were big and muscular, perhaps two and a half feet in height but more streamlined and with pointier snouts and narrower bodies than domestic hogs. This made them more adept at running through forest growth at high speed. The guide warned us that wild forest pigs could be aggressive, but these seemed almost tame. Still, I wasn't about to try anything stupid.

After an hour or so, we gave up on the orangs and hiked back to check out the camp museum, then returned to the boat for the night.

Before darkness set in we moved a bit upstream, anchoring in a beautiful sheltered spot. Fairly high trees formed a canopy where proboscis monkeys gamboled about, jumping and chasing each other.

When we came back aboard, our friendly and accommodating crew had a surprise for Indah and me. Although we had tried to be discreet last night, we apparently had fooled no one.

The upper deck had been rearranged for a special Valentine's evening. The two small individual mosquito nets were gone, replaced with one big enough to walk around in. Inside was a thin but comfortable futon mattress big enough for two. And as if this were not enough, in the middle of the futon bed lay a pillow as red as an American Beauty rose, with the two normal pillows placed side by side at one end. As an added touch, the captain told Indah that they would run the boat's small diesel generator for a couple of hours this evening. This way, we could watch a DVD movie on my laptop computer without completely draining the PC's remaining battery life.

The plan for the next two days was to make some long treks deeper into the forest, in the hope of finding some orangutans. Somehow, I knew that this goal of seeing these great apes—my main goal for the trip—would go unfulfilled. Soon, darkness fell, and another beautiful starlit night began. And as the whooping and chirring and clacking of the rain forest wind and rhythm section kicked into full gear, I felt that this would still be a memorable trip, orangs or no.

———

I left Indonesia in late February, on a short flight from Jakarta to Kuala Lumpur, the capital of Malaysia. In my cramped seat on Air Asia, the continent's super budget airline, I couldn't even put my knees together.

While sitting in this ridiculously cramped position, I studied my travel itinerary. To finish my travel project as efficiently as possible, I had laid out a spreadsheet with a "business plan" for my travels. My remaining objectives were color coded, with a detailed calendar for the horizontal axis running across the top of the spreadsheet. Below the calendar axis, my remaining objectives were positioned in the best seasonal windows for each particular activity, ordered according to priority.

My travel plan itinerary looked exhausting. It showed back-to-back journeys almost nonstop for the next eleven months, straight through to mid-January 2011. And then, with only a short breather, more back-to-back journeys for the rest of 2011. I realized I had a problem. I was burning out again, and I worried that I wouldn't be able to push myself through the home stretch.

As I had done a year earlier in Bangkok, I again thought about why I was doing my travel project, and all the same reasons why I couldn't stop now came up again. The most important reason was simply that I hadn't finished. I had put my whole life on pause to do this project. Everything I owned was in storage, and this opportunity would never come again. If I didn't finish, I would regret it for the rest of my days. This travel project was the fulfillment of my lifelong dream to do an extended period of uninterrupted travel—to really know the world. And most urgently of all my reasons, the rapidly accelerating changes taking place all over the world meant that much of what I sought to experience would soon be gone or, at best, become a vastly watered-down version of the real thing. I had to press on.

Later, while in Kuala Lumpur, I spent time with Ross. This was his favorite city in Southeast Asia, and he was here often. Since Ross and I first met, we had periodically shared with each other the personal challenges involved in our long-term travel situations, and sought each other's advice on how to deal with those challenges. One blazing-hot afternoon, we were walking along the running track at a large university. During our conversation, I mentioned to Ross some of my thoughts on the flight into Kuala Lumpur, when making the spreadsheet plan for my remaining travel objectives.

"It seems like almost every other day for the past few years, I've met someone who told me I was living something that they had always dreamed of doing," I said. "I know I'm really lucky to be able to do this long-term travel, and it has been a great experience, but it definitely comes with a price tag. In fact, sometimes I lose track of the dream part of it all."

I explained that for me, the biggest price was not the physical demands or the frequent bouts of tedium, but the loneliness and isolation that this constant travel necessarily entailed. I pointed out that in the past year my travels had become more socially oriented, including meeting a few really nice women along the way. Despite this, the isolation and loneliness were really starting to wear on me.

It didn't help that I still missed the closeness I once had with Achara.

"What about Indah in Borneo?" Ross asked. "She's beautiful and sounds like a winner. You should marry her!"

Perhaps he said this half in jest—I couldn't tell. I agreed with Ross that Indah was indeed wonderful, but it was not the right thing for me right now. For one thing, she was just too young for me—still in the process of becoming a woman and figuring out who she was. I wanted a woman who was established and already knew who she was and what she wanted in life.

"There'd be no future with Indah," I said. And indeed, she was smart enough to know this without any explanation. I told Ross that on our last evening together, Indah had been philosophical about our meeting each other. She cried a bit, but like me, she knew that we had had a wonderful, memorable short time together and that this was all it could ever be.

"Yeah, you're right," Ross said. "You're still a relatively young but nevertheless mature man." He stopped walking on the track and looked in my eyes. "To me, your problem right now is clear. You need to stop traveling for a while and connect with people—and, especially, connect with a woman."

Ross's solution was a practical one: to settle in one place for a while, maybe three months. He told me I should rent an apartment for that time, put out roots into the community, and go to some social events. "You have the money to afford it, so go to the elite clubs, even. Get to know people that you see on a regular basis. Meet some hot, quality women you can interact normally with, over time, where the woman will know you'll actually be around for a while."

I argued that I couldn't stop my travels, that I really needed to finish my travel project without delay so that I could get on with the next stage of my life.

"No. I'm telling you, I think you need to stop traveling now," Ross concluded. "Otherwise, you'll ruin the rest of your planned travels because you won't be happy."

I had to admit, he was probably right. But I wasn't sure how to do what he suggested. If I put my travel plans on hold, I'd have to delay finishing the project even longer. I was already looking at my project going two years longer than originally planned.

My next destination was the Philippines, where I planned to spend seven weeks on mostly rugged travel into a few of the wilder, remoter places of that amazingly diverse archipelago. I flew into the chaotic, polluted, traffic-choked capital, Manila. Because I arrived very early in the morning, my taxi managed to avoid the worst of the traffic as it brought me to the nice, highly recommended guesthouse I had reserved online. Ironically, although my guesthouse was officially in the modern financial area called Makati, it was actually on the edge of a large red-light district of brothels and girlie bars. Nevertheless, it was a comfortable and homey place, and I put off moving on to my first destination in the Philippines.

Shortly after settling into my guesthouse by the red-light district, I went out for the evening to an upscale popular restaurant and entertainment center in the Makati financial district. There, I happened to strike up an acquaintance with an amiable local businessman and some American expats. My new friends ultimately introduced me to their social circle, which included a salsa dance group. I wasn't especially into salsa dancing, but soon I was going out almost every evening to some sort of event or gathering. Also, a wonderful couple I had met in Gabon—a Frenchman and his Filipina wife—had returned to Manila. All of a sudden, I had a full social life again—something I had forgone the past three years. I continued to delay my real travel plans for the Philippines.

Through the salsa group, I met an attractive, accomplished, energetic Filipina woman. With her, I had what started to resemble a normal dating situation. She was a 40-year-old professional who owned a factory making bedding and linens, which she exported to the USA and Europe. It was a refreshing experience to feel almost settled again. She showed me many interesting places in Manila, and we had some nice times. Ross's prescription for me to settle down, dig into a community, and connect with a high-quality woman was starting to happen organically, almost by accident.

My impromptu stay in Manila ended up lasting six weeks. The facsimile of a normal life, a relationship with a woman that amounted to more than a one-night or -week stand, and a normal home (if you looked past the rows of seedy go-go and girlie bars) helped reenergize me. I probably could have stayed in Manila and the Philippines for a long time. The people were warm and hospitable, and the modern parts of the country, with all the widespread American influence, seemed very familiar to me. But by the end of April, I had to move on to continue my travel project.

Though Ross was probably correct in his prescription for my doldrums, I didn't want to take any more time off from my travels. Also, I felt it was unfair to start a relationship with a woman, knowing that sooner or later I would just up and leave.

Over the next few months, I was fully focused on my remaining travel objectives. I traveled in the Philippines and then went to Palau, a small island group in the western Pacific that was one of the objectives on my travel planning spreadsheet. From Palau, I went on to China to visit the World Expo in Shanghai, then back to Thailand for twelve days.

Thailand was roiling in crisis yet again. Large antigovernment protests had paralyzed Bangkok for the past seven weeks, threatening the well-being of the entire country. Thailand was more divided than ever, with no end in sight. While I was there, the government finally cracked down and moved the military into Bangkok to break the back of the siege that the protesters had the city under. It was a disaster. Riots broke out, with scores of people killed and a number of buildings burned, including the tony Central World shopping and entertainment center. It was painful to see the Land of Smiles in such anguish.

Against this backdrop, I reappeared briefly at Achara's house. As always, I got a warm welcome as part of the family. In late May, I left the scarred city of Bangkok for the clean solitude of Alaska, where I spent the summer. I spent part of that time in the Arctic National Wildlife Refuge, an area that had been the subject of long and heated political debate about whether oil drilling should be permitted in that amazing pristine wilderness. The untouched emptiness of the rugged Alaskan Arctic was a vivid reminder to me of the natural wonders I had originally sought to experience. It was a timely reminder. My next destination was a country with perhaps the most appallingly awful government on the planet: North Korea.

CHAPTER 17

North Korea: A Chilling Experience

*600,000 to 3,500,000: estimated range for the numbers of
people who starved to death in the North Korean famine
of 1994-98. This was out of an original population
estimated at 22 million at the time.*

*"Workers' Paradise": one of many propaganda terms
for North Korea coined by the same government
that oversaw the famine of 1994-98.*

My week in North Korea was the toughest trip of my entire travel project. It wasn't physically uncomfortable or demanding by any means, and nobody even tried to rob me. But much of what I experienced on the tour was weird beyond words, and the horrific repression of the country's people was the most chilling thing I have ever witnessed. It was so depressing, in fact, that only a couple of days into my tour, I was looking forward to getting out of there. For I had truly found hell on earth.

Over the years, I had read about North Korea, including some excellent books based on defectors' accounts. So in theory, I was ready. And there were no big surprises. You go to North Korea knowing that you will be lied to for the entire tour. And you figure that your North

Korean tour leaders—who are, in fact, your minders—know that they are lying, and, moreover, know that you know they are lying. But the whole charade proceeds more or less on schedule, as planned.

I had never intended to visit North Korea, officially called the Democratic People's Republic of Korea, or DPRK. I wouldn't go there, because I didn't want to contribute money to the horrific regime that oversaw the country. After all, any money from tours went straight to the government. I changed my mind, though, in May 2010, when I visited the North Korean country pavilion at the Shanghai World Expo.

The North Korean pavilion at the Shanghai Expo featured mostly drab and stagnant displays. One thing really caught my attention, though. To the left of the entrance into the pavilion was the DPRK national flag and a red banner proclaiming the "Workers' Paradise." Next to this was a row of four television monitors. The monitors were all the same and looked like old color television sets from the 1970s. All the monitors were showing propaganda videos about the amazing progress and modernity of the DPRK.

I watched the videos in fascination for perhaps an hour. Each video would play for about fifteen minutes and then restart. I viewed all four. Watching the videos, I thought to myself, *is this for real? Is this the best propaganda they can produce to show the outside world about how wonderful life is for citizens of the "Workers' Paradise?"* I had assumed that a regime that ran the largest maximum-security penal colony on the planet—the entire territory of North Korea— would at least have world-class propaganda wizards to be able to pull it all off.

The pathetically outdated monitors aside, the videos were hack jobs—a middle school film club could have put out a better product. A couple of video scenes showed happy consumers going to a "modern" foodstore that looked straight out of the 1970s. Corny video pans showed small, neat piles of vegetables and fruits and rows of very basic canned goods. Another video scene showed the modern neonatal facility in Pyongyang's flagship hospital. Here again, the technology on display looked like the state of the art from the early 1970s.

Another video scene showed a North Korean citizen's home: a small two-bedroom apartment with drab linoleum flooring, and a gleaming white flush toilet in a small bathroom complete with a little white porcelain sink. The video made a point of showing that the sink even had real hot and cold faucet handles. Other video scenes showed the city of Pyongyang with its wide boulevards, mostly empty of vehicles. The few somewhat stylish taller modern buildings of the otherwise drab city were also featured. The entire set of productions looked like something from a time capsule buried forty years ago.

This horrific antiquated system couldn't last much longer, I thought. I had to go see it.

I justified this decision, figuring it was better for the long-suffering inhabitants of North Korea to see and have at least some fleeting contact with outsiders. Tourists are the clearest evidence that other people in the world have the freedom and wealth to come to their country. But for the vast majority of North Koreans, the reverse is impossible— which goes a way toward refuting the state propaganda nonsense of North Korea as a superior system of a prospering workers' or people's "paradise."

The whole weird tour experience started with a forty-five-minute briefing, held the day before our tour group was to fly into the DPRK. (People can visit the country only as part of a government-licensed tour group.) This event was held by our tour company, Koryo Tours, in its office in Beijing. All thirty-five of us tour participants sat on folding chairs in the Koryo Tours briefing room. Our tour leader, a bright, easy-going twenty-something Englishwoman named Megan, then covered a long list of dos and don'ts that we should follow strictly during the tour.

These admonitions included instructions to take photographs only when given permission, and a warning that violators of this rule would be reported. Also, we were not to say anything derogatory about the DPRK government or ever wander off on our own during the tour. We learned the proper technique for photographing the many statues we would see of the country's leader, and not to talk about political issues or dispute the version of history being presented by our tour guides.

Some of the points Megan covered were downright comical. One of these regarded images of the North Korean leader, Kim Jong-il.

"Respect the portraits of the leader, Kim Jong-il," she said. "His picture is usually featured on the front page of the newspapers, including the English-language *Pyongyang Times*—depicting him doing something like visiting a factory, for instance. When you finish reading the paper or want to take a copy with you, don't fold it so that the crease is on the portrait. Fold the paper in such a way that the creases do not go through the portrait of the leader. And when you've finished with the paper in your hotel room, don't throw it in the garbage. Just leave it, without creasing the portrait, in your hotel room for one of the staff to collect and dispose of properly."

Megan confessed that she didn't know how the papers were actually discarded after the maids took them away. She then told the story of a hapless tourist who threw his copy of the *Pyongyang Times*, with its portrait of Kim Jong-il, into the trash bin. When the hotel staff discovered this transgression, he actually had to write an apology letter.

The morning after the briefing, our tour group flew to Pyongyang on Air Koryo, North Korea's national airline, in a small 1970s Russian Tupolev jet.

A comfortable air-conditioned tour bus picked us up from the airport and brought us through downtown Pyongyang, along Victory Boulevard, to our hotel. The city was mostly drab, dull, and monochrome. Most nongovernmental buildings were simple rectangular concrete affairs without much color. We passed some impressively wide boulevards that were strangely empty of cars. Old buses puttered down the boulevards while old-fashioned streetcars shrieked and clattered along the edges.

About the only color to be found in the city came in the form of the many propaganda signs along our route. One large billboard showed a square-jawed soldier on a white horse, charging skyward. Another showed a heroically stylized worker in a hardhat, a soldier, and a student all rushing toward a glorious socialist sunrise.

We arrived at the Yanggakdo Hotel, one of Pyongyang's main tourist hotels. The Yanggakdo was an austere yet imposing forty-seven-story structure of supremely unimaginative design. But its location—on an island in the Taedong River—was ideal for keeping its guests isolated from the city that surrounded it. The island's only ingress and egress were two bridges that took vehicles to and from the hotel. Megan, who would be with us all week, told us we were free to take a walk outside the hotel on our own, though we must stay on the island. Any attempt to leave would be blocked by guards on the premises.

That evening, for the first activity of our tour, we went to see the Mass Games. This performance spectacle came into widespread use as a propaganda tool throughout the Communist world during the mid-twentieth century. The purpose is to show the might of the state, depict its mythic glories, and demonstrate the people's discipline and unity in supporting the state. The most spectacular recent example of Mass Games was the opening ceremonies of the Beijing 2008 Olympics. That was a one-off spectacle, though—North Korea's Mass Games are now the only regularly scheduled events of this kind left in the world.

It was still daylight when we took our seats in Pyongyang's gigantic May Day Stadium, thought to be the largest in the world. The huge Mass Games propaganda show was just beginning. Across the vast field, the background scenery for the performance was changing.

Large stripes—red, dark blue, green, light blue, and yellow—stretched across the far side of the stadium. Interposed on this and running vertically were rows of Korean letters. Accompanying the scenery change, a low rumble like rolling thunder resounded from across the stadium. The scenery imaging seemed like a low-resolution video on a mega scale.

"How is the scenery accomplished?" I asked Herman, the man sitting next to me. "It doesn't appear to be a gigantic movie screen."

Herman, a Dutchman in his late thirties, was on his second tour to North Korea. He had been in Pyongyang at the same time a year ago, 2009, and had seen the Mass Games twice during that trip.

"If you look carefully," he said, "There are about twenty thousand schoolchildren sitting directly across from us, on the opposite side of the stadium. Each child has a specially made oversize book, with specific designs and colored pages. The children all hold up their books displaying a particular page—their infinitesimal contribution to that specific scene. It is the pages of these books, all held up together, that make up the scenic backgrounds we are seeing.

"When it's time for a scene change, a signal is given," Herman continued. "All the children then simultaneously turn to the particular page specified for the new scene. Since the books are huge and the pages are made of a hard material, the simultaneous turning of twenty thousand large, hard pages creates that low rolling thunderclap you hear."

I stared at him. "You mean, that scenery is made by all those thousands of schoolchildren turning pages of a big book in *perfect unison?*" I scrutinized the opposite end of the stadium, trying to make out the individual figures of all the young schoolchildren. "And they all are actually sitting there with such perfect discipline? Amazing!" I murmured.

"Yes, indeed it is." Then, turning to me, he said, "*Chilling*, isn't it?"

It was.

The Mass Games performance was the perfect introduction to our tightly controlled tour of this bizarre country. In the same way, throughout the tour, our guides and minders strove to show us tourists the fiction that the government wanted to present to the outside world.

The Mass Games performance was set to triumphally themed music and spectacular mood lighting. The ninety-minute performance featured a hundred thousand brightly costumed dancers and performers, moving in precisely synchronized patterns on the stadium's huge field. The storyline of the performance focused on the myth of Kim Il-sung, the Stalinist-styled first dictator of modern North Korea, and his son Kim Jong-il, the ruler at the time of my visit. Regardless of the show's message, the Mass Games were an amazing spectacle.

⸻

The morning after the Mass Games, our group was off on an early flight to the north of the country, where we would do a short three-day tour of two important places in the official North Korean lore. Our flight took us to Samji Airport near Lake Chon, along the Chinese border.

From the airport, we were driven for about an hour through a remote, rustic wooded area with small farm villages carved out of the forest. The houses in the villages looked small but neat and reasonably livable. The lack of modern farming operations and the spare, simple lives of the people in the countryside were obvious, though. There were few vehicles other than an occasional heavy truck that appeared to be associated with logging. The farmers seemed to rely on very basic tools such as rakes and hoes and small human-drawn wagons, or slightly larger ones drawn by oxen.

Our first stop was at an area high up on Mount Paektu, a sacred place of ancestral origin in Korean culture. There we visited an important propaganda location called the "Secret Camp," where, according to the official story line, Kim Jong-il was born.

The Secret Camp is in a clearing among tall trees and dark, lush greenery of the alpine forest. Rising majestically above this rustic setting is the face of the sacred Mount Paektu. Three large red Korean letters on it read "Jongilbon" (Jong-il peak). A small, sturdy log cabin stands in the clearing, flanked on one side by a North Korean flag.

Our guide was a short, chubby-faced woman wearing a green military cap and an olive drab uniform with a red "Great Leader" pin above her heart. (All North Koreans are expected to wear these pins, which depict a small portrait of Kim Il-sung with a beaming smile). She told us a story about patriotic Korean freedom fighters who, under Kim Il-sung's heroic leadership, battled the Japanese. The Secret Camp was used as a headquarters and hiding place during their long struggle. Amid this glorious but grim time, in the cold winter of 1942, Kim Jong-il was born in the log cabin. According to our guide, at the moment of the Dear Leader's birth, "A bright double rainbow shone over the mountain, and there were flashes of light and thunder. The Dear Leader grew up in this hut, amid the partisans and sounds of war."

The heroic story of the Secret Camp had one major flaw, though: it was a fairy tale. Objective historians place Kim Jong-il's birth somewhere in Siberia, when his father Kim Il-sung was serving, probably as a sergeant, in the Soviet Army.

This myth set the tone for the entire tour. It illustrated the absurd personality cult built up around the leader of the North Korean regime. The main focus centers on Kim Il-sung, who was instrumental in founding the DPRK in 1948. Known as the "Great Leader," he ran the country with an iron fist, in some ways modeling his regime after Stalin's system in the Soviet Union.

The personality cult of Kim Il-sung reached absurd proportions, elevating him to the status of a demigod who could do no wrong. This divine status and personality cult passed on to Kim Jong-il, who took over in 1994 upon his father's death. In the strange dystopian fantasyland of North Korea, Kim Il-sung is still considered the current "official" president of the country even though he has been dead for two decades.

We got another silly example of this extreme personality cult when we visited the Kim Il-sung museum near the Secret Camp. One of the museum exhibits was a small diorama map of the region around Mount Paektu. Our pleasant-looking middle-aged museum guide, wearing a white flowing dress and the standard red Great Leader pin on her left breast, explained the many pins and markers spread over the diorama map.

"These pins show the statues of the Great Leader," the guide said, pointing to a number of pins. She then spent time pointing to other site markers, giving numerical counts of visits to each site by one of the Great Leaders (father or son). The Great Leader Kim Il-sung visited this historic site forty-four times in his life, our guide explained, pointing to a marker; and this place twenty-six times, pointing to a another marker. And Kim Jong-il visited this place seventy-two times so far in his lifetime, and that town thirty-seven times, and so forth. She finished by giving us, in stirring tones, a numerical tally of the times that each Great Leader had visited the museum where we now stood.

It was absurd to me that anyone actually recorded such things or that anyone should think that we visitors cared.

Our tour in general seemed to show that the Kims were everywhere and responsible for everything (good) that happened in the country. An example of this occurred when our group visited a "Children's Palace" in a town near the Mount Paektu area. A Children's Palace is a big recreational building where the town's children can go after school. It houses various sporting facilities and grounds, such as a gymnasium, volleyball court, and places to study.

While our group was at the Children's Palace, our male guide, the principal of the facility, led us into the gym. There he told how the

Great Leader had visited this facility in a certain year and had given instructions during his visit.

"'This gym should be used for volleyball, basketball, and tennis,'" the principal said, recounting the Great Leader's sage words.

Apparently, it took a personal visit and instructions from the Great Leader for the local officials to figure this out.

A funny incident occurred on the next leg of our tour. We took a chartered twin-prop plane to Orang military airport, near Mount Chilbro. This is a few hours' drive from Chongjin, an important industrial city on the northeast coast. (Chongjin is in one of the regions hardest hit during the mass starvations in the late 1990s.)

As our plane came in on the final approach to the Orang airport, several of us looking out our windows noticed what appeared to be a large number of Soviet MIG fighter aircraft on the tarmac below. The MIGs were sitting on a separately paved area about 250 yards from the runway, among a number of camouflaged bunkers built to resemble small hills from the air. The bunkers were covered with live grass and appeared to be protective hangars for the aircraft. I got only a brief glimpse of the MIGs from my seat. I was surprised, though, that a tour group would be flown into what was obviously a military facility.

"Did you see the MIGs!" said Margaret, a cheerful middle-aged photography buff. As we stood around on the paved runway after getting off our plane, another tourist, an older Australian business-man named Austin, came up and also asked if I had seen the MIGs.

"Yes, but I only got a brief look," I replied, disappointed that my view wasn't better.

But many of my tour mates had gotten a clear look at the MIGs from their airplane seats. Our group huddled around on the runway under gloomy skies, waiting for our tour leaders to direct us. We dis-cussed the MIGs and estimated that there were about sixty of the fighters sitting outside the grass-covered bunkers.

Just for fun, to see the reaction I'd get, I asked our lead North Korean guide about the MIGs. Our lead guide was Mr. Lee, a tough-looking man who appeared to be in his late forties and had an ex-military demeanor.

"Mr. Lee, this must be a dual military-civilian-use airport," I said innocently. "Are those jets down that way Soviet-made MIGs?" I motioned toward the jets, which were quite visible in the distance.

Mr. Lee looked directly into my eyes, displaying a poker face and not batting an eyelash. He replied evenly, "This is only a civilian airport. Those are regular airplanes. There are no military jets here."

As he continued to look directly at me, I felt that he knew that I realized there was no other answer he could give.

Bravo! I thought. His answer was a hell of a performance, especially since only a hundred yards from where we were standing, two Russian Yak military training aircraft were parked in plain view for everyone to see.

Later, as our group was on the bus driving through an area of villages near Mount Chilbro, I asked Mr. Lee about housing in the countryside. The single-story homes that we saw, though modest, appeared quite livable.

"All citizens in the countryside are assigned to their respective houses," Mr. Lee answered. "The houses we see are all built by the state. They are purposely built as duplicates of each other in each village, though the styles in each village vary in different regions. Typically, three or four people will inhabit each home. They are about a thousand square feet in size [about 100 square meters]."

During the long bus rides through the countryside in the north, I began to experience one of the stranger aspects among the many strange things about this tour. This concerned the reactions of some of my fellow tourists. In one instance, our bus was driving past some villages, with their small, neat houses surrounded by fields of corn. I was sitting next to a retired schoolteacher, a woman from New York whom I'll call Lorraine, who often sat next to me on the tour buses. Lorraine was an extremely well-traveled woman and delightful company.

Looking at the village we were passing, she announced, "Things don't look that bad for the people."

"How do you mean?" I asked, mystified by her conclusion.

"The people don't seem unhappy," Lorraine replied. "I don't think it is so bad for them."

"That doesn't make much sense, Lorraine," I replied. "You know that these people are essentially kept in a huge prison by a government that treats them no better than farm animals. How can you possibly think things are '*not that bad for them*'!?"

"This is all they know," Lorraine said simply. "They probably don't know any better, since they've been spoon-fed the official propaganda nonstop since birth and don't have any other source of information to compare it to."

Lorraine then succinctly summed her argument by concluding, "In this case, ignorance really is bliss."

One evening in the north of the country, I had a similarly strange conversation with another fellow tourist at the group dinner. This person, whom I'll call Andrew, was a pudgy Londoner in his early thirties, who spoke with an infuriating air that he took for gravitas.

"Things do not appear to be that bad for the people in the countryside," he remarked to the general group sitting around him at our long tables. Since I was sitting directly across the table from him, I asked him how he could draw any meaningful assessment from the brief glimpses out bus windows as we zipped by.

"Well, the houses they live in look small but decent, there are fields full of corn, and nobody looks like they are starving," Andrew replied. He, too, expressed the sentiment that ignorance was bliss and, thus, the overall situation was okay for the people in the countryside.

"That doesn't make any sense, Andrew," I replied. I was seriously fighting back the temptation to blast him with a heavy dose of sarcasm in front of the others at the table. I had heard Andrew spouting this nonsense several times earlier in the day, and his fatuous pontificating was beginning to rankle. I had no respect for such an intellectually lazy rich-world dope. His asinine pronouncements on these wretched people who had been so royally screwed in the birth lottery fairly begged for someone to put him in his place.

"It's ridiculous, for one thing, to make conclusions based on a fleeting glimpse out a bus window," I said, resisting the urge to express how I *really* felt. "Plus, we all know that the tour in general is designed as a big propaganda show and a hard-currency generator for a bankrupt government. We tourists are allowed to see only what the regime wants us to see."

Of course, none of this altered Andrew's conviction that the "blissfully ignorant" country folk he saw were not that bad off after all.

In the Chongjin area, we did all the usual things for our tour. These involved visiting and being expected to bow to yet another huge statue of Kim Il Sung. Our group also visited another museum, where we once again heard the numerical counts of how many times the Great Leaders had graced the place with their semidivine presence. The city center in Chongjin was even drabber than in Pyongyang. The main street was mostly lined with nondescript squarish low-rise buildings. There were very few motor vehicles, though some people did have bicycles.

After our short time in the Chongjin area, we returned to the Orang airport to catch a flight back to Pyongyang. Ironically, as we walked onto the runway when our plane arrived, a half-dozen MIGs were in flight around the airport. Each fighter would come in and touch down, then accelerate again into takeoff, only to fly around the airport and repeat the exercise. The MIGs were doing their touch-and-go landings at a point only thirty yards from where we stood while waiting to board our plane. It was fun to watch these once feared mainstays of the old Soviet air force touch down time after time at such close range.

I decided not to ask Mr. Lee again about the MIGs or whether the airport was a military facility.

———————

Our first full day back in Pyongyang was Thursday, September 9, a major holiday known as National Day. Our first event of the day was a visit to the gigantic mausoleum for Kim Il-sung. In the mausoleum, the Great Leader's embalmed body lay inside a clear glass sarcophagus. It was another really weird tour experience.

The mausoleum, also called the Kumsusan Palace of the Sun (the sun is the symbol for Kim Il-sung), is the size of a small village. It is fronted by a huge square plaza about 1,600 feet on a side and bordered on two sides by a moat. Kim Il-sung used the palace as his office and residence, and after his death, Kim Jong-il spent hundreds of millions of dollars to renovate and convert it into a mausoleum. Meanwhile, hundreds of thousands were starving to death in famine-stricken parts of the country.

For North Koreans, visiting the Great Leader's mausoleum is a special event. The mausoleum draws an especially large crowd on National Day. In the pretour briefing, Megan had asked us to dress smartly for the mausoleum visit. She suggested that men wear ties, since the Koreans would all be dressed in their best clothes. So I donned my nifty new one-dollar-and-fifty-cent blue tie, which I had bought at a Beijing discount clothing bazaar.

Another tourist in our group, named Michael, went further. He actually had a custom Korean-style black dress suit made just for the occasion. Michael was an odd bird. A middle-Berliner who worked with the German customs agency, he was on his *fifth* trip to North Korea in the past seven years. He always came during the Mass Games and had seen them eight times before this trip. He had a bizarrely enthusiastic appreciation for everything he saw in North Korea. I found this as weird as anything on the tour. But it made sense. How had it not occurred to me that a place as strange as this would attract its own share of oddballs?

The mausoleum tour started with us passing over a machine that washed the soles of each visitor's shoes. Then we each went through a security scanner like those in airports. After this, we all stepped onto a series of long moving walkways that whisked us through the cavernous building to the rooms near where the dead Great Leader lay. Megan explained, "One doesn't walk to Great Leader; one is brought to him."

Finally, we arrived at a grand columned room with a large white statue of Kim Il-sung. Next to this was an elegant, moderately lit large room—a museum about the funeral and national mourning period after Kim Il-sung's sudden death in 1994. The museum was sparsely furnished, with bas reliefs on the walls depicting mourning soldiers, intellectuals, and farmers.

The museum offered a truly bizarre experience. Each of us was given a pair of headphones attached to a small playback device. A narrator's voice came on over the headphones, speaking in a shaking, tragically somber voice. He gave a heartrending account of the period of spontaneous mourning by the whole nation, which lasted for ten days following the announcement of Kim Il-sung's death in 1994. While we listened to this, dramatic photographs and historical video footage on display showed scenes of massive crowds of people wailing and crying. People were shown to be flailing their arms out in unspeakable grief and falling to the ground, unable to stand with the unbearable pain of losing their Great Leader.

The whole exhibit was laughably comical—and creepy. Accounts that I have read by defectors and escapees from North Korea tell how government agents and representatives observed people. They also encouraged people to report on their fellow citizens' behavior during the funeral and mourning ceremonies around the country. This was to ensure that people were indeed making the appropriate displays of grief. Anyone who did not show enough anguish could be reported. For those who did not give the proper display of grief, life could become yet harsher. Careers could be destroyed, and worse things could happen.

After this, we all passed through a large blower, to blow off any dust that we may have gathered. Then we entered the chamber where Kim Il-sung, the "official president" of the country, lay in his sealed glass case, dressed in an elegant black suit. Inside the chamber, we were expected to bow to the dictator's corpse from three sides before proceeding out of the chamber. We then took the moving walkways the long distance back to the museum entrance. Along the way, we passed large groups of officers of the DPRK armed forces, all looking very solemn, on their way to visit their departed Great Leader.

For us tourists, the whole goofy experience was insidiously comical. But the North Koreans had this junk pounded into their heads from birth. Many of them, at least at some point in their lives, probably really thought that this monstrous dictator was actually a benevolent demigod.

The final event of our tour, a visit to Pyongyang's Central Library, was fascinating. Called the Grand People's Study House, the central library is a very large building said to contain more than ninety thousand books. In a country where any non-government-sanctioned information is in short supply, the library is surely a welcome oasis to those lucky enough to have regular access.

The library contains a large room dedicated to computers connected to the country's intranet service. For almost all citizens of the DPRK, this was the only contact with anything resembling the World Wide Web. There is no outside world Internet access available to the ordinary citizen. A docent led our group through the large intranet room, past university-age students working diligently away at computer stations—

looking much like students one might find in the real world, accessing the real Web.

While there, I was curious to hear the official government explanation for why it denied its citizens access to the Internet. I figured a good Orwellian dictatorship like the DPRK would have a good explanation for why it refused its citizens a tool that most of humanity had access to. So I asked Mr. Lee for the official explanation of why the people of the DPRK were not allowed Internet access.

My question seemed to catch Mr. Lee off guard.

"Go ask Kim Jong-il," he replied abruptly.

I hadn't meant to cause Mr. Lee any discomfort. So, trying to inject a little levity, I said I'd send Kim Jong-il a note after the tour, to get the answer to my question.

Later, I asked Mr. Lee about the access to outside world news. He explained that there was one hour a week of world news on television. I believe he said it was broadcast every Saturday evening. I was curious what the government censors would let pass for "news."

During the library tour, I had my only real opportunity for conversation with an ordinary North Korean, one not associated in some way with our tour. This short encounter occurred when we visited the English-language learning room. A class had just ended, and a number of young male university-age students were milling around the doorway to the language room. As we were shown the room, a few of us tourists struck up conversations with these students.

I talked with a tall, slender student who wore baggy black slacks and a white long-sleeved shirt. We exchanged the usual introductory chat, sharing our names and the cities where we each lived. The student, who told me he studied computers and software, asked me what I did for work.

I replied that I was just traveling and not working at the moment.

"You are just traveling, not working?" the student asked with some surprise. "How long have you been traveling?"

"At this point, almost four years," I replied.

"Four years of travel!" he said. "Wow! What did you do for work before, which allows you to travel so long now without having to work?"

"I worked with a bank," I explained.

"What did you do for a bank that allowed you to make enough money to travel for so long?" he asked me.

"I created a small business within a larger business," I replied. "My business involved software and a special service to a certain type of company."

I further explained that I had some good luck with this business. It had caught on with a number of these types of companies across America, and so I was able to save enough money to travel for a while without working.

"After you finish your travels, will you go back to the bank and work again?" he then asked.

"No," I said. "I will not go back to the bank."

"Oh. What will you do for money, then?" he inquired.

"I don't know at this moment," I answered truthfully. "When I finish my travels I'll figure out something and start some new type of business or career."

Our group was then called away by our guides. My North Korean acquaintance had a quizzical look on his face as I walked away. I wondered what he must think about what he had just heard. As a North Korean, work was every citizen's primary obligation and focus in life. Once on a particular work path, one performed his function with little flexibility or choice in the matter. So hearing about such an impossibly freewheeling lifestyle had to be very strange indeed.

The next morning, Saturday, we were on board the Air Koryo flight back to Beijing, and not a minute too soon for me. I couldn't have stood much more time in a land with such a hellish, inhumane regime. And for the umpteen-thousandth time, I was reminded of the extreme fickleness of the birth lottery. The millions of unfortunate souls born into the nightmarish system of the DPRK had done nothing to deserve it, just as I had done nothing to deserve being born into a life of freedom and endless opportunity.

Back in Beijing a couple of days after the tour, I had dinner with one of my fellow DPRK tourists. Kevin was an academically inclined young Westerner who lived in China. He and I met in a popular Beijing Korean-Chinese fusion restaurant during happy hour one busy Thursday evening.

While discussing various aspects of the tour, I brought up what I thought was the weirdest aspect of the whole weird experience. I said that while much that we saw on the tour could be thought of as strange (such as the mausoleum to Kim Il-sung), still, most of it had been something along the lines of what I expected. What I had not expected, though, was for several people actually to tell me, near the end of the tour, what a great time they had.

Even more bizarre, I said, was that a couple of our tour mates told me how "*wonderful*" North Korea was, or how they felt that "*things didn't really seem that bad for the people*." Granted, only a minority of the tour participants had expressed such a view, but it still boggled the mind because every one of the thirty-five members on our tour were experienced to extremely experienced world travelers.

Kevin agreed that it was indeed hard to fathom. "Maybe they just fell for the propaganda," he reasoned. "After all, that is what the tour was about. I guess it worked on a few people."

"I think it's something shallower than that," I countered. "Let's call it the 'Disneyland effect.' North Korea is a pretty bizarre place, and quite different from anywhere else on earth. I think a certain percentage of travelers from the richer world find a thrill in what is different or exotic compared with what they know in their own lives. So when they find this exotic difference, whatever the circumstances of the people in the destination, it becomes a 'good' or 'great' time for them since it gave them the thrill they were seeking."

"Or maybe people just liked the nice food, service, and accommodations our tour provided," Kevin suggested. "For many people, those are the main things determining whether they had a good time on a trip. Since they were happy and comfortable, everything else would then appear fine to them."

A few days later, I flew from Beijing to a spot on the southeast coast of China. During the flight, I sat in an aisle seat. Across the aisle from me, an American in his mid-fifties was seated with his 18-year-old daughter. I happened to overhear them talking about North Korea, so I leaned over and struck up a conversation with them. Coincidentally, they had just completed a private tour in North Korea, and both were quite ebullient about their experience. I asked them what they thought about what they had seen on their tour.

"We had a *great time*," the father enthused. "North Korea is a *wonderful* country!"

Once again, I was taken aback by what I saw as an utterly bizarre reaction for someone from the rich world to the horrific situation in North Korea. But rather than question his enthusiasm, I decided first to find out a bit about the man. We talked for a while. I learned that he was an experienced traveler who had been to some areas in Central Africa that I was looking to visit. So I learned a bit from him to help in my upcoming plans for that region.

After getting a feel for him, I asked why he felt he had a great time on his North Korea tour and why he thought the country was "wonderful."

"My daughter and I did a private tour and were able to steer our tour guides away from the rote stuff of the tours—museums, statues and monuments, and such—and spend more time in public places," he explained. "This way, we got to have some contact with ordinary people."

"But how much contact did you really have, and did you really get to talk to anyone for more than a moment?" I asked. "Do you speak Korean?"

"No, I don't speak Korean," the father replied. "Most of our interchanges were quite short, with people we just happened to be near in the public places we visited in Pyongyang." (These were the same places our group tour visited: the bowling alley, the park, an amusement park, and along the street for the large-scale public dancing the day before National Day).

"It was so refreshing to see how nice and natural the North Koreans are, without airs or attitudes," the father enthused. "It was great to meet and have such contact with these people. I think the country is wonderful."

Our plane was landing soon, so I broke off our conversation as the crew bustled up and down the aisle, getting everything ready for touchdown. I was amazed, though, at the naïveté of this well-traveled man. For him, the spontaneous short, fleeting contacts in Pyongyang, with random strangers he could scarcely communicate with, was the exciting thing. And this was all it took to convince him that the tour was a "great time" and the country was "wonderful."

For me, on the other hand, the mere fact that anyone from the privileged, rich, and free Western world—especially a fellow American— could be so quick and shallow in their assessment of what they saw on tour in a hell world such as the DPRK was maybe the most chilling aspect of the tour.

CHAPTER 18

Rootless

There is a sort of script that travel memoirs of really long journeys like mine often seem to follow. The script involves the writer in an extended physical journey along with some sort of deep personal quest. Perhaps the traveler seeks inner peace after a tragedy or other huge life setback, to "find oneself," or to put meaning back into a life grown jaded or filled with meaningless routine. Such a memoir is as much a story about the author's personal journey as it is about the actual travels.

A few years into my travel project, I started hearing from many people I met that I should write a book about my journeys. At first, I struggled with what exactly I would write. Would my book be a travelogue? Or maybe a collection of short vignettes of different places and experiences? The thing missing from this equation for me was the "personal journey" aspect. I had set out to fulfill a lifelong dream to really know and experience the world, as well as to experience the parts of it that were fast disappearing. I had not undertaken this project to make a drastic change in who I was. I wasn't looking to "find myself," nor was I unhappy with my life or feeling some great lack or gap or disconnection.

Actually, it was quite the opposite. I was quite happy overall with my life and felt good about who I was as a person. Of course, I did expect to gain much wisdom from my travels, learn a lot, and have a great, fulfilling experience. But I assumed I would come back essentially the same person as when I left. Then I expected just to plug back into my life again and resume going forward.

After leaving North Korea, I spent several weeks traveling along the coast of China. From there I went onto Uzbekistan for a couple of weeks and then to Nepal, where I did some trekking in its famous scenic Himalayan landscapes. During this time, I often didn't sleep well at night. Indeed, for the first time since I started my travel project, I frequently lay awake at night, thinking about the future and what awaited me after this project was done.

I was beginning to realize that all my earlier thinking—that I would return from my long travels essentially the same person— was wrong. This travel experience had changed my life in major ways. Unlike the usual travel memoir scripts, though, some of these changes were not necessarily good ones. Instead of "finding myself"—since I already knew who I was when I started this project—I seemed actually to have *lost* part of myself.

The most profound change, of course, was that Achara would not be part of my daily life in the future. When she and I had launched this project with our trip to Papua New Guinea, I had a very firm picture of the future: After three years, we would return and do what was necessary for Achara to get her career on the path she needed. Or we would move and settle into one of the places in the States where she was considering studying for her PhD. This would most likely have been San Francisco, New York, or Washington, DC. In any event, the basic goal and strategy was the same: get Achara's life career goals on track. This gave me a definite path that I would have to pursue. I had a clear vision of a future.

But now that goal and path were gone, and I had no ready replace-ment. Instead, I was beginning to feel a nagging rootlessness. Sure, I now had much more freedom and, perhaps in some ways, easier options since my choices no longer involved someone else. Of course, I could always just return and live in Los Angeles. I had strong roots there and very much liked the lifestyle the area offered. But I didn't want to make the rest of my life there. I didn't want to spend the next phase of my life in the same crowds and smog where I had spent the previous chapter. Instead, I wanted to try something different and live in a beautiful place. But where? After all, I now knew of and had personally experienced many beautiful places.

Long-term rootlessness seemed to have become part of my inner core. Without a definite place to call home, I had too many choices. Once I got used to the seemingly unlimited freedom just to go wherever I wanted, I had a hard time seeing what "home" for me would look like when I stopped. The rootlessness that had become a part of my personality, and the illusion of unlimited opportunities, made trying to envision anything concrete much tougher.

A more practical challenge was how to handle the loneliness that continued to be an ever-present part of my experience. With neither a wife to return home to nor even a vision of an actual home, I felt alone and adrift. Some things helped. Throughout my travels, I tried to keep in regular touch with friends and some family members through Skype and e-mail when I had access to a good connection. But the most practical aspect was how to handle the absence of a woman in my life. As a young, healthy male, this was an ever-present element of the journey.

The most tempting thing to do was to take advantage of the relatively easy sex that seems to be on offer to the traveler almost everywhere. Since much of the world is poor, part of the reason this type of temptation even exists concerns the obvious calculus of a local woman seeing the traveler (in this case, me) as a source of money or a potential way to a better life. But this stereotypical view encompasses only part of the reality.

The truth is that a long-term traveler runs into many different occasions to meet and temporarily hook up with others of the opposite sex. In my travels, I would often, of course, cross paths with other long-term travelers. Other travelers of the opposite sex are frequently open to short-term flings. It just seems to go with the territory, the personality, of a long-term traveler.

The most common of these would be the backpacker set. Usually, since backpackers traveled on a shoestring and followed the ever popular Lonely Planet travel guides, I ran into these types only when on the "beaten path"—popular travel routes in cheaper locales. But there were still many times over the years of my travel project when I would be in places that also attracted the backpacker set.

From what I saw, this particular type of travel often appeared to be one big party for its more devout adherents. Backpacker travelers, who tend to be younger, follow similar travel routes and itineraries. In Southeast Asia, for instance, places included in popular routes are said to be on the "banana pancake trail." These travelers congregate at the same cheap hostels, go to the same small local restaurants and the same coffee shops and cafés, and do the same kinds of partying as most other backpackers. Often, despite the age gap between me and most backpackers, I often had the opportunity to join in the same festivities. I rarely did, though—it just wasn't my kind of deal.

I found, though, that the traveler in general, especially one who is not a backpacker, has an appeal that extends beyond the impoverished local woman looking for a way to improve her situation. After my divorce, I had many opportunities to meet—and occasionally had quick flings with—attractive, well-educated, successful professional women. (These were in addition to those I mention in this book.) The cliché that people are attracted to the exotic explains some of it. As a foreigner, I was exotic to local people, of course. Even during the short jaunts in Europe, I found this to be the case. (Europeans would hardly be expected to be hoping for a green card or looking at me as a source of money.) Lots of people find the long-term traveler interesting. Also, the long-term traveler represents a sort of freedom that many romanticize about wanting, though most would quickly find that such freedom comes at too high a price.

I was tempted to alter my travel plans now and again to take advantage of this type of opportunity. It would help alleviate (to a degree) the loneliness constantly nagging me, and perhaps also help me get over the still sharp pain of losing my marriage. But I didn't. After my unexpected downtime and short-term fling in the Philippines in spring 2010, I made a conscious decision to suppress any and all temptations to deviate from my travel objectives simply out of loneliness. In fact, when it came to women I pretty much just suppressed myself in general. I was afraid that to do otherwise could too easily lead me to veer off my travel plan and waste time. Also, I didn't want to hurt anyone who might be expecting more than I could offer at that rootless point in my life.

And, of course, I had not really gotten over the loss of my marriage. Even though I had been effectively apart from Achara for several years, and officially divorced for over a year and a half, I still missed the idea of what we were together.

Nevertheless, Achara's family represented a beacon of normality for me during my travels. I would look forward to the short, quick stays at her mother's house when I passed through Bangkok between journeys. There I would always be welcomed and reminded that I was family. This warm hospitality, especially from Achara's mother and aunt, helped offset the feeling of personal isolation I had to wrestle with. There was a black cloud to all this silver lining, though. I knew that when my travels ended and I returned to live in America, I would no longer see these wonderful people on the regular basis I had grown so accustomed to.

After North Korea, the next eleven months for me were a blur of almost nonstop travel. First, I went along the coast of China, then to Uzbekistan and Nepal, as I mentioned above. My travel project started to become scarily like work rather than a labor of love. I pushed and drove myself relentlessly, checking off one completed travel objective after another in order to finish. I was moving around so much that sometimes I would wake up and not know what continent I was on.

From Nepal, for example, I went on to northern India to see the great Sikh temple at Amritsar. *Check—another objective achieved.* Then, after a quick spell in Thailand, I spent seven weeks in Australia and Tasmania. Check. Then I flew across the world for another trip in the Amazon, this time in the Peruvian part of that great rain forest basin, visited the spectacular Iguazú Falls on the border between Argentina and Brazil, traveled through Central America, scuba dived in the Galápagos Islands, and traveled through Bhutan and then northern Laos. *Check, check, and check.*

Most of the places I traveled in this period were what I considered primary objectives that fit my Disappearing World Travel Project theme. I knew that I had to complete at least most of my primary objectives to feel successful about the project. It was basically a chunk of the itinerary that was on my spreadsheet plan that I had originally created on the flight from Jakarta to Kuala Lumpur back in February 2010 (and would follow till my entire travel project was finished).

The places on my spreadsheet plan tallied with my original goals for the project, which included spending time among a wide array of peoples who still retained strong cultural traditions and lifestyles, journeying in the world's great ecosystems of amazing biodiversity that were under severe threat, and seeing societies that still retained some of their historically colorful and exotic aspects but were changing rapidly due to globalization. Since it would have taken many more years of travel to try to experience everything in the world that might fit these goals, I made many arbitrary choices between possible objectives. For example, I chose to visit the Golden Temple at Amritsar because it was part of a colorful, dynamic, living, breathing Sikh culture that still thrives today. This seemed a higher priority than taking the time to see the amazing ruins of Petra, Jordan, which are now only dead remains from the distant past (although at some point in the future, I would definitely like to see this great archeological treasure).

The relentless pace I kept during this time wore on me physically. I began to suffer chronic back pains and often felt fatigued. I also inwardly worried about what the future would hold for me once I finished my travels. Without Achara as part of the picture, I had no clear idea what would be next. I knew that the rootlessness now in my personality, which seemed to offer me limitless opportunities, was equally a liability. Part of me longed to settle down again and have a normal life with routines and schedules and commitments. I just couldn't clearly see the what, where, or how. I also strongly worried that I would find a "normal" life boring and confining. But I knew that constant wandering around the world would ultimately be destructive, both psychologically and physically. Without becoming rooted again, there could be no meaningful future.

So I pressed relentlessly on to finish so that I might resume a "normal" life. Finally, around midsummer 2011, I began to see the finish line. I traveled in northern Laos in July. After Laos, I had the last big series of journeys for my travel project coming up, which would take me back to Africa. But I would also have yet another challenging setback. While staying in a town called Luang Namtha, in a scenic area of far northwestern Laos, I did some cycling through the countryside. During the trip, I noticed some dull pains in my left knee. I ignored the pain, figuring it was just muscle or tendon strain. Unfortunately, while in Africa I would find that I had actually sustained a serious injury—one that would come back to haunt me during my entire African journey.

CHAPTER 19

Back to Africa: My Music Moment, and Hobnobbing with Hunter-Gatherers

Nilikuonyesha nyota na uliangalia kidole tu. (I pointed out to you the stars, and all you saw was the tip of my finger.)
—Swahili Proverb

Early August 2011
Dakar, Senegal

It was a brilliant morning in Dakar, but as I sat in my top-floor room of the efficient budget hotel, my mood was anything but sunny. Earlier in the morning, I had walked down a rocky dirt street to a small, bare diner near my hotel for some eggs with papaya, a mango, and an unripe banana. During the short walk, my knee throbbed with pain. Returning to the hotel after breakfast, hurting even worse, I hobbled up the three floors to my room. After pulling off my shoes and socks to avoid tracking the grime of Dakar onto the clean white tile, I fought off a feeling of frustrated panic. These sharp knee pains just might scotch my plans for this African journey.

I had arrived a few days earlier in Dakar, the grimy capital of the impoverished nation of Senegal on Africa's northwest coast. My short time in Africa to this point had been a flurry of efficient activity. In a week's time, I had obtained three visas for countries I was planning to enter over the next several months of my journey. I intended to travel overland from Senegal through neighboring Mali, along the way visiting Timbuktu (the historic town that was sacked by Islamist insurgents in late 2012). Then I would continue into Niger, pass through a slice of Chad into Cameroon, and end up in the Central African Republic in mid-October. There, I would join a small group for my biggest objective on the trip: a lowland gorilla safari in the heart of the Congo Basin.

I really wanted to do everything right on this African trip, since it would be the last big journey of my six-year-long travel project. I was determined to savor to the hilt each grimy moment and remember every outstanding scene or vista. I vowed even to try to savor the frustrating times that would inevitably be involved. These, predictably, would include dealing with incompetent authorities and bribe-seeking police, brushing off the ubiquitous pesky touts, and dodging the usual scammers and pickpockets who preyed on foreigners. This trip was to be the culmination of a lifelong dream, and I intended to make the most of it.

But instead, I was sitting in my room, wanting to pound my fists on the table because I could hardly walk. The knee pain, which had started with the bicycle ride in Laos last month, was becoming chronic and sharp. I had thought I dealt with the problem already. During a short stop in Bangkok, after Laos and before coming to Africa, I had done some self-directed physical therapy for my knee. The small pain I had noticed in Laos seemed to dissipate, and I felt relatively fine. But now, in Dakar, it was suddenly back with a vengeance. So I breathed deeply, calmed my frustration, and decided to hole up for an extra week in this relatively nice budget hotel and rest my knee.

Contemplating this solution to my knee dilemma, I stepped into the bathroom. The bathroom floor had a thin pool of water, which was par for the course—budget guesthouses in sub-Saharan Africa, even the decent ones, often seemed to have leaking plumbing fixtures. So I walked around on the tiled floor room in wet bare feet to keep my socks dry. Moments later, I came out of the bathroom and walked to the head of my bed to move the small brass lamp on the nightstand. I wanted to sit on my bed and put my computer on the nightstand to do some Internet research.

When I grabbed the lamp with my left hand an overwhelming, crushing force surged up my arm. The full force of the 240 volts from the lamp instantly and completely paralyzed my upper body, making me vibrate violently. As the overpowering pulsations rushed up my arm, through my shoulder, and into my torso I thought, *So this is what it's like to be electrocuted!*

I tried to command my hand to let go of the lamp, but I couldn't move a thing. In my struggle to free myself from the crippling force, I desperately swiveled my midsection around since that part of me was not yet paralyzed. This action succeeded in yanking the lamp plug free from the socket.

My desperate motion flung the lamp hard across the room, where it smashed against the plaster wall and crashed to the floor. Amazingly, it didn't break—not even the lightbulb. But I was not so lucky. A searing pain shot through my lower back, as if I had torn a muscle. Collapsing onto my bed, almost unable to stand up, I sensed that I was really injured.

I lay there for hours. Finally, in midafternoon, I could hobble around my room. I knew I should seek professional medical help, especially for my knee. If I could hardly move, there was no way I could keep to my itinerary. Also, I felt suddenly vulnerable for one of the few times in my life. I was in a very poor place where so much was dysfunctional, where I didn't know a soul and, as a visibly handicapped foreigner, would be a conspicuous target to predators on the street. I grabbed my laptop and booked a flight out of Senegal to seek medical help in Nairobi, Kenya. Nairobi, Johannesburg, and Cape Town are perhaps the only places on the African continent where one can reliably get world-class medical care. Getting to Nairobi involved a stopover in Belgium since it was actually cheaper to fly up to Europe and back than just to go straight east across the African continent.

I was on an overnight flight to Belgium later that evening, with my big plans for Africa in tatters. During the flight, I decided to do an impromptu eight-day layover in Belgium. The lure of fantastic beer and the world's best chocolate was just too much to resist. Also, Belgium was a rich-world country with good medical care, where I could feel fairly safe in my crippled condition. Even though I could hardly walk, I figured on just using taxis to get around as I indulged myself with great beers.

Improbably, this unplanned stop seemed to give me a miraculous recovery. Apparently, the copious chocolate and many "cleansing ales" cured me of both my wrenched back and my knee problem. So I decided to skip the medical diagnosis of my knee in Nairobi (nor did I bother doing so while in Belgium). I redirected my booked flights to the exotic sun-drenched island of Zanzibar, off the coast of Tanzania. There, I figured I could do self-directed physical therapy to make my knee and back strong again. My goal, at all costs, was to be ready for the lowland gorilla safari in the Congo Basin in October.

I spent two weeks in Zanzibar once again, doing self-rehab on my knee. Unfortunately, while there and after seeming to recover, I reinjured myself. On my second to last night in Zanzibar, an attractive young professional woman I had casually befriended in the capital, Stone Town, had decided to make an unexpected late-night visit to my hotel. But she got lost while walking in the maze of narrow winding roads in the old-town section where I was staying. Panicked, she called me on my cell phone at around one a.m., pleading for me to come immediately and get her. She had stumbled into a dark spot near some unsavory drunk young men and was afraid to move.

I jumped out of bed, threw on pants and shirt and my hiking shoes, and ran full tilt for a quarter mile in the darkness through the maze of cobblestone streets. When I reached my woman friend, she appeared shaken but fine. I was not happy with her. Though I inwardly thought it cute and even flattering that my attractive new friend had intended to surprise me at my hotel so late at night, I wasn't interested in anything more than the casual friendship we had developed. It wasn't fair to have another quick fling that might create false expectations in someone I would never see again. I was also trying to control a sudden feeling of overwhelming exasperation. Because of the "rescue" run, my knee was once again throbbing in pain. All the recovery I thought I had achieved over the past three weeks, starting in Belgium and continuing in Zanzibar, had just been ruined.

A day later, I left Zanzibar and spent two weeks in the Usambara range in mainland Tanzania's northeast. This is a biodiverse forested highland with many rural villages, where I took it easy on my once again very sore knee. I worked my way toward the Serengeti Plains and Lake Eyasi in north-central Tanzania, just south of Kenya. There I wanted to visit a hunter-gatherer group called the Hadzabe, in the Lake Eyasi area, and do a Serengeti safari. I figured that these activities would be tame enough for my knee to continue recovering.

On my final day in the Usambara Mountains, I crammed into the usual transport for much of Tanzania: an overloaded beat-up minivan taxi with balding tires and cracked windows. I was making the seven-hour trip from a small mountain village to Arusha, a city near Tanzania's Serengeti. For much of the ride, the minibus bumped and lurched around winding mountain roads, often along steep ridges. I sat on a hard bench seat with no cushion, and the van was ripe with the usual smell of stale sweat. But gazing through the dirt-stained, flyspecked windows at the vivid beauty outside, I was quickly lost. Cheery puffs of cloud floated in brilliant blue skies over rolling forested mountains and canyons. Occasionally, we passed rustic farming villages, their neatly tended fields standing out among the scrub and forest of the mountains.

It was during this ride through the western edge of the Usambara Mountains that I had my "music moment." In movies involving a long drama or epic journey, there is often a time when the main character realizes some large goal, the completion of a quest, or some other major personal milestone. Dramatic music plays in the background, and grand scenery, memory flashbacks, or some idyllic scene is portrayed to illustrate the special realization. This is what I mean by "music moment."

I heard the music and had my special moment of realization. As I looked out the window at the grand landscape passing by, I finally *felt* the reality that I had done it. Despite all the unexpected troubles that had continually beset me since I started my long travel project years ago, I somehow had made it. I still had a way to go on this final African journey, but I knew I would complete my goal of having a worthwhile time on this trip, and do my gorilla safari in the Congo Basin no matter what. There in the crowded vehicle, I had a hard time keeping dry eyes. And I really heard the dramatic strains of a full orchestra in some far-off background ether. It was my music moment.

Mid-September 2011
Near Lake Eyasi, Central Rift Valley, Tanzania

The battered, sun-faded black pickup truck, its windshield cracked and a side mirror missing, rattled along the dirt road near Lake Eyasi, along the southern edge of the great Serengeti Plains. I was riding with Joseph, my jovial private guide and driver, and a chubby young guy named Peter, who was our interpreter for visits with the local tribespeople. It was early morning, and the sun was just up. It would soon be blazing hot. This was the dry season, so the small desolate villages and the trees and scrub wore a parched, dusty veneer.

Our destination was a camp of Hadzabe hunter-gatherers, a people I was very excited about visiting. Visiting them would be time travel in the extreme—a rare glimpse at how much of humanity once lived before the advent of domesticated animals and agriculture. When doing my research, I had been surprised to learn that many experts consider the Hadzabe the last remaining true hunting-gathering society in Africa. There were not many left, either. Their population had dwindled to around a thousand, with only about three hundred to four hundred who actually followed the traditional hunter-gatherer lifestyle.

A few centuries ago, however, the Hadzabe were far more numerous and covered a much larger geographic domain. This larger habitat ranged across much of north-central Tanzania, including the Serengeti and the Central Rift Valley region around Lake Eyasi. A disastrous population crash started in the late nineteenth century as more technologically advanced peoples encroached onto their lands. Large die-offs resulted from new contagions and more directly at the hands of outsiders who viewed them as inferior.

Ironically, it was two uniquely modern forces that saved the last remnant of the traditional Hadzabe from final oblivion. In 2001, documentaries by PBS and the BBC called attention to their plight, gaining them worldwide sympathy. This made the Hadzabe a tourist attraction, thereby placing a monetary value on preserving their way of life. I took comfort in the thought that perhaps my visit as a tourist might, in a tiny way, be helping them preserve their lifestyle.

The Hadzabe camp was just a clearing in the bush, with several crude igloo-shaped stick-and-bark structures perhaps five feet in height. Sitting on the ground around a few scattered campfires were about two dozen tribespeople. Surprisingly, no one came up to greet us or even looked in our direction. In my years of travel, I was accustomed to getting a reception from rambunctious, curious kids at least. Instead, the people, wearing an assortment of old clothes, rags, and beads, just continued with whatever they were doing. The men and boys, some wearing fur skin bands around their heads, were preparing for the hunt. The women were sitting separately, attending to babies and small children.

Joseph brought me over and introduced me to a group of men and boys sitting in a circle on the dirt. I took a seat next to one of the men and watched as they made arrows from sticks and fitted them with various tips to use on different prey. Other than a few cursory nods toward me, nobody paid me much attention, which made me feel a bit like an intruder.

After a moment of this awkwardness, I offered the leader of the group a pack of cigarettes that I had brought as a present. A strong, friendly-looking man who appeared to be in the prime of his life, he was shirtless and wore a thick headband of blue and yellow beads. This changed the atmosphere, and I could see right away that the Hadzabe enjoyed a smoke. The pack of cigarettes was promptly torn open and the cigarettes eagerly distributed to each member of the group. One of the boys then brought the remaining cigarettes to the others in the camp, including the women and children. I was happy and really curious when one of the men then ventured to ask Peter an actual question about me.

"They are asking if you brought any marijuana," Peter said. "They say that really like smoking marijuana but can only get it from visitors or in the wild since they don't grow or cultivate things."

This question was sort of a letdown for me. I would have expected an initial question from these people, who still lived the most primitive form of human lifestyle, to be about something more substantive than whether I had any dope.

But at least the ice was broken, I thought, as everyone lit up their cigarettes. A couple of the boys then showed me their hunting weapons.

"This is the most basic tip for an arrow," said one of the boys. He was slender, maybe 10 years old, and said his name was Alamo. He handed me a strong stick about thirty inches long, carved to a sharp point on one end and with feathers attached to the other end. "These are good for birds and small animals."

Alamo and his friend Maluca, who was also slender and around 10 years old, showed me several different types of arrowheads. Some were tipped with poison, and the most sophisticated were of metal. The boys explained that the metal arrowheads were used for larger game such as Kudu (a large antelope). They got the metal arrowheads by trading with neighboring Datoga people, who were famous for their blacksmithing skills.

As the men and boys continued to prepare for the hunt, Joseph and Peter showed me around the camp. Peter explained that the few remaining Hadzabe who still followed their traditional lifestyle were nomadic. They lived outdoors much of the year, building simple, temporary stick structures for use during the rainy season. Depending on the season, they moved to the best area for hunting and foraging. However, their territory was now very small compared to what it had been historically.

We then walked by a group of five women sitting on the sandy ground, tending to three small kids. One of the women, who was younger and topless and adorned with a wide band of bright yellow beads, was breast-feeding her baby. An elderly woman offered me a cigarette and invited me to sit with them. I sat down, smiled, and politely indicated that I didn't want to smoke. A very young boy, apparently unaccustomed to seeing white skin, came up to me and started touching my arms. I found it odd that the first person in the camp to show the slightest curiosity about me was a toddler.

While Peter and I sat with the women, Joseph described the daily routine of the Hadzabe. On the surface, life appeared very simple. Typically, the able-bodied males started their day off with a hunt while the women tended the children and then went into the bush to forage for berries, edible roots, and other foods and medicines. The men also foraged, often while hunting. After the morning hunt, they divided and ate the catch of the day, often doing another hunt in the evening.

For me, as a modern type-A multitasker, the Hadzabe lifestyle seemed simple indeed. Since they lived out in the open, there was no need to worry about keeping up a house. The only actual things they made, besides the weapons for hunting, were the crude igloo-shaped stick structures, which gave at least some relief from the rains during the wet season. And with no written language, they had no books to read or study. It appeared to me that there was truly nothing much to do when not hunting. I could see why they liked to smoke dope.

As I played with the little boy who was fascinated by my white skin, I wondered what lay in store for his life in the rapidly globalizing world.

"How do the Hadzabe plan for the future?" I asked. "What about schooling for the kids?" I nodded at the child now playing with my shoelaces.

"The Hadzabe have no planning for the future as there is no calendar in the modern sense," Peter replied. "For the most part, the children don't go to school. Those that do usually don't last long at it."

I asked Peter about religious beliefs. He explained that the Hadzabe were mostly animist, their main gods the sun and moon, and that they worshipped their ancestors. Interestingly, Joseph pointed out that when they went hunting, they didn't hunt hyena. This was because the Hadzabe traditionally left their dead out for the hyenas to eat. And now, even though they buried their dead because people of other cultures lived near them, the relationship between their ancestors and hyenas made the hyena off limits.

At this point, a whistling sound carried across the little encampment. It was time to get started. Six hunters—four men and Alamo and Maluca—along with Joseph, Peter, and me, all started walking fast along a dusty pathway. Soon, we were trotting through a forest of dried scrub, low thorn trees, and some large baobabs. As I would expect from energetic and precocious boys, Maluca and Alamo took a few wild arrow shots at some birds off in the distance. Alamo even tried to hit one in flight. Their arrows fell harmlessly after missing their targets, though, and the boys ran ahead and retrieved their arrows.

About twenty minutes into the hunt, the first kill happened. Maluca had shot a small bird. He brought it over to me, bleeding and hanging on the tip of his arrow. The forlorn creature looked as though it might provide the amount of meat found on a single chicken wing.

I quickly realized that there was no limit to the kinds of animals hunted. Anything edible that moved, except hyenas (if indeed they are edible), was fair game. Also, snakes were not hunted. This meant that most kills would be small or even tiny animals or birds—barely a few shreds of meat.

After an hour of running about the scrub, through small patches of forest and along a dried riverbed, everyone suddenly became excited. The hunters started shouting, whistling, making clicking sounds at each other, and waving their hands at a nearby copse of trees and bushes. The group broke out into an all-out sprint into the bushes. I followed the oldest hunter, A-Bala, a muscular fellow with a receding hairline.

With growing excitement, I thought it must be a big animal. Perhaps a kudu had been spotted! I followed A-Bala into a thicket. He hunched down, motioning for me to do the same. Joseph and Peter, both visibly out of shape and huffing away, were left way behind.

As everyone closed in on the unseen beast, I thought about the unfolding reality. It would be so different from what is popularly imagined by those in the modern world. The kill would not be a dramatic scene such as seen in a movie. In a movie scene, the heroic hunter-gatherer takes cool and measured aim at the majestic beast. He draws back his bow and fires a precise kill shot. The beast's poignant death throes ensue.

Instead, what I assumed was about to unfold would likely be a drawn-out, gory affair. Probably the first arrow shot would hit somewhere on the poor animal's shoulder, leg, or midsection. The creature would howl and squeal in blind panic and become dangerous, fighting for its life, with no real comprehension of the lethality of its wounds. The proud hunter-gatherers would take more shots at the wounded, terrified, exhausted animal. When it collapsed, one of the hunters would then come up to it and deliver the coup de grâce with a spear, a club, or an arrow shot at close range, putting the poor thing out of its misery.

The Hadzabe hunters continued to crawl and scramble through the bush and thorn thicket, giving sharp whistling and clicking signals as they closed in on the surrounded but still unseen beast. A-Bala backed out of the thicket, and I followed him, tearing the shoulder of my shirt in the process. He then crouched in waiting outside the bush area, poised to kill the panicked beast if it managed to bolt past its pursuers.

Then came shouts of triumph. I could imagine, in the modern world, the hunters slapping each other's hands in high fives. I waited in eager anticipation as they emerged from the thicket with the great beast they had just killed!

Well, sort of.

Again, Alamo came over to proudly display the kill so I could take a picture. The source of all the excitement was a small squirrel that hung bleeding, in its pitiful last spasms, on the end of his arrow. The poor creature was maybe enough for eight or nine bites. I solemnly took a few photos of the pathetic thing, suppressing the urge to laugh at how ridiculous all the commotion made over it now seemed.

After a few more small-animal kills, the hunters took a break at their resting spot, a shallow cave with some old rock paintings, near the top of a steep hill. I was hobbling badly. My left knee had become severely sore during the run after the squirrel in the thorn bushes. Walking was now terribly painful as I struggled to keep pace going up the hill.

Damn it, I thought: I knew right then that my trip in Tanzania was to come to an abrupt halt. I would have to return to the modern world for corrective surgery. I suppressed my anger and pain, determined not to show that anything was wrong, not to spoil the experience.

At the top of the hill, a young man named Kwakama explained that this group of Hadzabe often used the cave as a place of shelter from heavy rains during the wet season. We all sat down to rest around the cave opening, which gave us a few moments to converse, with Peter interpreting.

I asked them about their lives and their thoughts on various things. At one point, I asked Alamo and Maluca if they went to school.

"They say they don't go to school," Peter said. "They say all they need to know is how to hunt to be able to live. They'd rather be out hunting then sitting in school."

From this conversation, the most surprising thing to me was the hunters' lack of curiosity about the world outside their familiar surroundings. While I asked them lots of questions about their lives, they had no questions for me except for the usual one: how many children did I have?

Puzzled by this lack of interest in anything outside their life realm, I told Peter, "Please let them know they are free to ask me anything they might be curious about. Is there anything they want to know about the outside world—maybe different lifestyles they might want to hear about? Or is there anything at all about me they might be curious about?"

I figured that the hunters might think it impolite to ask me such questions. Peter explained to them that I would be happy to tell them anything about the outside world or about myself. Kwakama said something in response.

Oh, good, I thought, *a real question!*

"They are curious why you did not bring any marijuana," Peter said. "They really enjoy smoking it, but it is difficult for them to get."

"Oh. Well, I didn't know to bring any," I said. "But if I come back and visit them again, I'd be happy to bring some."

Somewhat deflated at this rather mundane feedback, I tried one more time.

"There is really *nothing* they are interested in hearing about from the modern world?" I said to Peter. "Please ask them why they are not curious about anything in the outside world. Also maybe you can ask if any of them have ever wanted to visit areas outside their familiar surroundings."

So Peter asked them these questions for me. He got back a few cumulative quick responses.

"They say that they have no interest in learning about other lifestyles or the other parts of the world, because they are happy with their lives here," Peter told me.

I guess I shouldn't have been so surprised. Over the past century, the Hadzabe had had a disastrous experience with the outside world.

Altogether, the hunt lasted around three and a half hours. The take for the morning's work: two sparrow-size birds, one baby squirrel, and two bush babies (small nocturnal primates that look a bit like tree squirrels).

As everyone walked back toward their camp, we crossed paths with two Datoga men herding a group of goats. The animals kicked up a small dust cloud as they passed. The Datoga are a pastoral people who resemble the more well-known Maasai in both physique and lifestyle. The two young Datoga men doing the herding were tall and slender, with dark black skin. They wore tattered modern clothing and each carried a long stick to guide their goats forward.

The Hadzabe group just walked past these people of a completely alien culture, paying them no attention. Perhaps they didn't care. Or perhaps their indifference was their only defense against an outside world that was already upon them.

The next day, Joseph and Peter took me to a village of Datoga people. On the way, we stopped by a small shop on the side of the dusty dirt road we were following. A young woman friend of Joseph's came over to the truck for a moment to say hello. She was plump, with a round, pleasant face. Peter went into the shop to buy some candy, and Joseph's friend walked away from the truck. Always the accommodating tour guide, Joseph motioned toward the plump woman and asked me if I'd like an African girl for the evening.

"Maybe ten dollars is all that would be needed for her to spend the night," he offered with a knowing grin.

I graciously declined.

We drove for another half hour along a dirt road through dry scrub, past a few forlorn-looking villages. Arriving at the Datoga village, we pulled into a compound of several small houses built of mud and cow dung plastered over a frame of sticks. The compound was surrounded by a fence of thick brush and bushes planted close, with an opening for a gate, and a big dirt yard in front. Off to the side of the main house, a few men were working under a crude awning of sticks—a "blacksmith factory," Peter explained.

I admired the view from the compound property, which sat on a shallow hill overlooking a large valley. A few other home compounds and brush corrals were scattered across the valley, among large rolling fields of dried brown grass, scrub, and clumps of short, leafless trees. Sere-looking round hills with black dirt-and-gravel surfaces formed a backdrop to this grand vista.

Two old women, who appeared almost bald, came out to meet us. They both wore orangish golden capes over their bare shoulders, and a midlength orange-gold cotton cloth wrap cut up into long ribbons at the bottom. Both women also wore several colorful beaded necklaces. They were quite friendly and invited me into their home. I liked them immediately.

The inside of the mud-and-dung house was one big room with a little separate room off to the side. Some basic round and gourd-shaped food containers of baked clay, and a few rudimentary cooking utensils hung neatly from one wall. The younger of the two old women then started grinding maize into flour with a stone roller on a stone block. I sensed that this was a sort of "tourist demonstration" that perhaps she felt obliged to do for me. The other old woman sat quietly on the ground against the wall, with two small children beside her. It all seemed a little awkward and uncomfortable.

With Peter interpreting, I asked the two women their names. The younger old woman introduced herself as Deleah and said she lived here with one of her daughters and her family. The other woman, Didi, was a visiting friend. To try to break the ice, I asked more questions.

"How many people live in this house?" I asked. The two women started to appear a bit more relaxed.

Deleah replied that ten people lived here, including her, her married daughter, and four of her grandchildren by the daughter. Three men also lived here. They were working in the blacksmith shop outside. Deleah also said she had seven children altogether and many grandchildren.

I could sense that the two women were very warm people but had no idea how to relate to the strange white alien sitting on their floor. I continued asking them questions about their lives and the Datoga, trying to create a real dialogue.

Deleah explained that for the Datoga, cattle were the most important possession, and cow's milk was a major food (as with the Maasai). They also grew maize and ate goats that they raised. Blacksmithing was also very important work for them, she said.

I then asked Didi where she was visiting from. She came from a village over the hills and through the forest, she said, waving in that direction. To get here, she had walked seventy kilometers, for two days on dirt roads through the hills.

"Oh, that sounds like a serious effort to visit your friend," I said. "I guess you did not just come to have a meal and then go home."

Everyone laughed as Peter interpreted. Didi then explained that she had no car, and so the only way to get around was by walking. The two women now appeared much more at ease. I asked Didi about her family.

She had borne twelve children altogether, although four had died. One died giving birth to her fourth child, one died as a young adult, and the other two died as young children, she said. I winced internally at the harshness of life in her world.

But she was fortunate to have many, many grandchildren by her surviving eight children, she said. One of her daughters alone had eight children, and one of her sons had six.

"Where are you from, and what brought you here?" Deleah asked.

I explained that I was from America and had been traveling for many years, that I was interested in visiting different peoples and lands and knowing about their ways of life.

Both Didi and Deleah said that they would love to be able to travel. I was genuinely beginning to respect these two women. Their lives were circumscribed in many ways by their allotted situations, but they seemed to have an unbounded spirit.

I asked them if they had ever traveled anywhere outside their home area.

Didi had once traveled in one of her son's trucks to Karatu (a small town about seventy miles away, near Tanzania's famous Ngorongoro Crater National Park.) Otherwise, both women said they had never been out of their homeland environment.

"Would you like to see what another part of the world looks like?" I asked. "I have some pictures in my camera here of where I recently visited, which I can show you in the little screen."

"Yes!" Both women's eyes lit up. "Please come sit here and show us." Now completely at ease, they motioned to me to sit between them against the mud-and-cow-dung wall.

"This is Stone Town, the capital of Zanzibar Island," I explained, showing on the preview screen pictures that were stored in the camera's memory. Their eyes lit up again at the beautiful old Islamic-style buildings from the late Middle Ages that Stone Town is famous for.

"This is not a modern or big city by any means, I said. I then explained that Zanzibar was an island off the coast of Tanzania.

They chatted back and forth excitedly, both pointing to the small camera preview screen. The two small boys, also, were excited and visibly animated by the pictures.

"We have never seen anything like this," Deleah said. "Didi and I both think it is beautiful. I have heard some young people from around here that have gone away and then returned, describe the big faraway villages that they saw. But I could never really imagine what they look like until now." For these two women with no television or Internet, the pictures of Zanzibar were a wonder of the world.

"Can you show us pictures of America?" Didi asked. I told her that I was sorry but I had only the pictures of Zanzibar stored in my camera. I then spent some time trying to describe some aspects of America and the modern city. To them, the idea that buildings could be hundreds of feet high was almost unfathomable. I couldn't help reflecting on what an amazing contrast this curiosity was to the Hadzabe people's indifference.

After a couple of hours sitting in the small house talking, the two women brought me out to meet the men working in the blacksmith shop. Six young men dressed in long cotton robes of orange, purple, or reddish checkered patterns were hard at work. Their tools were crude and simple: some hammers that looked to be from the early Iron Age, a few metal bars, awls, chisels, and picks, along with a small fire pit and a hand bellows for stoking the forge. Their raw material was old junk metal from various sources, but a large assortment of what appeared to be well-made metal pieces were lined up on a table. These were mostly assorted arrowheads, cutlery, and large round earrings and other sorts of metal adornment bands.

As I looked at the arrowheads, a young man in a purple checkered robe asked if I wanted to buy one.

"How long does it take to make an arrowhead?" I asked, figuring it took perhaps an hour or so.

He said it took only about ten minutes to make a fairly intricate arrowhead with several shaft barbs.

I didn't believe him. "Ten minutes and you can make this?" I asked, pointing to an arrowhead with many small barbs in its shaft. "If you can make one right now in front of me in ten minutes, I'll buy two arrowheads," I said, laying down the challenge.

"No problem," the young man said. He grabbed a piece of scrap metal and shoved it into the fire. After a few moments, he had it set on a small anvil and was chopping away excess superheated metal. Within perhaps seven minutes, he had pounded, scraped, chiseled, and filed to a nice finish a very sharp arrowhead, complete with several extremely sharp shaft barbs. I happily bought this arrowhead and another as souvenirs of such expert craftsmanship.

It was then time to leave. The two women, along with the two children and the six blacksmiths, all came out into the dirt front yard to see me off. As we drove away, I looked back at all the people waving to me. Seeing Didi's and Deleah's faces still lit up with beaming big smiles, I thought about the magic of travel: how such simple encounters as the one I just had could be so wonderfully enriching to everyone involved.

———

A week after my visit with the Hadzabe hunter-gatherers, I was in the medical offices of the Sport Sciences Institute in Cape Town, the well-known sports medicine center used by the Springboks, the South African national rugby union team. After an MRI test, the doctor told me my knee needed corrective surgery to get better and that the problem would only get worse the longer I waited. He gave me two surgery options. One was the standard procedure usually done with injuries such as mine, and the second was a pioneering new technique that would fix the problem much better in the long run but was riskier and required that I not make the injury any worse.

I chose the second surgery option. But I told the doctor about my planned gorilla safari in the Congo Basin next month and that I would pay almost any price not to miss it. Having the surgery now would kill my chance for this trip. So the doctor had me fitted with a state-of-the-art athletic knee and leg brace that would support and relieve pressure on my knee during the Congo gorilla safari. Walking would be awkward, though, and I would be fairly stiff-legged on my left side. He cautioned that I had to be very careful not to make the problem worse. Then, after the gorilla safari, I would return to Cape Town for my surgery.

Walking stiff-legged in a brace wasn't the best way to make an arduous journey in one of the world's great, physically challenging wilderness areas. But I was determined to make this African trip a success, and I really wanted to see the gorillas of the Congo Basin.

CHAPTER 20

Jungle and General Dysfunction in the Congo Basin

What is said over the dead lion's body could not be said to him alive.
—Congolese proverb

October 2011
Central African Republic

An endless carpet of green stretched in all directions below us. The view from our chartered ten-passenger twin-engine plane, at ten thousand feet above the primeval jungles, was awe inspiring. A brown ribbon of water snaked its way through the green infinity, and cottony puffs of cloud floated here and there above. Flying into the Congo Basin at the southwestern tip of the Central African Republic (CAR), the view reminded me of several flights I had made over the Amazon Basin. After the mighty Amazon, the Congo Basin contains the world's second-largest expanse of undisturbed rain forest, with areas still considered unexplored.

Our small group consisted of eight participants and the lead guide, Jean-Pierre, a middle-aged man from neighboring Cameroon. We were flying from CAR's capital, Bangui, to the Dzanga Sangha National Park in the southwest corner of the country. This great park is part of the wilderness area called the Tri-State Protected Area, an immense expanse of wilderness in the northern Congo Basin that sprawls over the borders of CAR, Congo Republic, and Cameroon. We were beginning a twelve-day expedition-style journey into the CAR and Congo Republic sections of this vast protected but highly threatened area. Like my entire trip in Africa for the previous two and a half months, this excursion would not be the smoothest of journeys.

Gazing out on the endless green below, I thought it looked misleadingly peaceful, belying the almost constant survival struggles taking place under its cover. For me, the time-travel aspect of journeying in the Congo Basin was one of the greatest leaps backward into the world's ancient history. Uniquely among the planet's great tropical rain forests, high numbers of large land mammals still roam its expanse. It is home to the biggest population of gorillas in Africa, as well as to legions of forest elephants and forest buffalo. Humanity itself still carries on its most primeval lifestyles in the forest-dwelling Pygmies who inhabit its vast reaches.

But the struggle for survival is not just with the life under its peaceful green cover. This wonderland of nature sits in a huge expanse of the world's failed or semifailed states and ungovernable territories. The geographical extent of human dysfunction starts in the east with Somalia and continues across the continent, through northern Kenya, Sudan and South Sudan, and into the Congo Basin itself, with the monumental failure of nationhood that is the Democratic Republic of the Congo, and the near failure CAR. Failed states and wilderness protection do not usually go well together, making this entire region of nature's treasures a potential tragic entrant to the Disappearing World.

All of us participating in this journey had rendezvoused yesterday afternoon in Bangui. Shabby, run-down Bangui is really just a poor big town, certainly nothing resembling a capital city. The center of town is a collection of tumbledown buildings with peeling paint. Its roads in many areas are nothing more than a thin veneer of crumbling pavement, slapped over red dirt and clay. A motley collection of even more dilapidated vehicles plies those roads. As a first-time visitor to Bangui, it was obvious to me that the country was not a normally functioning place. But CAR doesn't see lots of casual visitors.

One of the least-developed countries in the world, CAR is often described as a failed state in permanent crisis, and its people are among humanity's poorest.

"There is still low-level fighting going on in many villages in sections of the north," Jean-Pierre had said over a beer at dinner last night. "The French have troops here, and there are some international peacekeepers. But I think the French mostly just worry about how to profit from this country and don't really help otherwise."

Jean-Pierre, a somber man, was voicing a sentiment shared by others I had met in my short time in Bangui. CAR had been in a continual state of instability for decades. Since independence from France in 1960, it had been plagued by rebellions, mutinies, a proliferation of illegal weapons, and a long-running insurgency. The current insurgency that Pierre was talking about had displaced thousands of CAR citizens in large parts of the country's north, many of whom had fled to neighboring Chad. The fighting included elements of the Lord's Resistance Army, which had been waging a deadly, low-level insurgency in Uganda for over two decades, and other armed groups. Along with the international peacekeepers, Ugandan troops operated on CAR territory, opposing the Lord's Resistance Army.

"The country has so much potential wealth in minerals, diamonds, and gold, though—it could be much better off," Jean-Pierre concluded, referring to the common situation of resource-rich countries with dirt-poor masses.

In other words, CAR was a mess and not a top choice for many outsiders to visit.

Our plane rumbled in for landing near a village called Bayanga, bouncing along a dirt-and-grass clearing that served as a landing strip. While we unloaded our food and gear onto the ground, some local villagers gathered casually around, though none of us paid them much attention—in the poor world, there always seemed to be a lot of locals hanging around with not much to do.

We then shoved the gear into two waiting four-by-fours and piled in. Our group rode in the four-by-fours along dirt roads through the forest, to a nearby dock on the Sangha River, a major tributary of the mighty Congo. Without delay, we hauled our stuff onto a broad-beamed old motorized wooden canoe. The old outboard sputtered to life, and we were off, heading downriver on the chocolate-brown waters of the Sangha. It was midmorning, and the sun was scorching hot. I took off my high-tech leg brace and stretched my legs out from my boat stool, ready to enjoy the jungle scenery and the light, cooling breeze from the boat's motion downriver.

Our first destination was a Wildlife Conservation Society (WCS) research camp near Bomassa in the Congo Republic, an eight-hour motorized canoe trip from Bayanga. The research camp was at the edge of the famous Noubale Ndoki National Park, part of the Tri-State Protected Area that we would journey through.

Twenty minutes after we started, Jean-Pierre, who was slouched over and dozing off near the front of the canoe, suddenly jolted awake. He called out to the boatman, "Turn around! Return to Bayanga!"

Overhearing this, I asked him what was wrong.

"I just realized, a big box with much of our food, including our breakfast things, is not on the canoe," Jean-Pierre said. "I think it was stolen by one of the villagers hanging around when we unloaded from the airplane."

We returned to the dock at Bayanga, and sure enough, the food box was gone. Since we were in such a remote place, there was no practical way to replace the stolen food. So we just got back on our canoe and took off without our breakfast and some other food supplies. A local woman had come to the dock with several bags of peanuts for sale, so two Russians in the group and I each bought a few bags. It was a lousy way to start a journey.

Our motorized canoe swung back out into the wide, brown Sangha, into endless green jungle that appeared ready to swallow us. We passed a local woman standing in the stern of a small dugout canoe, paddling downriver with a big bundle. Periodically, we passed wooden shacks with grass thatch roofs, built along the high dirt riverbank. People would stop what they were doing and wave as we passed, and cute naked children called out excitedly.

Our canoe, typical for poor sub-Saharan Africa, was a bare-bones deal, simple, with no sunroof or covering of any kind, so the equatorial sun beat down mercilessly the entire time. Long before midday, the wiser passengers had covered up, but the two Russian men, in shorts and shirtless, seemed unconcerned as they drank down their bottle of vodka. Predictably, by midafternoon they were bright pink all over and suffering.

About five hours downriver from our starting point, Jean-Pierre announced that we were approaching the CAR river border check-point.

"Please put your cameras away inside your bags so that they cannot be seen," he instructed, shouting above the whine of the canoe engine. "Keep them away while I take care of business with the border agents."

I leaned over and asked discreetly, "Hey, Jean-Pierre, how much will this border business cost us?"

"Don't say anything to the others, Gary," he murmured. "I'll take care of it. I am hoping to get by with a payment of only eight euros for each expedition participant."

He then walked up the sloping dirt riverbank to the border station shack, where two agents in faded green uniforms stood waiting. Jean-Pierre handed one of them our small stack of passports, no doubt with a small packet of money. It had the feel of business as usual. Ten minutes later, he was back on the boat and we were on our way again.

Later that afternoon, we came to a clearing in the dense jungle along the river shoreline. Several efficient-looking buildings of wood and corrugated metal, with real window screens and a large satellite dish, were set in the clearing. The WCS research camp at Bomassa looked surprisingly homey. As we docked our canoe, a tall, friendly-looking German of perhaps 40 came out to greet us. He introduced himself as Thomas and asked us to join him for a briefing in a large screened room in the main dining and conference building.

At our briefing, it sounded as though the WCS camp had done some remarkable conservation work.

"When I first came here over a decade ago, the nearby village of Bomassa was primarily sustained by poaching and the bush-meat trade," said Thomas. "This included the killing of elephants (for ivory) and gorilla from the forest. However, with patient and persistent effort, most of the village inhabitants now seem won over to the idea of conserving the animals."

Thomas described how the village had recently experienced rapid growth from the steady earnings of the park's small tourist business.

"The inhabitants of Bomassa have come to see that the gorillas, elephants, and other animals are worth more alive than being sold dead on the black market," he said.

But progress was still far from assured or total. He told the story of how, just four weeks before our visit, poachers had killed a large silverback gorilla—shot through the chest. The ensuing investigation implicated the village chief, who was also a WCS *staff member* for Thomas. The chief had illegally sold the gun used in the crime to a "hunter."

"The hunter, it seems, was a safari tourist who *just wanted to kill a gorilla*," Thomas said. "He apparently offered enough money that the chief decided to give him the gun used for the crime."

An Australian woman with the group then asked Thomas about bush-meat hunting.

"It is now illegal to hunt bush meat," he said, referring to duiker, monkeys, forest buffalo, bushpig, and other animals besides the protected species. "But bush-meat hunting still does happen. For the people who live in forest villages, it is a primary source of animal protein and practically impossible to stop completely."

For all the WCS camp's earnest and worthwhile achievements, it could do only so much. The abject poverty of the local inhabitants, the corruption of local officials, and the horrendous senselessness of tourists who took pleasure in killing great animals created an almost overwhelming tide against its conservation efforts.

Early the next day, we were on the move again, to Mondika, another WCS research camp. The forests around Mondika and the next stop along the way, Mbelli Bai, were considered among the most pristine areas in Central Africa. These places would give us the best opportunity of the whole trip to see lowland gorillas.

Getting to Mondika was a chore. Our group loaded into two dusty WCS four-by-fours and bounced along dirt-and-rock roads through high scrub, grass, and patchy forest. An hour later, we came to the end of the road. From this point, it was a ten-kilometer walk through dense rain forest and swamp to Mondika.

Everyone else donned their backpacks, and I paid one of the local WCS guides to carry mine—my injured knee and leg brace would be enough to manage. We filed along a narrow path through dense jungle. It was hot, humid, and overcast. After an hour and a half, we came to a big swamp with thigh-deep water, where we all took off our hike boots and waded through clear tea-colored water for a half hour. Normally, I wouldn't have found a hike like this especially challenging, but schlepping through the swamp stiff-legged in a leg brace was a lot of work.

After we slogged through the swamp it started to rain, as if to ensure that we all stay wet and sticky the rest of the several-hour jungle trek. But our group had a nice surprise at the end of the trek. The Mondika camp was, surprisingly, almost plush for an isolated research camp in remote deep forest. It had several modest wooden buildings for dining and the researchers' work, and a number of raised wooden platforms with large tents for sleeping quarters. But for all of us, the main draw at Mondika was the two habituated gorilla groups living in the surrounding forest.

Early the next morning, we were off, separated into small groups of four expedition participants each. Each group was led by four local Ba'aka Pygmy men—traditional forest dwellers who knew the jungle intimately. It was encouraging to see these local people involved in the tourist business, having a stake in preserving the forest habitat and the gorillas. Two of the Pygmy guides went ahead, trying to track one of the gorilla groups. It was drizzling and cool as we hiked along narrow twisting paths through dense jungle. We non-forest dwellers slipped and slid occasionally in the wetness, moving at a much slower, noisier pace than our little sure-footed guides.

After an hour of hiking, our Pygmy guides came to an abrupt halt and signaled us to be still and quiet. I looked up through the foliage. Blocking our path not more than twenty-five feet ahead of us was a magnificent sight: a huge male gorilla. Around 350 pounds, he had a massive build with an amazingly muscular upper torso.

The huge male, known as Kingo among the local Pygmies, had fluffy black body hair, a high forehead with rust-colored hair, and a broad black face with a full, squat nose and prominent nostrils. When he moved at an angle to us, we could see the silvery-gray hair on his back. Kingo hunched on all fours, just looking at us, as if silently appraising the interlopers who had disturbed his morning.

Kingo is a "famous" gorilla. He was once featured in a *National Geographic* story and had appeared in several documentaries on gorillas and his Congo Basin forest home. Known as an aggressive fighter, Kingo had several "wives" as a result of his prowess. To me, he looked confident, like someone who knew that he was lord and master of his realm.

"Be quiet. Move slowly when you walk or work with your cameras," whispered our main Pygmy guide, who had learned some English.

"Kingo is accustomed to people, but you don't want to get too close. If he charges you, you must stand your ground and not show fear," he added, repeating instructions we had heard at a briefing in the camp.

We all stood still, silently watching the massive gorilla. Incredibly, Kingo began to climb up some trees and vines. I half expected the flimsy-looking support to give way, but, these giant animals were master climbers, and barely a leaf broke.

Kingo was not alone. Nearby, a small round-faced baby with fluffy black hair was climbing up a branch. One of Kingo's harem, looking perhaps half his size, sat silently in a clump of vegetation not far from where we stood. This was only a small part of Kingo's extended family, and judging by how he looked and carried himself, it would be a long time before any challenger took away his harem and his mating prerogative.

To this amateur gorilla watcher, these western lowland gorillas seemed very similar to the mountain species I had seen in Uganda a few years ago. The two types differ in small ways, though. Lowland gorillas are a bit smaller than their mountain cousins, and their fur is lighter colored and thinner due to the higher humidity and temperatures of their habitats. There are also dietary and behavioral differences, and the nature of the food supply in the lowland jungles gives the lowland species a larger range.

In the two days we spent at the Mondika camp, I did three gorilla treks, two involving Kingo's group. It was exhilarating to see these great apes up close in the wild. It was also sobering to realize that, despite their appearance of gentle indifference, we were here only because they allowed it.

At one point, though, the two Russian men and I came through some thick underbrush and almost ran into Kingo. As we and Kingo came face to face maybe eleven feet apart, the two Russians, without thinking of their situation, abruptly raised their cameras to grab a photo. Kingo instantly went from casual, nonthreatening giant to ferocious, scary wild beast. Roaring, he feigned a charge. Comically, the cameras instantly went down. This time, all three of us did exactly what we were supposed to do. We held our ground—mostly because we were frozen in alarm at the giant creature's feigned attack.

Later that evening in camp, reviewing photos of this majestic creature, I found it hard to believe how fragile and threatened his existence really was. Estimates put the number of lowland gorillas as high as perhaps 130,000 still in the Congo Basin. But the entire ecosystem is under such heavy pressures from so many different causes—logging, mining, hunting, poaching, and road construction—that many experts fear that these gorillas' numbers could crash to perhaps only ten thousand as soon as the year 2030.

Although the gorillas were spectacular during our time in Mondika, the food was not. For laughs, I started keeping notes on what we had to eat. I would show this to some friends back home who were fine-food buffs, in case they were curious about what one ate on a trip like this. For the five days we spent in the Congo Republic, our breakfast consisted of bland white bread, margarine, jam, liquid chocolate, tea, and coffee. One day, we got a couple of cans of tuna. Lunches and dinners, too, were mostly empty starches: white bread and pasta, and a small piece of chicken or smelly fish thrown in with some lentils.

On remote trips like this, I usually brought my own supply of nuts and dried fruit to keep up good nutrition. But for weight limitation purposes, I had only a small bag of dates, another of raisins, and another of mixed nuts. So to make these luxurious treats last, I rationed them down to six dates, a pinch of raisins, and ten nuts each day. This little stash lasted only through day six—halfway through the expedition.

From Mondika, we did another all-day jungle/swamp hike and canoe journey to a well-known *bai* called Mbeli. A bai is a natural clearing in the forest, with small lakes or patches of water. It is where animals congregate to drink. But we had bad luck. Virtually no animals, and not a single gorilla, came to Mbeli Bai on our day there, so it was a bust.

Despite the lack of wildlife, I still managed to get attacked at Mbeli camp—not by big animals but by some nasty, fast-moving ants. Our "camp" at Mbeli was actually a set of simple wood cabins on high stilts. After dinner our first night there, I walked with my roommate, Max, an Italian bodybuilder and wildlife photography buff, back to our cabin in the dark. Somewhere along the short path from the dinner building to our cabin, we both unknowingly stepped into a stream of ants crossing the path.

As I got to the veranda by the entrance to our room, I felt biting and burning sensations spreading quickly up my ankles. I reacted by pulling up my pant legs and trying to brush off the ants, but this proved useless—they just kept coming and soon were in my pants and crawling up to potentially very uncomfortable places. Instantly, I flung off my boots and clothes, right there on the veranda, so I could brush off the ants. Max had to do a similar panicked and contorted withdrawal from his clothes. It was comically undignified—just the kind of screw-up that would quickly go viral on the Web if caught on video.

After our time in Mbeli, we journeyed back by canoe and through the forest to Bomassa and clambered into our motorized canoe for the long trip up the Sangha, back to Bayanga in CAR. This time, rather than a beating hot sun, a potent storm appeared to be building upriver ahead of us. As we chugged along, the clouds began to gather and the skies darkened, promising torrents of driving rain. I eagerly anticipated the storm, which would be a welcome relief from the heat.

Just before the downpour hit, some of our group needed to stop for a pee break. So we pulled up at a small clearing along the shore.

It was an eerie-looking place.

Weird objects were dangling from thin ropes strung up on trees lining the shoreline. One of the hanging objects looked like a curled-up small, thick burnt snake. Another appeared to be a very large long-necked glass bottle filled with a brown murky substance, and dangling a few feet away from this was a an elongated bundle roughly the size of an ear of corn, wrapped in dried twine. Behind the trees were several closed and boarded-up old wooden shacks. A smaller dried twine bundle hung in front of the entrance to the main shack.

"This is a fishing camp," Jean-Pierre said in response to my inquiry about the place. "You can see the fishing tools by the side of the main hut there." He motioned to a half-dozen fishing spears stacked against the main wooden shack.

"What are those things hanging from the trees and in front of the main shack?" I asked.

"Fetishes," Jean-Pierre replied. "The fetish hanging by the entrance to the wooden hut is designed to bring great pain and injury to a person's innards if they dare enter the building."

"And those"—he pointed to the fetishes hanging from the trees by the water—"are to bring good luck to the fisherman."

This fit. We were still on the Congo Republic part of the Sangha River, and from my readings, the use of fetishes was quite widespread throughout the country. But knowing this didn't subtract from the creepy aura of the place.

I then asked Jean-Pierre if he, too, being from Cameroon, believed in the power of the fetishes.

"It is better not to tempt fate," he said, with a slight grin. This seemed to me a practical mind-set.

Several hours later, after being drenched by refreshing rains along the way, we arrived back at Bayanga in the CAR. Bayanga was a bustling village of maybe a thousand inhabitants, with wide dirt roads and old wooden bungalows. Around it were many small villages populated by displaced Ba'aka Pygmies. In a common theme in many places in Sub-Saharan Africa, they had been "persuaded," which is to say, moved outright from their ancestral lands in the forest. They came from a culture cocooned in dense, deep jungle, where the passage of time hadn't meant change in any meaningful sense for centuries upon centuries. But now many modern Ba'aka live in harsh conditions in villages on the edge of their traditional homelands in the forest. Their lives bear only a passing resemblance to what they used to be. Like rapidly vanishing forest-dwelling peoples across the planet, they are casualties of modernization—another cultural jewel joining the ranks of the Disappearing World.

The Dzangha Sangha Protected Area, next to Bayanga, is the CAR part of the Tri-State Protected area. For the remainder of the excursion, our group would stay in a jungle lodge near the village and do day trips into the Dzangha Sangha National Park, part of the protected area.

Early the next morning, four of us, a couple of local guides, and a driver took off in a beat-up old four-by-four pickup. We were taking a two-hour ride into the jungle, to an area known for good gorilla viewing. With branches and foliage slapping against the windshield and side windows, we jounced and sloshed along a cratered, sometimes submerged muddy path through the deep forest.

It started raining hard. In the spirit of ill luck that seemed to plague our group when in Bayanga's environs, our truck got stuck in the mud. Compounding this inconvenience, the driver foolishly spun the wheels for about an hour, trying to rock or just muscle the vehicle out of the mire. All of us expedition participants stood outside the truck, advising him that his actions were only making things worse, but to no avail. He continued to do this even as clouds of white smoke billowed from under the truck.

Worse, the driver was not equipped to deal with the obvious potential emergency of being severely stuck in deep mud. He had no shovel, no winch, no rope, nor any support base, such as a thick board, to set the truck's jack on. This actually didn't matter, though, since the jack had no handle anyway. Our small group was two hours away from our starting point, in thick, remote jungle under steady rain, without any equipment to extract the truck, and no way to call for help.

Finally we "outsiders" became assertive and took control of the situation. I suggested that we use some machetes in the truck to dig a trench through the mud around the tires. This way, the truck's wheels would not be buried in mud. An older Australian man with us suggested putting big pieces of wood, chopped up from some trees, under the tires to give traction. These actions worked, and an hour later, we were finally free and moving again. We drove a whole mile when we were forced to halt—our rear transmission differential had been ruined by the wheel spinning.

This time, our driver displayed the sort of astonishing Sub-Saharan ingenuity that only a life of continual adversity can inspire. As I watched in disbelief, he proceeded to do a jungle roadside repair of the differential. Amazingly, he did have a basic toolkit. Without a jack, the driver and his helper removed the rear differential completely—a job requiring some skill even in a well-equipped auto garage. He then patched it back together right there in the mud, rain, and thick jungle. Strange that someone capable of such a feat would not have prepared for the inevitable miring in the mud.

After the repairs, the truck could motor forward using only front-wheel drive. This was risky, though, since we had a high probability of getting stuck during the ensuing two-hour drive in intermittent pouring rain. Luckily, we made it back to town.

The next day, we made it without incident to a large wetland clearing in the forest, called Dzangha Bai. A major gathering point for forest elephants, it was the primary place researchers used to observe these animals in the Congo Basin. A large rectangular wooden platform, used for discreetly viewing wildlife in the bai, had been built at one edge of the huge clearing.

Forest elephants are slightly smaller than those seen on the African savannah. They are a species under great pressure, facing an ongoing loss of habitat and, in many areas, large-scale poaching for their tusks—often by well-organized groups using automatic weapons. Some are hunted by rich-world miscreants who just want to kill a big animal.

It was a beautiful sunny day, and the bai was noisy with snorting, low rumbling, and periodic splashing sounds. The distinctive trumpeting calls of the adult elephants boomed out at times. Out in the bai, large, majestic beasts with prominent white tusks strode in from the surrounding forest. Some would be leading their families to the drinking spot. They often filed in with the bull in front, followed by several slightly smaller cows and some appealing little calves, trotting to keep up behind. As they splashed through, the elephants would stop and plunge their trunks deep into the shallow, muddy water.

Rust-colored sitatunga, a type of swamp-dwelling antelope found all over Central Africa, lazed about, generally keeping a respectful distance from the much bigger elephants. Brown-hued forest buffalo, with horns much smaller than their savannah cousins, the cape buffalo, mingled with the sitatunga. From our viewing platform, it looked like a big convention for forest animals.

Like many conventions, this one had its interpersonal dramas. In one exciting spectacle, a big bull elephant covered in white mud charged a big dark-colored bull. There was loud trumpeting as the huge beast charged, and the clack of tusks. Within a few moments, the dark elephant had managed to lock tusks with its attacker and twist the white-coated bull's head around to the point that it had to back off. The losing elephant, like the loser in a schoolyard brawl, backed away, then raised its head and made indignant trumpeting calls at the winner from a distance. Eventually, the dark bull chased the loser back into the forest.

Just after this elephant fight, I met the well-known WCS forest elephant expert Andrea Turkalo. She lived in a camp near the bai with two Pygmy trackers and assistants and had happened to walk onto the viewing platform just moments earlier. She was from the East Coast of the USA and had spent ten months each year since 1991 studying and monitoring the Dzangha Bai activity for the WCS. I immediately felt Andrea's passion for the elephants to which she had devoted most of her adult life.

"You are very lucky to have seen this," Andrea said about the fight. "Real fights between two bulls are unusual. Most of the confrontations, or *jousting*, we call it, are about establishing, challenging, and maintaining hierarchy as the dominant bull." Actual fights were rare, she said, because they were dangerous and could lead to serious injury or death.

Later, I asked Andrea her thoughts on the future of the Dzangha Bai, a critical habitat for the forest elephants in this part of the Congo Basin.

"I am not optimistic about the future of the bai—or the entire forest, for that matter," she said. "There are so many threats and pressures from seemingly all directions on the whole regional forest. Just twenty kilometers east of here, right at the park's boundary, a French company is doing large-scale logging, which threatens the bai's very existence. And park boundaries don't mean much here anyway. Plus, there is the usual difficult problem with poachers. A large bull was actually shot last year right here in the bai. If you look over there, towards the middle of the field, its bones are still visible.

"And the bush-meat trade, as everywhere in the Congo Basin forests, continues to deplete wildlife at an alarming rate," Andrea said, continuing the long and dismal litany of factors destroying this amazing wilderness. "Perhaps the toughest challenge, though, is getting a cultural change to occur in the local people. Without this, nothing can save the forest or the animals."

I asked her what she meant by "cultural change" in the locals.

"The villagers may now wear modern clothes, but their minds still think in the ways of primitive times," Andrea said in a quiet, poignant voice. "Magic is a big thing for the Central and West Africans in explaining how life works. Exploitation of the forest and its animals has been the way of life for the local people since time immemorial. So the idea of 'education' to instill modern concepts of habitat and species conservation is a very difficult proposition. The poverty here is so deep, even what would seem a very small amount of money to rich-world citizens is a huge deal to the local people. For example, take the two Ba'aka Pygmy men I have working for me. When they return periodically from here to visit their home villages, they get swamped by practically everyone, requesting or demanding money. Everyone in the village knows that they have received money from their work with me and the WCS."

"If their modest salaries are considered riches to be targeted by many others in the village, then imagine the temptations of poaching, and the sheer survival needs involved in the bush-meat hunting." Andrea sounded hopeless about the whole situation.

After hearing this dismal prognosis, I spent the rest of the day watching the amazing spectacle in the bai. A still truly wild place, with nature as it had been since time immemorial, carried on its rhythms and its constant primal drama amid indescribable beauty. But for how much longer?

During our time in Bayanga, I had many occasions to visit some Ba'aka villages. This provided mostly a sobering experience, for the harshness of life there was palpable. The village-dwelling Ba'aka suffered from living sedentary lives in conditions they were not accustomed to. For example, I commonly saw numerous bumps and scabs on the exposed legs of many of the Ba'aka in the villages. This was caused by chiggers, Jean-Pierre explained—tiny larval mites that attach and feed under the skin of their hosts.

Traditionally, Jean-Pierre explained, the Ba'aka were nomadic, moving through the forest to various hunting grounds, living only in temporary camps. Thus, they never stayed in one place long enough for a chigger infestation to build. Now, in their village homes, it was a different story.

Other problems, too, were apparent with the Ba'aka's village life. Jean-Pierre explained that the new sedentary life brought people together into a denser proximity, requiring sanitation practices they had not needed as forest-dwelling nomads. Now the Ba'aka suffered from many communicable diseases that were not common in their past, and they also suffered from an inability to treat these ailments.

"In the forest, they had access to lots of plant and herbal remedies for their ailments (including malaria)," Jean-Pierre said. "Now, these things are hard to come by, and modern medicine is in short supply in poor forest-side villages. It is the same with nutrition. As with medicine, the forest provided a nutritious variety of foods for the Ba'aka. But now, living in villages outside the forest, they often have a difficult time eating a nutritious diet."

Another problem marginalizing the Ba'aka was their small size. (Men ranged from four and a half feet to perhaps five and a half feet tall.) Jean-Pierre explained that the Ba'aka's small stature adapted them better than peoples of normal stature to the forest environment, allowing them to run through trees and bush faster and more easily. But outside the forest, in villages and towns of mixed ethnicities, they were often subject to discrimination. They were physically vulnerable to people of larger stature and were often looked down on as inferior. Thus, these people went from being evolutionary winners in their native environment to big losers in the modern-era birth lottery.

On the last day of our twelve-day expedition, we did a fun activity with the Ba'aka: we took some of them out on a hunt. At first, I thought it strange: foreign visitors taking the locals out on a hunt. But the new reality was that the Ba'aka now lived in villages a fair distance from their forest hunting grounds, with no practical means of transport. So when outside visitors came to the area with trucks to take them to their hunting grounds, the occasion was a festive and special one.

On the day of the hunt, our group took two trucks to two Ba'aka villages near Bayanga. We pulled up to the first village, which had several small stick-and-mud houses with grass thatched roofs sitting in tall grass. At once, a stream of Ba'aka surrounded our trucks. Young women in old cotton wraparounds, breast-feeding their babies, a well-built middle-aged man with a mustache, wearing a blue jersey with the number "24" and the name "West" imprinted on it, and many more people streamed up to us. The atmosphere was like a carnival. Everyone was animated and excited. Clearly, the Ba'aka relished the opportunity to go on a hunt.

Many in the festive crowd carried big coils of netting. When the lucky group that was going on the hunt loaded onto the backs of our trucks, they started singing boisterously. This joyous merriment continued all the way down the dirt road as we drove deeper into the forest, toward the day's hunting grounds.

Upon arrival at the hunting grounds, everyone jumped out of the truck in an even more animated mood. As I got out of the truck, a middle-aged woman a little over four feet tall, wearing a gray tank top with the word "Replay" printed across the chest, said something to me. Not understanding, I asked our driver to interpret.

"She is very happy. This reminds her of their real way of life," the driver explained. "If the hunt is successful, there will be a big barbecue feast of the freshly caught meat later today in their villages. The hunters will share their catch with their families and fellow villagers."

I figured that the hunt was also a welcome change from what must be a stiflingly dull routine of daily village life, with nothing to do most of the day.

Very quickly, the hunters were off running, whooping and hollering. They charged nimbly through the forest, not following any visible paths. Their short stature was an obvious advantage in the thick forest, where they scampered under low branches and through narrow gaps in the brush without even having to watch where their feet were stepping. I, on the other hand, like my fellow visitors, lumbered through the brush, crashing between vines and tripping over roots. And, of course, the leg brace amplified the challenge. But I clumsily soldiered on.

After about ten minutes of stiff-legged running, I caught up with the hunters. Several had stopped and begun spreading out the nets they had been carrying. The nets, which were quite long and only a yard high, were strung above the ground to create a long, low, level fence. Then the Ba'aka women and men all moved quickly away from the net. The few non-Pygmies among us crouched behind some brush and trees, watching quietly.

Continuing to make a great racket, the hunters fanned out. Then they began to stir and disrupt the bushes and vegetation around them, slowly moving back together toward the net. Using sticks, the women beat at imaginary things along the ground, creating as much disturbance as possible. The idea was to scare prey into coming out of hiding and making a run for it toward the net fence.

After about ten minutes of this, a huge commotion erupted from several of the hunters some distance away. They were celebrating the first catch! Following the net line, I ran through the trees to see what they had caught. Several of the hunters gathered around a duiker, a small antelope, that had gotten entangled in the net. One of the men quickly took the terrified animal by the hind legs, and another then smashed its head with a machete, killing it.

Within a few moments, another set of whoops and hollers rang out farther down the net line. I walked over to see the catch. The woman with the "Replay" T-shirt was pinning down another small duiker entangled in the net. The stunned animal sat completely still, its brown eyes staring wide in what appeared to be uncomprehending terror. Another women hunter came over and calmly snapped the poor animal's hind legs, incapacitating it, then clubbed it to death with a machete.

The nets were gathered up and moved to another spot, where the process was repeated, ensnaring more duiker.

The method of hunting we witnessed was one type of hunt in the traditional Ba'aka lifestyle of the past. I had read that this method of hunting was usually done by women, though. Typically, the men, as in most hunter-gatherer societies, would go off some distance from camp for long periods, hunting for larger game. The women stayed around the home encampment doing their various chores, which included hunts in the manner just described.

Men's hunts traditionally could involve the use of weapons, such as bows and arrows. In a similar concept to the hunt method used by women, nets would be strung up, creating a fencelike barrier. But the barrier would resemble the shape of a long funnel in the forest. The men would then go a distance away from the large opening and attempt to flush animals into the funnel, where they would be trapped and ultimately killed by the hunters. From my understanding, this hunting method was still practiced in some other parts of the Congo region.

After the hunters had caught five duiker, the hunt was over. Everybody got together in a small clearing for a rest, which turned into a sort of impromptu celebratory party. The men sat back and smoked cigarettes and marijuana while several women danced energetically. The women held branches and brush, making sweeping motions and beating the ground, stylistically imitating the hunt they had just done. It all was accompanied by lots of whooping, laughing, and general merriment.

At the same time, several women quickly butchered the five duiker that had been caught. The cut-up pieces were wrapped in large leaves and divided among the group. Nothing was wasted; every edible part of the animal would be consumed. The two villages where the hunters lived would feast that afternoon on the freshly barbecued meat.

It was time to bring the happy hunters back to their villages. They could escape the reality of their new sedentary lifestyle only for a very short while.

Early on the morning after the hunt, we were on our chartered bush flight back to Bangui. Looking out the window at the endless expanse of forest below, it seemed hard to believe that this was truly a disappearing world.

But the trends of deforestation and other pressures from modern-world development on this amazing ecosystem are relentless and seemingly unstoppable. The jungles of the Congo Basin represent the first romanticized image that non-Africans think of when they imagine what Africa is like. How profoundly, ironically tragic that, perhaps soon, this romanticized image will be no more than a memory.

Shortly after arriving in Bangui, CAR, I flew back to Cape Town for my knee surgery. After a week there, I returned to Bangkok in a knee brace and on crutches. Once again, Thailand was in crisis. This time, though, it was catastrophic flooding that plagued the country.

A few days before my return, Achara e-mailed me to say that her family had to move from their homes. Big sections of Bangkok were underwater, and the floodwaters had reached the areas around her family's homes. She also sent me a recent satellite photo taken of the country. Rather than the normal green terrain broken up by cities, roads, river, and lakes, the photo showed what appeared to be a gigantic blue lake where much of the northern half of Thailand used to be.

Back in Bangkok, I stayed in Sukhumvit, one of the main financial and business districts. It and Silom, the other big nearby financial section, were still not flooded. Once again, the city felt like a place under siege. Piles of sandbags lined the streets in front of the buildings and storefronts. In my hotel room, I watched televised reports showing images of people piloting boats along the major highways in nearby parts of the city. One news feature showed kids frolicking on inner tubes and blow-up rafts at a submerged major highway intersection. This festive counterpoint to the grim situation impressed on me yet again that typically Thai knack for making the best of whatever fate brings.

A week after my return to Bangkok, Achara and her mother could move back into their home, and I joined them. While there, still recovering from my knee surgery, I suffered severe muscle tears in my left hip and then in my left quadriceps—perhaps from the muscles growing so stiff and strained from all the rigorous running around stiff-legged in Africa. My injuries were so bad, I couldn't walk for over a week. I lay in my bed most of each day with my feet and legs propped high up almost vertically against the wall at the head of the bed, which helped lessen the searing pain. It was so bad that I had to cancel my flight back to the States, scheduled for three weeks after my arrival in Bangkok.

As always, Achara's mother was there for me, bringing me meals and handling anything I couldn't do by computer from my strange inverted position on the bed. She also brought me to a wonderfully talented Thai doctor and physical therapist. After a short period of therapy, I could walk and sit well enough to fly back to Los Angeles. My painful slog in Africa had been the last seriously challenging journey of my almost six-year Disappearing World travel project. It had been a super-ultra-megamarathon, with me barely limping across the finish line.

CHAPTER 21

Our Disappearing World

I stood on the outside forward deck of the MV *Ortelius*, a midsize Russian ice-reinforced ship. The sturdy vessel cut a straight, sure path through the deep-blue mild chop of the Southern Atlantic. I was with a group of ninety-six participants on a twenty-six-day expedition-style voyage to some of the world's great natural wonderlands, in the Falkland Islands, South Georgia, and the Antarctic Peninsula. It was the first day of the last journey in my travel project.

A clean, bracing sea breeze whipped refreshingly against my face as I watched an entourage of seabirds follow us toward the Falklands. Beautiful black-speckled pintado petrels soared effortlessly alongside against vibrant blue skies, and southern giant petrels soared majestically by like huge, hunchbacked gliders. A number of black-browed albatrosses, other types of petrels, and smaller petrels called prions also drafted alongside the ship.

After the sticky heat, bugs, grime, and general chaos of my recent African trip, the cool, pristine beauty of the faraway Antarctic seemed the perfect prescription.

Visiting the Antarctic also seemed a particularly appropriate way to finish my long Disappearing World travel project. Earth's southernmost continent is perhaps the largest region left on earth that, on casual inspection, bears almost no sign of mankind's footprint. The main reason for this is simply that it's not easy to get there or, once there, to stay for long.

Especially for civilians not actively working there, reaching the Antarctic Peninsula (whose northern tip comes almost within six hundred miles of South America) is real work. The journey entails two long, seasick days through the roughest stretch of open ocean in the world: the Drake Passage. This is two-thirds the amount of time it took the Apollo astronauts to reach the moon.

Because of this great distance and the brutally harsh climatic conditions of almost the entire continent, Antarctica is practically the only land on the planet that has never known any kind of indigenous or other permanent human settlement. How precious, then, I thought while standing on the deck of the *Ortelius*, to be able to experience a vast part of the world that was still as nature had wrought it.

Being on a long trip to a place so remote from the rest of humanity gave me time to pause and reflect on my travels of the past six years. Back when I started this journey, I never dreamed of writing a book about it. My main motivation was a personal one: to experience those cultural and natural wonders of the planet that seem to be disappearing altogether or changing irrevocably into something quite different. Then, along the way, I met many people who encouraged me to write a book about my experiences.

But it was while on the deck of this ship plowing through the Southern Ocean that I finally realized I must.

So I embarked on another long journey: the writing of this book. This was not to be a screed exhorting humanity to change its ways, or a prescription for what must be done to save the many wonders of the world that still exist. There are already whole libraries of such volumes, written by far abler scientific and policymaking minds than mine. Instead, I have tried to share the experience the best I could with those interested in following my journey or maybe undertaking one of their own. But after such a long and comprehensive effort to really know our world, I have, of course, developed certain opinions and conclusions from the experience.

On a personal level, I naively started this odyssey with the idea that after three years or so, I would return home and just sort of plug back into my old life. I thought I would still be essentially the same person. And, of course, I assumed I would still be with my wife, Achara. These assumptions mostly turned out wrong. No one does something so all-consuming and returns as the same person.

I have lived out a childhood dream and been freed from a lifelong obsession. I had conducted my adult life to this point with the idea that I would undertake such a long journey, and this affected all my long-term plans—pivotal plans, such as what career to embark on and whether to become a parent. But now, as I look at my life going forward, I can do so without the worry that at some point I will disrupt it through another total uprooting. Though I met many people along the way who remarked how I was "living the dream," I learned first-hand a reality that should perhaps be obvious: the freedom of being able to travel constantly at will, without the constraints of a home or other responsibilities, comes at a price. Looking forward after this experience, I know I will always be a traveler, but a traveler with a real physical home.

Still, during the Antarctic voyage, while reflecting on my six-year epic, I couldn't give myself a high-five for accomplishing it. The same urgency that had finally pushed me to go after my lifelong dream made it a bittersweet experience. The name I have hung on it, "Our Disappearing World," is certainly not an optimistic one.

Broadly, the two main categories of what is so rapidly changing and potentially disappearing in the modernizing world are traditional cultures and nature itself, especially true wilderness and endangered animal and plant species. Before starting my travel project, I had little optimism that the rapid changes and losses in each of these broad categories would or could be mitigated in any significant way. And indeed, afterward, I'm even more pessimistic. But the picture is not altogether bleak by any means, and I see many positive trends also taking place as the world rushes headlong toward its modern future. Though massive cultural changes and disappearances and the wholesale alterations to the world's natural environments are usually inextricably linked, I'll try to start first with some observations about human cultures.

Cultural change has always been a natural part of human existence. Cultures and languages will continue to disappear regardless of the loss to the world's diverse legacy. The history of humankind is full of examples of one wave of people displacing another, who likely had supplanted a yet earlier culture, and so on back to the first foraging protohumans ever to wander into a region. Tens of millennia ago, for example, modern humans are reckoned to have displaced Neanderthals in Europe, the Middle East, and Central Asia. Since then, ensuing waves over the centuries have displaced and uprooted the "original" inhabitants of regions through mass migrations and conquest. In modern times, the cultures of many indigenous peoples all over the New World were effectively wiped out or quarantined into tiny enclaves by the diseases and superior weapons of European conquistadors and settlers. Today, local cultures worldwide are being subsumed by yet another conquest, in the form of modernization and globalization. Viewing things from the long haul, thus, we see that cultural change, whether through dilution from alien cultures, absorption into another culture, or sheer obliteration, is the norm.

Cultural change is certainly not all bad, either. From what I have experienced, most people—though certainly not all—regardless of their culture or homelands, want and welcome some of the changes and things that modernization brings. One of the more striking sights I have seen in my travels, and that is now increasingly common in media photographs and videos, is that of a tribesperson in exotic traditional garb, talking on a cell phone. It is and, except where blocked by deep religious or cultural conviction, has probably always been all but universal human nature to want things that make our lives better, easier, and more secure.

In many cases, modern culture and ways of life bring huge benefits to those whom it has begun to engage. People will live longer because of access to the miracles that modern health care can bring, for example. And the newly spreading abilities to communicate and travel offer people in less modern locales vastly more life choices. With more modern ways, women in particular are often freed from traditional lives that put them in a vastly inferior position to men. Abhorrent traditional practices, such as female genital mutilation and the practice that has been grossly misnamed "honor killing," which still are common in many parts of Africa and Asia, will hopefully one day be relegated to the scrap heap of history.

The same can be said for the equally abhorrent treatment of women in all too many societies—not only in tribal societies but also some more modern societies in the Middle East and even Europe. In too many regions, the inhabitants still have attitudes toward women that are primitive almost beyond our ability to imagine in a modern world. In these cases, the spreading of modern global cultural norms will eventually, we can hope, free women of the crippling hobbles on their life possibilities.

The losers in all this, though, are often those relatively isolated peoples who have massive change from the outside world thrust abruptly on them. The end result of the crashing in of alien values and religions can be disaffection, alcohol and drug addiction, juvenile delinquency, and breakdown in the social order. And it can engender mass movements of youth with no coherent view of the future, to the sprawling shantytowns now so common around many major cities in the poorer world. All too often, traditional peoples go from being rich in their old world order to being "modern" and impoverished. These are the tragedies that modernization has brought to too many people already, whether displaced forest-dwelling Pygmies or the inhabitants of once remote island paradises in the South Pacific.

But perhaps a majority of people still leading challenging and difficult lifestyles in their traditional cultures will ultimately either welcome or have to adapt to the modern world. Since the process of change is inevitable, we can hope that the world might still keep something of the exotic and colorful lifestyles of the more traditional peoples, and—crucially, perhaps—some of the wisdom, sense of community, and cohesiveness of those societies.

How can this happen? How can the best things of the many varied and fascinating cultures that still exist on this planet be preserved? The best, least traumatic way for those still in very traditional societies to experience change is organically, in a process that happens over time and is freely and willingly absorbed into the affected society. From my experience, if the color and rich tapestry of traditional cultures are to be preserved in this fast-globalizing world, the main thrust to preserve the best of original traditional cultures will have to be mostly homegrown efforts by those from within those cultures.

This, indeed, is the reality in many places. Many peoples over the years have made strong efforts at cultural preservation. A virulent and high-profile case of a mostly homegrown effort at cultural preservation could be the Iranian Revolution in 1979, which was driven, in part, by a theme of preserving Persian culture and traditions from alien Western modernization. Another salient example of this is the radical militant Islamism that features so prominently and tragically in so many modern acts of terrorism. This type of extremism, with its willingness to commit mass murder against random innocents, may (justifiably) seem sheer insanity to outsiders. Nevertheless, the roots of these types of militant Islam are partly a reaction to encroaching modern alien cultures, with the vain hope of returning to some ancient ideal.

More positive mostly homegrown efforts at cultural preservation, though, can be seen with groups like the First Nations peoples in

Canada, aboriginal peoples in Australia, the Maori of New Zealand, and several forest-dwelling groups in the Amazon. A key part of each of these indigenous peoples' efforts at cultural preservation is that they now have large areas where they exercise a degree of governing autonomy. This allows them to have some control over how to live and what type of development and resource exploitation to allow on their lands. In addition, various efforts are being made in reviving and passing their original languages on to their children, and celebrating traditional holidays and rituals. Some of these arrangements, while not ideal, seem to work better than similar concepts done with indigenous groups in the United States.

For indigenous peoples to achieve some type of control over parts of their traditional homelands and other key aspects of their cultures, ironically, often means learning to work the modern political systems effectively. For example, the Achuar, an indigenous forest-dwelling group in a remote section of southeastern Ecuador's incredibly biodiverse upper Amazon rain forest, use a practical approach. To deal effectively with the threat of outsiders—especially logging and mining interests—seeking to exploit their homelands, the tribe regularly sends a few of its best and brightest young people to the modern world to be educated. There they learn the ways and laws of modern society. These adolescents grow into adults who can understand how the modern economic and political world functions, and work within it looking out for the Achuar people's interests. I have come across this strategic concept of way-of-life self-preservation in a number of situations around the world.

And, of course, there is plenty of room for outside help. Traditionally living forest peoples, for example, cannot continue their lifestyles outside their home environment. Trying to do one's part on a daily level to preserve old-growth forest regions, such as the still vast areas of the Amazon, Congo, New Guinea, and Indonesia, to name just some of the largest ones, will help these forest peoples. One practical way for modern-world citizens to help in this direction is to strive to buy only those lumber and wood products grown and harvested in a certified sustainable manner. This obviously helps preserve both the culture and the wilderness itself.

But there are many ways to help just by being responsible consumers. Buying specialized products made by indigenous or traditionally living peoples can have an impact. This can range from buying specialized sustainable rain forest-derived products such as soaps and shampoos or food products such as acai juice and herbs. Or trying to purchase products through "fair trade" oriented companies—for example, chocolate or coffee grown by more traditionally living small growers in the Guatemala highlands. Many of these types of strategies allow consumers to help people of traditional cultures to retain their lifestyles while making a dignified living.

Another way that outsiders can help is by being responsible tourists. The funds from modern tourism can be powerful inducements for societies to preserve traditional cultures and pristine habitats. The Hadzabe hunter-gatherers in Tanzania, for example, still exist probably only because of their "earning ability" for tourist dollars. The Achuar people run the Kapawi Ecolodge in their part of the Ecuadorian Amazon, bringing in hard money to help pay for the effort to preserve their forest homelands.

In these examples and countless other similar experiments around the world, outsiders, through ecotourism, are a direct part of the equation. As with the idea of consumer-directed "activism" noted above, the key idea behind all this is to make the preserved lands "pay off," usually in terms of the rich-world money economy. Just as importantly, making the forest "pay" for the local people also has the practical effect of lessening their temptation to join hands with, or be bought off by, outside business interests such as oil, logging, or mining companies.

The concept of traveling responsibly in alien lands is a positive trend that has taken deep hold in the world of tourism over the past generation. Outsiders who want to visit some of the most interesting, colorful, and remote cultures still left in the world now have a smorgasbord of options to choose from that can help both cultural and ecological preservation in many small ways. As many experienced travelers already know, being a responsible tourist means striving to be as "local" as possible. This means always trying to use local operators, guides, and services when visiting areas of more traditional peoples. The same goes when visiting the still magnificent great wildernesses left on earth. If local people make money bringing people into their preserved areas, this creates advocacy groups for those areas' continued preservation.

These are some of the positive factors working to preserve at least some of the more interesting aspects of the world's various traditional cultures. Nevertheless, many of the world's remaining traditional and indigenous peoples will continue to be degraded at an accelerating rate. This will happen by outright displacement, such as with the Pygmies in many parts of the Congo Basin, or through destruction and takeover of their homelands by the modern world. The most common way that cultural loss will happen, though, is through the relentless process of absorption of traditional lifestyles into the modern world and, in many cases, the morphing of these cultures into new forms as they blend with modernity.

The end result is that in too many cases, the colorful cultures, ways of life, practices, languages, dress, and cosmologies of indigenous tribal and traditional peoples will vanish. Their only visible remnants will be in history books and as depicted in cartoonish "cultural shows" that are becoming the fodder for many modern travelers seeking the exotic.

———

During the Antarctic and sub-Antarctic journey, I saw the natural world in its most extravagant abundance. For the first sixteen days, our group spent time in the Falklands and South Georgia. Fur seals, sea lions, southern elephant seals, blizzards of penguins and albatrosses, and an amazing assortment of seabirds and raptors were our daily fare. At the small island of Steeple Jason in the Falklands, for example, perhaps a hundred thousand breeding pairs of black-browed albatrosses were congregated along the island's northeastern edge. Birds of prey flew or strutted boldly about, and rockhopper and gentoo penguins cavorted among the breeding hordes of albatrosses. It looked like a pelagic avian paradise.

South Georgia was simply a wildlife wonderland. At St. Andrews Bay, our group gazed in awe at what is estimated to be the densest concentration of wildlife on the entire planet. In a single coastal valley, an immense king penguin colony, numbering perhaps six hundred thousand birds, went about its life rhythms against the backdrop of a gorgeous glacier-covered mountain. As our group journeyed and made stops along South Georgia's rugged and forbidding eastern coast, huge fur seal rookeries, hordes of penguins and seabirds, and majestic glaciers became almost commonplace. This was what nature could look like without the interfering hand of man. It was, like much of the sub-Antarctic and essentially all the Antarctic Peninsula itself, an increasingly rare thing on earth: still a vast region of true wilderness.

On the seventeenth day of our journey, as our ship headed toward the Antarctic Peninsula, we began to pass through a vast stretch of giant icebergs in the Weddell Sea. All of us stood on the outside decks, that day and late into the evening, gazing in awe at the huge floating mountains and mesas. Vast flat-topped, or *tabular*, icebergs stood majestically on the dark blue waters, glowing against the clear powder blue skies. The biggest of these looked like landmasses that could hold small cities. These bigger tabular icebergs had lengths measuring in the dozens of miles and stood as high as five hundred feet, according to one of our expedition leaders. They were majestic and also somehow sinister in their alien beauty.

As we gazed spellbound at the amazing ice formations, our expedition leader explained that the tabular icebergs had their distinctive flat tops and appearance of being part of a landmass because they were. They were, in fact, huge tracts that had broken away from ice shelves—which are sheets of ice extending over the sea from the edge of land. The tabular icebergs we were seeing most likely came from recently broken-up parts of the Larsen Ice Shelf, a long shelf extending along the northeast coast of the Antarctic Peninsula. Two of the three sections that historically composed the Larsen Ice Shelf—one of them the size of Rhode Island—have broken up in the past two decades, due to increasing global temperatures.

After hearing this from our expedition leader, I thought about the irony of the situation: that the gorgeous spectacles we were now beholding in wonder may have been created by human technology's destructive effect on the natural world. It was yet another sign that no place on earth, no matter how far away from humans, can escape our reach and our propensity for dangerously altering the natural world.

It is perhaps not yet possible to know for certain what events are being caused directly by human-generated greenhouse gases. Some things that occur because of climate warming, such as the breakups of the Larsen Ice Shelf, and the receding sea ice in both Antarctic and Arctic waters, also can happen to varying degrees even without the effects of greenhouse gases. However, uncertainty does not change the fact that humans are performing a huge experiment on the very atmosphere that sustains all life, with no real way of guessing the outcome.

This is also just part of the grand experiment that humans are making on the world's biosystems. Through direct predation and environmental transformation, we are causing, or coming close to causing, extinctions on a scale paralleled only a few times in the earth's geological history. This grand and reckless experiment involves changing the fundamental nature of the very ecosystems that sustain life itself. We cannot know with any certainty what might be the breaking point in this grand experiment. Nor can we know what will happen once this point is passed: whether the damage can be reversed or arrested, or whether the threat may simply overwhelm life on earth and, ultimately, us.

What is clear to me from my travels is that nature on earth is changing dramatically, and mostly not for the better. My boyhood worries about the earth being blown up in a nuclear war, or the Amazon rain forest being totally burned down, have, thankfully, not yet occurred. But as a traveler, I could see clearly that the world faces serious threats from the accelerating wholesale environmental destruction. Many of the world's great treasures and remaining wildernesses suffer constant wholesale assaults—for example, the relentless destruction in Borneo, the multifold assaults on the Congo Basin, and the constant nibbling, from every direction, on the Amazon. These are not just a few isolated high-profile examples. The same destructive trend is taking place at varying speeds in most of the places I wrote about in this book—and, indeed, almost everywhere I have ever been.

Essentially, here is the big trend, on a broad scale, of what is going on in the world: To stave off degradation or utter destruction of many natural treasures in the world, humans have undertaken to section off patches of wilderness and nature in many places across the planet. These national parks, preserves, and protected areas will hopefully remain true vestiges of some of the great natural wonders of the world. From an optimistic standpoint, much of humanity understands and appreciates the need to do so. And often, these protected areas can work well if properly protected and managed. Some once highly threatened species, for instance, are in the process of rebounding or have even come back from the edge of oblivion, thanks to being in protected habitats.

A related and newer positive trend is that people are starting to understand that preserved places need to be connected to each other, to create large stretches of nature for animals to roam and for different habitats to exist naturally next to each other. A prime example of this is the large reach of Amazonia protected by the Mamirauá reserve and two adjoining large reserves. Also, there is a growing realization that nonarable places such as swamps and wetlands are not wastelands but actually fundamental parts of the natural world. Even in the world's oceans, which face massive assaults just as land habitats do, marine preserves and protected areas are starting to become more common, and in them, fish and other sea life often rebound and flourish. But despite these signs of promise, what will almost certainly become quite scarce is real, true wilderness.

My own conclusion is that the trends of environmental destruction are so entrenched and so overpowering that they cannot be reversed at this point in history. From my travels, I have come to see the world as starting to become something akin to a giant garden that requires tending. In the richer sections of this garden, the naturally occurring parts of nature will be highly tended to resemble something acceptable, clean, and pleasant. These patches of nature will be nice to have, and wild plants and creatures will live there. But most of them won't be what we can call wildernesses.

In the poorer parts of the world garden, the nice patches will be smaller and sparser. They, too, will be nice places, though often not as nice or as protected as in the richer world. In between these nice places, in growing sections of the garden, the environment will continue to collapse, diminish, and be degraded beyond recognition. Some of these highly degraded zones will be largely devoid of life and horribly polluted. Some places like this already exist, such as around the Aral Sea in Central Asia—considered one of the world's greatest environmental disasters. Stay tuned; more are on the way.

Finally, some oases of great and real wildernesses will still exist. As the world continues to degrade, these oases of wilderness will also continue to face pressures. Perhaps, in the ultimate play-out of this scenario, the only true wildernesses that will continue to exist will be those that are just too remote, or have climates too harsh, for humans to operate on a large scale. These pockets of remaining wilderness will be mostly at the poles or deep in the center of the remaining parts of the Amazon, in the extremes of Siberia, or, for example, in the remote highlands of Papua New Guinea. But even in these places, the environments will continue to degrade noticeably as global warming, ocean degradation (which changes the food chain), and other systemic human-made problems snowball ahead.

This dismal scenario does not have to play out. Humankind can change things and slow or even reverse the decline of the world's great natural jewels that still exist. Individuals can and should join and support well-run and -managed environmental advocacy groups, lobby their government officials about needed environmental protections or actions, and become activists in other ways. Many of the earth's wonders still exist today in all their glory because of environmental activism. Individual actions and everyday choices can and do make a difference. Also, improving and new technologies can and will no doubt make things cleaner, less polluting, and more fuel efficient and even help turn highly degraded environments back to more natural forms.

But my ultimate gut assessment of what the future holds for real wilderness and many of the world's cultural wonders is easy to see. I made it clear just by doing this six-year travel epic.

I have one parting piece of advice for anyone who really wants to experience this beautiful, awesome planet's remaining great wilderness. This includes all who yearn to travel in places of still-deep mystery, indescribable beauty, and sheer primevalness. To all whose childhood dreams were filled with visions of magical, wondrous wildernesses and great beasts that still roam the earth or swim the waters, and to those restless souls who yearn for an idea of the world as it once was, when it was still filled with remote, exotic lands that promised adventure and awe to any who ventured there . . .

My advice is, go do it now.

Acknowledgments

After my travels, writing this book became a whole new journey—and, by its nature, a mostly solitary one. But, of course, many people provided support, encouragement, and crucial help along the way. At the start of my travels, the idea of writing it all down for others to read had never occurred to me. But so many people I met along the way, when they heard what I had been doing, told me I had to write it all down.

On a more personal level, all my family, friends, and former colleagues were urging, nudging, practically shoving me in that direction. My longtime friend Greg Zook gave me a blank Moleskine writing book on my birthday. Another friend, Ron Johnson, encouraged me in a different way. Toward the end of my travel project, I was seriously contemplating writing a book but hadn't a clue how to organize or even make sense of such a long, often chaotic experience. So Ron suggested creating a Web site and blog as a way to start getting some thoughts and stories down. I did. And eventually, that, along with my travel notes and many e-mails sent along the way, became the source material for this manuscript.

Once I started drafting the manuscript, I got vitally important feedback from my aunt Gwen. She pointed out that I was going about it all wrong—this should be a much more personal account than the dry reportage I was writing. Being a very private person, I found this an enormous added challenge. As I got deeper into the project, several people gave me constructive feedback on what I was writing, and encouraged me to stick with it. Among these was Jaylyle Redmon, who had written a couple of books and could identify with my pursuit. My mother, Pat, was a wellspring of moral support. She seemed genuinely excited that I was writing this book. The same with my father, George, and his wife, Connie, who became tireless readers for many of the chapters. They were always there to buoy my spirits during the inevitable episodes of despair.

I thoroughly enjoyed working with my editor, Michael Carr. Before this project, my writing experience was limited to school, graduate school, and the business world—very different stuff from what I was trying to do here. Through Michael's kind but meticulous coaching, I learned that simply relating what happened is never enough—you must also put the reader *there.*

Finally, my heartfelt thanks go to the Salonites family: Robert, LaJean, Conrad, Nick, and John. Before starting the book, my life was the sort of ceaseless kinetic activity seen in the very outgoing—some might even say *hyper*—person who is constantly seeking new challenges. But this book project required something far more alien to me than any of the places I had traveled: to live a hermit's life and actually sit still all day and, often, late into the night. For most of this project, rather than return to my old haunts of West Los Angeles, I took temporary lodgings down the street from the Salonites family, in a semirural setting in Northern California, far from the old chums and exciting distractions of home. These lovely people provided a much-needed social outlet during my self-imposed exile. They also encouraged me every step of the way, becoming a vital though unobtrusive part of this book-writing journey. Robert and LaJean read each iteration of the manuscript and gave me critical in-depth feedback. The thing I treasured most, though, was that I had become part of their family—a family that gave me the support I needed to complete this project.

Gary Mancuso
November 18, 2013
Los Angeles, California

About the Author

Gary Mancuso yearned to travel ever since he was a boy. Then, the summer before his senior year in high school, he left his family home in Ohio and drove to California. Arriving in Los Angeles with four dollars in his pocket, he slept on the beach for a spell until he got his footing. When he wasn't off wandering somewhere, he studied economics, communications, and  political science and got a master's degree in International Relations from the University of Southern California. Before setting off on the journey that became the subject of this book, Gary headed business development in the trading room of a large regional bank. Along with his passion for travel, he is an avid trekker, swimmer, scuba diver, environmentalist, and private pilot.

Journeys in Our Disappearing World ...

A sampling of the locations the author has traveled to with their corresponding chapters. (locations approximate.)

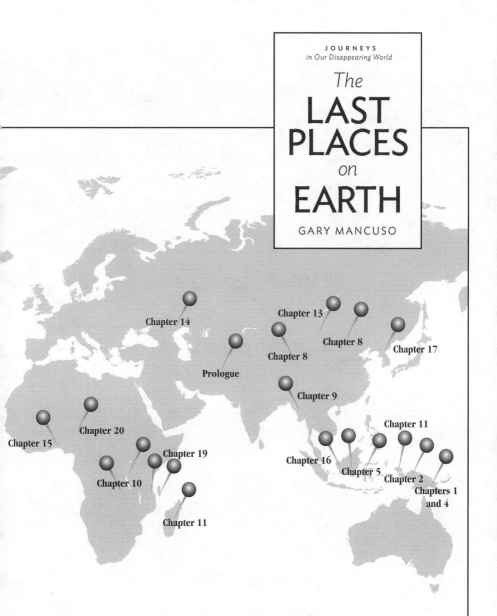

JOURNEYS
in Our Disappearing World

The
LAST
PLACES
on
EARTH

GARY MANCUSO

Chapter 14

Chapter 13

Chapter 8

Chapter 8

Chapter 17

Prologue

Chapter 8

Chapter 9

Chapter 20

Chapter 11

Chapter 15

Chapter 19

Chapter 16

Chapter 10

Chapter 5

Chapter 2

Chapters 1 and 4

Chapter 11

Visit www.thelastplacesonearth.com
to view extensive photo galleries; read essays, stories and more
about Our Disappearing World.